United Nations Peacekeeping and the Principle of Non-Intervention

Using a unique application of Third World Approaches to International Law (TWAIL), this book provides a critical, interdisciplinary, examination of the contemporary practice of UN peacekeeping.

Is peacekeeping intervention? Since its conception in the mid-1950s, peacekeeping has significantly evolved from traditional, lightly armed, passive operations to robust, multi-dimensional stabilisation peacekeeping operations. This raises questions as to whether this is simply a natural evolution of peacekeeping or whether it marks an expansion of the concept beyond its boundaries, pushing it into the realm of peace enforcement or intervention. In response, this book examines the frameworks which govern UN peacekeeping and seeks to understand the relationship between peacekeeping and the principle of non-intervention. Providing practical examples from the United Nations' operations in the Democratic Republic of the Congo and drawing upon interviews with key international actors including UN personnel, the book explores the boundaries of peacekeeping, contending that peacekeeping, at times, becomes a form of intervention. This, the book argues, is detrimental both to the concept of peacekeeping and to the host state, and it concludes by offering a series of recommendations to re-affirm peacekeeping's boundaries and amplify the effectiveness of contemporary peacekeeping.

This book will be of interest to scholars and students in international law, international relations, politics, history and criminology.

Jennifer Giblin PhD is Associate Head of the School of Law, Criminology and Policing, Edge Hill University, UK.

United Nations Peacekeeping and the Principle of Non-Intervention

A TWAIL Perspective

Jennifer Giblin

Routledge
Taylor & Francis Group
a GlassHouse Book

First published 2024
by Routledge
4 Park Square, Milton Park, Abingdon, Oxon OX14 4RN

and by Routledge
605 Third Avenue, New York, NY 10158

Routledge is an imprint of the Taylor & Francis Group, an informa business

a GlassHouse book

British Library Cataloguing-in-Publication Data
A catalogue record for this book is available from the British Library

Library of Congress Cataloging-in-Publication Data
Names: Giblin, Jennifer, 1992- author.
Title: United Nations peacekeeping and the principle of non-intervention: a TWAIL perspective/Jennifer Giblin.
Description: Abingdon, Oxon [UK]; New York, NY: Routledge, 2024. | Includes bibliographical references and index.
Identifiers: LCCN 2023047957 (print) | LCCN 2023047958 (ebook) | ISBN 9781032442884 (hardback) | ISBN 9781032443386 (paperback) | ISBN 9781003371649 (ebook)
Subjects: LCSH: United Nations–Peacekeeping forces. | Peacekeeping forces (International law) | Intervention (International law)
Classification: LCC KZ6376 .G53 2024 (print) | LCC KZ6376 (ebook) | DDC 341.5/84–dc23/eng/20231012

LC record available at https://lccn.loc.gov/2023047957
LC ebook record available at https://lccn.loc.gov/2023047958

ISBN: 978-1-032-44288-4 (hbk)
ISBN: 978-1-032-44338-6 (pbk)
ISBN: 978-1-003-37164-9 (ebk)

DOI: 10.4324/9781003371649

Typeset in Sabon
by Deanta Global Publishing Services, Chennai, India

For Gill and Paul

Contents

Acknowledgements

This project would not have been possible without the considerable support of my family, friends and colleagues, to whom I am greatly indebted.

To my family and friends, thank you for your endless love and encouragement. To my constant pillar of support, Adam, thank you for always being there. To my colleagues at Edge Hill University, thank you for giving me the space and encouragement to grow. And finally, to my PhD supervisors, Professor Nigel White and Professor Olympia Bekou, thank you for the many years of guidance, wisdom and kindness.

Chapter 1

Introduction

Introduction

Is peacekeeping intervention? This is the central theme which runs throughout this book. Since its conception in the mid-1950s, peacekeeping has significantly evolved from traditional, passive, monitoring and observing operations to robust, multi-dimensional stabilisation operations, with seemingly endless lists of mandated tasks. In recent years, despite the continued existence of some traditional models of peacekeeping operations,[1] the United Nations has increasingly deployed multi-faceted operations to 'stabilise' complex, fragile settings and enable state institutions to flourish, reflecting a state-centric, stabilisation approach to peacekeeping.[2] This noticeable drift from the traditional understanding of peacekeeping raises questions as to whether this is simply a natural evolution of peacekeeping or whether it marks an expansion of the concept of peacekeeping beyond its boundaries, pushing it into the realm of peace enforcement or intervention. Put simply, has peacekeeping evolved too far?

As a tool for maintaining international peace and security, peacekeeping was designed as a consensual activity far removed from the non-consensual, forceful interventions prohibited under the principle of non-intervention. As this book will examine, the extensive broadening of peacekeeping's principles is problematic as it results in peacekeeping, at times, becoming a form of intervention which takes peacekeeping far beyond its intended purposes and results in a weakening of the principle of non-intervention and strengthening of hegemony within the international system.

Using the Democratic Republic of the Congo (DRC) as a case study, this book seeks to understand the relationship between UN peacekeeping and the principle of non-intervention. It explores the boundaries between

1 For example: UNFICYP, UNSC Res 2561 (29 January 2021) UN Doc S/RES/2561.
2 AC Day and CT Hunt, 'UN Stabilisation Operations and the Problem of Non-Linear Change: A Relational Approach to Intervening in Governance Ecosystems' (2020) 9(1) Stability 1–23, 1.

DOI: 10.4324/9781003371649-1

peacekeeping and intervention, questioning whether, at times, peacekeeping becomes a form of coercive action designed to influence change in the host state and, therefore, intervention. In doing so, the book begins by examining the history of intervention and the development of the principle of non-intervention, before outlining the evolution of peacekeeping, clarifying its legal and normative frameworks which, together, form a complex red boundary line around peacekeeping, separating it from intervention and thus preventing it from violating the principle of non-intervention. This analysis is then taken further, through an exploration of the interpretation and application of peacekeeping's norms and legal principles in the DRC – the largest arena within which UN peacekeeping has evolved.

The aim of this book is to provide an overview of the contemporary peacekeeping frameworks and to understand, firstly, how an application of these frameworks impacts the relationship between peacekeeping and the principle of non-intervention and, secondly, how the fluidity of these frameworks has allowed peacekeeping to, at times, be used by dominant powers in the furtherance of their interests, with peacekeeping being used to legitimate intervention. Put simply, the book presents: (1) an overview of the legal and normative frameworks which govern peacekeeping; (2) an exploration of the relationship between peacekeeping and the principle of non-intervention; and (3) an alternative theoretical understanding of peacekeeping through a TWAIL lens.[3]

Overall, this book will question whether there needs to be a redrawing of peacekeeping's boundary lines to reaffirm the distinction between peacekeeping and intervention. It will also highlight key recommendations – to move towards a people-centred approach to peacekeeping, with realistic, streamlined mandates – which may help to reaffirm peacekeeping's boundaries and support initiatives that seek to amplify peacekeeping's effectiveness.

Methodology

Both the principle of non-intervention and the concept of peacekeeping are ill-defined, with no formal, legal basis rooted in a definitive Charter, Act or body of law. Instead, the principle of non-intervention has developed, predominantly, from UN General Assembly Resolutions and Declarations[4] and interpretations by the International Court of Justice (ICJ)[5] and regional organisations.[6] Similarly, peacekeeping was conceived through interpretations

3 Third World Approaches to International Law.

4 For example: Declaration on Principles of International Law Concerning Friendly Relations and Cooperation among States in Accordance with the Charter of the United Nations, UN Doc A/Res/2625 (XXV) (24 October 1970).

5 For example: *Corfu Channel Case (UK v Albania)* (Merits) [1949] ICJ Rep 4, 132–169.

6 Such as the Organisation of African Unity and African Union.

of the UN Charter, the implied powers of the Security Council,[7] General Assembly[8] and Secretary-General[9] and decisions from the ICJ[10] and is based upon the three fundamental principles of consent, impartiality and non-use of force.[11] The book will therefore consult and interpret primary sources such as Security Council and General Assembly Resolutions, Secretary-General Reports and Bulletins and case law of the ICJ. It will 'seek out, discover, construct or reconstruct rules and principles'[12] relating to intervention and peacekeeping, to clarify the current legal and normative frameworks and to set the basis for further theoretical analysis.

When identifying the legal rules and principles governing intervention and peacekeeping, the book will take this doctrinal approach further by adopting a socio-legal approach. In so doing, it will consider the wider, historical and social structures which have influenced the concepts of non-intervention and peacekeeping, rather than just assuming or accepting the legal rules and legal doctrine as autonomous or internally constructed.[13] Indeed, within Chapters 2, 3 and 4, as the development of the principle of non-intervention and the concept of peacekeeping are explored, respectively, broader social and historical events which influenced their development are considered. The book will therefore examine both the 'intrinsic' and 'extrinsic' history of intervention and UN peacekeeping.[14] That is, it will explore the development of these two concepts within international law (resolutions, declarations, case law) and, simultaneously, the 'extrinsic' history of their relationship to general history and other social phenomena. Allott argues that by examining the history of international law itself ('intrinsic' history) it will 're-form our consciousness of the identity, the functioning, and the potentiality of international law as law'.[15] Whilst writing the 'extrinsic' history 'will re-form our consciousness of the role of international law in the forming, re-forming, and re-making of international society'.[16] Mapping the historical development of the principle of non-intervention and UN peacekeeping will therefore offer a better understanding of how the principle and peacekeeping operate today.

7 See: Articles 24(1), 36(1), 40 UN Charter.
8 See: Articles 10, 11(2), 12, 14 UN Charter.
9 See: Articles 97–99 UN Charter.
10 *Certain Expenses of the United Nations (Article 17, Paragraph 2 of the Charter)* (Advisory Opinion) [1962] ICJ Rep 151.
11 UNGA, 'Summary Study' A/3943 (9 October 1958) UN Doc A/3943.
12 R Banakar and M Travers, 'Law, Sociology and Method' in R Banakar and M Travers (eds) *Theory and Method in Socio-Legal Research* (Hart 2005) 7.
13 CM Campbell and P Wiles, 'The Study of Law in Society in Britain' (1976) 10 L&SR 547–578, 553.
14 P Allott, 'International Law and the Idea of History' (1999) 1 JHistIntLaw 1–22.
15 ibid 20.
16 ibid.

Third World Approaches to International Law (TWAIL)

The law of international organisations 'is still somewhat immature', in that there is no convincing theoretical framework governing the area.[17] In particular, as Klabbers notes, 'international legal doctrine has a hard time coming to terms with the relationship between an international organisation and the very states which are its members'.[18] Indeed, this is a central issue within this book – the relationship between the United Nations, its member states and the state host to a peacekeeping operation. To address this matter, this book will invoke critical legal theory to illuminate this tension within UN peacekeeping. The decision to apply critical legal theory, or to think critically about the law in this area, was inspired by Foucault's insistence that most claims which were presented as 'truth' can be viewed simply as expressions of power by the actor making the claim, who is attempting to shape the knowledge and undermine competing claims.[19] Indeed, it is argued that the UN Charter is a 'living instrument' which is 'like every constitutional instrument, continuously interpreted, moulded and adapted to meet the interests of parties'.[20] It therefore follows that as UN peacekeeping stems from interpretations of the Charter, particularly Chapters VI and VII, peacekeeping can also be interpreted, moulded and adapted to meet the needs of the relevant parties, who, as this book will demonstrate, are typically the dominant permanent five members of the Security Council. The book thus seeks to challenge the dominant Western narrative of international law, opening it up to different interpretations in order to ascertain a true understanding of intervention and UN peacekeeping. As Kennedy notes, it is only after 'pushing past international law's classic self-conception' as the 'highest experience of universal values, the best map of the world's political actors and their powers, and toolkit of policy solutions' that international lawyers will be able to use international legal materials to illuminate global processes.[21]

In adopting this critical lens, the book will apply the philosophy of TWAIL. This has been chosen, in part, given that the case study for this book – the DRC – is a Global South or Third World state and partly because TWAIL is a scholarly movement committed to challenging the existing international order.[22] Whilst there is no coherent and distinctive 'Third World approach' to international law, there are common features or characteristics which may be

17 J Klabbers, *An Introduction to International Institutional Law* (CUP 2009) 3.
18 ibid 3–4.
19 See: M Foucault, *Ethics: Subjectivity and Truth: Essential Works of Michel Foucault 1954–1984. Volume I* (Penguin 2000).
20 O Schachter, *International Law in Theory and Practice* (Martinus Nijhoff 1991) 118–119.
21 D Kennedy, 'Law and Political Economy of the World' (2013) 26(1) LJIL 7–48, 37.
22 See: OC Okafor, 'Newness, Imperialism, and International Legal Reform in Our Time: A TWAIL Perspective' (2005) 43(1/2) OHLJ 171–191, 176–177.

seen as an overarching 'Third World approach'.[23] Indeed, all TWAIL scholars or 'TWAIL-ers' are united in their opposition to the 'unjust global order' and the furtherance of their common goal of eradicating international laws' subordination of the Third World and its peoples.[24] As Mickelson notes, such a movement is best imagined as a 'chorus of voices that blend, though not always harmoniously' to make a shared collection of concerns heard.[25] TWAIL scholars therefore have a 'shared ethical commitment' to expose and reform features of international law which maintain an unequal order.[26] In seeking to expose the 'unjust relationship between the Third World and International Law',[27] TWAIL also illuminates the perspective of those who are often unheard – in this instance, the peoples of the Third World. As with other critical theorists, TWAIL scholars therefore strive to give a voice to 'the poor, the disadvantaged, the voiceless, the unrepresented, [and] the powerless'.[28]

The origins of TWAIL, for some, can be traced to the decolonisation period, in particular, the Bandung Conference of 1955.[29] Generally, a distinction can be made between TWAIL I scholarship produced by this first generation of post-colonial international lawyers, such as Georges Abi-Saab and Taslim Elias,[30] and post-1996 TWAIL II scholarship.[31] Regardless of this distinction, for all TWAIL scholars, 'international law makes sense only in the context of the lived history of the peoples of the Third World'.[32] Two key characteristics of TWAIL thinking then stem from this. Firstly, that colonialism and

23 K Mickelson, 'Rhetoric and Rage: Third World Voices in International Legal Discourse' (2011) 16(2) WisIntlLJ 353–419, 353.
24 M Mutua, 'What Is TWAIL?' (2000) 32 ASILProc 31–38, 36–37.
25 Mickelson (n23) 360.
26 Okafor (n22) 177.
27 MA Attar and R Thompson, 'How the Multi-Level Democratisation of International Law-Making Can Effect Popular Aspirations towards Self-Determination' (2011) 3(1) TradeL&Dev 65–102, 67.
28 E Said, *Representation of the Intellectual* (Vintage 1994) 84.
29 Whilst Mutua argues that 'Bandung was the symbolic birthplace of TWAIL', others such as Gathii consider it to be a more recent phenomenon, tracing its origins to around 1996 at Harvard Law School. See: Mutua (n24) and JT Gathii, 'TWAIL: A Brief History of Its Origins, Its Decentralised Network, and a Tentative Bibliography' (2011) 3(1) TradeL&Dev 26–64.
30 TO Elias, *New Horizons in International Law* (Springer, 2nd edn, 1992) and G Abi-Saab, *The Development of International Law: An Introduction by the United Nations* in F Snyder and S Sathirathai (eds) *Third World Attitudes to International Law: An Introduction* (Martinus Nijhoff 1987).
31 A group of Harvard Law School graduate students initiated a series of meetings. The group consisted of Celestine Nyamu, Balakrishnan Rajagopal, Hani Sayed, Vasuki Nesiah, Elchi Nowrojee, Bhupinder Chimni and James Thuo Gathii.
32 A Anghie and BS Chimni, 'Third World Approaches to International Law and Individual Responsibility in International Conflicts' (2003) 2(1) ChinJIL 77–103, 78.

neo-colonialism have made Third World peoples 'acutely sensitive to power relations among states' and to how international rules and institutions 'will actually affect the distribution of power between states and peoples'.[33] And, secondly, the 'interpretive prism through which these rules of international law are to be evaluated' is the 'actualised experience' of Third World peoples and 'not merely that of states'.[34] TWAIL therefore examines international law and the distribution of power from the perspective of the Third World and its peoples. Taking this TWAIL approach, this book will question: if international law is 'the principal language in which domination is coming to be expressed in the era of globalisation', can this domination be found within intervention and UN peacekeeping?[35] In particular, is peacekeeping used, at times, to legitimate intervention to further the interests and agendas of the dominant powers?

In answering these questions, the book will apply some important tenets of both TWAIL I and TWAIL II scholarship. Firstly, TWAIL I, *inter alia*, stressed the importance of the principles of sovereignty and non-intervention and focused on colonial international law legitimising the subjugation and oppression of the Third World.[36] The book will therefore generally highlight both the importance of the principle of non-intervention and the use of international law by dominant states to oppress the Third World. Secondly, this book will focus on a main proposition of TWAIL II scholarship: that colonialism is not external or incidental to international law but, rather, that it is central to the formation of international law.[37] In doing so, the book will draw heavily on Antony Anghie's work on imperialism, sovereignty and the making of international law as his combination of theory, history and colonialism, when examining both international law and sovereignty, could be applied to the principle of non-intervention, given that it is a corollary of sovereignty.[38] Anghie broadly argues that colonialism was central to the formation of international law, with many of the basic doctrines of international law (in particular, the doctrine of sovereignty) being forged out of the colonial confrontation and the attempt to create a legal system which

33 ibid.

34 ibid.

35 BS Chimni, 'Third World Approaches to International Law: A Manifesto' (2006) 8 ICLR 3–7, 3.

36 See: RP Anand, *International Law and the Developing Countries* (Banyan Publications 1987).

37 Anghie and Chimni (n32); see also: A Riles, 'Aspiration and Control: International Legal Rhetoric and the Essentialization of Culture' (1993) 106(3) HarvLRev 723–740; A Anghie, 'Finding the Peripheries: Sovereignty and Colonialism in Nineteenth Century International Law' (1999) 40(1) HarvIntlLJ 1–71.

38 A Anghie, *Imperialism, Sovereignty and the Making of International Law* (CUP 2007). See also: A Anghie, 'Rethinking International Law: A TWAIL Retrospective' (2023) 34(1) EJIL 7–112.

could manage relations between European and non-European worlds.[39] This book will therefore take this hypothesis and apply it to the principle of non-intervention and UN peacekeeping to ascertain the extent to which, if at all, colonialism has animated the principle and the concept of peacekeeping.

In adopting this TWAIL approach, the book does not seek to deliberate on the merits of TWAIL scholarship. That is, it will not engage in discussions about the risk of TWAIL 'simply rehashing, not reimagining old debates'[40] or its potentially paradoxical argumentative logic that is said to ultimately rely upon the very underlying assumptions of the conservative system which it seeks to transcend.[41] Instead, the book will uniquely apply a TWAIL lens to intervention and peacekeeping to provide an alternative view to the prevailing Western-centric narratives. Similarly, it must also be noted that whilst the TWAIL story is one of the frustrations, disappointments and exploitation of the Third World by international law and international institutions, 'it is also a story of hope in the moments of resistance'.[42] Therefore, the purpose of this book's application of TWAIL to UN peacekeeping is not to present a totalising, destructive critique of peacekeeping but, rather, to provide new insights and constructive criticisms in the hope that it will offer a more pluralistic interpretation, contributing to the reimagining and reinvigoration of peacekeeping.

The Congo

The DRC has been chosen as a case study for this book as both peacekeeping and the Congo are inextricably linked. That is, the United Nations has been deployed within the Congo, intermittently, since 1960 – two weeks after the country gained its independence and a few years into the birth of peacekeeping. As peacekeeping has shaped the Congo, so too has the Congo shaped peacekeeping. Indeed, the DRC has been used as a test-bed for UN peacekeeping with three operations deployed – ONUC (1960–1964) shortly after the Congo gained independence; MONUC (1999–2010) after the First Congo War and the signing of the Lusaka Ceasefire Agreement and MONUSCO (2010–present day) which was an evolution of MONUC into a stabilisation peacekeeping operation. These operations have been some of the largest and most expensive peacekeeping operations in UN history, with MONUSCO, in particular, continually reinventing itself[43] in an attempt to

39 ibid, 3.

40 AG Kiyani, 'Third World Approaches to International Criminal Law' (2016) 109 AJILUnbound 255–259, 257.

41 JD Haskell, 'TRAIL-ing TWAIL: Arguments and Blind Spots in Third World Approaches to International Law' (2014) 27(2) CJLJ 383–414, 386.

42 M Fakhri, 'Law as the Interplay of Ideas, Institutions, and Interests: Using Polyani (and Foucault) to Ask TWAIL Questions' (2008) 10 ICLR 455–465.

43 Such as deploying the Force Intervention Brigade and engaging in protection of civilian tasks.

adapt to changing conflict dynamics and demands from the Security Council, Congolese government and regional actors.

Throughout its turbulent history, the Democratic Republic of the Congo has also been known by various names. During colonisation, it was named the Congo Free State and, later, the Belgian Congo; after gaining independence, initially, it was known as the Republic of Congo and then the Democratic Republic of the Congo until 1971 when the then-president, Mobutu, changed its name to the Republic of Zaire under his 'Africanisation' programme.[44] The country remained as Zaire until Mobutu's dictatorship ended in 1997, when it was again renamed as the Democratic Republic of the Congo, as it is still known today. Throughout this book, the country will be referred to as 'Congo' or 'DRC' interchangeably. This is not to be confused with the Republic of Congo (or Congo-Brazzaville) which lies across the Congo River from the DRC's capital city, Kinshasa. It must also be noted that the use of 'the' may also be invoked ('the Congo') and whilst this does form part of Congo's official name, it must be recognised that some find it to be problematic, as it denotes colonial remnants.[45] The usage of 'the Congo' or 'the DRC' within this work is therefore to be understood not in support of a colonial legacy but simply for grammatical purposes.

Similarly, throughout the book, whilst the term 'Global South' is predominantly used, it may, at times be interchanged with 'Third World', particularly within Chapter 2 when the historical development of the principle of non-intervention is explored. In the post-Cold War era, many academics were sceptical of the term 'Third World' and proclaimed that it had ceased to exist as a category.[46] However, as Chimni argues, a critique of the term is an 'old divide and rule strategy' used by hegemonic states to 'misrepresent and undermine the unity of the Other' in order to exercise their own dominance.[47] Other commentators have also stressed the importance of understanding the term as a direct attack on Western hegemony in the world order.[48] Therefore, the category of 'Third World' remains crucial, provided that it is not fixed to a geographical space and peoples continue to self-identify with the term.[49]

Empirical Research

The doctrinal, socio-legal, theoretical and jurisprudential research within this book is also supported by qualitative empirical research in the form of

44 See: M Wrong, *In the Footsteps of Mr Kurtz* (Harper Collins 2000).

45 See, for example, S Autesserre, *The Trouble with the Congo* (CUP 2010) 36.

46 See: D Otto, 'Subalternity and International Law: The Problems of Global Community and the Incommensurability of Difference' (1996) 5(3) SocLegStud 337–364, 353.

47 Chimni (n35) 6.

48 Mutua (n24) 36.

49 Okafor (n22) 175.

semi-structured interviews, which are interwoven throughout the book.[50] That is, rather than containing a separate chapter of research findings, data from the interviews is dispersed throughout the book, informing how the law is applied in practice and providing an external perspective which will be compared and contrasted with the author's analysis of intervention, peacekeeping and the frameworks which govern the two concepts. The purpose of this empirical research is to provide an additional layer of analysis, to potentially fill any gaps left by the theoretical and doctrinal parts of the book and to, ultimately, provide a more nuanced appreciation of the UN decision-making process for peacekeeping both in general and specifically within the DRC.

Participants for this research consist of UN personnel from various departments and organs of the United Nations within the organisation's headquarters in Geneva and New York, including the Department of Peace Operations, the Office of Legal Affairs, the UN Development Programme, the Office of the High Commissioner of Human Rights and the Office of the Special Representative on Conflict Related Sexual Violence. Furthermore, beyond the UN headquarters, numerous current and former MONUSCO personnel were also interviewed, including personnel within the Office of the Special Representative of the Secretary-General to MONUSCO, former deputy and force commanders, current and former senior military personnel within MONUSCO's Force component and numerous civilian personnel, such as gender and child protection advisers and political affairs and human rights officers. Outside of the United Nations, interviews were also conducted with personnel from international organisations, such as the International Committee of the Red Cross, non-governmental organisations and independent experts, including Congolese actors.

This combination of UN and non-UN actors was chosen as a data sample as it this ecology of 'First United Nations' (member states), 'Second United Nations' (staff members of international secretariats) and 'Third United Nations' (supportive non-state actors such as NGOs and consultants) which, together, formulate and refine ideas and decision making on UN policies, including peacekeeping matters.[51] Focusing on a mixture of these actors therefore provides a greater understanding of the politics of knowledge and norm production which shape UN directives on peacekeeping and the ideas and narratives which drive or underpin them.[52]

50 See: J Giblin, 'United Nations Peacekeeping Raw Interview Data' (University of Nottingham Research Data Management Repository, June 2021) DOI: <http://doi.org/10.17639/nott.7119>.

51 TG Weiss, T Carayannis and R Jolly, 'The "Third" United Nations' (2009) 15(1) GG 123–142.

52 T Carayannis and TG Weiss, *The 'Third' United Nations: How a Knowledge Ecology Helps the UN Think* (OUP 2021) 1–2.

Thus, the aim of these interviews and the broader purpose of the book is to ascertain the 'what', 'why' and 'how' of peacekeeping – what constitutes the peacekeeping frameworks, why are they peacekeeping's boundaries and how are they interpreted and applied in practice? Whilst the author offers an interpretation of these questions, the interviews with personnel who engage in these frameworks at the institutional and field level provide further views on both their interpretations of these frameworks and their understanding of the United Nations' interpretations. Furthermore, the interviews have focused on actors at the institutional level, rather than at the field level, as it is these actors who set the legal and normative frameworks which govern intervention and peacekeeping and which this book seeks to clarify. Interview questions therefore focused on ascertaining what frameworks the individuals perceived themselves to be operating within, what they believed to be the high and low points or strengths and weaknesses of the United Nations' current operation in the Congo (MONUSCO) and whether they believed that there are any lessons which could be learnt from the United Nations' experiences in the Congo.

Structure of the Book

The structure of this book can be likened to a three-tiered pyramid with intervention or the principle of non-intervention forming the top of the pyramid, whilst UN peacekeeping forms the second layer, with peacekeeping in practice (the Congo case study) constituting the third and final layer. Chapter 2 will therefore begin by providing a definition of intervention and an examination of the historical development of the principle of non-intervention. It will highlight how the concept and practice of intervention have been somewhat cyclical, with a constant fluctuation in intervention and non-intervention rhetoric, often coupled with a disparity between rhetoric and practice. That is, whilst the principle of non-intervention may have been emphatically supported, in practice interventions have often occurred. The chapter therefore argues that these cycles of interventionist practice have had the impact of either supporting or undermining the principle of non-intervention. When exploring contemporary interventions, the chapter noted that UN peacekeeping as a form of collective security intervention is the most prevalent form of intervention today.

As such, Chapters 3 and 4 move on to explore the second layer of the pyramid – UN peacekeeping – finding that, despite the lack of an explicit framework, there exist legal principles and norms which, together, form a complex peacekeeping framework. Chapter 3 identifies the 'holy trinity' of consent, impartiality and non-use of force as the three legal principles which formulate peacekeeping's legal framework, whilst Chapter 4 argues that the newer, more controversial norms of democracy promotion, protection of civilians (PoC) and the prohibition of sexual exploitation and abuse (SEA) form part of peacekeeping's normative framework. The chapters argue that the legal framework sits at the core of peacekeeping and is surrounded by the much broader normative framework. However, the chapters note that these frameworks do not exist in total isolation but, rather, overlap at certain points, particularly when the norms invoke elements of international humanitarian, criminal and human rights law, thereby providing a secondary contribution to peacekeeping's legal framework. Furthermore, the chapters argue that these principles and norms do not exist harmoniously and instead 'exist in a competitive arena' with the normative composition of a peacekeeping operation being 'rebalanced each time'.[53] As such, an interpretation and application of one norm or principle may have an impact on another. Indeed, Chapters 3 and 4 highlight how the six principles and norms are continually re-interpreted and re-shaped which results in peacekeeping's frameworks being repeatedly contracted and expanded. That is, where the principles and norms are interpreted narrowly, generally, this results in a constriction of the peacekeeping frameworks, thereby firming the boundary between peacekeeping and intervention and consequently reinforcing the principle of non-intervention. However, when the principles and norms are interpreted more broadly, as is frequently the case with contemporary, multi-dimensional stabilisation operations, this expands peacekeeping's frameworks, blurring the line between peacekeeping and intervention and therefore undermining or, at times, potentially contravening the principle of non-intervention.

Following this, Chapters 5 and 6 take this analysis further by examining peacekeeping in practice, through an exploration of the United Nations' operations in the Congo. Whilst Chapter 5 focuses on the interpretation and application of peacekeeping's legal frameworks in the DRC, Chapter 6 examines the normative frameworks. Both chapters again demonstrate how these frameworks are constantly re-interpreted, reimagined and contorted, resulting in a continual fluctuation of peacekeeping's boundaries and the dividing line between peacekeeping and intervention. It is argued that, at times, ONUC, MONUC and MONUSCO have expanded peacekeeping's frameworks to their very limits and beyond, resulting in peacekeeping becoming intervention. As such, the book argues that there may need to be a narrowing or retraction of some of peacekeeping's principles and norms, and therefore the peacekeeping frameworks, to shrink the invisible red boundary line surrounding peacekeeping and to reaffirm the boundaries between peacekeeping and intervention. The concluding Chapter 7 therefore offers recommendations – to adopt a people-centred approach to peacekeeping, with realistic, streamlined mandates – in order to amplify peacekeeping's effectiveness as a tool for maintaining international peace and security in the modern era.

53 J Karlsrud, 'Special Representatives of the Secretary-General as Norm Arbitrators? Understanding Bottom-up Authority in UN Peacekeeping' (2013) 19(4) GG 525–544, 527.

References

Abi-Saab G, 'The Development of International Law: An Introduction by the United Nations' in F Snyder & S Sathirathai (eds) *Third World Attitudes to International Law: An Introduction* (Martinus Nijhoff 1987)

Allott P, 'International Law and the Idea of History' (1999) 1 JHistIntLaw 1–22

Anand RP, *International Law and the Developing Countries* (Banyan Publications 1987)

Anghie A, 'Finding the Peripheries: Sovereignty and Colonialism in Nineteenth Century International Law' (1999) 40(1) HarvIntlLJ 1–71

Anghie A, *Imperialism, Sovereignty and the Making of International Law* (CUP 2007)

Anghie A, 'Rethinking International Law: A TWAIL Retrospective' (2023) 34(1) EJIL 7–112

Anghie A and Chimni BS, 'Third World Approaches to International Law and Individual Responsibility in International Conflicts' (2003) 2(1) ChinJIL 77–103

Attar MA and Thompson R, 'How the Multi-Level Democratisation of International Law-Making Can Effect Popular Aspirations Towards Self-Determination' (2011) 3(1) TradeL&Dev 65–102

Autesserre S, *The Trouble with the Congo* (CUP 2010)

Banakar R and Travers M, 'Law, Sociology and Method' in R Banakar and M Travers (eds) *Theory and Method in Socio-Legal Research* (Hart 2005)

Campbell CM and Wiles P, 'The Study of Law in Society in Britain' (1976) 10 L&SR 547–578

Carayannis T and Weiss TG, *The "Third" United Nations: How a Knowledge Ecology Helps the UN Think* (OUP 2021)

Certain Expenses of the United Nations (Article 17, Paragraph 2 of the Charter) (Advisory Opinion) [1962] ICJ Rep 151

Chimni BS, 'Third World Approaches to International Law: A Manifesto' (2006) 8 ICLR 3–7

Corfu Channel Case (UK v Albania) (Merits) [1949] ICJ Rep 4

Day AC and Hunt CT, 'UN Stabilisation Operations and the Problem of Non-Linear Change: A Relational Approach to Intervening in Governance Ecosystems' (2020) 9(1) Stability 1–23

Declaration on Principles of International Law Concerning Friendly Relations and Cooperation among States in Accordance with the Charter of the United Nations, UN Doc A/Res/2625 (XXV) (24 October 1970)

Elias TO, *New Horizons in International Law* (2nd edn, Springer 1992)

Fakhri M, 'Law as the Interplay of Ideas, Institutions, and Interests: Using Polyani (and Foucault) to Ask TWAIL Questions' (2008) 10 ICLR 455–465

Foucault M, *Ethics: Subjectivity and Truth: Essential Works of Michel Foucault 1954–1984. Volume I* (Penguin 2000)

Gathii JT, 'TWAIL: A Brief History of its Origins, its Decentralised Network, and a Tentative Bibliography' (2011) 3(1) TradeL&Dev 26–64

Giblin J, 'United Nations Peacekeeping Raw Interview Data' (University of Nottingham Research Data Management Repository, June 2021) DOI: <http://doi.org/10.17639/nott.7119>

Haskell JD, 'TRAIL-ing TWAIL: Arguments and Blind Spots in Third World Approaches to International Law' (2014) 27(2) CJLJ 383–414

Karlsrud J, 'Special Representatives of the Secretary-General as Norm Arbitrators? Understanding Bottom-up Authority in UN Peacekeeping' (2013) 19(4) GG 525–544

Kennedy D, 'Law and Political Economy of the World' (2013) 26(1) LJIL 7–48

Kiyani AG, 'Third World Approaches to International Criminal Law' (2016) 109 AJILUnbound 255–259

Klabbers J, *An Introduction to International Institutional Law* (CUP 2009)

Mickelson K, 'Rhetoric and Rage: Third World Voices in International Legal Discourse' (2011) 16(2) WisIntlLJ 353–419

Mutua M, 'What Is TWAIL?' (2000) 32 ASILProc 31–38

Okafor OC, 'Newness, Imperialism, and International Legal Reform in Our Time: A TWAIL Perspective' (2005) 43(1/2) OHLJ 171–191

Otto D, 'Subalternity and International Law: The Problems of Global Community and the Incommensurability of Difference' (1996) 5(3) SocLegStud 337–364

Riles A, 'Aspiration and Control: International Legal Rhetoric and the Essentialization of Culture' (1993) 106(3) HarvLRev 723–740

Said E, *Representation of the Intellectual* (Vintage 1994)

Schachter O, *International Law in Theory and Practice* (Martinus Nijhoff 1991)

UN Peacekeeping, 'A4P+ Priorities for 2021–2023' <https://peacekeeping.un.org/sites/default/files/a4p_background_paper.pdf>

UNGA, 'Summary Study' A/3943 (9 October 1958) UN Doc A/3943

UNSC Res 2561 (29 January 2021) UN Doc S/RES/2561

Weiss TG, Carayannis T and Jolly R, 'The "Third" United Nations' (2009) 15(1) GG 123–142

Wrong M, *In the Footsteps of Mr Kurtz* (Harper Collins 2000)

Chapter 2

The Principle of Non-Intervention

Defining Intervention

In the broadest sense of the term, everything that anyone does which has an effect or influence on another is an intervention. Within international law, intervention is a contentious concept directly linked to the principles of sovereignty, self-determination and non-use of force. Intervention is a 'continuum, ranging from criticism to coercion'.[1] It is both a legal and political concept[2] and is a 'corollary of every state's right to sovereignty, territorial integrity and political independence'.[3] Within international law, there is no singular, authoritative definition of intervention. It is an ambiguous, 'blurred, controversial and disputed' legal term[4] and, as a concept, is described as 'one of the vaguest branches of international law'.[5] As Argentinian jurist Carlos Calvo wrote in 1870, on the matter of intervention 'there are almost as many opinions as there are authors'.[6] This remains true today. The definition is also further complicated by states' frequent use of the term in political rhetoric, condemning the acts of other states as intervention in their internal affairs,[7] and it has been the subject of much debate in recent times following the Russian invasion of Ukraine.

1 MNS Sellers, 'Intervention under International Law' (2014) 29(1) Maryland JIL 6.
2 For a discussion of the legal and political aspects of intervention, see: H Bull (ed) *Intervention in World Politics* (Clarendon 1984).
3 RY Jennings and AD Watts, *Oppenheim's International Law* (9th ed, OUP 2008) 428.
4 G Hafner, 'Sub-Group on Intervention by Invitation, Preliminary Report, 26 July 2007' (2007) Yearbook of the Institute of International Law, Sanitago Session 226, 236.
5 PH Winfield, 'The History of Intervention in International Law' (1922–1923) 3 BYIL 130.
6 Translation quoted in: A Heraclides and A Dialla, *Humanitarian Intervention in the Long Nineteenth Century: Setting the Precedent* (MUP 2015) 14.
7 Such as the Trump administration's foreign policy dialogue. See: S Siddiqui, 'Donald Trump Praises Syria Strikes and Declares: "Missions Accomplished"' (*The Guardian*, 14 April 2018) <https://www.theguardian.com/us-news/2018/apr/14/donald-trump-syria-strikes-mission-accomplished>; M Zenko, 'Donald Trump Is a Magical (Foreign Policy) Realist' (*Foreign Policy*, 7 June 2016) <foreignpolicy.com/2016/06/07/donald-trump-is-a-magical-foreign-policy-realist/>.

DOI: 10.4324/9781003371649-2

Within the UN system, a practical, working definition of intervention is adopted, with intervention defined as any 'action along a wide continuum from the most pacific to the most coercive' by one state against another.[8] However, as this book is examining the legal norms or principles within UN peacekeeping, a normative definition will be taken instead. 'Intervention' will therefore be defined as any situation where coercive action is taken by a state, state actor or international organisation to try to enforce a change in the internal affairs of another state. This definition follows the general definition stated by Oppenheim, that 'intervention is dictatorial interference by a State in the affairs of another State'.[9] It is also in-keeping with the International Court of Justice's (ICJ) understanding of the principle of non-intervention, which it stated in *Nicaragua* 'involves the right of every sovereign State to conduct its affairs without outside interference'.[10]

When examining both the principle of non-intervention and, later, UN peacekeeping, 'intervention' will be defined as any action taken by a state, state actor or international organisation, such as the United Nations, that may be deemed coercive, in order to force change within the host state. Coercive action will be further understood as activities which override the element of voluntariness. That is, pressure on the host state (either directly or indirectly) to change or demand a change to their behaviour, without the state being able to reject the change or to decide whether or not to comply. Coercion is therefore distinguishable from persuasion, criticism, public diplomacy and propaganda as they are aimed at a voluntary change, unlike coercion which removes this element of voluntarism. For example, a peacekeeping operation which instructs a host state to remove certain personnel from its armed forces or it will withdraw its support could amount to direct coercive action as the ultimatum removes the element of voluntarism from the United Nations' request. Similarly, indirect coercive action may occur through the development of sub-economies around peacekeeping bases as these create host state dependency or reliance on the peacekeeping operation which, in turn, may result in subsequent UN ultimatums becoming coercive. Indeed, it is this concept – UN peacekeeping as intervention – which will run as the red thread throughout this book. That is, when examining the development of UN peacekeeping, this book will highlight instances when peacekeeping has crossed the threshold into intervention. More importantly, it will explore how the functions of contemporary stabilisation peacekeeping operations may, on occasions, amount to intervention.

8 UN Press Release, 'Secretary-General Presents His Annual Report to General Assembly' (SG/SM/7136, GA/9596).

9 IL Oppenheim, *International Law: A Treatise* (Longmans, Green and Co 1905) 221.

10 *Case Concerning Military and Paramilitary Activities in and against Nicaragua (Nicaragua v United States of America)* [1986] ICJ Rep 14, para 202.

Furthermore, this chapter will also be informed by Third World approaches to international law (TWAIL). As previously explored,[11] for TWAIL scholars, 'international law makes sense only in the context of the lived history of the peoples of the Third World'.[12] Uniquely applying TWAIL, the chapter will focus on the importance of the principle of non-intervention and the use of international law by dominant states to oppress the Third World or Global South. It will also focus on the role colonialism has played in shaping the principle of non-intervention.[13] In particular, it will draw upon Anghie's work on imperialism, sovereignty and the making of international law to ascertain the extent to which, if at all, colonialism has animated the principle of non-intervention.[14] More specifically, this chapter will highlight the power relations embedded both within the principle and within its application, focusing on the concept of 'othering'[15] – distinguishing between 'us' and 'them'/'others', with the latter group viewed as lesser, thereby justifying domination by the enlightened 'us'.[16] Anghie argues that 'over the centuries' international lawyers have maintained a basic dichotomy between 'the civilised and the uncivilised' and have 'continually developed techniques' to civilise the uncivilised.[17] As other scholars have noted, the civilising mission or the 'standard of civilisation' identified 'those that belong to [a] particular society from those that do not' and those nations that did not measure up were excluded 'as "not civilised" or possibly "uncivilised"'.[18] Throughout the early development of international law, this division resulted in those deemed to be 'uncivilised' as falling 'outside the bounds of international society and thus lacking equal recognition in international law'.[19] These 'uncivilised' societies were either rejected from the remit of international law or given a quasi-legal status – partially subjected to international law but afforded only minimal protection. The classical standard of civilisation was therefore 'well and truly entrenched in the annals of international law'.[20] This

11 Chapter 1, Section 2.

12 A Anghie and BS Chimni, 'Third World Approaches to International Law and Individual Responsibility in International Conflicts' (2003) 2(1) Chinese JIL 77–103, 78.

13 ibid; See also: A Riles, *Aspiration and Control: International Legal Rhetoric and the Essentialization of Culture* (1993) 106 HarvLRev 723; A Anghie, 'Finding the Peripheries: Sovereignty and Colonialism in Nineteenth Century International Law' (1999) 40(1) HarvIntlLJ 1.

14 A Anghie, *Imperialism, Sovereignty and the Making of International Law* (CUP 2007).

15 See: E Said, *Orientalism* (Penguin Books 2003).

16 See: E Said, *Culture and Imperialism* (Vintage 1994). For contemporary discussion in international law, see: A Orford (ed) *International Law and Its Others* (CUP 2006).

17 Anghie (n14) 4.

18 GW Gong, *The Standard of 'Civilization' in International Society* (Clarendon Press 1984) 3.

19 B Bowden, 'The Colonial Origins of International Law: European Expansion and the Classical Standard of Civilization' (2005) 7 JHIL 1–23, 20.

20 ibid.

endless process of creating a gap between two cultures ('demarcating one as 'universal' and civilised and the other as 'particular' and 'uncivilised') and then seeking to close this gap by normalising the 'aberrant society' is what Anghie refers to as the 'dynamic of difference'.[21] He argues that this dynamic animated the development of core doctrines of international law, in particular sovereignty doctrine, and continues to operate within international law today. Anghie further argues that this characterisation of 'non-European societies as backward and primitive legitimised European conquest of these societies' and justified intervention.[22] It is this concept that this chapter, and the remainder of this book, will therefore build upon. Indeed, this chapter will highlight how the principle of non-intervention, like sovereignty, also acquired its character through colonialism and was shaped, and continues to be shaped, by the 'dynamic of difference'. It will note examples of when this dynamic has been created and then used to justify intervention, primarily on the basis of needing to bridge the gap between the civilised and uncivilised or, more recently, the developed and developing. The chapter will therefore employ Anghie's theory and a broader TWAIL lens to highlight the contradictions and inherent power biases throughout the evolution of the principle of non-intervention, its uneven application (both past and present) and the potential for it to be used as a tool by dominant powers (including the United Nations as an autonomous actor) to extend their self-interests.

Taking this theoretical approach and the previously discussed definition, this chapter will examine the legal development and application of the principle of non-intervention. The aim of the chapter will be to analyse this development and application with reference to the broader global issues where relevant. The chapter will begin by examining the historical development of non-intervention and, then, its advancement through international organisations, conventions, charters and case law, before examining the principle in the modern era. It will identify key tipping points or periods throughout this evolution, such as colonialism, the Bandung conference, decolonisation and, more recently, the War on Terror. The chapter will examine various forms and justifications for intervention, such as collective security intervention, and will identify examples of Anghie's dynamic of difference throughout the development and operation of non-intervention. It will conclude by summarising the principle of non-intervention today before the book moves on to explore UN peacekeeping as a specific form of intervention. Throughout this exploration, it must be noted that whilst a critical lens is applied, this is not a totalising critique aimed at dismantling the principle of non-intervention. As noted in the introduction to this book, the adoption of a critical lens is a constructive critique, designed to clarify the legal and normative boundaries

21 Anghie (n14) 4.
22 ibid.

of the principle – the red elastic band which surrounds the principle – and to explore the justifications or legitimisations which puncture this red line, thereby challenging or undermining the principle of non-intervention. This chapter therefore provides a greater understanding of the principle of non-intervention which will be taken further in subsequent chapters when examining the concept of peacekeeping.

Historical Development

During the 'Age of Discovery' in the fifteenth century intervention occurred on a grand scale in the form of conquest and discovery. Led by Portuguese and Spanish explorers, the 'discovery' of the 'New World' facilitated European expansion and laid the foundations for the subsequent colonial project.[23] Intervention was also a common method for dealing with foreign affairs and, in particular, enforcing impartial and papal rules in the Middle Ages.[24] As European exploration intensified, questions arose as to how the 'New World', 'which was not part of the '*respublica Christiana*', but also not classed as the "enemy"', should be perceived.[25] Whilst some kingdoms had 'a sophisticated and well-developed state',[26] these were disregarded on the basis of the Europeans' belief in their superior ontological status and divine or natural right to hegemonic power – a mentality which has endured throughout history, as this chapter will highlight. A distinction – or a dynamic of difference[27] – was therefore created between the hegemonic Western powers and the newly 'discovered' Global South states, or the 'other'.

Peace of Westphalia

This changed in 1648 with the Peace of Westphalia – a trinity of treaties which ended the Thirty Years' War in Europe and marked a turning point in international relations and the law of nations. It is generally argued that the Peace established the concept of sovereignty and a 'Westphalian system' of equal, sovereign states which refrained from intervening in each other's domestic

23 See: E Hobsbawm, *The Age of Empire: 1875–1914* (Abacus 1989).

24 See: W Preiser, 'History of International Law, Ancient Times to 1648' (Max Planck Encyclopedia of Public International Law, 2008) <http://opil.ouplaw.com/view/10.1093/law:epil/9780199231690/law-9780199231690-e716>.

25 G Baars, 'From the Dutch East India Company to the Corporate Bill of Rights: Corporations and International Law' in U Mattei and J Haskell (eds) *Research Handbook on Political Economy and Law* (Edward Elgar 2015) 263.

26 A Hochschild, *King Leopold's Ghost: A Story of Greed, Terror and Heroism in Colonial Africa* (Pan Books 2012) 9.

27 Anghie (n14).

affairs.[28] Westphalia is therefore crucial for the principle of non-intervention as it established the concept of sovereignty within international law and, by corollary, non-intervention. However, as Milton argues, by including France and Sweden's 'foreign crowns' in the treaties, 'a right to intervene for the protection of constitutional and religious rights within another state was enshrined in positive treaty law'.[29] The Westphalian treaties therefore legalised intervention in a foreign state in order to protect the legal rights of subjects. Similarly, the concept of sovereignty and therefore this tentative principle of non-intervention were only applicable to the European powers; as such, intervention in non-European territories was perceived as more permissible. This was particularly the case when it was justified on the basis of expanding European (international) law to the 'uncivilized' or 'primitive' societies of the 'New World'.[30] The complexities of these relationships were noted during this period by Vitoria who attempted to address the problem of difference, asserting the 'humanity of the Indians of the "New World"'.[31] From a TWAIL perspective, this exemplifies the formulation and operation of the dynamic of difference 'at the very beginning of the discipline of international law' as the Global South states are firstly characterised as the primitive other and then a series of legal principles are outlined to justify intervention on the basis of the need to 'civilise' the other and close the gap between the two cultures.[32]

Similarly, whilst European lines of hegemony were being demarcated across the globe in the sixteenth and seventeenth centuries, trading companies became increasingly important interventionist actors in aiding states' attempts to colonise any unclaimed land.[33] Corporations such as the Dutch and British East India Companies became key components of the colonial expansion as their 'indistinct legal status' made them 'perfect agents to police' the 'transitional' colonialism.[34] Corporations were therefore significant interveners, with their interventionist activities moulding the earliest

28 See: D Philpott, *Revolutions in Sovereignty: How Ideas Shaped Modern International Relations* (PUP 2001) 4, 30, 85; cf D Croxton, 'The Peace of Westphalia of 1648 and the Origins of Sovereignty' (1999) 21(3) Int Hist Rev 569; S Beaulac, 'The Westphalian Legal Orthodoxy – Myth or Reality?' (2000) 2 JHIL 148–177.

29 P Milton, 'Guarantee and Intervention: The Assessment of the Peace of Westphalia in International Law and Politics by Authors of Natural Law and of Public Law c. 1650–1806' in S Zurbuchen (ed) *The Law of Nations and Natural Law 1625–1800* (Brill 2019) 186–226, 199.

30 Bowden (n19) 13.

31 A Anghie, 'The Evolution of International Law: Colonial and Postcolonial Realities' (2006) 27(5) TWQ 739–753, 742–744.

32 Anghie (n14) 9.

33 C Miéville, *Between Equal Rights: A Marxist Theory of International Law* (Pluto Press 2006) 182; W Grewe, *The Epochs of International Law* (Walter de Gruyter & Co; Rev Ed 2000) 181.

34 ibid, Miéville, 182.

formations of international law. As Grewe notes, whilst states used these actors, who were considered more or less independent, to annex conquered territories, they consequently constructed a 'particularly elastic system of colonial international law'.[35] At the same time as corporations and states were exploring and expanding, the Trans-Atlantic slave trade – the most illustrative and interventionist form of colonial violence – was spreading across Africa.

The slave trade also perfectly exemplifies Anghie's dynamic of difference. The trade solidified the dichotomy of 'civilised' and 'uncivilised' and crystallised the concept of the 'other'.[36] Western intervention in the 'New World' was then justified on the basis of 'civilising' the 'barbarians' or 'savages' thereby seeking to close the gap in Anghie's so-called dynamic of difference.[37] The slave trade was therefore animated by the European belief, in particular, in African's 'inferiority' and 'backwardness', resulting in a lasting effect on how Europeans viewed and treated Africans.[38] This narrative also perpetuated the concept of the 'White Man's burden'[39] within international relations. That is, the belief that powerful, predominantly Western states are tasked with the 'burden' of 'civilising' the 'barbarous' Third World and therefore intervention in these states is a necessary and legitimate task. This rhetoric of enlightened civiliser and uncivilised natives was also furthered during the Age of Discovery by Christian missionaries who sought to convert natives to Christianity. During this period, intervention therefore occurred extensively and was predominantly based or justified on a sense of moral righteousness – the European belief in their duty to enlighten the inferior 'new world' – a theme which has arguably permeated the principle of non-intervention and remains embodied within it today. It is within this context that international law and the principle of non-intervention emerged.

Formulating a Principle of Non-Intervention

In the seventeenth century, scholars such as Hugo Grotius began to support the notion of intervention (within European states) to protect individuals within another state from violations of natural law, on the basis that they

35 Grewe (n33) 346.

36 See: Said, *Orientalism* (n15); Orford (n16).

37 These terms are in quotation marks as they were part of the ordinary discourse of many international lawyers, commentators and actors from the fifteenth to nineteenth century, such as Francisco de Vitoria and James Lorimer. See, for example: J Lorimer, *The Institutes of the Law of Nations Vol 1* (Adamant Media Corporation 2001).

38 K Somerville, *Africa's Long Road since Independence: The Many Histories of a Continent* (Penguin 2017) 6.

39 R Kipling, *The White Man's Burden: A Poem* (Doubleday and McClure Co 1899).

were unable to defend themselves from their sovereign.[40] However, others such as Wolff believed that intervention within the concept of natural law was impermissible, arguing that to interfere in another state 'is opposed to the natural liberty of nations'.[41] Post-Westphalia, the principle was therefore still subject to much debate. Whilst the Peace of Westphalia established a system of sovereign states and, by extension, an unofficial agreement of non-interventionism, rather than curtailing internal interventions, Westphalia 'strengthened them by increasing the scope of the basis upon which interventions could take place'.[42] The Westphalian system therefore established a system which favoured non-intervention, on the basis of sovereignty, but permitted intervention if a legal basis existed. This formulation of a general prohibition of intervention but with specific legal justifications or exceptions has persisted throughout the development of the principle of non-intervention.

During this period, it is Emer de Vattel, a founding father of modern international law,[43] who is often credited with being the first to formulate the principle of non-intervention in 1758 in his work *Le droit des gens*.[44] Within this, Vattel 'inaugurated the terms in which we continue to carry on debates about intervention'; that is, a system of 'legally equal and independent sovereign states that warrant protection from outside intervention in order to develop autonomously'.[45] However, despite some codification of the principle,[46] in the midst of the French Revolution, France, for example, failed to limit its own interference in the internal affairs of other states, with the French government claiming a right to intervene in all cases where interference was necessary to assist people's struggle for liberty.[47]

Even during its early conception, then, the paradox within the intervention principle is evident. This contradiction between intervention in theory

40 See: GP van Nifterik, 'Religious and Humanitarian Intervention in Sixteenth and Early Seventeenth Century Legal Thought' in R Lesafer and G Macours (eds) *Sovereignty and the Law of Nations (16th–18th Centuries)* (Peeters Publishers 2006).

41 Quoted in J Pitts, 'Intervention and Sovereign Equality: Legacies of Vattel' in S Recchia and JM Welsh (eds) *Just and Unjust Military Intervention: European Thinkers from Vitoria to Mill* (CUP 2013) 143.

42 Milton (n29) 201.

43 There are numerous histories of international law (such as Chinese international law or Islamic international law) but it is European law, now known as modern international law, which has come to dominate.

44 E Vattel, *Droit des gens ou principes de la loi naturelle* (Londres 1758) I para 37.

45 Pitts (n41) 132.

46 For France, non-intervention was integrated in Article 4 of its Constitutional Act and in its Declaration of the Rights of Man and of the Citizen. See: RR Ludwikowski, 'The Beginning of the Constitutional Era: A Bicentennial Comparative Study of the American and French Constitutions' (1989) 11(1) MJIL 167.

47 See: WE Lingelbach, 'The Doctrine and Practice of Intervention in Europe' (1900) 16 AnnAmAcadPolSocSci 1–32.

and intervention in practice or, more specifically, the dominant powers' manipulation of a caveated principle of non-intervention, has persisted throughout the evolution of the principle. That is, states purport to be non-interventionist yet intervene extensively under various auspices. Indeed, the French justification for intervention – the protection of nationals and individual liberties[48] – has persisted throughout the development of the principle of non-intervention and can be seen in contemporary justifications such as humanitarian intervention and the responsibility to protect. All of these justifications seek to protect the rights of individuals and invoke a similar sense of moral righteousness, as espoused during the Age of Discovery, albeit in a different context. For TWAIL scholars, the creation of international law during this period was based on European and Christian values, with 'Europe as the centre, Christianity as the basis for civilisation, capitalism as innate in humans and imperialism as a necessity'.[49] The selective use of intervention by the dominant European powers therefore exemplifies the European and Christian origins of international law.

Whilst the concept of a non-intervention principle was discussed again by scholars such as Kant in the late eighteenth century,[50] states continued to intervene extensively in other nations. In Europe, the Holy Alliance[51] claimed the right to intervene in situations involving European revolutionary governments, on the basis of protecting the legal establishment[52] – a justification similar to today's rule of law. Beyond Europe, the right of intervention was also established in multilateral treaties such as the Treaty of Berlin 1878, which permitted European powers to interfere in the internal affairs of Turkey and Africa, primarily based on a form of 'humanitarian' intervention, to guarantee a minimum of rights of the inhabitants.[53] In international legal scholarship, Oppenheim's classic commentary on international law also addressed the issue of intervention.[54] Following Lauterpacht's approach, Oppenheim noted that intervention was, 'as a rule, forbidden by the Law of

48 ibid.

49 M Mutua, 'What Is TWAIL?' (2000) 94 ASILPROC 31–38, 33.

50 See for example: FH Hinsley, *Power and the Pursuit of Peace* (CUP 1963); FR Tesón, 'The Kantian Theory of International Law' (1992) 92(1) ColumLRev 53–102; A Franceschet, 'Kant, International Law and the Problem of Humanitarian Intervention' (2010) 6(1) JIntPolTheory 1–22.

51 See: WP Cresson, *The Holy Alliance: The European Background of the Monroe Doctrine* (OUP 1922); A Brisku, 'The Holy Alliance as "An Order of Things Conformable to the Interests of Europe and to the Laws of Religion and Humanity"' in T Hippler and M Vec (eds) *Paradoxes of Peace in Nineteenth Century Europe* (OUP 2015).

52 Austrian intervention was justified in the Troppau Proposal of 19 November 1821. See: PW Schroeder, *The Transformation of European Politics, 1763–1848* (OUP 1994) 610–612.

53 Treaty between Austria-Hungary, France, Germany, Great Britain, Italy, Russia and Turkey for the Settlement of Affairs in the East (13 July 1878).

54 Oppenheim (n9).

Nations' but only if it was 'forcible or dictatorial interference'.[55] Interference 'pure and simple' was not enough to be considered illegal intervention.[56] Oppenheim also noted that, in addition to forceful or dictatorial interference, intervention could be justified on the basis of protecting a state's nationals, humanitarian reasons or collective intervention in the general interest.[57] It is this concept of intervention which has generally prevailed.

An Emerging Principle

The principle of non-intervention eventually began to gain significant support from states, with the introduction of numerous doctrines in the late nineteenth century.[58] This change in approach to intervention was a direct reaction to the excess and abuse of intervention which occurred with the emergence of new nation states. In particular, the Latin American Wars of Independence forced a shift in the colonial global power order and marked the first wave of decolonisation, with most Latin American states gaining their independence by 1825.[59] During this time policies such as the Monroe Doctrine were proclaimed, in this instance, as a US policy against European colonialism in the Americas, appearing to declare a strong non-interventionist stance.[60] However, in practice, the doctrine was used by the United States to exert American hegemony over Latin America and justify intervention.[61] The Monroe Doctrine could be viewed, then, as an agreement between dominant states in the Global North to mutually respect each other's sovereignty and, in particular, to refrain from intervening in each other's spheres of influence – namely, the Global South. It therefore was a selective form of the principle of non-intervention, supporting the notion that both non-intervention and sovereignty were only applicable to select states, thereby marginalising and excluding the 'other' states who were not granted the protection of the principles and, again, re-creating Anghie's dynamic of difference. Indeed, the United States' application of the Monroe Doctrine has been referred to as 'imperial anticolonialism';[62] that is, whilst the Doctrine rejected European

55 ibid s134, 221.
56 Jennings and Watts (n3) 428.
57 ibid.
58 For example, the Calvo Doctrine/Calvo Clause (1868); Monroe Doctrine (1823) and Drago-Porter Convention (1907).
59 See: R Harvey, *Liberators: Latin America's Struggle for Independence* (Overlook Books 2002).
60 See: J Sexton, *The Monroe Doctrine: Empire and Nation in Nineteenth-Century America* (Farrar, Straus and Giroux 2011).
61 See: MR Gilderhus, 'The Monroe Doctrine: Meanings and Implications' (2006) 36(1) PSQ 5–16.
62 A term used by historian William Appleman Williams in his work 'The Tragedy of American Diplomacy', see: HW Berger (ed) *A William Appleman Williams Reader: Selections from His Major Historical Writings* (Ivan R Dee 1992).

colonialism, it simultaneously permitted American imperialism. Again, the development and application of the Monroe Doctrine supports Anghie's argument that doctrines of international law grew out of and were shaped by the colonial encounter, with the endless dynamic of difference creating gaps between states.[63]

Colonialism

The contradictory development of the principle of non-intervention is exemplified by the fact that during the mid- to late nineteenth century, whilst Latin America was gaining its independence and the United States was emerging as a great power, throughout the African continent, colonialism was at its height with the 'Scramble for Africa', culminating in the Berlin Conference of 1884–1885.[64] Therefore, whilst the Global North states enjoyed the full protection and benefits of the principles of sovereignty and non-intervention (including the protection of their nationals when in the Global South), Latin American states gained a quasi-form, whilst colonised states fell outside the remit of the principles and were instead subject to extensive intervention. This reflected the hierarchy of states (and states' rights) which was prevalent at that time, that is, the distinction between civilised, semi-civilised and uncivilised states with each of these, respectively, enjoying either full, limited or no international legal personality.[65] The principle of non-intervention at this point could therefore be compared to an exclusive club which was still in its infancy, with the terms of its membership, including who qualified for admittance, still undecided.

The colonial era marked the height of Western intervention, with states occupying and exploiting vast amounts of territory in the non-Western world in order to expand their empires or boost their economies. During this period, international law permitted, legitimated and legalised extensive intervention through, for example, legal instruments or institutions such as treaties or trade agreements and, more profoundly, the Berlin Conference of 1884–1885.[66] Colonial conquest therefore represented 'the first pertinent *global* model of intervention'.[67] Through explorers or private chartered companies,[68] treaties

63 Anghie (n14).

64 See: T Packenham, *The Scramble for Africa* (Abacus New Ed 1992).

65 See: Lorimer (n37) and G Simpson, *Great Powers and Outlaw States: Unequal Sovereignty in the International Legal Order* (CUP 2004) 116.

66 See: M Craven, 'Between Law and History: The Berlin Conference of 1884–1885 and the Logic of Free Trade' (2015) 3(1) LRIL 31–59.

67 HJ Richardson III, 'Critical Perspectives on Intervention' (2014) 29 Maryland JIL 12–49, 14.

68 By the conclusion of the Berlin Conference, or the Scramble for Africa, over 75% of British acquisitions in sub-Saharan Africa had been acquired by chartered companies. See: M Koskenniemi, *The Gentle Civilizer of Nations* (CUP 2009) 117–121.

between native tribal leaders and Western states were established and used exploitatively to allow Western states to formally obtain land.[69] These treaties, again, highlight a striking paradox within the law. Whilst Europeans acknowledged that the natives were capable of entering into legal obligations to grant Western powers sovereignty over their territory, within international law the natives were also characterised as lacking any form of legal status.[70] Indeed, Anghie notes how the natives were granted a 'quasi-sovereignty for the purposes of enabling them to *transfer* rights, property and sovereignty' to the Western imperial powers.[71] For the principle of non-intervention, natives were evidently capable of falling within the ambit of international law in order to transfer their property or sovereignty but were not afforded the right or protection of the principle as they were subject to extensive intervention from the West. It is within this two-tiered level of international law, with its uneven evolution and application of sovereignty, that the principle of non-intervention developed.

At the Berlin Conference this power differential between the Western colonisers and the native peoples was exacerbated further, with international law again permitting and legitimising such actions. The conference determined the future of Africa, dividing the continent into artificial countries which could be more easily controlled by European states, with not one African involved in the process. Indeed, 'the most irrelevant factor in deciding the fate of the continent was the Africans themselves'.[72] As occurred with the early European explorers, the Western states showed complete disregard for any pre-existing kingdoms, systems of governance or ethnic, tribal or national interests. The arbitrary boundary lines, pencilled on a map,[73] divided kingdoms and ethnic groups and contrived an 'unnatural division of Africa'.[74] These colonial borders still have a profound influence on contemporary African politics, as is particularly evident with the ethnic tensions in the Great Lakes region.[75] It could therefore be argued that intervention, in this instance, has had a significant, long-term impact, again based on the superiority of Western standards and interests which were forced upon the non-Western world, with international law providing a veneer of legitimacy to these interventionist activities.

69 For an example of a treaty see: H Sanford, 'Declaration by the International Association of the Congo. April 22, 1884' (1909) 3(S1) AJIL 5.
70 Anghie (n31) 745.
71 ibid.
72 UO Umozurike, *International Law and Colonialism in Africa* (Nwamife 1979) 26.
73 D Van Reybrouck, *Congo: The Epic History of a People* (Fourth Estate 2015) 58–59.
74 R Anand, *New States and International Law* (Vikas 1972) 33.
75 As seen with the conflict between the Tutsi and Hutu tribes in Rwanda and its neighbouring countries; see: M Mamdani, *When Victims Become Killers: Colonialism, Nativism, and the Genocide in Rwanda* (PUP 2002).

In particular, the process of intervening and dividing the African continent was addressed through the rhetoric of free trade and 'civilising' which were enshrined in Acts such as the 'General Act of the Berlin Conference Respecting the Congo'.[76] This Act focused on ensuring the provision of free trade for the European states operating in the area and pledged to 'civilize' the native population, making them 'understand and appreciate the advantages of civilization'.[77] Again, Anghie's dynamic of difference is presented here through the 'civilising mission', with the Europeans presented as the 'civilisers' or 'saviours' in contrast to the 'barbaric' or 'uncivilised' non-Europeans.[78] Grewe notes that the term 'civilisation' 'embodied an attempt to place the global political supremacy and colonial mission of the white man on a new basis of legitimacy'.[79] Indeed, the General Act, and other international treaties at that time, 'included a pathetic invocation of the European powers' mission to promote civilization'.[80] This rhetoric of free trade and civilising simply allowed Western states, leaders and corporations to 'pursue contradictory and inconsistent goals'.[81] Therefore, intervention during this period was again based on a sense of moral righteousness and the colonial or imperialistic narrative of the 'civilised self' against the 'savage', 'barbaric' other which TWAIL scholars seek to challenge.[82] This polarisation was then glossed over by international law, with instruments such as the General Act of the Berlin Conference legitimating these justifications for intervention and thereby perpetuating the civilised-barbaric narrative.

International law's relationship with colonialism and imperialism is thus evident. For TWAIL scholars, imperialism is said to be 'ingrained in international law as we know it today'.[83] In particular, Anghie's dynamic of difference – the clash between two cultures – is both animated and justified by international law.[84] Understanding both this relationship between international law and colonialism and the use of international law to subjugate and

76 (signed 26 February 1885) (1885) 165 CTS [485]; see especially the preamble: 'Wishing to regulate in a spirit of good mutual understanding the conditions most favourable to the development of commerce and of civilization in certain regions of Africa'.

77 ibid, Article 6.

78 Again, quotation marks are used here to denote terms frequently invoked at that time. See: Frantz Fanon, *The Wretched of the Earth* (Penguin Classics 2001); Said (n15).

79 Grewe (n33) 455.

80 ibid, 451.

81 P Ala'i, 'Leopold & Morel: A Story of "Free Trade" and "Native Rights" in the Congo Free State' 37 (2005) Stud Transnat'l Legal Pol'y 33–46, 33.

82 M Mutua, 'Savages, Victims, and Saviors: The Metaphor of Human Rights' (2001) HarvIntLJ 201–245.

83 JT Gathii, 'Neoliberalism, Colonialism, and International Governance: Decentering the International Law of Governmental Legitimacy' (1999–2000) 98 MichLRev 1996–2065, 2020.

84 Anghie (n14).

oppress Third World peoples is a central objective of TWAIL.[85] Mutua notes how European states justified the colonisation of independent, non-European lands, whether by military conquest, fraud or intimidation, through international law.[86] As colonisation was viewed as 'part of the manifest destiny of Europeans and "good" for non-Europeans', 'any method deployed in its pursuit was morally and legally just'.[87] In an age of 'frenetic' expansion, international law therefore provided 'an ethical rationalisation' of the European will for global power.[88] Fisch notes that although 'the colonial acquisition of Africa needed no justification', as the right of conquest was 'widely accepted both in theory and state practice', it was understood that there should be proper justification[89] – hence the conference and subsequent General Act. Koskenniemi also argues that the Berlin Conference marked a shift in the European approach to intervention. He contends that the Conference was a result of a 'new imperialism' whereby European powers 'suddenly took active steps for the creation of formal empires'.[90]

The colonial period was therefore a crucial time for both the delimitation of the principle of non-intervention and the development of international law more broadly. In particular, it established the principle of non-intervention between European states but not between European states and non-European territories, once again reflecting the balance (or imbalance) of power during that period. As the remainder of this chapter will demonstrate, the influence of colonialism on shaping international law and the colonial dichotomy of civilised and uncivilised have remained firmly entrenched within international law.

Into the Twentieth Century

During the start of the twentieth century, a wealth of international conventions were produced after the First World War which endorsed the principle of non-intervention. After many years of battling with the concept, firm commitments were made to recognise the importance of non-intervention and respect for the sovereign equality of states. Regional and international treaties

85 See for example: Mutua (n49); K Mickelson, 'Rhetoric and Rage: Third World Voices in International Legal Discourse' (2011) 16(2) WisIntlLJ 353–419; B Rajagopal, 'International Law and Its Discontents: Rethinking the Global South' (2012) 106 ASILPROC 176–181.

86 M Mutua, 'Why Redraw the Map of Africa: A Moral and Legal History' (1995) 16 MichJIntlL 1113–1176.

87 Mutua (n49) 33.

88 M Mazower, *Governing the World: The History of an Idea, 1815 to the Present* (Penguin 2012) 67.

89 J Fisch, 'Africa as *Terra Nullius*: The Berlin Conference and International Law' in Förster et al (eds) *Bismarck, Europe and Africa: The Berlin Africa Conference 1884–1885 and the Onset of Partition* (OUP 1988) 360.

90 Koskenniemi (n68) 117.

were created, alongside international institutions, which further solidified the status of the principle within international law. It is during this period that the principle of non-intervention began to firmly take shape and states which had previously been excluded from the principle's ambit now fell within the protection of the law as they gained sovereign status.

The first affirmative condemnation of intervention came in 1933 with Article 8 of the Montevideo Convention which proclaimed that 'no State has the right to intervene in the internal or external affairs of another'.[91] The subsequent Additional Protocol Relative to Non-Intervention also affirmed the principle.[92] Parties to the Protocol declared inadmissible 'the intervention of any one of them, directly or indirectly, and for whatever reason, in the internal of external affairs of any other of the Parties'.[93] In the Americas, the Good Neighbour Policy, which favoured anti-imperialism, economic internationalism and political non-interventionism,[94] appeared to reaffirm sovereignty for Latin American states.[95] However, similar to the application of the Monroe Doctrine, non-intervention was only restricted within the boundaries set by the political elites in the United States. This later became evident with the United States' numerous Cold War interventions, despite Latin American states' attempts to challenge US intervention through coordinated diplomatic manoeuvring.[96] The principle of non-intervention was therefore tentatively but unevenly developing. In particular, there remained a significant gap between the West and 'the rest', with the latter, non-Western states typically falling outside of the remit of the principle, thereby remaining subject to intervention and perpetuating Anghie's dynamic of difference.

In addition to this distinction, there were also differing approaches to intervention amongst Western states, with the language or justifications put forward for intervention varying between Europe and the United States. Whilst European countries favoured the 'monopolistic protectionism' of colonies as exclusive sources of raw material, the United States advocated for freedom of commerce unfettered by territorial or sovereign claims of control.[97] As

91 The Montevideo Convention of 1933 on Rights and Duties of States 159 LNTS 199. For the events of the Montevideo Conference, see also: D Jones, *Code of Peace: Ethics and Security in the World of the Warlord States* (UCP 1991) 79–82.

92 Affirmed Protocol Relative to Non-Intervention 1936 188 LNTS 31.

93 ibid.

94 RD Johnson, 'Anti-Imperialism and the Good Neighbour Policy: Ernest Gruening and Puerto Rican Affairs, 1934–1939' (1997) 29(1) JLatAmStud 89–110, 93.

95 See: IF Gellman, *Good Neighbour Diplomacy. United States Policies in Latin America, 1933–1945* (JHUP 1979).

96 MP Friedman and T Long, 'Soft Balancing in the Americas: Latin American Opposition to US Intervention, 1898–1936' (2015) 40(1) IntSecur 120–156.

97 JT Gathii, 'How American Support for Freedom of Commerce Legitimized King Leopold's Territorial Ambitions in the Congo' (2005) 37 StudTransnat'lLegalPol'y 97–107.

TWAIL scholar Gathii notes, whilst the USA's approach implied they were an 'enlightening power' and in opposition to European territorial expansion and intervention, it 'effectively legitimised the very colonial occupation it regarded as illiberal'.[98]

Again, to use the analogy of the principle of non-intervention as a club, the club's handbook had begun to be drafted (by the hegemonic powers) but, as colonialism still existed, membership remained limited and was reserved for the most dominant states. It was only with the formation of the United Nations and the body of law which it and the International Court of Justice produced that the principle of non-intervention began to solidify and be more uniformly applied. At the end of the Second World War, an increase in state cooperation and the rise of internationalism led to the further development of the principle. Non-intervention was defined as prohibiting intervention through the use of force but also interference through economic, political and diplomatic means,[99] thereby laying the foundations of the principle which is prevalent today. This broader understanding of intervention also reflected the political climate at that time. As cooperation between states increased, interference was possible in a more subtle manner without the need for the use of force.

The United Nations

The creation of the United Nations, with an increase in cooperation between states, marked a turning point for the principle of non-intervention. Whilst the International Law Commission was the first institution to stipulate non-intervention as a duty of states,[100] the establishment of the United Nations in 1945 set the stage for what would later become a pivotal institution for the principle of non-intervention. Whilst non-intervention is 'not, as such, spelt out in the Charter' of the United Nations, it is a 'corollary of the principle of the sovereign equality of States' contained in Article 2(1) of the UN Charter.[101] It is therefore generally implied that if a state has sovereign powers, by extension, it is granted the protection of the principles of non-use of force and non-intervention.[102] Conversely, without the prohibition on intervention, the principle of sovereignty, with its 'two complementary and mutually dependent dimensions' of 'internal sovereignty' (the power to make

98 ibid 103.

99 See: *Nicaragua* (n10).

100 Article 3, UNGA Res 375 (IV) Draft Declaration on Rights and Duties of States (6 December 1949) UN Doc A/RES/375.

101 *Nicaragua* (n10) para 202.

102 For a discussion on the concept of sovereignty and its relationship with international law see, for example: G Kreijen, M Brus et al, *State, Sovereignty and International Governance* (OUP 2002).

decisions on domestic matters) and 'external' sovereignty (that 'a sovereign power obeys no other authority')[103] cannot be realised.

Within the UN Charter, the principle of non-intervention can therefore be viewed as being enshrined in Article 2(1), as a corollary of sovereignty, and is also read into Articles 2(4) and 2(7) of the Charter. Thus, the introduction of the United Nations and its founding Charter encapsulated the principle of non-intervention into a legal document on a much broader scale than ever before. Indeed, it went further than its predecessor, the League of Nations, whose Covenant contained weaker provisions that indirectly supported the early conception of non-intervention by abolishing the 'right of conquest' for members of the league,[104] protecting members from 'external aggression' and preserving their 'domestic jurisdiction'.[105] Therefore, whereas non-intervention had previously only been found in *ad hoc* conventions and policies, predominantly at a regional level,[106] now it had gained a global and 'universal' recognition through the United Nations.

Whilst the prohibition on the use of force, contained within Article 2(4), can be seen within the principle of non-intervention in the prohibition on the use of armed or military intervention (including military occupation of a territory, naval blockades, seizure of assets and embargos),[107] the only direct reference to intervention within the Charter is found in Article 2(7). This states that the Charter does not authorise the United Nations to 'intervene in matters which are essentially within the domestic jurisdiction of any state', excluding enforcement measures under Chapter VII.[108] Although this could be viewed as a notable development for the principle of non-intervention, as it enshrined the concept within the Charter of an international institution, for some, no other Article within the Charter 'has caused more trouble than this one' as 'its relatively simple terms contain a dual danger'.[109] That is, the United Nations is prohibited from intervening but only in 'domestic' matters and neither 'intervention' nor 'domestic jurisdiction' have been sufficiently defined as to clarify what forms of intervention this encompasses. This has then led to different constructions of the Article which makes its 'content elusive' and results in contradictions or self-negating outcomes.[110] For some,

103 B Fassbender, 'Purposes and Principles, Article 2(1)' in B Simma et al, *The Charter of the United Nations: A Commentary Vol 1* (OUP 3rd ed 2012) 136.

104 Q Wright, 'Effects of the League of Nations Covenant' (1919) 13(4) APSR 556–576, 559.

105 Articles 10 and 15(8) The Covenant of the League of Nations (28 April 1919).

106 Such as: the Calvo and Monroe Doctrines (n58).

107 See: M Kunig, *Prohibition of Intervention* (MPEPIL 2008).

108 Charter of the United Nations (26 June 1945) Article 2(7).

109 DR Gilmour, 'The Meaning of "Intervene" within Article 2(7) of the United Nations Charter – An Historical Perspective' (1967) 16 ICLQ 330–351, 331.

110 N Tsagourias, 'Security Council Legislation, Article 2(7) of the UN Charter, and the Principle of Subsidiarity' (2011) 24 LJIL 539–559, 549.

the Charter's focus on the 'limits instead of the forms of intervention' avoids 'the intractable problem of distinguishing intervention from the legitimate and necessary efforts of states to influence the behaviour of other states'.[111] There has also been debate as to whether this provision is applicable only to the United Nations or whether it also applies *a fortiori* to member states.[112] Therefore, what initially appears to be a development in the strengthening of the principle of non-intervention is, arguably, not as significant as first appears.

The contribution of Article 2(7) to the development of the principle of non-intervention is further weakened by the inclusion of the caveat that it does not preclude enforcement measures under Chapter VII. As such, Article 2(7) is effectively placed into the hands of the United Nations' executive body – the Security Council – as it is the Council which determines the exercise of Chapter VII measures. This is problematic when the composition of the Security Council, in particular the permanent five members' veto power, is considered.[113] Gifted to the most dominant states at the time of the United Nations' creation,[114] the veto power of the five permanent members (P5) has been referred to as 'the mother of all powers of the UN' as it provides the P5 with a right to veto proposed resolutions or decisions.[115] A disproportionate amount of power therefore lies with these dominant five states which are able to act in their own self-interests or in the interests of their allies, using the veto power to protect their agendas, often to the detriment of smaller states, thus maintaining a level of inequality amongst member states of the United Nations.[116] The veto power, then, is a permanent reminder of the domination of hegemonic powers, which TWAIL opposes. Indeed, 'TWAIL regards the structure of the United Nations, and in particular its Security Council, as completely indefensible', with scholars such as Mutua arguing that the United Nations legitimises Western global hegemony through 'the cloak of universality'.[117] The veto power could also be viewed as a perpetual example of Anghie's dynamic of difference both in its fundamental composition (the five dominant states' advantage against the remaining members) and

111 NG Onuf, 'The Principle of Non-Intervention, the United Nations and the International System' (1971) 25(2) IntOrgan 209–227, 214–215.

112 ibid and UN Documents A/AC.119/SR.26, pp6–8; A/AC.119/SR.3-, pp4–6; A/AC.119/SR.31, pp11–12.

113 J Wouters and T Rhys, 'Security Council Reform: A New Veto for a New Century?' (2005) Egmont Paper 9, 1–35.

114 See: B Fassbender, *UN Security Council Reform and the Right of Veto: A Constitutional Perspective* (Kluwer 1998).

115 I Arias, 'Humanitarian Intervention: Could the Security Council Kill the United Nations?' (1999) 23(4) Fordham Intl L J 1005–1027, 1020.

116 B Simma (ed) (in collaboration with H Mosler, A Randelzhofer, C Tomuschat, R Wolfruh) *The Charter of the United Nations: A Commentary* (2nd ed, OUP 2002) 508.

117 Mutua (n49) 37.

in its operation – in this instance, in its potential to be implemented in relation to Article 2(7). Indeed, this was an issue which was considered during the drafting of this provision, in particular, in relation to the interpretation of 'domestic jurisdiction'. As Abi-Saab notes, when drafting the provision, smaller states attempted to widen the scope of 'domestic jurisdiction' both to safeguard their own independence and 'as a bar and a limitation to the extensive powers that could be exercised by the directorate' of the permanent five members.[118] The creation of the United Nations and the inclusion of the principle of non-intervention within the UN Charter therefore assisted with the development of the principle of non-intervention, but this was limited by the inherent power imbalances within the UN system. It is only with decolonisation and the inclusion of more Global South states that the United Nations became a greater tool or instrument for the development of the principle of non-intervention, albeit with the enduring and ever-looming hegemony of the Security Council.

Decolonisation and the Rise of the Global South

Decolonisation marked a significant shift in the history of intervention and the formation of the principle of non-intervention. It was during this period that the principle expanded from essentially a European/Western principle to an international doctrine, starting with the Bandung Conference, and then primarily through the United Nations and the body of law which it produced predominantly from 1960 until 1985. The creation of the United Nations combined with the decolonisation period resulted in an expansion of sovereign states and consequently an increase in states which were subject to the principle of non-intervention. This led to an expansion of the geographical scope of the principle and also required a re-balancing within the 'international community' as the Northern or Western states' domination within global politics and international law was now challenged by the newly sovereign Third World states.[119] As Grewe has argued, this period became 'an oscillation between international community and the hegemony of a single superpower'.[120] That is, both international law and the international community[121] were adjusting to the new world order – learning how to balance the newly independent states of the Third World, the reduction in

118 G Abi-Saab, 'The Newly Independent States and the Scope of Domestic Jurisdiction' (1960) 54 ASILPROC 84–90, 86.

119 See: Richardson (n67) 24.

120 Grewe (n33) 703–706.

121 In this chapter the term 'international community' will be used to refer to the community of states. For a discussion on the term see: G Abi-Saab, 'Whither the International Community?' (1998) 9 EJIL 248–265 and E Lagrange, 'The Thoughts of René-Jean Dupuy: Methodology or Poetry of International Law?' (2011) 22(2) EJIL 425–440.

Western hegemonic power and the body of UN and ICJ law on the principle of non-intervention.

As has been a recurring theme throughout the development of the principle, during this period there was a paradox between non-intervention rhetoric and interventionist activities. Whilst colonial intervention ended and the principle was emphatically supported, intervention still occurred but in a less obvious, more subtle form.[122] States moved from overt, unilateral military intervention to multilateral intervention or proxy interventions through insurgents, armed groups, mercenaries and private military and security companies (PMSCs).[123] Reverting back to the analogy of the principle of non-intervention as a club, membership had expanded to include almost all states but sub-groups had begun to grow, resulting in a fracturing of the forms of intervention, with seemingly just as many interventionist activities albeit in a less invasive form.

Bandung and Decolonisation

In 1955, against the 'backdrop of crumbling European colonies', representatives from 29 Asian and African states gathered in Bandung (Indonesia) and sought to use new norms of non-intervention to regain their sovereignty.[124] The conference represented approximately two-thirds of the world's population and became viewed as an 'event'[125] or, more abstractly, a 'spirit',[126] which has influenced numerous contemporary movements and institutions. Indeed, within international law scholarship, it is considered to be the 'symbolic birthplace' of TWAIL.[127] More broadly, it sparked the 'Afro-Asian movement', leading, in the early 1960s, to 'the Non-Aligned Movement' before the birth of the 'Group of 77' (G-77).[128] The latter of these saw the Latin American states joining the Asian and African states which shared the same economic and political predicaments. The Bandung Conference was therefore a key catalyst for mobilising non-Western states to oppose the agenda of

122 For example, Belgium granted the Congo independence but retained significant control within the mineral-rich province of Katanga. See: Reybrouck (n73).

123 See for example: PW Singer, *Corporate Warriors: The Rise of the Private Military Industry* (Cornell University Press 2003).

124 L Eslava, M Fakhri and V Nesiah (eds) *Bandung, Global History and International Law* (CUP 2018).

125 S Pahuja, 'Decolonisation and the Eventness of International Law' in F Johns et al (eds) *Events: The Force of International Law* (Routledge 2011) 101.

126 V Prashad, *The Darker Nations: A People's History of the Third World* (New Press 2008) 45–46.

127 Mutua (n49).

128 The group was established by the 'Joint Declaration of the Seventy-Seven Developing Countries Made at the Conclusion of the United Nations Conference on Trade and Development' (Geneva, 15 June 1964).

the dominant hegemonic powers. More specifically, in relation to the principle of non-intervention, those states at the conference, which had already gained independence, sought to challenge history's most illustrious form of intervention – colonialism. Noting the 'evils arising from the subjection of peoples to alien subjugation, domination and exploitation', these newly independent states declared that 'colonialism in all its manifestations is an evil which should speedily be brought to an end'.[129] This demand was then later reiterated in the General Assembly in its 1960 Declaration on the Granting of Independence.[130] Thus, Global South states were challenging the long-standing practice of Western domination and simultaneously expanding the scope of the principle of non-intervention to now include the Global South.

For TWAIL scholars, this decolonisation period, beginning with the Bandung Conference, marked 'the emergence of a new voice and the quest for a new paradigm'.[131] Third World states were therefore contesting 'the universality and legitimacy of the international legal system' which had been developed without their participation and used to justify their subjugation.[132] This did not, however, mean that the 'new' Asian-African states rejected the whole body of international law; rather, 'the occasional outbursts' and 'demand for its adaptation' reflected only protests against the inequities within the system.[133] Again, this reflected the broader TWAIL initiative of opposing the global hegemony of the West and advocating for the full representation of all voices, particularly those which constitute the 'Third World'.[134] These 'new' states therefore wished to actively participate in international law and assist in its transformation into a more equitable body of law. Indeed, Anand argues that the newly independent states believed international law to be a protection for them as 'weaker members of international society', despite recognising that the system was developed by 'Western Christian civilisation' in accordance with their cultures and philosophies.[135] Nowhere is this tension more evident than with the development of the principle of non-intervention, which, during this period, was transformed from a 'European into a universal rule of international law'.[136] That is, as Global South states gained

129 'Final Communiqué of the Asian-African Conference' (2009) 11(1) Interventions 94–102, 99.

130 Declaration on the Granting of Independence to Colonial Countries and Peoples, UNGA Res 1514 (XV) (14 December 1960).

131 G Abi-Saab, 'The Third World Intellectual in Praxis: Confrontation, Participation, or Operation behind Enemy Lines' (2016) 37(11) TWQ 1957–1971, 1959.

132 ibid 1960.

133 RP Anand, 'Role of the "New" Asian-African Countries in the Present International Legal Order' (1962) 56 AJIL 383–406, 388.

134 Mutua (n49) 37.

135 ibid 388–389.

136 Grewe (n33) 40.

independence they entered the international arena as sovereign states, falling within the ambit of international law. Thus, they ostensibly gained the same status as their former colonial rulers and also obtained the benefits of this status, including the protection of the principle of non-intervention.

Decolonisation therefore marked a tipping point for the concept of non-intervention, and it was 'professed equally emphatically in the East, West and Third World'.[137] Where the principle had previously only been applicable to the West, it was now also applicable to the Global South, thereby representing 'the utilisation of existing international law to craft a more pluralistic, tolerant international system'.[138] In this instance, international law was effectively used by Third World states to reject colonial intervention and protect their own legal, political and cultural interests. However, whilst the principle of non-intervention was now applicable to both the North and South, this did not necessarily translate into an equal application. Indeed, the dichotomy of the colonial relationship did not instantly vanish when colonised states gained their independence and became sovereign entities. For some, the decolonisation period was viewed as a 'Revolt against the West'[139] – a term loaded 'with a sense of dismay and disapproval at anti-colonialism, decolonisation and the emergence of a demanding, unsettled and unruly "Third World"'.[140] Whilst decolonisation eliminated military occupation and sovereign control over African territories by European powers, it has been argued that 'political influence, economic preponderance, and cultural conditioning' remained.[141] Whilst states granted their former colonies their independence, in reality they simply fostered a transition from formal control to informal control through less conspicuous means of intervention.[142] In some instances, these interventions were legitimated under international law through legal instruments such as 'Treaties of Friendship'.[143] International law was therefore used by the dominant actors to legitimate intervention, supporting the TWAIL assertion that international law provides powerful states with a legal pretext to exercise their domination over the weak. During this period, then, whilst the Global South had gained the same rights and protections as the

137 ibid 654.

138 ibid.

139 The phrase emerged in Britain in the late 1950s, see: H Seton-Watson, *Neither War nor Peace: The Struggle or Power in the World* (Kessinger Publishing 2010) and G Barraclough, *An Introduction to Contemporary History* (Penguin 1990).

140 I Hall, 'The "Revolt against the West" Revisited' in T Dunne and C Reus-Smit, *The Globalization of International Society* (OUP 2017) 346.

141 W Zartman, 'Europe and Africa: Decolonization or Dependency?' (1976) 54 Foreign Affairs 325–343.

142 S Metz, 'American Attitudes toward Decolonization in Africa' (1984) 99(3) PolSciQ 515–533, 515.

143 Treaty of Friendship between Belgium and the Congo, reprinted in EW Lefever, *Crisis in the Congo: A United Nations Force in Action* (Brookings Institution 1965) 199–200.

Global North, the playing field was not levelled, with the North-South divide maintained even as the South entered the international law arena.

Non-Intervention through the United Nations

This battle or readjustment between the North and South states also unfolded within the UN system as almost a third of the world's population (750 million people) and more than 80 former colonies gained their independence through decolonisation.[144] This subsequently led to a significant increase in UN membership, with the original 51 members growing to 127 by 1970 with 44 states admitted during the high point of decolonisation.[145] Membership to the United Nations provided newly independent states with a seat in the General Assembly, thereby also providing them with voting powers and a platform to promote their interests. For some TWAIL scholars and Third World states, the United Nations was thus viewed as a 'shield for the protection of the small Powers'.[146] These newly independent states were also said to have adopted a 'very liberal and functional interpretation of the Charter'[147] and powers of the UN organs to 'change the *status quo*' and strive to 'restructure their societies and the international society to reach a more equitable situation'.[148] As such, the UN system offered Third World states a tool to challenge the dynamic of difference and attempt to reduce the gap between themselves and the dominant powers through their engagement in the development of international law. As international institutions, such as the United Nations, are 'ideologically charged to validate and legitimate world order norms',[149] they are able to include Global South leaders and absorb counter-hegemonic initiatives.[150] The institutions can therefore play a crucial role in levelling the playing field and developing international law. From a TWAIL perspective, membership in the United Nations could therefore be viewed as an opportunity for the newly independent Global South states to contest the dominant states' monopoly and to influence international law-making 'through participation in debates, decisions and cooperate activities'

144 See: UN and Decolonisation, 'List of Former Trust and Non-Self Governing Territories' <https://www.un.org/dppa/decolonization/history/former-trust-and-nsgts>.
145 See: UN, 'Growth in United Nations Membership, 1945–present' <https://www.un.org/en/sections/member-states/growth-united-nations-membership-1945-present/index.html#1960s>.
146 Abi-Saab (n118) 90.
147 ibid 88–90.
148 Anand (n133) 390.
149 Ananthavinayagan (n178) 4.
150 RW Cox, 'Gramsci, Hegemony and International Relations: An Essay in Method' in S Gill (ed) *Gramsci, Historical Materialism and International Relations* (1st ed, CUP 1993) 49–66.

undertaken in the United Nations.[151] This influx of Global South states thus challenged the domination of the hegemonic powers, particularly within the General Assembly as, for the first time, Global South states held the voting majority.

For the principle of non-intervention, this growing presence of the Global South meant these states could engage in the development and formation of the principle, promoting their interests and therefore making the principle ostensibly more universal, rather than a European or Western creation. In particular, as the Cold War 'precluded the potential directorate' of the five permanent members of the Security Council, the General Assembly (GA) became 'the stronghold of the small Powers' as they enjoyed 'absolute equality' with the big Powers and 'numerical superiority'.[152] As such, when the inherently biased hegemonic organ of the Security Council was paralysed, the playing field was levelled somewhat, with the Global South able to promote their agendas without having to compete with the P5 and their veto power.

This was epitomised in the adoption of the United Nations' pivotal 1960 Declaration on the Granting of Independence to Colonial Countries and Peoples which declared the need to bring colonialism to a 'speedy and unconditional end'.[153] It expressly stated many of the concerns identified during the Bandung Conference and reflected the informal alliance between these states, the non-aligned Bloc and the Group of 77, thus signalling a shift in the majority within the UN General Assembly. Whilst the General Assembly's 'Essentials of Peace' could be viewed as the United Nations' first postulation of non-intervention,[154] it was the Assembly's 1960 Declaration on Independence which was the first UN document to significantly contribute to the principle of non-intervention by explicitly and vehemently rejecting the most prevalent form of intervention at that time – colonialism – 'in all its forms and manifestations'.[155] This then established a platform which allowed the broader UN system to more coherently develop the principle of non-intervention through Declarations and Special Committees, which remain active today.[156]

151 DP Fidler, 'Revolt against or from within the West?: TWAIL, the Developing World, and the Future Direction of International Law' (2003) 2(1) CJIL 29–76, 38.

152 Abi-Saab (n118) 87.

153 UNGA Res 1514 (XV) (14 December 1960).

154 'Essentials of Peace' called upon every state to 'refrain from any threats or acts, direct or indirect, aimed at impairing the freedom, independence or integrity of any state or at fomenting civil strife and subverting the will of the people in any State'. UNGA Res 290 [V] (1 December 1949) para 2.

155 Declaration on Independence (n130).

156 See: Special Committee on Decolonisation (C-24) UNGA Res 1654 (XVI) (27 November 1961); International Decade for Eradication of Colonialism in 1990–2000, 2001–2010 and 2011–2020.

Building upon the 1960 Declaration on Independence, the United Nations' main contribution to the principle of non-intervention came with the 1965 Declaration on the Inadmissibility of Intervention, which provided a more authoritative elaboration of the norm of non-intervention.[157] This declared that 'no State has the right to intervene, directly or indirectly, for any reason whatever, in the internal or external affairs of any other State'.[158] During General Assembly debates, the Declaration was viewed as 'one of great importance, particularly for the smaller countries, which did not feel safe from intervention by more powerful countries', in spite of the Charter provisions on self-determination and 'categorical assurances and virtuous professions'.[159] The Declaration could therefore be viewed as an important development within international law not only for the principle of non-intervention but also for the promotion of the Third World voice as it built upon Bandung and the 1960 Declaration by including recommendations from the former colonised states. This again demonstrated how, through General Assembly debates, newly independent states, which had struggled against colonial intervention, were able to voice their concerns and interests.[160] Ghana, for example, noted that the emergence of new states from colonisation 'revealed other more subtle forms of intervention in the internal affairs of those States'.[161] This included economic dependence resulting in political pressure and foreign military bases which enabled external states 'to run the affairs of other States from the sidelines in their own interests'.[162] As such, it was recognised that the Declaration needed to include these forms of intervention as prohibited acts. Again, from a TWAIL perspective, these resolutions were 'momentous' as they concerned matters 'of utmost interest to the Third World' and, as they were developed within the UN General Assembly, newly independent states could play a significant role in 'renegotiating the rules' and developing international law.[163]

Within the UN system, the development of the principle of non-intervention was also supported by the General Assembly's establishment of the Special Committee on Principles of International Law concerning Friendly Relations and Cooperation among States in 1963.[164] This culminated in the Friendly

157 UNGA Res 2131 (XX) (21 December 1965).

158 ibid para 1.

159 UNGA First Committee (20th Session, 1402nd Meeting) (8 December 1965) UN Doc A/C.1/SR.1402, para 1.

160 On the importance of the UN General Assembly for the Global South, see NA Adams, *Worlds Apart: The North-South Divide and the International System* (Zed Press 1993) 53–55.

161 UNGA Sixth Committee (28th Session, 1402nd Meeting) (1 October 1973) UN Doc A/C.6/SR.1402, para 13.

162 ibid.

163 Abi-Saab (n118) 1959.

164 UNGA Res 1966 (XVIII) (16 December 1963).

Relations Declaration of 1970, which expressly stated that the principles of the UN Charter, which were embodied in the Declaration, including non-intervention, 'constitute basic principles of international law'.[165] Within the preamble, it also developed the principle of non-intervention further by linking non-intervention and international peace and security, noting that a 'strict observance by States' not to 'intervene in the affairs of any other State' is an essential condition for nations to live in peace.[166] It also re-emphasised the overlap between the principles of non-intervention and non-use of force by stating that forceful or 'armed' intervention and 'all other forms of interference or attempted threats' against the personality of the state violate international law.[167] The Declaration then went on to maintain a somewhat broader interpretation of non-intervention by stating that 'No State may use or encourage the use of economic, political or any other type of measures to coerce another State' in order to 'obtain from it the subordination' of any of its sovereign rights and secure advantages.[168] Therefore, the Declaration clarified that intervention amounted to more than merely forceful or military intervention, simultaneously reinforcing the notion that coercion is the essence of intervention.

In addition to these notable legal contributions to the development of the principle, the Declaration again highlighted the Global South states' newfound ability to contribute to the development of international law. As with the 1960 Declaration, during committee meetings on the core principles of the Friendly Relations Declaration, statements on self-determination were included, largely at the insistence of newly independent African and Asian states.[169] The Declaration, like the earlier GA resolutions and declarations, demonstrated both the development of the principle of non-intervention and the reconfiguration of the relationship between the dominant powers and the newly independent states, with an increased involvement of the Global South. However, as has been identified as a common pattern within the development of the principle, all is not as first appears with discourse not matching practice. Whilst the principle was being legally and normatively strengthened, in practice the United Nations was intervening extensively in Africa with its largest and most forceful peacekeeping operation to date,[170] thus, again highlighting the recurring contradiction between the principle of

165 UNGA Res 2625 (XXV) (24 October 1970) section 3.
166 ibid.
167 ibid.
168 ibid.
169 UNGA, 'Report of the Special Committee on Principles of International Law Concerning Friendly Relations and Co-operation among States' (24th Session, Supplement No 19 A/7619) (October 1969) UN Doc A/AC.125/L.24, para 4(c).
170 See: J Boulden, 'United Nations Operation in the Congo (ONUC)' in JA Koops, T Tardy, N MacQueen and PD Williams (eds) *The Oxford Handbook of United Nations Peacekeeping Operation* (OUP 2015).

non-intervention in theory and in practice. Furthermore, whilst there had been an increase in states entering the international system, and thereby a greater possibility of them contributing to the development of the principle, this did not necessarily translate into a counter-hegemonic narrative to juxtapose that of the dominant states. This was highlighted in 1981, ten years after the Friendly Relations Declaration, when a General Assembly Resolution containing a Declaration on the Inadmissibility of Intervention in the Domestic Affairs of States was issued.[171] Whilst this resolution provided a much more comprehensive definition of intervention than previous resolutions, it was opposed by most Western states.[172] Again, this reflected the lingering dynamic of difference between the West and the rest and a reluctance by the dominant states to place limitations on their powers and close the dynamic gap.

This then leads us to the broader and inescapable issue of the intrinsic power relations embedded within the UN system. As noted earlier, the Security Council holds a disproportionate amount of power within the United Nations and for TWAIL scholars 'the primacy of the Security Council' over the General Assembly makes 'a mockery of the notion of sovereign equality among states'.[173] It is further argued within TWAIL scholarship that the United Nations was used as a front by the big powers and 'simply changed the form of European hegemony, not its substance'.[174] Indeed, Mazower goes as far as to argue that the United Nations was created both to promote liberal internationalism and to preserve the interests of empire.[175] He argues that at the founding of the United Nations, many believed the organisation was deeply hypocritical, viewing its 'universalising rhetoric of freedom and rights as all too partial'.[176] Mazower proposes, therefore, that the United Nations may not have begun as an instrument to end colonialism but, rather, 'at least in the minds' of some of the drafters, as a means to preserve it.[177] This is reflected in the development of the principle of non-intervention with, for example, the Western opposition to the most comprehensive proposed definition of intervention and the continual, uneven application of the principle between states. Further, as the remainder of this book will highlight,

171 UNGA Res 36/103 (9 December 1981).

172 AV Lowe, 'The Principle of Non-Intervention: Use of Force' in V Lowe and C Warbrick (eds) *The United Nations and the Principles of International Law: Essays in Memory of Michael Akehurst* (Routledge 1994) 69.

173 Mutua (n49) 34.

174 D Otto, 'Subalternity and International Law: The Problems of Global Community and the Incommensurability of Difference' (1996) 5 Soc&LegStud 337–364, 340.

175 M Mazower, *No Enchanted Palace: The End of Empire and the Ideological Origins of the United Nations* (PUP 2009).

176 ibid 7.

177 ibid 31, 19–21, 28–65.

UN peacekeeping is a prime example of both this tension and the use of selective intervention, based on the dominant states' agenda. That is, if the United Nations can be viewed as being taken 'hostage by powerful states and exploited for their geo-political and economic interests',[178] with the Security Council holding a disproportionate power, then, as it is the Security Council that sets the peacekeeping agenda, by extension it could be argued that peacekeeping, as a form of intervention, is driven by the interests of the dominant powers. Building upon the TWAIL perspective that interventions are staged on a tableau of hegemonic or Western justifications (such as human rights), yet espoused to be part of a 'universal progress narrative',[179] the subsequent chapters will explore how peacekeeping, as a form of intervention, has developed in this same vein. Put simply, is peacekeeping another example of intervention in the Global South, based on the interests of the dominant powers?

Evolution in the International System

Whilst the United Nations is the main institution within the international system to have contributed to the development of the principle of non-intervention, other entities such as the ICJ and regional organisations have also contributed to its development. The creation of regional entities such as the Organisation of American States (OAS), Association of Southeast Asian Nations (ASEAN)[180] and Organisation of African Unity (OAU)[181] reinforced the interests of the Global South and further developed the principle of non-intervention through their constitutive acts and charters. This provided the principle with greater legal and normative support and created a more nuanced understanding of its composition. In particular, it also explored the application of the principle to the Global South and began to highlight a somewhat new form of intervention – intervention by the Global South within the Global South – which started to become more prevalent in the late Cold War and post-Cold War era.[182]

178 TV Ananthavinayagan, 'Uniting the Nations or Dividing and Conquering? The United Nations' Multilateralism Questioned – A Third World Scholar's Perspective' (2018) 29 IrishStudIntAff 1–17, 2.

179 V Nesiah, 'The Specter of Violence that Haunts the UDHR: The Turn to Ethics and Expertise' (2009) 24(1) MJIL 135–154, 148.

180 See: AC Wilgus, 'James G Blaine and the Pan American Movement' (1922) 5(4) HAHR 662–708.

181 Charter of the Organisation of African Unity (25 May 1963).

182 Such as: the Economic Community of West African States (ECOWAS) intervention in Liberia and Sierra Leone. See: W Ofuatey-Kodjoe, 'Regional Organisations and the Resolution of Internal Conflict: The ECOWAS Intervention in Liberia' (2007) 1(3) IntPeacekeep 261–302 and PA Dumbuya, 'ECOWAS Military Intervention in Sierra Leone: Anglophone-Francophone Bipolarity or Multipolarity?' (2008) 25(2) JThirdWorldStud 83–102.

International Court of Justice

Within the ICJ, Articles 62 and 63 of the Court's Statute envisage the possibility of third-state intervention in specific circumstances, that is, when a 'legal interest' may affect the intervening party[183] or for the purposes of interpreting a multilateral treaty to which the intervening state is a party.[184] The Statute therefore takes a relatively strong non-interventionist stance, rendering intervention permissible only within these limited circumstances. Indeed, within its judgments in cases pertaining to intervention, the Court's refusal to permit intervention in *Corfu Channel* and the *Continental Shelf Cases* reflects a non-interventionist stance,[185] thereby buttressing the principle of non-intervention. Similarly, the Court also reiterated the understanding of intervention outlined in the Friendly Relations Declaration, namely that there must be an element of coercion and the intervention must bear on matters which each state is freely permitted to decide, including political, economic, social and cultural systems and 'the formulation of foreign policy'.[186] The decisions by the Court solidified the understanding of non-intervention, with its discussions on the use of force and self-defence in *Nicaragua* crystallising the law in this area and remaining valid today in regards to humanitarian and collective security intervention.[187]

In defence of the principle and its boundaries, the ICJ also noted it would 'certainly lose its effectiveness as a principle of law if intervention were to be justified by a mere request for assistance made by an opposition group in another State'.[188] More specifically, it argued that it would 'be difficult to see what would remain of the principle of non-intervention in international law' if intervention, which is already allowable at the request of the host state government, were also to be allowed at the request of the opposition.[189] It was believed that this would 'permit any State to intervene at any moment in the internal affairs of another State', either at the request of the government or the opposition.[190] The ICJ therefore clarified and reaffirmed the boundaries of the principle of non-intervention, highlighting its importance within international law. Furthermore, as the subsequent chapter will explore, this assertion of state sovereignty and state consent for intervention is also replicated within UN peacekeeping, whereby the host state must consent to the presence of a

183 Statute of the International Court of Justice (1946), Article 62(1).

184 ibid Article 63(1).

185 See: *Corfu Channel Case (UK v Albania)* (Merits) [1949] ICJ Rep 4, 132–169; LF Del Duca, 'Reviewed Work(s): L'Intervento davanti alla Corte Internazionale di Giustizia by Angelo Davi' (1987) 81(2) AJIL 465–467, 466; *Nicaragua* (n10) 14–150.

186 ibid 202, 288–89.

187 M Kohen, 'The Principle of Non-Intervention 25 Years after the Nicaragua Judgment' (2012) 25(1) LJIL 157–164.

188 *Nicaragua* (n10) 246.

189 ibid.

190 ibid.

peacekeeping operation. Therefore, this notion of state sovereignty and consent within the principle of non-intervention is carried through into collective security intervention. More specifically, as will be explored in Chapters 5 and 6, this interpretation has been upheld when, for example, consent for the presence of peacekeepers is only requested from the host state and not from prevalent non-state actors or armed groups, who have significant territorial control.

Once again, the ICJ reasserted the boundaries of the principle of non-intervention and applied the principle to support the Global South states, thereby cultivating its universal application and demonstrating how the international arena had expanded in the post-Second World War era. Furthermore, through a TWAIL lens, the court's decision in *Nicaragua* could be viewed as a defence of the Global South (Nicaragua) against a hegemonic power (USA). As Richardson argues, *Nicaragua* was important not only for reaffirming the principle of non-intervention but also for condemning the 'hegemonic subordination of small, regional "other" states and peoples'.[191] Returning to the analogy of non-intervention as a club, whereas the Global South had gained membership through decolonisation and the UN system, there was still disparity between its members and the application of the principle to these members. However, this changed slightly through the decisions of the ICJ which applied the principle of non-intervention to all members of the club, including the Global South, and elaborated on the conditions of their membership. Indeed, the ICJ developed the application of non-intervention in the Global South further in *Democratic Republic of Congo v Uganda*,[192] where it reaffirmed the principle of non-intervention, finding that 'by actively extending military, logistic, economic and financial support to irregular forces' in the DRC, Uganda had violated both the principle of the non-use of force and the principle of non-intervention.[193] This decision therefore supported the development of the principle of non-intervention and provides one of the first examples of the international system engaging in a debate on intervention within the Global South by the Global South, instead of the previously typical pattern of hegemonic power intervention in the South. This once again reflects the broadening of the application of the principle of non-intervention and the increased engagement of the Global South in the international system.

Diversifying Forms: From Theory to Practice

Despite the significant development of the principle of non-intervention through the UN system and the ICJ, the instability and conflicts during the

191 Richardson (n67) 23.

192 *Case Concerning Armed Activities on the Territory of the Congo (Democratic Republic of the Congo v Uganda)* Judgment of 19 December [2005] ICJ Rep 168–283.

193 ibid para 345.

decolonisation period created an opening for a diverse range of Cold War interventions.[194] These interventions differed from the typical, direct military interventions and instead took the form of proxy wars (often involving private military contractors), economic interventions and a small number of UN peacekeeping operations. During this period, as the composition of the international community had shifted with the inclusion of the Global South, the rules of the game began to change. That is, whilst the principle of non-intervention had been firmly established and the most illustrious form of intervention (colonialism) had ceased, in practice, intervention continued to occur but in more subtle forms. A splintering occurred whereby intervention, instead of taking the form of direct, military action, began to occur in less overt but numerous different forms which, in turn, continued to perpetuate the long-standing power imbalances and dynamic of difference. Again, as has been highlighted throughout this chapter, within the development of the principle of non-intervention a gap between theory and practice remained. Thus, whilst the principle had gained strong legal underpinnings and there was a significant non-intervention rhetoric, this did not translate in its application.

Peacekeeping as Collective Security Intervention

Perhaps the most notable of these 'new' forms of intervention is collective security intervention through UN peacekeeping which, amongst other things, highlights the dichotomy between intervention in theory and intervention in practice. As was discussed in the previous section, the United Nations has been a key actor in developing and strengthening the principle of non-intervention through its organs, particularly the General Assembly. However, in contradiction to this, whilst espousing non-intervention and producing resolutions and declarations, it simultaneously began to develop peacekeeping as a tool for maintaining international peace and security. The United Nations was therefore creating a new form of intervention whilst also supporting the creation of the principle of non-intervention. This was done through the concept of collective security intervention – something which was 'not unique to the twentieth century' but has since become synonymous with the United Nations.[195]

When the Cold War geo-political tensions paralysed the UN Security Council, peacekeeping was invented as a mechanism to ensure that the United Nations could fulfil its role of maintaining international peace and security.[196] Thus, a 'new' form of intervention was introduced based upon

194 E Schmidt, *Foreign Intervention in Africa: From the Cold War to the War on Terror* (CUP 2013) 22–29.

195 AJ Bellamy and PD Williams, *Understanding Peacekeeping* (2nd ed, Polity Press 2010) 71.

196 M Goulding, 'The Evolution of United Nations Peacekeeping' (1993) 69(3) IntAff 451–464; JA Koops, T Tardy, N MacQueen and PD Williams, *The Oxford Handbook of United Nations Peacekeeping Operations* (OUP 2015).

multilateral action through an international organisation, ostensibly based on the collective interests of the international community but, again, driven by dominant actors, namely the P5. Indeed, Simpson argues that the United Nations (like the Concert of Europe and League of Nations which came before it) is predicated on a 'legalised hierarchy', whereby the international community conferred special rights and responsibilities upon the great powers and enshrined them in law – such as through the UN Charter.[197] It is then further posited that the dominant powers have a special responsibility to maintain international peace and security,[198] with peacekeeping providing a way in which this responsibility could be achieved.

Traditionally, peacekeeping began as simple observation and monitoring operations, designed to oversee ceasefire agreements as part of the United Nations' 'preventive diplomacy' to avoid local conflicts escalating into global confrontations.[199] Whilst the United Nations deployed personnel to the Balkans, the Middle East, Kashmir and Korea, mostly to monitor adherence to armistice agreements or ceasefires, it is UNEF I that is generally considered to be the first UN peacekeeping operation.[200] UNEF, deployed in the Sinai to help diffuse the Suez Crisis of 1956, established the traditional model of UN peacekeeping operations, contributing to the establishment of the core peacekeeping principles of host state consent, impartiality and non-use of force.[201] As the following chapter will explore in detail, this 'new' form of intervention seemingly adopted a tentative, non-interventionist stance as the three fundamental principles placed a limit on the extent of peacekeeping as an intervention in the host state. That is, the principles, together, created a red boundary line around peacekeeping, similar to that which had developed around the principle of non-intervention. In particular, the need to obtain host state consent for a peacekeeping's presence mirrored the emphasis on state sovereignty which had been evident throughout the development of the principle of non-intervention. As such, the initial peacekeeping operations could be characterised as a passive, non-threatening, disinterested form of intervention which did not penetrate, interfere or seek to impose any changes within the host state. Instead, they simply played a supportive role, aiding the host state in the implementation of ceasefire agreements and thereby contributing to the maintenance of international peace and security. For the principle of non-intervention, the creation of peacekeeping, justified under the umbrella of collective security intervention, could be viewed, at this point,

197 Simpson (n65) 170–171.
198 Bellamy and Williams (n195) 91.
199 Bellamy and Williams (n195) 85.
200 UNGA Res 998 (ES-I) (4 November 1956).
201 See: UN Peacekeeping, 'Principles of Peacekeeping' <https://peacekeeping.un.org/en/principles-of-peacekeeping>; N Tsagourias, 'Consent, Neutrality/Impartiality and the Use of Force in Peacekeeping: Their Constitutional Dimension' (2007) 11 JCSL 3, 465–482.

as an acceptable exception to or justifiable expansion of the principle of non-intervention.

However, the exception to this was the United Nations' peacekeeping operation in the Congo – ONUC – which was deployed in 1960, during the height of decolonisation. Unlike the UNEF-style peacekeeping operation, ONUC quickly evolved from a traditional peacekeeping operation to become a large, highly robust, more complex and multi-faceted operation composed, at its peak, of almost 20,000 troops, alongside civilian components.[202] ONUC also used high levels of force, essentially engaged in armed conflict,[203] and became embroiled in the country's internal affairs.[204] The peacekeeping operation was therefore highly interventionist, broadly interpreting the fundamental principles that acted as a boundary around peacekeeping and consequently expanding the interventionist nature of peacekeeping, thereby constricting the principle of non-intervention by creating a broader exception to the principle. This expansion of peacekeeping was at odds with the non-intervention narrative that the United Nations was espousing during that period. Furthermore, it also created significant tensions within the United Nations, particularly between the two Cold War superpowers, with the Soviet Union arguing that ONUC was a proxy for the United States, rather than an agent of the Security Council.[205] Indeed, ONUC reflected the differing views of what peacekeeping meant at that time. For the United States, peacekeeping 'meant an agency for "stability" and thus the spread of communism', whilst for the Soviet Union it meant 'a convenient agency for pacification of situations that become uncontrollable' and therefore dangerous to Soviet interests 'as long as peacekeeping operations themselves remain controllable'.[206]

This tension during the early stages of peacekeeping highlights a recurring issue both within the UN system and peacekeeping – the balance or concentration of power and the differing state views on intervention. The disagreement amongst the superpowers supports TWAIL scholars' assertions that dissemination functions of international institutions are 'steered by the dominant coalition of social forces and States to legitimise their vision of world order'.[207] That is, for peacekeeping, as will be explored in

202 See: A James, 'The Congo Controversies' (1994) 1(1) International Peacekeeping 44–58 and G Abi-Saab, *The United Nations Operation in the Congo 1960–1964* (OUP 1978).

203 See: M Kennedy and A Magennis, *Ireland, the United Nations and the Congo* (Four Courts Press, 2014).

204 See: Abi-Saab (n202); R Dayal, *Mission for Hammarskjöld: The Congo Crisis* (OUP 1976).

205 Bellamy and Williams (n195) 87; UNGA (15th Session, 882nd Plenary Meeting) (3 October 1960) UN Doc A/PV.882, paras 24–25.

206 LP Bloomfield, 'The United States, the Soviet Union, and the Prospects for Peacekeeping' (1970) 24(3) *International Organization* 548–565, 551.

207 BS Chimni, 'Marxism and International Law: A Contemporary Analysis' (1999) 34(6) EPW 337–349, 345.

later chapters, it is the dominant actors, namely the P5, who set the peacekeeping agenda, deploying peacekeeping operations (and therefore interventions) in the Global South. This, from a TWAIL perspective, is Anghie's dynamic of difference. The dominant powers recognise a gap between the dominant and weaker (South) states, creating a division of 'us' (UN peacekeeping) and 'them' (the host state), with the former sent to the latter to bridge the gap by normalising or transforming the 'other' to meet the dominant powers' agendas. There is not, however, one uniform agenda as the interests of the P5 can differ greatly, with China and Russia typically staunch defenders and rigid interpreters of the principle of non-intervention.[208] In more recent years, China's behaviour in the Security Council and its participation in peacekeeping operations have also evolved to 'assist its interests in being universally viewed as a "responsible great power"'.[209] This has resulted in China framing peacekeeping as a 'rare area for multilateral cooperation',[210] setting up training centres to prepare personnel for UN service and contributing to peacekeeping practices such as peacekeeper safety and security.[211]

This is then further exacerbated by the fact that peacekeeping operations predominantly consist of troops from the Global South, whilst the hegemonic powers primarily fund and dictate peacekeeping activities.[212] Whilst there may be many explanations for this disparity, including Global South states' desire to advance their public image, gain recognition and prestige, benefit financially or support regional cooperation,[213] there are some who perceive it as 'racism in peacekeeping'.[214] Indeed, this 'colour line' within peacekeeping generally results in the Global South troops primarily taking the risks, whilst the dominant powers adopt senior or management positions – a case of 'you

208 AK Larssen, 'Russia: The Principle of Non-Intervention and the Libya Case' in D Henriksen and AK Larssen (eds) *Political Rationale and International Consequences of the War in Libya* (OUP 2016) 67–85; M Barelli, 'China and Peacekeeping: Unfolding the Political and Legal Complexities of an Ambivalent Relationship' (2022) *Asian Journal of International Law* 1–20.

209 CJ Fung, *China and Intervention at the UN Security Council: Reconciling Status* (OUP 2019); see also: R Foot, *China, The UN, and Human Protection* (OUP 2020).

210 R Gowan, 'China's Pragmatic Approach to UN Peacekeeping' (Brookings, 14 September 2020) <https://www.brookings.edu/articles/chinas-pragmatic-approach-to-un-peacekeeping/>.

211 CJ Fung, 'Peace by Piece: China's Policy Leadership on Peacekeeping Fatalities' (2022) 43(4) Contemporary Security Policy 572–593.

212 TG Weiss and G Kuele, 'The Global South and UN Peace Operations' (*E-International Relations* 3 Feb 2019) <https://www.e-ir.info/2019/02/03/the-global-south-and-un-peace-operations/#_ftn2>.

213 ibid.

214 D Malone and R Thakur, 'Racism in Peacekeeping' (*Global and Mail* 30 October 2000) <https://www.theglobeandmail.com/opinion/racism-in-peacekeeping/article1340656/>.

lead, we bleed'.[215] For some, the inclusion of these Global South armed forces into the global military systems of the imperial powers also constitutes somewhat of a 'dependent militarisation'.[216]

The inherent power dynamics which animated the principle of non-intervention and the creation and expansion of the United Nations during decolonisation can therefore also be said to have filtered down into the concept of peacekeeping. In particular, as UN peacekeeping is driven by the P5's agendas, its deployment within a host state could be viewed as an attempt to alter or force change within the host state, to meet hegemonic interests. Whilst the nuances of this argument will be explored in more detail in the subsequent chapters, for the development of the principle of non-intervention, the birth of peacekeeping created a further justification for intervention which was legitimated by international law and consequently narrowed the principle of non-intervention.

Cold War Interventions and Regional Organisations

The introduction of peacekeeping as a new form of intervention, under the umbrella of collective security, thus permitted the United Nations to continue to fulfil its role in maintaining international peace and security during the Cold War. In a similar vein, as the Cold War superpowers refrained from engaging in direct conflict, other forms of intervention evolved. During this period, intervention began to take the form of proxy wars, with external, allied powers supporting internal actors, such as Cuba's involvement in Angola and Ethiopia[217] and its attempted intervention in the Congo (then called Zaire) in support of Congolese independence.[218] The Cold War and decolonisation period also brought about a revival of mercenaries[219] who found 'opportunities in the power vacuums created by colonial transitions'.[220] This also marked another form of military intervention but one which differed from the usual direct state intervention and therefore fell into a grey

215 UNA-UK, 'The Colour Line' (*UNA-UK Magazine* 19 October 2018) <https://una.org.uk/magazine/2018-1>.

216 P Cunliffe, *Legions of Peace: UN Peacekeepers from the Global South* (C Hurst & Co Publishers Ltd 2013) 155–163.

217 See: P Gleijeses, 'Moscow's Proxy? Cuba and Africa 1975–1998' (2006) 8(4) J Cold War Stud 98–146.

218 'From Cuba to Congo, Dream to Disaster for Che Guevara' (*The Guardian*, 12 August 2000) <https://www.theguardian.com/books/2000/aug/12/cuba.artsandhumanities>.

219 See: M Hoare, *Congo Warriors* (Paladin Press 1991) and M Hoare, *The Road to Kalamata: A Congo Mercenary's Personal Memoir* (Paladin Press 2008).

220 A McIntyre and T Weiss, 'Weak Governments in Search of Strength' in S Chesterman and C Lehnardt (eds) *From Mercenaries to Market: The Rise and Regulation of Private Military Companies* (OUP 2007) 68.

area within international law,[221] raising questions as to how the principle of non-intervention could or should apply in these instances.

From a TWAIL perspective, it could also be viewed as a loss of some of the gains that had previously been made – a classic example of one step forward and two steps back. That is, just as the principle of non-intervention had been substantially developed in the United Nations and ICJ and Global South states had managed to gain independence from the most illustrious form of intervention, the rules of the game changed again. Therefore, the Third World's challenge of the North's dominance and shaping of international law and its principles (including non-intervention) was somewhat stalled. Despite the Global South states ostensibly gaining the same rights and protections as the Northern states, the dominant powers, particularly the two Cold War superpowers, continued to intervene to maintain their dominance, this time fighting to gain spheres of influence in the South.[222] Intervention thus offered a 'potentially attractive means to pursue relative gains', particularly in the '"grey zones" of the Third World'.[223] The United States, in particular, viewed Africa 'through the prism of white-minority rights and the Cold War and considered radical nationalist movements to be Soviet proxies'.[224] This narrative was therefore used to justify extensive intervention in order to protect hegemonic interests and maintain benefits gained through the colonial encounter – in essence maintaining significant elements of colonialism. Indeed, it is noted that 'some of these interventions resembled past imperial practices with more powerful nations attempting to exploit Africa and its riches for their own ends'.[225]

Similarly, the dominant powers (particularly Western powers) often remained involved in the political structures of the newly independent states, such as Belgium and the United States' alleged assassination of the DRC's first democratically elected president.[226] This could be viewed as an example of what TWAIL scholar Chimni refers to as a 'Northern subversive strategy' designed to undo regimes which were not favourable to hegemonic states.[227] This, consequently, prevents an 'effective Third World coalition from emerging

221 See: PW Singer, 'War Profits, and the Vacuum of Law: Privatized Military Firms and International Law' (2003–2004) 42 ColumJTransnatlL 521–550; C Lehnardt, 'Private Military Companies and State Responsibility' (2007) in Chesterman and Lehnardt (n220) 155.

222 See: D Richterova and N Telepneva, 'An Introduction: The Secret Struggle for the Global South – Espionage, Military Assistance and State Security in the Cold War' (2021) 43(1) IntHistRev 1–11.

223 SN MacFarlane, 'Intervention During the Cold War' (2002) 42(350) AdelphiPapers 33–45.

224 Schmidt (n194) 23.

225 ibid 8.

226 See: E Gerard and B Kuklick, *Death in the Congo: Murdering Patrice Lumumba* (HUP 2015).

227 BS Chimni, 'Third World Approaches to International Law: A Manifesto' (2006) 8 ICLR 3–27, 6.

as a counterweight to the unity of the First World'.[228] Therefore, for the principle of non-intervention, this has the knock-on effect of limiting the ability of the Global South to both meaningfully contribute to its development and seek protection when faced with the prospect of an intervention from the dominant powers. These hegemonic interventions during the Cold War can also be viewed as another example of Anghie's ever-changing dynamic of difference – on this occasion, the hegemonic powers identified the Global South states as siding with the Cold War opposition, thereby justifying intervention in order to close the gap and alter the 'other' to prevent them from joining the adversary.

South-South Intervention

These Cold War interventions also led to further interventions in the form of regional and neighbouring interventions,[229] that is, intervention in the Global South by the Global South. The influx of weapons and money within the newly independent states throughout the Cold War and its proxy wars[230] 'entrenched power differentials and rendered local conflicts far more lethal'.[231] At the end of the Cold War, unstable, post-colonial states were therefore left with a wealth of weapons 'that fuelled new competition for riches and power'.[232] This then resulted in intervention between these states and, thus, intervention by the Global South within the Global South. Within the Great Lakes region, for example, the ending of a 32-year dictatorship in the Congo by a Kabila-led rebel insurgency supported by Rwanda[233] escalated into the 'First Congo War'.[234] This marked the beginning of an extensive period of intervention within the region, with Angola, Namibia, Chad and Zimbabwe supporting the Kabila government and Uganda and Rwanda supported the opposing rebels. These interventions then escalated into 'Africa's World War' or the 'Second Congo War', one of the deadliest conflicts since the Second World War, with five million deaths from 1998 to 2003.[235]

228 ibid.

229 Such as: African Union interventions (regional) and ECOWAS interventions (neighbouring). See: S Bamidele, 'Regional Approaches to Crisis Response, the African Union (AU) Intervention in African States: How Visible Is It?' (2017) 73(1) IndQuart 114–128; Ofuatey-Kodjoe (n182) and Dumbuya (n182).

230 See: P Gleijeses, 'Moscow's Proxy? Cuba and Africa 1975–1998' (2006) 8(4) J Cold War Stud 98–146.

231 Schmidt (n194) 11.

232 ibid.

233 M Deibert, *The Democratic Republic of Congo: Between Hope and Despair* (Zed Books Ltd 2013) 63.

234 See for example: T Turner, *The Congo Wars: Conflict, Myth and Reality* (Zed Books 2007); T Cooper, *Great Lakes Holocaust: First Congo War, 1996–1997* (Hellon and Company 2013).

235 See: G Prunier, *Africa's World War: Congo, the Rwandan Genocide, and the Making of a Continental Catastrophe* (Oxford University Press 2011).

This Great Lakes example therefore highlights the 'new' form of neighbouring or inter-African intervention which emerged at the end of the Cold War. In particular, it was during this period that the notion of 'African solutions to African problems' began to occur, legitimising the practice of inter-African interventions,[236] that is, the notion that 'long-term-solutions could only come from Africans themselves'; thus, internal, African solutions were preferable over imported, dictated or external foreign solutions and interventions.[237] This therefore juxtaposed the typical patterns of Northern intervention in the South that had significantly shaped the principle of non-intervention up until this point.

This initiative and the practice of Global South intervention was then given further weight with the development of regional organisations, such as the African Union (AU). Officially launched in 2002 as a successor to the OAU, the AU developed an 'elaborate institutional framework to implement the right to intervene'.[238] Whereas the AU's predecessor, the OAU, had no legal power to intervene in internal conflicts within the continent, Article 4(h) of the AU's Constitutive Act gave the AU the right to intervene unilaterally and forcefully if one of its member states is subject to war crimes, genocide and crimes against humanity.[239] It also permits the AU to intervene when a member state requests intervention to restore peace and security.[240] The AU's approach to intervention thereby significantly contributed to the development of the principle of non-intervention, being realistic of the needs of its member states. The AU was also the first regional institution to propose a comprehensive collective security and intervention regime which was normatively more advanced than any other regional organisation, including the North Atlantic Treaty Organization (NATO).[241] This could therefore be viewed, not only as a development for the principle of non-intervention and its regional application, but also as an example of the Global South making a notable contribution to the international system and the shaping of international law. Indeed, the AU's development of the principle of non-intervention could be viewed as an example of what TWAIL scholar, Abi-Saab, referred to as the Third World states 'renegotiating the rules'.[242] That is, the Global

236 A Mazuri, *Towards a Pax Africana: A Study of Ideology and Ambition* (UCP 1967) 203.

237 See: GBN Ayittey, 'The Somalia Crisis: Time for an African Solution' (1994) CATO Institute, Policy Analysis No 205.

238 International Refugee Rights Initiative, 'From Non-Interference to Non-Indifference: The African Union and the Responsibility to Protect' (September 2017) 4 <https://reliefweb.int/sites/reliefweb.int/files/resources/AU%20R2P%20-%20final.pdf>.

239 Constitutive Act of the African Union (11 July 2000).

240 ibid.

241 O Emeka, 'Analyzing Humanitarian Intervention from an African Point of View' (2012) 1 Vestnik RUDN IR 22–26, 24.

242 Abi-Saab (n131).

South states, which had entered an international legal system which had been formed without their input,[243] were now attempting to redress the balance and re-define principles and norms to meet their interests.[244]

Furthermore, AU intervention again supports the concept of 'African solutions to African problems', promoting intervention by the Global South over intervention by the dominant powers.[245] The OAU, in particular, was said to have 'guarded' Article 33 of the UN Charter,[246] strongly advocating that African solutions should be sought first, before conflicts were referred to the UN Security Council.[247] This became known as 'try Africa first'[248] – the origins of the norm of African solutions to African problems – which was legitimised through the notion of 'continental jurisdiction', with the concept of *Pax Africana* asserting that 'the peace of Africa is to be assured by the exertions of Africans themselves'.[249] A distinction was therefore drawn between illegitimate foreign intervention and inter-African intervention which, through Mazuri's understanding of 'racial sovereignty', was a more legitimate form of intervention.[250] Whilst these forms of intervention therefore further developed the principle of non-intervention, by creating a more nuanced understanding of intervention in the Global South, it also raises concerns about the applicability of the principle and how to reconcile this form of intervention with the TWAIL narrative that intervention is predominantly exercised by the dominant powers, often the Global North. Indeed, as Adebajo notes, these interventions were simply an 'African "Monroe Doctrine"';[251] that is, it prohibited intervention from external actors (essentially those from outside the continent) whilst simultaneously permitting intervention by internal actors (neighbours or those within the continent). Consequently, it perpetuated a similar level of intervention as foreign interventions, which arguably risked contravening the principle of non-intervention, as was seen in the ICJ's case of the *DRC v Uganda*.[252] The concept of 'African solutions to African problems' and its usage to justify or legitimate

243 See: JT Gathii, 'International Law and Eurocentricity' (1998) 9 EJIL 184–211.

244 See: T Maluwa, 'International Law Making in Post-Colonial Africa: The Role of the Organisation of African Unity' (2002) 49 NILR 81–103.

245 See: TM Mays, 'African Solutions for African Problems: The Changing Face of African-Mandated Peace Operations' (2003) 23(1) JConfStud 106–125; L Gelot, *Legitimacy, Peace Operations and Global-Regional Security: The African Union-United Nations Partnership in Darfur* (Routledge 2013).

246 UN Charter (n108) Article 33.

247 Gelot (n245) 47.

248 ibid.

249 Mazuri (n236) 203.

250 ibid.

251 A Adebajo, 'The Revolt against the West: Intervention and Sovereignty' (2016) 37(7) TWQ 1187–1202, 1188.

252 *DRC v Uganda* (n192).

interventions are therefore as 'problematic and riddled with hidden agendas as traditional interventions'.[253] Thus, the TWAIL narrative which has run throughout this exploration of the development of the principle of non-intervention is seemingly challenged.

The Empire Strikes back

As the Cold War ended, the nature of intervention once again altered, albeit within the framework or boundaries of the principle which had been set predominantly within the UN system during decolonisation. Intervention in the post-Cold War era underwent another oscillation period, this time as interventions shifted from predominantly unilateral interventions to multilateral interventions. The collapse of the Soviet Union and Western 'victory' changed the Cold War consensus which had sanctioned intervention[254] and led to increased optimism about the potential for the United Nations and the international community to ensure peace.[255] Intervention therefore became reliant on a 'coalition of partners, shared costs and UN-led multilateral forces',[256] as opposed to direct and unilateral intervention. As Falk notes, 'the renunciation of [unilateral] intervention' did 'not substitute a policy of non-intervention'; rather, it involved the development of some form of collective intervention.[257] Indeed, towards the end of the Cold War, there was a revival of UN peacekeeping, with more operations undertaken between 1988 and 1993 than in the previous 40 years.[258] In the subsequent decades, peacekeeping rapidly developed from traditional peacekeeping to 'robust' peacekeeping operations and, more recently, multi-dimensional or 'stabilisation' operations.[259] In turn, these developments of peacekeeping created further nuances within the principle of non-intervention by permitting broader, more ambiguous forms of intervention, legitimised under the auspices of UN peacekeeping. Furthermore, as collective security intervention (which typically takes the form of UN peacekeeping) has now replaced

253 C Ero, 'The Problems with "African Solutions"' (*International Crisis Group*, 2 December 2013) <https://www.crisisgroup.org/africa/problems-african-solutions>.

254 RJ Barnet, *Intervention and Revolution: America's Confrontation with Insurgent Movements around the World* (Meridan 1968).

255 See, for example, the optimism within: UNGA, 'Report of the Secretary-General. An Agenda for Peace: Preventive, Diplomacy, Peacemaking and Peacekeeping' (31 January 1992) UN Doc A/47/277-S/24111.

256 WQ Morales, 'US Intervention and the New World Order: Lessons from Cold War and Post-Cold War Cases' (1994) 15(1) TWQ 77–101, 78.

257 R Falk, *Legal Order in a Violent World* (PUP 1968) 339.

258 Twenty peacekeeping operations during this period. See: UN Peacekeeping <https://peacekeeping.un.org/en>.

259 See: A Gilder, 'The Effect of "Stabilization" in the Mandates and Practice of UN Peace Operations' (2019) 66 NILR 47–73.

unilateral intervention as the main method of intervention in the modern era, then an understanding of the legal and normative boundaries of peacekeeping is essential in order to understand the boundaries or composition of intervention today. Indeed, it is this very issue which the subsequent chapters will explore – how the legal principles and norms, which constitute a peacekeeping framework, may support or contravene the principle of non-intervention.

In a similar vein, alongside this shift in military or forceful intervention, there was also a further diversification of the forms which intervention took, namely economic intervention. During the 1990s, as globalisation brought states closer together, foreign intervention into African economies became 'the critical backdrop to the crises of the 1980s and 1990s, which stimulated a new wave of external political and military intervention in the continent'.[260] Intervention therefore took the form of humanitarian aid, market expansion investments[261] and the extraction of natural resources through mining companies.[262] For the principle of non-intervention, whilst these interventions may appear to have marked a shift from the typical patterns of intervention which had been prevalent up until this point, they were arguably not a new form of intervention. That is, the practice of intervening to exploit natural resources for the intervening states' benefit was a historic practice which had been a key feature of colonial intervention, and this had been recognised and included within the concept of intervention as it developed in the UN system. Indeed, as noted earlier, as the principle of non-intervention evolved through UN General Assembly Resolutions and Declarations, the definition of intervention was expanded, often at the insistence of the Global South states, to include these subtler forms of intervention. It could therefore be argued that the main framework for the principle of non-intervention had been set during the decolonisation period, with more contemporary interventions simply adding further nuances to the understanding of the principle in practice, rather than adding any significant, new developments to its boundaries. Returning, once again, to the analogy of the principle as a club, membership to the club was now open to all, with a well-established handbook or manual to guide proceedings. However, in order to keep up-to-date with changing practices, interpretations of the handbook and additional appendices were possible. Whilst some of these amendments remained within the club's boundaries,

260 Schmidt (n194) 10–11.

261 See for example: J Vidal, 'Construction of World's Largest Dam in DR Congo Could Begin within Months' (*The Guardian*, 28 May 2016) <https://www.theguardian.com/environment/2016/may/28/construction-of-worlds-largest-dam-in-dr-congo-could-begin-within-months>.

262 See for example: D Stringer and T Biesheuvel, 'Tesla Strikes Deal to Buy Cobalt from Glencore for EV Plants' (*Bloomberg*, 16 June 2020) <https://www.bloomberg.com/news/articles/2020-06-16/glencore-agrees-deal-to-sell-cobalt-to-tesla-for-new-car-plants>.

others contravened the club rules, falling outside the boundaries and thereby undermining the values of the club.

Consensual Intervention: A Humanitarian Veneer

Whilst the principle of non-intervention significantly developed during decolonisation and the Cold War period, with a relatively strong rhetoric of non-intervention, this began to soften at the end of the twentieth century and the beginning of the twenty-first century. As the Cold War ended and the concept of an 'international community' took root, intervention again became more acceptable but within the framework or justification of collective security action, such as UN peacekeeping. From a TWAIL perspective, this changing attitude towards intervention was reflected in the shift in power dynamics within the UN system. That is, as the Security Council's Cold War paralysis dissolved, the General Assembly, which had allowed the newly independent Third World states to play a significant role during decolonisation, 'lost its own as legal oracle of the international community'.[263] Therefore, whilst the Global South had been able to play a greater role in the development, interpretation and application of international law, including the principle of non-intervention, thus challenging the dominance of the hegemonic powers, the latter began to re-take some of their dominance, effectively silencing the Third World again. Indeed, prominent TWAIL scholar Georges Abi-Saab refers to this immediate post-Cold War period as 'the empire strikes back' – the second act in the three-part 'psychodrama' of the North-South confrontation.[264]

A Return of the Civilising Mission?

This re-balancing of the global order was highlighted in the 1990s as the international community received criticism for failing to intervene in atrocities such as the Rwandan genocide and the Srebrenica massacre.[265] Therefore, whilst Global North or hegemonic intervention in the Global South had been strongly condemned during decolonisation, there was now a general consensus that dominant states should be intervening in less dominant states, on the basis of humanitarian needs. This was then legitimised within international law in the form of the 'responsibility to protect' doctrine[266] – the notion of

263 Abi-Saab (n131) 1960.

264 ibid 1959.

265 See: S Stein, 'The UN and Genocide: A Comparative Analysis of Rwanda and the Former Yugoslavia' in F Attinà (ed) *The Politics and Policies of Relief, Aid and Reconstruction* (Palgrave Macmillan 2012).

266 See for example: S Chesterman, *Just War or Just Peace? Humanitarian Intervention and International Law* (OUP 2001) and A Orford, *Reading Humanitarian Intervention: Human Rights and the Use of Force in International Law* (CUP 2008).

'coercive action against a state to protect people within its borders from suffering grave harm'.[267] Thus, the intervention rhetoric shifted from one which supported the independence of the Global South against hegemonic interventions, to one which now welcomed intervention in the South, based on a perceived duty of the dominant states to protect vulnerable citizens of the world, through collective intervention.[268] The principle of non-intervention, then, was constricted or eroded during this period as these potentially broad humanitarian-based justifications chipped away at the red boundary line that had demarcated the principle and limited intervention. Indeed, it was similarly recognised that these interventions had eroded state sovereignty, particularly within African states, which were forced to 'dilute notions of absolute sovereignty to allow military interventions for humanitarian purposes'.[269]

From a TWAIL perspective, these forms of intervention also raise numerous issues. Firstly, it could be argued that the basis or criteria for a humanitarian-based intervention are essentially based on European or Western standards and ideals. That is, determining what constitutes a gross human rights violation and an affront to civilised standards (thus justifying intervention) involves the imposition of a standard of 'civilised' behaviour which 'to some degree is likely to reflect culturally specific values'.[270] As collective intervention is primarily carried out by the United Nations, it follows that decisions on when and where to intervene are determined by the United Nations, specifically the Security Council and thus the veto-wielding members of the Security Council. Decisions on humanitarian-based interventions are therefore ultimately determined by the dominant states and, as such, are based predominantly upon Western rather than universal values. This, in turn, leads to criticisms about the selectivity of these interventions, with the 'international community' accused of determining targets selectively, 'ignoring human rights violations of equal or even greater magnitude elsewhere'.[271] Again, applying a TWAIL lens, humanitarian intervention and R2P can be critiqued as a form of European/Western standard setting which is presented as 'supposedly universal values' but is used 'to conquer and colonise parts of the Third World'.[272] Indeed, both concepts have been identified as

267 G Evans and M Sahnoun, 'The Responsibility to Protect' (2002) 81(6) Foreign Affairs 99–110, 99.

268 See for example the multinational operations in Libya and Cote d'Ivoire: UNSC Res 1973 (17 March 2011) UN Doc S/RES/1973 and UNSC Res 1975 (30 March 2011) UN Doc S/RES/1975.

269 Adebajo (n251) 1187.

270 TM Franck, 'Humanitarian Intervention' in S Besson and J Tasioulas (eds) *The Philosophy of International Law* (OUP 2010) 531–532.

271 M Ayoob, 'Humanitarian Intervention and International Society' (2001) 7 GG 225–230, 225.

272 R Bachand, 'Critical Approaches and the Third World: Towards a Global and Radical Critique of International Law' (Speech at University McGill, 24 March 2010).

tools which could be 'indirectly used as an intervention instrument'[273] or a 'weapon of imperial intervention at will'.[274] Thus, international law has once again provided a veneer of legitimacy to hegemonic intervention in the Global South, simultaneously legitimising 'the intrusion of international law in the internal affairs of a state'.[275] Put simply, humanitarian-based interventions permit intervention in the Global South on the basis of standards set by the dominant states.

This then leads to a similar, second notable issue with these types of intervention, which is that these forms of intervention, from a TWAIL perspective, are comparable to the colonial civilising mission as both are based on the notion of 'the White Man's burden',[276] with an enlightened dominant state civilising or altering a weaker state to match the standards of the former. For some, this points to the broader evolution and purpose of international law in the modern era. As Koskenniemi notes, international law, instead of 'being dressed as a project for civilisation', now 'appears as a modernising project, a state-building project, a project for economic and technological development, for human rights protection, for conserving natural resources and seeing to global security'.[277] Thus, the same themes and power structures are present but are simply re-packaged into a more palatable form. Furthermore, humanitarian-based interventions could also be viewed as a replication of Anghie's dynamic of difference as they are, once again, an example of the hegemonic powers identifying a gap with the 'other' and then using that gap as a justification for intervention in order to alter the 'other'. As Anghie argues, as the international system changes, so too does the dynamic of difference, which continuously acquires a new form.[278] In the modern era, then, 'the familiar pattern of the colonial encounter, the division between civilised and uncivilised' is replicated as the 'developed' and the 'developing'.[279] In this instance, the dynamic is replicated within these humanitarian-based interventions. This, in turn, also has the effect of maintaining the hierarchical power structures which have been prevalent throughout the development of the principle of non-intervention. As a result, despite the increased involvement of the Global South in the development and application of the principle, the power dichotomy remains.

273 Mazower (n88) 396.

274 N Chomsky, 'Statement by Professor Noam Chomsky to the United Nations General Assembly Thematic Dialogue on the Responsibility to Protect' (UN, 23 July 2009) 4 <https://www.un.org/en/ga/president/63/pdf/calendar/20090723-resptoprotect.pdf>.

275 Anghie (n70) 749.

276 Kipling (n39).

277 M Koskenniemi, 'Histories of International Law: Dealing with Eurocentrism' (2011) 19 Rechtsgeschichte 152, 159.

278 Anghie (n14) 203.

279 ibid, 244.

From Military to 'Security', through Peacekeeping?

Alongside these humanitarian-based interventions, further nuances have developed within the principle of non-intervention through a revival of UN peacekeeping[280] and a shift towards a 'security' culture following the 9/11 terrorist attacks and the subsequent 'War on Terror'.[281] At the turn of the century, the 'War on Terror' led to an increase in interventions, such as the United States-led war in Iraq which, for some, changed the 'way the world viewed international military action'.[282] Beyond military action, intervention through cyberspace, such as electoral interference, has also led to international lawyers questioning whether the principle of non-intervention now also extends to the cyber context – a matter which goes beyond the scope of this book but indicates how the principle is continually evolving and may be expanded to apply to differing forms of intervention.[283] Therefore, as noted within the previous discussion of humanitarian interventions, whereas the decolonisation period could be characterised as having a strong non-interventionist rhetoric, this softened within the post-Cold War era, particularly after the 9/11 attacks, when numerous justifications for intervention began to arise.

Whilst decolonisation was a tipping point for the principle of non-intervention, it could also be argued that the 9/11 attacks and the subsequent 'War on Terror' were a further tipping point for the principle. In contrast to decolonisation, which promoted non-intervention and the Global South voice, the War on Terror promoted intervention and the dominance of the hegemonic (typically Northern) powers. Thus, through a TWAIL lens, the War on Terror era offers a further example of the empire striking back, with the hegemonic powers seeking to regain and retain their prominence in the international arena. It is within this backdrop, as intervention became more permissible again, that the reinvigorated UN peacekeeping operations were increasingly expanded and used as a primary tool for engaging in collective security intervention in the twenty-first century. As the strategic context for peacekeeping operations shifted, peacekeeping adapted, with significant internal assessments of its capabilities undertaken at the turn of the century

280 See: A Adebajo and C Landsberg, 'Back to the Future: UN Peacekeeping in Africa' (2000) 7(4) IntPeacekeep 161–188.

281 H Duffy, '"Terrorism" in International Law' in H Duffy, *The 'War on Terror' and the Framework of International Law* (CUP 2015) 29–74. See also: ND White and C Henderson, *Research Handbook on International Conflict and Security Law: Jus ad Bellum, Jus in Bello and Jus post Bellum* (Edward Elgar 2013).

282 JT Gathii, 'Humanizing the Pax-Americana Global Empire' (2005) 4(1) GlobalStudLRev 121–134.

283 N Tsagourias, 'Electoral Cyber Interference, Self-Determination, and the Principle of Non-Intervention in Cyberspace' in D Broeders and B van den Berg (eds) *Governing Cyberspace: Behavior, Power and Diplomacy* (Rowan & Littlefield 2020).

to strengthen its capacity to create peace and stability in complex environments.[284] Put simply, peacekeeping evolved in line with interventionist trends (such as humanitarian intervention and security interventions) which were, again, dictated by the dominant powers.

Multi-Dimensional Peacekeeping

The move towards a security culture was reflected in the development of peacekeeping in the post-Cold War era, which simultaneously further exemplified the underlying power structures within both the concept of peacekeeping and the principle of non-intervention. As the deployment of peacekeepers became more frequent at the end of the Cold War, peacekeeping operations also began to evolve from the traditional, passive model to multi-faceted operations which engaged in numerous activities that typically fell within the host state's jurisdiction, thereby resulting in a greater or deeper level of intervention in the host state. These multi-dimensional operations were mandated to not only maintain peace and security but also to facilitate peace processes, protect civilians, assist in the disarmament, demobilisation and reintegration of former combatants, promote human rights and support democratisation.[285]

In addition to the expansion of peacekeeping to include these tasks, the concept of 'robust peacekeeping' was also introduced during this period.[286] This permitted peacekeeping to use force to defend both the mission's components and the operation's mandate, including the ever-growing list of operational tasks.[287] Whilst the subsequent chapters (in particular Chapters 5 and 6) will explore the interventionist nature of some of these tasks, more generally, as the following two chapters highlight, this evolution began to raise concerns as it became a 'mix of peacekeeping, peacebuilding and peace enforcement',[288] thereby blurring the boundaries between peacekeeping and intervention. More specifically, it expanded the possibility of intervention (coercive action to influence change in a state), simultaneously contracting the principle of non-intervention. Indeed, this development of robust peacekeeping and the introduction of protection of civilians as an operational task fit within the broader intervention rhetoric at the time as it came after the United Nations was criticised for failing to intervene in the numerous

284 Such as: UNGA, 'Report of the Panel on United Nations Peace Operations' ('Brahimi Report') (21 August 2000) UN Doc A/55/305-S/2000/809.

285 See: UN, *United Nations Peacekeeping Operations: Principles and Guidelines* ('The Capstone Doctrine') (DPKO 2008) Chapter 2.

286 Brahimi Report (n284).

287 ibid.

288 J Reynaert, 'MONUC/MONUSCO and Civilian Protection in the Kivus' (IPIS 2010) 14.

atrocities of the 1990s.[289] The discourse of humanitarian-based interventions had therefore permeated the concept of peacekeeping, primarily through concepts such as robust peacekeeping and the protection of civilians. Again, this, in turn, expanded the remit of peacekeeping, consequently expanding the concept of collective security intervention and thereby constricting the principle of non-intervention.

Put differently, if there is an invisible red boundary line which surrounds the principle of non-intervention, collective intervention could be viewed as a main gateway which permits an opening of this boundary. Peacekeeping could then be viewed as a central vessel which runs from this, creating space for further intervention, with the varying tasks contained within a peacekeeping mandate seen as additional interventionist threads. If collective intervention is the overarching exception to non-intervention, then peacekeeping and its complex mandates with its numerous tasks are the arteries, veins and capillaries which extend UN intervention into the host state even further. This is compounded by the fact that, often, UN peacekeeping operations are deployed simultaneously with the imposition of UN sanctions – a form of economic intervention.[290] Under Article 41 of the UN Charter, the Security Council is authorised to impose sanctions to maintain or restore international peace and security. This may include economic and trade sanctions or more targeted measures such as arms embargoes, travel bans and asset freezes.[291] An additional layer of intervention is therefore imposed upon the host state, in an attempt to coerce change within the host state, simultaneously buttressing military, collective security intervention which also attempts to alter the state. For the principle of non-intervention, whilst this may appear to be another form of contemporary intervention, it could be viewed as simply a replication of pre-existing interventionist practices. That is, the sanctions can be categorised as simply another form of economic intervention, alongside the extraction of natural resources, investments or trading which, as previously discussed, have also typically occurred together with military or forceful intervention. However, what makes the UN sanctions a more significant form of intervention is that they stem from the United Nations, thereby carrying with them the weight of the organisation, and are frequently imposed alongside the deployment of a peacekeeping operation. The sanctions therefore add additional pressure to coerce the host state into altering

289 UNSC, 'Chairman of Independent Inquiry into United Nations Actions During 1994 Rwanda Genocide Presents Report to Security Council' (14 April 2000) Press Release SC/6843.

290 Economic intervention may take various forms, such as the imposition of sanctions, embargos, counter-measures or trade restrictions between states. The difficulty with economic intervention lies in determining whether or not it is legitimate under international law.

291 See: UNSC, 'United Nations Security Council Consolidated List' <https://www.un.org/securitycouncil/content/un-sc-consolidated-list>.

as the United Nations sees fit, thus amounting to an additional layer of intervention designed to force a change in behaviour which is, ultimately, based on the agenda of the UN Security Council.

Both the expansion of peacekeeping into multi-dimensional operations and the use of sanctions therefore lead back, once again, to the TWAIL narrative of a regime of domination and subordination. As discussed in previous sections, the inescapable, disproportionate hierarchy of power which underpins the United Nations results in the veto-wielding P5 states ultimately determining both the deployment and general composition of a peacekeeping operation and the imposition of UN sanctions. Therefore, as with the humanitarian-based interventions, two further issues arise with these multidimensional operations: firstly, the list of mandated tasks and, secondly, the selectivity of deployment. For the former, it could be argued that, like humanitarian interventions, the prioritisation of certain tasks within a peacekeeping mandate, including the advancement of human rights[292] and democratisation,[293] is based upon Western values and standards. As TWAIL scholars such as Mutua have argued, human rights and democracy are 'the universalised version of the other', both of which are projects that are devoid of the input of Third World states and are 'essentially infinite, open-ended, and highly experimental in nature'.[294] Thus, the inclusion of these within peacekeeping tasks creates not only an ambiguous and potentially open-ended justification for intervention, but also a potentially limitless justification for the hegemonic powers' dominance over the Global South. Similarly, the decision on where and when to deploy a peacekeeping operation is, as with humanitarian-based interventions, premised on the interests, values and motivations of the hegemonic powers within the Security Council. Once again, this reinforces the power dynamics and provides another example of Anghie's dynamic of difference – the dominant actor identifies a gap in the subordinate other and subsequently sets about closing the gap, in this instance, by deploying a peacekeeping operation. Indeed, this is strongly evidenced within UN peacekeeping with the predominance of operations in Africa and the frequent clashes between members of the P5 over the deployment of peacekeepers to countries such as Syria – a crisis which has invoked the use of the veto by Russia and China on numerous occasions, thereby also highlighting the differing views on intervention within the P5 of the Security Council.[295]

292 Mutua (n82).

293 See: B Jahn, 'The Tragedy of Liberal Diplomacy: Democratization, Intervention, Statebuilding (Part II)' (2007) 1(2) JIntervStatebuilding 211–229.

294 ibid 593.

295 See: UNSC, 'Belgium and Germany: Draft Resolution' (10 July 2020) UN Doc S/2020/667 and (13 July 2020) UN Doc S/2020/693.

For the principle of non-intervention, then, these multi-dimensional peacekeeping operations represent both a broadening and deepening of intervention which contracts the boundaries of the principle but which, in turn, is limited by the selectivity of the deployment of peacekeeping operations. That is, the expansion of peacekeeping to multi-dimensional operations undoubtedly increases peacekeeping's interventionist possibilities, thereby widening or broadening the gateway that opens the non-intervention boundary line. However, this opening is narrowed again by the fact that the operations are predominantly only deployed within one geographical location. The shift to multi-dimensional peacekeeping could therefore be best described as a deepening, rather than a broadening, of intervention as it permits greater levels of intervention but within a narrower geographical scope. This therefore creates a further nuance or dimension within the development of the principle of non-intervention but one which, ultimately, continues to support the TWAIL narrative of a system predicated on subordination and domination.

Stabilisation Peacekeeping: Intervention by Invitation?

Multi-dimensional peacekeeping operations were given a further interventionist veneer in 2010 when some were re-packaged into 'stabilisation' peacekeeping operations – now one of the most prevalent forms of intervention in contemporary peacekeeping. Peacekeeping therefore evolved again, with operations now able to take numerous forms – traditional, multi-dimensional, robust or stabilisation. Since 2010, the Security Council's new generation of 'stabilisation' peacekeeping operations have been mandated to support the host government, protect civilians and combat armed groups, often in joint operations with the host state forces, such as MONUSCO's Force Intervention Brigade, which Chapter 5 explores in greater detail.[296] Despite the increased use of the term 'stabilisation' and its inclusion in the title of peacekeeping operations in the DRC, Mali and the Central African Republic (CAR), it is undefined within the United Nations,[297] creating a flexibility that opens a window for a broad range of interventionist activities to be undertaken, as subsequent chapters will explore. Generally, four main elements have been identified as forming part of these operations – 'robustness', counter-terrorism, cooperation with the host state, extending state authority and control and entrenching the rule of law and ending impunity.[298] Again, as with multi-dimensional operations, the same TWAIL lens could be applied,

296 UNSC Res 2098 (28 March 2013) UN Doc S/RES/2098 and UNSC Res 2502 (19 December 2019) UN Doc S/RES/2502, para 29(i)(e); S Sheeran and S Case, 'The Intervention Brigade: Legal Issues for the UN in the Democratic Republic of the Congo' (IPI 2014).

297 See: A Gilder (n254) 47–73; A Gilder, *Stabilization and Human Security in UN Peace Operations* (Routledge 2022).

298 ibid.

with arguments made about how these tasks or components stem from an agenda set by the dominant powers in the Security Council, with only the element of cooperation with the host state potentially invoking the input of the Global South.

Indeed, this apparent cooperation with the host state raises further questions for peacekeeping's legal basis or framework. Whilst stabilisation operations could be viewed as an evolution or extension of UN peacekeeping from its traditional or robust models, some have argued that these types of operations 'should be understood as a qualitatively distinct form of UN-mandated intervention by invitation'.[299] That is, whilst peacekeeping's legal basis is generally found under Chapter VI (consensual peacekeeping) or Chapter VII (non-consensual enforcement) of the UN Charter, Labuda argues that the legal basis for stabilisation operations could be tied to host state consent rather than Chapter VII.[300] This is based on the fact that the Security Council cannot order the host state to provide troops, use force or conduct joint operations with a peacekeeping operation in its territory, regardless of how broadly its powers are interpreted.[301] Therefore, when peacekeepers are 'authorised' to conduct joint operations with the host government forces, it implies that the Security Council is permitting or mandating host troops to use force alongside peacekeepers, which is a power that the Council does not possess.[302]

As such, Labuda argues that where a host state plans and conducts joint operations with a stabilisation operation, as has occurred within MONUSCO in the DRC, this should instead be viewed as 'a function of the host state's consent' for UN intervention[303] and, thus, the government's support for external intervention or an invitation to intervention. This, in turn, raises numerous issues pertaining to the use of force, the invocation of rules of international humanitarian law and the traditional peacekeeping principles of impartiality and consent – all of which will be discussed in further detail in the subsequent chapters. For the principle of non-intervention, it also creates a further nuance within the concept and creates a complex paradox of extensive, consensual intervention, which renders the boundaries of the principle of non-intervention unclear, thereby leaving room for extensive, potentially unlawful, intervention. The evolution of peacekeeping to these stabilisation operations therefore, again, highlights a key theme of this book – whether contemporary peacekeeping operations are, at times, intervention,

299 PI Labuda, 'United Nations Peacekeeping as Intervention by Invitation: Host State Consent and the Use of Force in Security Council-Mandated Stabilisation Operations' (2020) JUFIL 1–37, 3.

300 ibid.

301 ibid, 32.

302 ibid, 32–33.

303 ibid, 33.

and thereby contravene or, at the very least, constrict the boundaries of the principle of non-intervention. Indeed, it could be argued that as peacekeeping has created a justified or legitimate gap in the invisible red boundary line around the principle of non-intervention, every evolution of peacekeeping expands this gap further. It follows, then, that there must come a point where this gap cannot be expanded anymore without snapping the red elastic band boundary, resulting in a violation of the principle of non-intervention and eroding its validity. As such, it is essential to establish the framework or boundaries surrounding peacekeeping in order to assess how today's most prevalent form of intervention impacts the principle of non-intervention in the modern era.

Conclusions: Intervention Today

An exploration of the development of the principle of non-intervention highlights how intervention is best characterised as a concept or practice which has been cyclical in nature. That is, whilst intervention was overt and extensive during colonialism, the decolonisation period saw a decline in intervention, only for it to increase again in the post-Cold War/'War on Terror' era. There has been a constant fluctuation, then, in intervention and non-intervention rhetoric, with, at times, rhetoric failing to match practice. During decolonisation, for example, when the concept of non-intervention was supported emphatically, intervention was still occurring in the form of UN peacekeeping operations and economic or political interventions by colonial powers in their former colonies. All the while, as these patterns of intervention have occurred, the principle of non-intervention has been developed, primarily through international institutions such as the United Nations and ICJ. Indeed, it was during the decolonisation period, when the Cold War paralysed the hegemonic powers and intervention was at a low point (except within the superpowers' spheres of influence), that the newly independent Global South states gained a seat at the table, thereby being able to contribute to the development of the principle. This period was therefore a significant tipping point for the principle of non-intervention, firmly establishing its legal framework and importance as a principle of international law. It could be argued, then, that this creation of the red boundary line around the principle of non-intervention has remained in place ever since, even when interventions began to increase again. That is, once established as a principle of international law during this period, subsequent interventionist practices have provided a more nuanced understanding of the concept of non-intervention and its application, which has had the dual effect of both supporting and undermining the principle but, ultimately, not eradicating it as an established principle of international law. Therefore, regional organisations, humanitarian-based interventions and UN peacekeeping have all contributed to the development of the principle of non-intervention, not through adding anything substantially new to the principle but, rather, by providing a greater understanding of the pre-existing elements of the principle.

This then leads to further noticeable dynamics which have arisen throughout the development of the principle. From a TWAIL perspective, the unequal global order, the lack of a Third World voice within the international system and the use of international law to maintain these hierarchies are all present within the principle of non-intervention and interventionist practices.[304] Indeed, TWAIL scholars such as Tzouvala argue that international law is simultaneously 'a locus of oppression' and a 'constant promise for liberation'.[305] Nowhere is this dichotomy more evident than within the principle of non-intervention whereby the principle has both protected the Global South from intervention whilst simultaneously permitting intervention by the dominant actors within the Global South, primarily through the justification of collective security intervention. Furthermore, as Anghie argues, international law is animated by colonialism with the colonial dichotomy of civilised and uncivilised continually replicated in what Anghie refers to as a 'dynamic of difference'.[306] Again, both the influence of colonialism and the replication of the dynamic of difference can be found within the development of the principle of non-intervention and contemporary interventions, as this chapter has demonstrated. In particular, it is arguable that some elements of colonialism or, rather, practices which occurred during colonialism, remain within the concept of intervention today, in particular, through UN peacekeeping. Thus, comparisons may be drawn between the two forms of intervention. Indeed, just as colonialism was the most illustrious form of intervention in the nineteenth and twentieth centuries, so too is peacekeeping the most illustrious form of intervention in the twenty-first century. Both invoke elements of domination and subordination, both are largely motivated or led by the interests and will of the hegemonic powers, both invoke justifications based on notions of values or standards which are predominantly Western-centric and both have gained varying degrees of legitimacy through international law. This comparison, however, is not to condemn peacekeeping and its purported well-intentioned efforts. Rather, it is to join the TWAIL movement in exposing or acknowledging the 'imperial character' of international law and the remnants of colonial practice which linger within the international system,[307] in order to then promote or increase the Global South's participation, creating a truly universal international law.

304 See, for example: Mutua (n49).

305 N Tzouvala, 'TWAIL and the "Unwilling or Unable" Doctrine: Continuities and Ruptures' (2015) 109 AJIL Unbound 266–270.

306 Anghie (n14).

307 BS Chimni, 'International Institutions Today: An Imperial Global State in the Making' (2004) 15(1) EJIL 1–37, 1–2.

Having tracked the development of the principle of non-intervention, then, the following chapter will take this analysis a level deeper by examining today's most prevalent from of intervention – UN peacekeeping. It will explore how interpretations of peacekeeping's legal principles and norms either expand or contract the boundaries of peacekeeping and thus undermine or support the principle of non-intervention. That is, if peacekeeping is a form of intervention, thereby constituting an exception to the principle of non-intervention, the form which peacekeeping takes arguably has a direct impact on the boundaries of the principle of non-intervention. As this chapter has demonstrated, whilst the traditional concept of peacekeeping did not pose a significant challenge to the principle, the same cannot be said for contemporary, multi-dimensional operations, particularly the stabilisation operations which some consider to be intervention by invitation.[308] The following two chapters will therefore outline the evolution of peacekeeping, identifying its legal and normative frameworks. Chapters 5 and 6 will then go on to examine these principles and norms in practice, using the DRC as a case study, with the purpose of providing specific examples of how peacekeeping in practice may impact the principle of non-intervention, possibly, at times, contravening it and, thus, amounting to intervention.

References

——, 'Final Communiqué of the Asian-African Conference' (2009) 11(1) Interventions 94–102

——, 'From Cuba to Congo, dream to disaster for Che Guevara' (*The Guardian*, 12 August 2000) <https://www.theguardian.com/books/2000/aug/12/cuba.artsandhumanities>

Abi-Saab G, 'The Newly Independent States and the Scope of Domestic Jurisdiction' (1960) 54 ASILPROC 84–90

Abi-Saab G, *The United Nations Operation in the Congo 1960–1964* (OUP 1978)

Abi-Saab G, 'Whither the International Community?' (1998) 9 EJIL 248–265

Abi-Saab G, 'The Third World Intellectual in Praxis: Confrontation, Participation, or Operation Behind Enemy Lines' (2016) 37(11) TWQ 1957–1971

Adams NA, *Worlds Apart: The North-South Divide and the International System* (Zed Press 1993)

Adebajo A and C Landsberg, 'Back to the Future: UN Peacekeeping in Africa' (2000) 7(4) IntPeacekeep 161–188

Adebajo A, 'The Revolt Against the West: Intervention and Sovereignty' (2016) 37(7) TWQ 1187–1202

'Affirmed Protocol Relative to Non-Intervention' (1936) 188 LNTS 31

Ala'I P, 'Leopold & Morel: A Story of "Free Trade" and "Native Rights" in the Congo Free State' 37 (2005) Stud Transnat'l Legal Pol'y 33–46

308 Labuda (n299).

Anand A, *New States and International Law* (Vikas 1972)
Ananthavinayagan TV, 'Uniting the Nations or Dividing and Conquering? The United Nations' Multilateralism Questioned – A Third World Scholar's Perspective' (2018) 29 IrishStudIntAff 1–17
Anghie, A, 'Finding the Peripheries: Sovereignty and Colonialism in Nineteenth Century International Law' (1999) 40(1) HarvIntlLJ 1
Anghie A, 'The Evolution of International Law: Colonial and Postcolonial Realities' (2006) 27(5) TWQ 739–753
Anghie, A, *Imperialism, Sovereignty and the Making of International Law* (CUP 2007)
Anghie, A and BS Chimni, 'Third World Approaches to International Law and Individual Responsibility in International Conflicts' (2003) 2(1) Chinese JIL 77–103.
Anand RP, 'Role of the "New" Asian-African Countries in the Present International Legal Order' (1962) 56 AJIL 383–406
Arias I, 'Humanitarian Intervention: Could the Security Council Kill the United Nations?' (1999) 23(4) Fordham Intl L J 1005–1027
Ayittey GBN, 'The Somalia Crisis: Time for an African Solution' (1994) CATO Institute, Policy Analysis No 205
Ayoob M, 'Humanitarian Intervention and International Society' (2001) 7 GG 225–230
Baars, G, 'From the Dutch East India Company to the Corporate Bill of Rights: Corporations and International Law' in U Mattei and J Haskell (eds) *Research Handbook on Political Economy and Law* (Edward Elgar 2015)
Bachand, 'Critical Approaches and the Third World: Towards a Global and Radical Critique of International Law' (Speech at University McGill, 24 March 2010)
Bamidele S, 'Regional Approaches to Crisis Response, the African Union (AU) Intervention in African States: How Visible Is It?' (2017) 73(1) IndQuart 114–128
Barelli M, 'China and Peacekeeping: Unfolding the Political and Legal Complexities of an Ambivalent Relationship' (2022) Asian Journal of International Law 1–20
Barnet RJ, *Intervention and Revolution: America's Confrontation with Insurgent Movements Around the World* (Meridan 1968)
Barraclough G, *An Introduction to Contemporary History* (Penguin 1990)
Beaulac, S, 'The Westphalian Legal Orthodoxy – Myth or Reality?' (2000) 2 JHIL 148–177
Bellamy AJ and PD Williams, *Understanding Peacekeeping* (2nd edn, Polity Press 2010)
Berger HW (ed) *A William Appleman Williams Reader: Selections from His Major Historical Writings* (Ivan R Dee 1992)
Bloomfield LP, 'The United States, the Soviet Union, and the Prospects for Peacekeeping' (1970) 24(3) International Organization 548–565
Boulden J, 'United Nations Operation in the Congo (ONUC)' in JA Koops, T Tardy, N MacQueen and PD Williams (eds) *The Oxford Handbook of United Nations Peacekeeping Operation* (OUP 2015)
Bowden, B, 'The Colonial Origins of International Law: European Expansion and the Classical Standard of Civilization' (2005) 7 JHIL 1–23
Brisku, A, 'The Holy Alliance as 'An Order of Things Conformable to the Interests of Europe and to the Laws of Religion and Humanity' in T Hippler and M Vec (eds) *Paradoxes of Peace in Nineteenth Century Europe* (OUP 2015)

Bull H, (ed) *Intervention in World Politics* (Clarendon 1984)

Case Concerning Military and Paramilitary Activities in and Against Nicaragua (Nicaragua v United States of America) [1986] ICJ Rep 14

Case Concerning Armed Activities on the Territory of the Congo (Democratic Republic of the Congo v Uganda) Judgment of 19 December [2005] ICJ Rep 168-283

Charter of the Organisation of African Unity (25 May 1963)

Charter of the United Nations (26 June 1945)

Chesterman S, *Just War or Just Peace? Humanitarian Intervention and International Law* (OUP 2001)

Chimni BS, 'Marxism and International Law: A Contemporary Analysis' (1999) 34(6) EPW 337–349

Chimni BS, 'International Institutions Today: An Imperial Global State in the Making' (2004) 15(1) EJIL 1–37

Chimni BS, 'Third World Approaches to International Law: A Manifesto' (2006) 8 ICLR 3–27

Chomsky N, 'Statement by Professor Noam Chomsky to the United Nations General Assembly Thematic Dialogue on the Responsibility to Protect' (UN, 23 July 2009) 4 <https://www.un.org/en/ga/president/63/pdf/calendar/20090723-resptoprotect.pdf>

Constitutive Act of the African Union (11 July 2000)

Cooper T, *Great Lakes Holocaust: First Congo War, 1996–1997* (Hellon and Company 2013)

Corfu Channel Case (UK v Albania) (Merits) [1949] ICJ Rep 4, 132–169

Cox, 'Gramsci, Hegemony and International Relations: An Essay in Method' in S Gill (ed) *Gramsci, Historical Materialism and International Relations* (1st ed, CUP 1993) 49–66

Covenant of the League of Nations (28 April 1919)

Craven M, 'Between Law and History: The Berlin Conference of 1884–1885 and the Logic of Free Trade' (2015) 3(1) LRIL 31–59

Cresson, WP, *The Holy Alliance: The European Background of the Monroe Doctrine* (OUP 1922)

Croxton, D, 'The Peace of Westphalia of 1648 and the Origins of Sovereignty' (1999) 21(3) Int Hist Rev 569

Cunliffe P, *Legions of Peace: UN Peacekeepers from the Global South* (C Hurst & Co Publishers Ltd 2013)

Dayal R, *Mission for Hammarskjöld: The Congo Crisis* (OUP 1976)

Declaration on the Granting of Independence to Colonial Countries and Peoples, UNGA Res 1514 (XV) (14 December 1960)

Deibert M, *The Democratic Republic of Congo: Between Hope and Despair* (Zed Books Ltd 2013)

Del Duca LF, 'Reviewed Work(s): L'Intervento davanti alla Corte Internazionale di Giustizia by Angelo Davi' (1987) 81(2) AJIL 465–467

Devlin L, *Chief of Station, Congo* (Public Affairs 2007)

Duffy H, 'Terrorism in International Law' in H Duffy (ed) *The 'War on Terror' and the Framework of International Law* (CUP 2015)

Dumbuya PA, 'ECOWAS Military Intervention in Sierra Leone: Anglophone-Francophone Bipolarity or Multipolarity?' (2008) 25(2) JThirdWorldStud 83–102

Emeka O, 'Analyzing Humanitarian Intervention from an African Point of View' (2012) 1 Vestnik RUDN IR 22–26
Ero C, 'The Problems with "African Solutions"' (*International Crisis Group*, 2 December 2013) <https://www.crisisgroup.org/africa/problems-african-solutions>
Eslava L, M Fakhri and V Nesiah (eds) *Bandung, Global History and International Law* (CUP 2018)
Evans G and M Sahnoun, 'The Responsibility to Protect' (2002) 81(6) Foreign Affairs 99–110
Falk R, *Legal Order in a Violent World* (PUP 1968)
Fanon F, *The Wretched of the Earth* (Penguin Classics 2001)
Fassbender B, *UN Security Council Reform and the Right of Veto: A Constitutional Perspective* (Kluwer 1998)
Fassbender B, 'Purposes and Principles, Article 2(1)' in B Simma et al (eds) *The Charter of the United Nations: A Commentary Vol 1* (3rd edn, OUP 2012)
Fidler DP, 'Revolt Against or From Within the West?: TWAIL, The Developing World, and The Future Direction of International Law' (2003) 2(1) CJIL 29–76
Fisch J, 'Africa as *Terra Nullius*: The Berlin Conference and International Law' in S Förster et al (eds) *Bismarck, Europe and Africa: The Berlin Africa Conference 1884–1885 and the Onset of Partition'* (OUP 1988)
Foot R, *China, The UN, and Human Protection* (OUP 2020)
Franceschet, A, 'Kant, International Law and the Problem of Humanitarian Intervention' (2010) 6(1) JIntPolTheory 1–22
Franck TM, 'Humanitarian Intervention' in S Besson and J Tasioulas (eds) *The Philosophy of International Law* (OUP 2010)
Friedman MP and T Long, 'Soft Balancing in the Americas: Latin American Opposition to US Intervention, 1898–1936' (2015) 40(1) IntSecur 120–156
Fung CJ, *China and Intervention at the UN Security Council: Reconciling Status* (OUP 2019)
Fung CJ, 'Peace by Piece: China's Policy Leadership on Peacekeeping Fatalities' (2022) 43(4) Contemporary Security Policy 572–593
Gathii JT, 'International Law and Eurocentricity' (1998) 9 EJIL 184–211
Gathii JT, 'Neoliberalism, Colonialism, and International Governance: Decentering the International Law of Governmental Legitimacy' (1999–2000) 98 MichLRev 1996–2065
Gathii JT, 'How American Support for Freedom of Commerce Legitimized King Leopold's Territorial Ambitions in the Congo' (2005) 37 StudTransnat'lLegalPol'y 97–107
Gathii JT, 'Humanizing the Pax-Americana Global Empire' (2005) 4(1) GlobalStudLRev 121–134
Gellman IF, *Good Neighbour Diplomacy: United States Policies in Latin America, 1933–1945* (JHUP 1979)
Gelot L, *Legitimacy, Peace Operations and Global-regional Security: The African Union-United Nations Partnership in Darfur* (Routledge 2013)
Gerard E and B Kuklick, *Death in the Congo: Murdering Patrice Lumumba* (HUP 2015)
Gleijeses P, 'Moscow's Proxy? Cuba and Africa 1975–1998' (2006) 8(4) J Cold War Stud 98–146

Gilder A, 'The Effect of "Stabilization" in the Mandates and Practice of UN Peace Operations' (2019) 66 NILR 47–73

Gilder A, *Stabilization and Human Security in UN Peace Operations* (Routledge 2022)

Gilderhus MR, 'The Monroe Doctrine: Meanings and Implications' (2006) 36(1) PSQ 5–16

Gilmour DR, 'The Meaning of "Intervene" within Article 2(7) of the United Nations Charter – An Historical Perspective' (1967) 16 ICLQ 330–351

Gleijeses P, 'Moscow's Proxy? Cuba and Africa 1975–1998' (2006) 8(4) J Cold War Stud 98–146

Gong, GW, *The Standard of 'Civilization' in International Society* (Clarendon Press 1984)

Goulding M, 'The Evolution of United Nations Peacekeeping' (1993) 69(3) IntAff 451–464

Gowan R, 'China's Pragmatic Approach to UN Peacekeeping' (Brookings, 14 September 2020) <https://www.brookings.edu/articles/chinas-pragmatic-approach-to-un-peacekeeping/>

Grewe, W, *The Epochs of International Law* (Rev edn, Walter de Gruyter & Co 2000)

Hafner G, 'Sub-Group on Intervention by Invitation, Preliminary Report, 26 July 2007' (2007) Yearbook of the Institute of International Law, Sanitago Session 226.

Hall I, 'The "Revolt" against the West Revisited' in T Dunne and C Reus-Smit (eds) *The Globalization of International Society* (OUP 2017)

Harvey R, *Liberators: Latin America's Struggle for Independence* (Overlook Books 2002)

Heraclides A and A Dialla, *Humanitarian Intervention in the Long Nineteenth Century: Setting the Precedent* (MUP 2015) 14

Hinsley, FH, *Power and the Pursuit of Peace* (CUP 1963)

Hoare M, *Congo Warriors* (Paladin Press 1991)

Hoare M, *The Road to Kalamata: A Congo Mercenary's Personal Memoir* (Paladin Press 2008)

Hobsbawm, E, *The Age of Empire: 1875–1914* (Abacus 1989)

Hochschild, H, *King Leopold's Ghost: A Story of Greed, Terror and Heroism in Colonial Africa* (Pan Books 2012)

International Refugee Rights Initiative, 'From Non-Interference to Non-Indifference: The African Union and the Responsibility to Protect' (September 2017) 4 <https://reliefweb.int/sites/reliefweb.int/files/resources/AU%20R2P%20-%20final.pdf>

Jahn B, 'The Tragedy of Liberal Diplomacy: Democratization, Intervention, Statebuilding (Part II)' (2007) 1(2) JIntervStatebuilding 211–229

James A, 'The Congo Controversies' (1994) 1(1) International Peacekeeping 44–58

Jennings, RY and AD Watts, *Oppenheim's International Law* (9th edn, OUP 2008).

Johnson RD, 'Anti-Imperialism and the Good Neighbour Policy: Ernest Gruening and Puerto Rican Affairs, 1934–1939' (1997) 29(1) JLatAmStud 89–110

Jones D, *Code of Peace: Ethics and Security in the World of the Warlord States* (UCP 1991)

Kennedy M and Magennis A, *Ireland, the United Nations and the Congo* (Four Courts Press 2014)

Kipling, R, *The White Man's Burden: A Poem* (Doubleday and McClure Co 1899)

Koops JA, T Tardy, N MacQueen and PD Williams, *The Oxford Handbook of United Nations Peacekeeping Operations* (OUP 2015)

Kohen M, 'The Principle of Non-Intervention 25 Years after the Nicaragua Judgment' (2012) 25(1) LJIL 157–164

Koskenniemi M, *The Gentle Civilizer of Nations* (CUP 2009)

Koskenniemi M, 'Histories of International Law: Dealing with Eurocentrism' (2011) 19 Rechtsgeschichte 152

Kreijen G, M Brus et al, *State, Sovereignty and International Governance* (OUP 2002)

Kunig M, *Prohibition of Intervention* (MPEPIL 2008)

Labuda PI, 'United Nations Peacekeeping as Intervention by Invitation: Host State Consent and the Use of Force in Security Council-Mandated Stabilisation Operations' (2020) JUFIL 1–37

Lagrange E, 'The Thoughts of René-Jean Dupuy: Methodology or Poetry of International Law?' (2011) 22(2) EJIL 425–440

Larssen AK, 'Russia: The Principle of Non-Intervention and the Libya Case' in D Henriksen and AK Larssen (eds) *Political Rationale and International Consequences of the War in Libya* (OUP 2016)

Lefever EW, *Crisis in the Congo: A United Nations Forces in Action* (Brookings Institution 1965)

Lingelbach, WE, 'The Doctrine and Practice of Intervention in Europe' (1900) 16 AnnAmAcadPolSocSci 1–32.

Lorimer, J, *The Institutes of the Law of Nations Vol 1* (Adamant Media Corporation 2001)

Lowe AV, 'The Principle of Non-Intervention: Use of Force' in V Lowe and C Warbrick (eds) *The United Nations and the Principles of International Law: Essays in Memory of Michael Akehurst* (Routledge 1994)

Ludwikowski, RR, 'The Beginning of the Constitutional Era: A Bicentennial Comparative Study of the American and French Constitutions' (1989) 11(1) MJIL 167.

MacFarlane SN, 'Intervention During the Cold War' (2002) 42(350) AdelphiPapers 33–45

Malone D and R Thakur, 'Racism in Peacekeeping' (*Global and Mail*, 30 October 2000) <https://www.theglobeandmail.com/opinion/racism-in-peacekeeping/article1340656/>

Maluwa T, 'International Law Making in Post-Colonial Africa: The Role of the Organisation of African Unity' (2002) 49 NILR 81–103

Mamdani M, *When Victims Become Killers: Colonialism, Nativism, and the Genocide in Rwanda* (PUP 2002)

Mays TM, 'African Solutions for African Problems: The Changing Face of African-Mandated Peace Operations' (2003) 23(1) JConfStud 106–125

Mazower M, *No Enchanted Palace: The End of Empire and the Ideological Origins of the United Nations* (PUP 2009)

Mazower M, *Governing the World: The History of an Idea, 1815 to the Present* (Penguin 2012)

Mazuri A, *Towards a Pax Africana: A Study of Ideology and Ambition.* (UCP 1967)

McIntyre A and T Weiss, 'Weak Governments in Search of Strength' in S Chesterman and C Lehnardt (eds) *From Mercenaries to Market: The Rise and Regulation of Private Military Companies* (OUP 2007)

Metz S, 'American Attitudes Toward Decolonization in Africa' (1984) 99(3) PolSciQ 515–533

Mickelson K, 'Rhetoric and Rage: Third World Voices in International Legal Discourse' (2011) 16(2) WisIntlLJ 353–419

Miéville, C, *Between Equal Rights: A Marxist Theory of International Law* (Pluto Press 2006).

Milton, P, 'Guarantee and Intervention: The Assessment of the Peace of Westphalia in International Law and Politics by Authors of Natural Law and of Public Law c. 1650–1806' in S Zurbuchen (ed) *The Law of Nations and Natural Law 1625-1800* (Brill 2019) 186–226

Montevideo Convention of 1933 on Rights and Duties of States 159 LNTS 199

Morales WQ, 'US Intervention and the New World Order: Lessons From Cold War and Post-Cold War Cases' (1994) 15(1) TWQ 77–101

Mutua M, 'Why Redraw the Map of Africa: A Moral and Legal History' (1995) 16 MichJIntlL 1113–1176

Mutua, M, 'What is TWAIL?' (2000) 94 ASILPROC 31–38

Mutua M, 'Savages, Victims, and Saviors: The Metaphor of Human Rights' (2001) HarvIntLJ 201–245

Neiman S, 'The Dangers of Deteriorating Relations Between Rwanda and Uganda' (*World Politics Review*, 17 October 2019) <https://www.worldpoliticsreview.com/articles/28272/the-dangers-of-deteriorating-relations-between-rwanda-and-uganda>

Nesiah V, 'The Specter of Violence that Haunts the UDHR: The Turn to Ethics and Expertise' (2009) 24(1) MJIL 135–154

Nifterik, GP, 'Religious and Humanitarian Intervention in Sixteenth and Early Seventeenth Century Legal Thought' in R Lesafer and G Macours (eds) *Sovereignty and the Law of Nations (16th–18th Centuries)* (Peeters Publishers 2006).

Ofuatey-Kodjoe W, 'Regional Organisations and the Resolution of Internal Conflict: The ECOWAS Intervention in Liberia' (2007) 1(3) IntPeacekeep 261–302

Onuf NG, 'The Principle of Non-Intervention, the United Nations and the International System' (1971) 25(2) IntOrgan 209–227

Oppenheim, IL, *International Law: A Treatise* (Longmans, Green and Co 1905)

Orford, A (ed) *International Law and its Others* (CUP 2006)

Orford A, *Reading Humanitarian Intervention: Human Rights and the Use of Force in International Law* (CUP 2008)

Otto D, 'Subalternity and International Law: The Problems of Global Community and the Incommensurability of Difference' (1996) 5 Soc&LegStud 337–364

Pahuja S, 'Decolonisation and the Eventness of International Law' in F Johns et al (eds) *Events: The Force of International Law* (Routledge 2011)

Packenham T, *The Scramble for Africa* (Abacus New Ed 1992)

Philpott, D, *Revolutions in Sovereignty: How Ideas Shaped Modern International Relations* (PUP 2001)

Pitts, J, 'Intervention and Sovereign Equality: Legacies of Vattel' in S Recchia and J.M. Welsh (eds) *Just and Unjust Military Intervention: European Thinkers from Vitoria to Mill* (CUP 2013).

Prashad V, *The Darker Nations: A People's History of the Third World* (New Press 2008)

Preiser, W, 'History of International Law, Ancient Times to 1648' (Max Planck Encyclopedia of Public International Law 2008) <http://opil.ouplaw.com/view/10.1093/law:epil/9780199231690/law-9780199231690-e716>

Prunier G, *Africa's World War: Congo, the Rwandan Genocide, and the Making of a Continental Catastrophe* (Oxford University Press 2011)

Rajagopal B, 'International Law and Its Discontents: Rethinking the Global South' (2012) 106 ASILPROC 176–181

Reynaert J, *MONUC/MONUSCO and Civilian Protection in the Kivus* (IPIS 2010)

Richardson III HJ, 'Critical Perspectives on Intervention' (2014) 29 Maryland JIL 12–49

Richterova D and N Telepneva, 'An Introduction: The Secret Struggle for the Global South – Espionage, Military Assistance and State Security in the Cold War' (2021) 43(1) IntHistRev 1–11

Riles, A, 'Aspiration and Control: International Legal Rhetoric and the Essentialization of Culture' (1993) 106 HarvLRev 723.

Said, E, *Culture and Imperialism* (Vintage 1994).

Said, E, *Orientalism* (Penguin Books 2003).

Sanford H, 'Declaration by the International Association of the Congo. April 22, 1884' (1909) 3(S1) AJIL 5

Schmidt E, *Foreign Intervention in Africa: From the Cold War to the War on Terror* (CUP 2013)

Schroeder, PW, *The Transformation of European Politics, 1763–1848* (OUP 1994)

Sellers MNS, 'Intervention under International Law' (2014) 29(1) Maryland JIL.

Seton-Watson H, *Neither War not Peace: The Struggle or Power in the World* (Kessinger Publishing 2010)

Sexton J, *The Monroe Doctrine: Empire and Nation in Nineteenth-Century America* (Farrar, Straus and Giroux 2011)

Sheeran S and S Case, *The Intervention Brigade: Legal Issues for the UN in the Democratic Republic of the Congo* (IPI 2014)

Siddiqui, S, 'Donald Trump Praises Syria Strikes and Declares: "Missions Accomplished"' (*The Guardian*, 14 April 2018) <https://www.theguardian.com/us-news/2018/apr/14/donald-trump-syria-strikes-mission-accomplished>

Simma B, (ed) (in collaboration with H Mosler, A Randelzhofer, C Tomuschat, R Wolfruh) *The Charter of the United Nations: A Commentary* (2nd edn, OUP 2002)

Simpson G, *Great Powers and Outlaw States: Unequal Sovereignty in the International Legal Order* (CUP 2004)

Singer PW, *Corporate Warriors: The Rise of the Private Military Industry* (Cornell University Press 2003)

Singer PW, 'War Profits, and the Vacuum of Law: Privatized Military Firms and International Law' (2003–2004) 42 ColumJTransnatlL 521–550

Somerville, K, *Africa's Long Road Since Independence: The Many Histories of a Continent* (Penguin 2017)

Stein S, 'The UN and Genocide: A Comparative Analysis of Rwanda and the Former Yugoslavia' in F Attinà (ed) *The Politics and Policies of Relief, Aid and Reconstruction* (Palgrave Macmillan 2012)

Stringer D and Biesheuvel T, 'Tesla Strikes Deal to Buy Cobalt From Glencore for EV Plants' (*Bloomberg*, 16 June 2020) <https://www.bloomberg.com/news/articles/2020-06-16/glencore-agrees-deal-to-sell-cobalt-to-tesla-for-new-car-plants>

Tesón, FR, 'The Kantian Theory of International Law' (1992) 92(1) ColumLRev 53–102

Tsagourias N, 'Consent, Neutrality/Impartiality and the Use of Force in Peacekeeping: Their Constitutional Dimension' (2007) 11 JCSL 3, 465–482

Tsagourias N, 'Security Council Legislation, Article 2(7) of the UN Charter, and the Principle of Subsidiarity' (2011) 24 LJIL 539–559

Tsagourias N, 'Electoral Cyber Interference, Self-Determination, and the Principle of Non-Intervention in Cyberspace' in D Broeders and B van den Berg (eds) *Governing Cyberspace: Behavior, Power and Diplomacy* (Rowan & Littlefield 2020)

Turner T, *The Congo Wars: Conflict, Myth and Reality* (Zed Books 2007)

Tzouvala N, 'TWAIL and the "Unwilling or Unable" Doctrine: Continuities and Ruptures' (2015) 109 AJIL Unbound 266–270

Umozurike UO, *International Law and Colonialism in Africa* (Nwamife 1979)

UNA-UK, 'The Colour Line' (*UNA-UK Magazine*, 19 October 2018) <https://una.org.uk/magazine/2018-1>

UN, 'Growth in United Nations Membership, 1945-present' <https://www.un.org/en/sections/member-states/growth-united-nations-membership-1945-present/index.html#1960s>

UN, *United Nations Peacekeeping Operations: Principles and Guidelines* ("The Capstone Doctrine") (DPKO 2008)

UN Document A/AC.119/SR.26

UN Document A/AC.119/SR.3

UN Document A/AC.119/SR.31

UN Peacekeeping <https://peacekeeping.un.org/en>

UNGA (15th Session, 882nd Plenary Meeting) (3 October 1960) UN Doc A/PV.882

UNGA First Committee (20th Session, 1402nd Meeting) (8 December 1965) UN Doc A/C.1/SR.1402

UNGA Sixth Committee (28th Session, 1402nd Meeting) (1 October 1973) UN Doc A/C.6/SR.1402

UNGA, 'Report of the Special Committee on Principles of International Law Concerning Friendly Relations and Co-operation Among States' (24th Session, Supplement No 19 A/7619) (October 1969) UN Doc A/AC.125/L.24

UNGA, 'Report of the Secretary-General. An Agenda for Peace: Preventive, Diplomacy, Peacemaking and Peacekeeping' (31 January 1992) UN Doc A/47/277-S/24111

UNGA, 'Report of the Panel on United Nations Peace Operations' ("Brahimi Report") (21 August 2000) UN Doc A/55/305-S/2000/809

UNGA Res 290 [V] (1 December 1949)

UNGA Res 375 (IV) Draft Declaration on Rights and Duties of States (6 December 1949)

UNGA Res 998 (ES-I) (4 November 1956)

UNGA Res 1514 (XV) (14 December 1960)

UNGA Res 1654 (XVI) (27 November 1961)

UNGA Res 1966 (XVIII) (16 December 1963)

UNGA Res 2131 (XX) (21 December 1965)

UNGA Res 2625 (XXV) (24 October 1970)

UNGA Res 36/103 (9 December 1981)
UN Peacekeeping, 'Principles of Peacekeeping' <https://peacekeeping.un.org/en/principles-of-peacekeeping>
UN Press Release, 'Secretary-General Presents his Annual Report to General Assembly' (SG/SM/7136, GA/9596)
UNSC, 'United Nations Security Council Consolidated List' <https://www.un.org/securitycouncil/content/un-sc-consolidated-list>
UNSC, 'Chairman of Independent Inquiry into United Nations Actions During 1994 Rwanda Genocide Presents Report to Security Council' (14 April 2000) Press Release SC/6843
UNSC, 'Belgium and Germany: Draft Resolution' (10 July 2020) UN Doc S/2020/667 and (13 July 2020) UN Doc S/2020/693
UNSC Res 1973 (17 March 2011) UN Doc S/RES/1973
UNSC Res 1975 (30 March 2011) UN Doc S/RES/1975
UNSC Res 2098 (28 March 2013) UN Doc S/RES/2098
UNSC Res 2502 (19 December 2019) UN Doc S/RES/2502
UN and Decolonisation, 'List of Former Trust and Non-Self Governing Territories' <https://www.un.org/dppa/decolonization/history/former-trust-and-nsgts>
Van Reybrouck D, *Congo: The Epic History of a People* (Fourth Estate 2015)
Vattel, E, *Droit des gens ou principes de la loi naturelle* (Londres 1758).
Vidal J, 'Construction of World's Largest Dam in DR Congo Could Begin Within Months' (*The Guardian*, 28 May 2016) <https://www.theguardian.com/environment/2016/may/28/construction-of-worlds-largest-dam-in-dr-congo-could-begin-within-months>
Vitoria, F, *De Indis et De Ivre Belli Relectiones* (first publication 1532, Ernest Nys tr, Oceana 1964).
Weiss TG and G Kuele, 'The Global South and UN Peace Operations' (*E-International Relations*, 3 February 2019) <https://www.e-ir.info/2019/02/03/the-global-south-and-un-peace-operations/#_ftn2>
White ND and C Henderson, *Research Handbook on International Conflict and Security Law: Jus ad Bellum, Jus in Bello and Jus post Bellum* (Edward Elgar 2013)
Wilgus AC, 'James G Blaine and the Pan American Movement' (1922) 5(4) HAHR 662–708
Winfield PH, 'The History of Intervention in International Law' (1922–3) 3 BYIL 130
Wouters J and T Rhys, 'Security Council Reform: A New Veto for a New Century?' (2005) Egmont Paper 9, 1–35
Wright Q, 'Effects of the League of Nations Covenant' (1919) 13(4) APSR 556–576
Zartman W, 'Europe and Africa: Decolonization or Dependency?' (1976) 54 Foreign Affairs 325–343
Zenko M, 'Donald Trump is a Magical (Foreign Policy) Realist' (*Foreign Policy*, 7 June 2016) <foreignpolicy.com/2016/06/07/donald-trump-is-a-magical-foreign-policy-realist/>

Chapter 3

Peacekeeping – In Search of a Legal Framework

Searching for a Peacekeeping Framework

As the UN Charter makes no reference to peacekeeping, there is no pre-determined constitutional, institutional or normative framework or guidelines governing peacekeeping. Instead, it has developed from interpretations of the Charter, the implied powers of the Security Council,[1] General Assembly[2] and Secretary-General[3] and decisions from the International Court of Justice[4] and is based upon the three fundamental principles of consent, impartiality and non-use of force.[5] Therefore, as with the principle of non-intervention, peacekeeping has evolved through international organs which have established a piecemeal red boundary line around the concept that separates peacekeeping from intervention. That is, it creates a line between, on the one hand, peacekeeping, as a form of collective security intervention[6] (thus a justified exception to the principle of non-intervention), and, on the other hand, intervention in the form of coercive action designed to influence change within a state, which violates the principle of non-intervention. This chapter and the subsequent chapter will therefore explore how collective security is the main gateway opening the red boundary line around intervention, with peacekeeping an extension of this, an additional gateway that permits intervention. Its principles and norms then act as veins, arteries and capillaries that further expand a peacekeeping operation's interventionist potential, thus simultaneously undermining or contravening the principle of non-intervention.

Continuing the approach taken in the previous chapter's exploration of non-intervention, this chapter will identify instances in which peacekeeping's

1 See: Articles 24(1), 36(1), 40 Charter of the United Nations (24 October 1945) ('UN Charter').
2 See: Articles 10, 11(2), 12, 14 UN Charter.
3 See: Articles 97–99 UN Charter.
4 *Certain Expenses of the United Nations (Article 17, Paragraph 2 of the Charter)* (Advisory Opinion) [1962] ICJ Rep 151.
5 UNGA, 'Summary Study' A/3943 (9 October 1958) UN Doc A/3943.
6 See: N Tsagourias and ND White, *Collective Security Theory, Law and Practice* (CUP 2013).

DOI: 10.4324/9781003371649-3

red boundary line has been expanded, contorted and, at times, stretched to its limits. It will then note how this, in turn, has a direct impact on the principle of non-intervention as, if peacekeeping breaches its limits, it risks crossing the intervention line, becoming a form of coercive action and thereby violating the principle of non-intervention. It is therefore important to clarify what the legal and normative frameworks surrounding peacekeeping are in order to ascertain the interventionist nature of peacekeeping and the extent to which peacekeeping's principles and norms may reinforce or undermine the principle of non-intervention.

Furthermore, identifying the legal and normative frameworks is also important for both the operation and function of peacekeeping. In particular, clarifying peacekeeping's legal framework is important as 'in general, third party activity is much less likely to raise objection if it rests on legal authority and is brought within the framework' of the UN Charter.[7] Similarly, it is argued that a peacekeeper may find invoking legal obligations and prescriptions persuasive when facilitating negotiations or undertaking tasks,[8] with a 'legal foundation for the necessary activities' proving to be 'essential to effective performance'.[9] Peacekeeping's legal framework is therefore essential both for relations with the host state, for the legitimacy and legality of the operation and for regulating and guiding the peacekeepers during the deployment of an operation.

Peacekeeping's Legal Basis

Generally, peacekeeping finds its constitutional basis within Chapters IV, VI and VII of the UN Charter, although it has been argued that the more fitting categorisation is 'Chapter VI and a half operations'.[10] Similarly, as seen in Chapter 2, some have suggested that the legal basis for contemporary stabilisation operations could be tied to host state consent, thereby a form of intervention by invitation.[11] Whilst Chapter IV deals with the powers of the UN General Assembly (UNGA), it is only on very rare occasions that the Assembly has mandated peacekeeping operations.[12] Instead, the UNGA undertakes a

7 O Schachter, 'The Uses of Law in International Peacekeeping' (1964) 50(6) VLR 1096–1114, 1098.
8 O Schachter, 'Dag Hammarskjold and the Relation of Law to Politics' (1962) 56(1) AJIL 1–8, 5–6.
9 Schachter (n7) 1099.
10 See: JF Hillen III, 'UN Collective Security: Chapter Six and a Half' (1994) 24(1) Parameters 27–37.
11 See: Chapter 2, Section 4 and PI Labuda, 'United Nations Peacekeeping as Intervention by Invitation: Host State Consent and the Use of Force in Security Council-Mandated Stabilisation Operations' (2020) JUFIL 1–37, 3.
12 UNEF: UNGA Res 377 (V) (3 November 1950); ONUC: UNGA Res 1474 (ES-IV) (20 September 1960).

key role in the financing of operations and monitoring peacekeeping performance through its Special Committee on Peacekeeping Operations, with the Security Council tasked with establishing peacekeeping operations.[13] Within Chapter VI, the Security Council is authorised to deal with the 'pacific settlement of disputes' that may endanger international peace and security, including recommending 'appropriate measures or methods of adjustment'.[14] Peacekeeping operations authorised under this Chapter therefore follow the traditional, passive, consensual model, such as UNEF and UNFICYP,[15] and thus reinforce the principle of non-intervention. Through Chapter VII, however, the Council is given broad powers to determine breaches or threats to peace and then to take military, coercive action to combat these in order to 'maintain or restore international peace and security'.[16] Operations mandated by the Council under Chapter VII are thus, typically, non-consensual enforcement operations,[17] which, at times, blur the boundaries between peacekeeping and peace enforcement and thus undermine the principle of non-intervention by pushing peacekeeping closer to the interventionist boundary line.[18]

Despite this general distinction, in reality, the constitutional basis of peacekeeping operations is not as clear-cut, with recurrent, inconclusive debates about the Charter basis of peacekeeping,[19] leading to an uncertainty about the coercive or interventionist nature of peacekeeping. For some, peacekeeping operations may be initiated on the basis of recommendations made by the Security Council on 'procedures or methods of adjustments' under Article 36(1); thus, Chapter VI may provide a legal basis for the establishment of a peacekeeping operation.[20] However, for others, it is impossible for

13 See: UN Peacekeeping, 'Role of the General Assembly' <https://peacekeeping.un.org/en/role-of-general-assembly>.

14 Article 36(1) UN Charter. Confirmed by the ICJ in *Certain Expenses* (n4).

15 UNGA Res 998 (ES-I) (4 November 1956); UNSC Res 186 (4 March 1964) UN Doc S/RES/186.

16 Articles 39–42 UN Charter.

17 Articles 39 and 40 envisage recommendations and provisional measures as well as decisions, and therefore a Chapter VII operation is not automatically non-consensual. On the legality and enforceability of Security Council powers, see, for example: D Whittle, 'The Limits of Legality and the United Nations Security Council: Applying the Extra-Legal Measures Model to Chapter VII Action' (2015) 26(3) EJIL 671–698 and E De Wet, *The Chapter VII Powers of the United Nations Security Council* (Hart Publishing 2004).

18 UNSC Res 143 (14 July 1960) UN Doc S/RES/143; UNSC Res 1279 (30 November 1999) UN Doc S/RES/1279; UNSC Res 1925 (28 May 2010) UN Doc S/RES/1925.

19 See, for example: ND White, 'The UN Charter and Peacekeeping Forces: Constitutional Issues' (1996) 3(4) IntPeacekeep 43–63; A Orakhelashvili, 'The Legal Basis of the United Nations Peace-Keeping Operations' (2003) 43 VaJIL 485–524; D Ciobanu, 'The Power of the Security Council to Organize Peacekeeping Operations' in A Cassese (ed) *United Nations Peacekeeping: Legal Essays* (Springer 1978) 15, 17, 40.

20 H Kelsen, *The Law of the United Nations: A Critical Analysis of Its Fundamental Problems* (Frederick A Praeger 1964) 401; Orakhelashvili (n19).

peacekeeping's constitutional foundations to lie in Chapter VI as the potential use of force by peacekeepers is not an element of the pacific settlement of disputes contained within the Chapter.[21] Instead, it is argued that peacekeeping's basis lies in Chapter VII, in particular Article 39 which permits the Security Council to 'take coercive measures or make recommendations'.[22] Further, although the International Court of Justice stressed that peacekeeping operations are not enforcement actions and, as such, cannot find their legal basis in Articles 41 and 42,[23] there remain debates as to whether measures can be taken by peacekeeping operations pursuant to these two Articles.[24]

To further complicate matters, within contemporary peacekeeping, the multi-dimensional, stabilisation or 'third generation' operations are frequently deployed with a Chapter VII mandate in complex, intra-state conflicts.[25] However, the explicit reference to the Charter often comes in the form of a singular phrase – 'Acting under Chapter VII' – which is invoked in the introductory clause or chapeau of the resolution.[26] This then creates the misleading impression that peacekeeping and peace enforcement have become one (with some even referring to these stabilisation operations as 'Chapter VII and a half' operations) when, instead, the invocation of Chapter VII is to authorise the use of force for specific tasks, such as the protection of civilians.[27]

Today's operations are therefore a complex infusion of Chapter VI and VII elements, exploiting the space between the two Chapters.[28] This chapter will not, however, engage in these well-trodden debates over peacekeeping's Charter basis.[29] Instead, it will focus on the legal principles of peacekeeping as it is these principles which, combined with the normative framework discussed in the subsequent chapter, determine the interventionist nature of peacekeeping as they form peacekeeping's frameworks and thus peacekeeping's boundary line.

The Birth of the 'Holy Trinity'

The first UN peacekeeping operation, UNEF, was a lightly armed, several thousand-strong monitoring and observing operation deployed to the Sinai

21 Ciobanu (n19).
22 Orakhelashvili (nxix).
23 *Certain Expenses* (n4) 166, 171. Ciobanu (n19) 18.
24 Orakhelashvili (n19) 492–493.
25 MW Doyle and N Sambanis, 'Peacekeeping Operations' in TG Weiss and S Daws (eds) *The Oxford Handbook on the United Nations* (OUP 2007) 325.
26 Such as in MONUSCO: UNSC Res 2502 (19 December 2019) UN Doc S/RES/2502.
27 ibid. On Chapter VII and a half: J Karlsrud, 'United Nations Stabilization Operations: Chapter VII and a Half' (2019) 18(5) Ethnopolitics 494–508.
28 ND White, 'Peacekeeping Doctrine: An Autonomous Legal Order?' (2019) 88(1) NJIL 86–110, 94.
29 See, for example: ND White (n19); A Orakhelashvili,(n19); D Ciobanu (n19) 15, 17, 40.

in 1956 to oversee the Suez peace agreement and act as a buffer between the four formerly hostile states.[30] Following UNEF, the then-Secretary-General (UNSG/SG), Dag Hammarskjöld, set out the 'basic principles and rules which would provide an adaptable framework' for peacekeeping operations in his *Summary Study* report.[31] Within this, Hammarskjöld set out the three fundamental principles of peacekeeping, the 'Holy Trinity' of consent, impartiality and non-use of force. Initially, these principles were narrowly interpreted and therefore, cumulatively, suggested a non-interventionist approach which echoed the United Nations' agenda at that time and epitomised Hammarskjöld's own personal, philosophical beliefs.[32] Indeed, this formulation of peacekeeping was occurring during the height of the decolonisation period which, as explored in the previous chapter, was also a pivotal time for the development of the principle of non-intervention, with a general non-interventionist rhetoric dominating the international system. The principles therefore created a red boundary line around the concept of peacekeeping, placing limits on peacekeeping's activities and, consequently, its ability to intervene, thereby supporting the principle of non-intervention.

The principles are also frequently invoked by member states, including Russia and China, in part for political reasons but also 'to establish clear boundaries' linked to the fact that peacekeeping can become an intrusive tool 'wielded by the West in particular to sort of dictate what should happen in some sovereign countries'.[33] Indeed, China vehemently opposed the deployment of UNEF II in 1973 arguing that the deployment of peacekeeping operations would 'only pave the way for further international intervention and control with the superpowers as the "behind-scenes-boss"'.[34] The Holy Trinity thus serves not only as a boundary line between peacekeeping and intervention but, from a TWAIL perspective, as a useful tool for limiting the power of the hegemonic states and consequently limiting their ability to use peacekeeping to push their agendas or use coercive action to influence change in host states (in other words, to intervene). Once again, it therefore highlights how the power dynamics, which the previous chapter identified as prevalent within the United Nations and the principle of non-intervention, also exist within peacekeeping.

The interpretation and application of the fundamental principles are therefore crucial for the legality of the peacekeeping operation and for determining the interventionist nature of the operation. Whether taken individually

30 UNGA Res 998 (ES-I) (n15); UNGA Res 1000 (ES-I) (5 November 1956).

31 UNSG, 'Address by Secretary-General Dag Hammarskjöld at University of California Convocation, Berkeley' (13 May 1954) Press Release SG/382.

32 See: B Urquhart, *Hammarskjöld* (Alfred A Knopf 1972) 17–45.

33 Interview with Senior Political Affairs Officer, UN DPO ('Interviewee 16') (New York, 10 December 2019) DOI: <http://doi.org/10.17639/nott.7119> pg 42.

34 UNSC Verbatim Record (25 October 1973) UN Doc S/PV.1750, 2, para 13.

or combined, the principles may restrict or permit peacekeeping as intervention, depending on how they are interpreted. Peacekeeping operations which maintain a narrow interpretation of the principles, such as UNEF, are classified as traditional models of peacekeeping and are typically consensual, non-interventionist and non-coercive. However, as the remainder of this chapter will explore, these principles have been significantly expanded over the years, thereby widening both the boundaries and the interventionist nature of peacekeeping. Indeed, this expansion or interpretation of the principles began even during Hammarskjöld's tenure with the deployment of ONUC in the DRC in 1960. Whilst ONUC initially began as a traditional model of peacekeeping, following a narrow reading of the fundamental principles which Hammarskjöld had only recently laid out, escalating conflict, demands from the host state and pressure from UN members forced Hammarskjöld to interpret his principles more broadly. As later sections will explore, Hammarskjöld, in his position as UNSG, struggled to balance the maintenance of his original understanding of the fundamental norms with the complexities of the Congo crisis, leading to a somewhat inevitable expansion and re-interpretation of the principles or norms. This broadening of the peacekeeping principles also, simultaneously, stretched the thin red boundary line surrounding peacekeeping, expanding the sphere of collective security intervention and thereby undermining or perhaps contravening the principle of non-intervention.

As the remainder of this chapter will explore, successive Secretaries-General have re-interpreted the fundamental principles, helping to drive the evolution of peacekeeping operations, as Chapter 2 noted, from the traditional model to multi-dimensional, robust operations, with an expanded use of force, questionable impartiality and dubious host state consent. Similarly, the successive UN Secretaries-General, as the 'chief administrative officer',[35] 'manager, investigator, chief mediator diplomat'[36] and norm entrepreneur,[37] have introduced new norms within peacekeeping. These norms emerged from a consensus or understanding of interventionist practices, that were highlighted in the previous chapter, and have then been crystallised by the Secretary-General, highlighting how the SG can play a significant role in developing and shaping peacekeeping. For example, in the post-Cold War optimism, with the re-emergence of peacekeeping and the rise of liberal democracy in a post-ideological world,[38] under Secretary-General Boutros Boutros-Ghali democracy

35 Report of the United Nations Preparatory Commission, December 23, 1945 (HM Stationary Office, London, 1946).

36 EJ Ravndal, '"A Force for Peace": Expanding the Role of the UN Secretary-General Under Trygve Lie, 1946–1953' 23(3) (2017) Global Governance 443–459, 445.

37 I Johnstone, 'The Secretary-General as Norm Entrepreneur' in S Chesterman (ed) *Secretary or General? The UN Secretary-General in World Politics* (CUP 2007) 123–138.

38 F Fukuyama, *The End of History and the Last Man* (Penguin 2020).

promotion was introduced into peacekeeping operations and is now a common feature within peacekeeping operations.[39] Shortly after, when the post-Cold War optimism began to fade and the United Nations was embroiled in a series of catastrophic failures in the 1990s, Boutros-Ghali's successor, Kofi Annan, championed the concept of 'responsibility to protect', leading to the introduction of protection of civilians within peacekeeping mandates.[40] Again, the introduction of this norm reflected a broader consensus within the international community and amongst member states for humanitarian-based interventions. More recently, following numerous allegations of sexual exploitation and abuse (SEA) by UN peacekeepers and calls for action to be taken to eradicate this from peacekeeping operations, a 'zero tolerance policy' against SEA was introduced.[41]

Cumulatively, these principles and norms form a patchwork framework upon which peacekeeping operations are based. This chapter will therefore focus on mapping the evolution of the fundamental principles, demonstrating how the varying interpretations and applications of the principles are often in line with interventionist trends or rhetoric discussed in Chapter 2. It will also highlight how an interpretation and application of one principle may have a causal effect on another principle, further highlighting the interconnectedness and fluidity of the frameworks.

Consent

Consent is a cornerstone of international law and plays a key role in generating legal obligation,[42] based on the notion that the rules which bind sovereign states 'must emanate from their own free will'.[43] It has also long been established that consent must be 'internationally attributable to the State'; that is, it must come from a person 'whose will is considered, at the international level, to be the will of the State' and such a person must be 'competent to manifest that will'.[44] It is usually accepted, then, that it is the government who may provide such consent, based on a long-standing presumption that

39 See: UNGA, 'Report of the Secretary-General. An Agenda for Peace: Preventive, Diplomacy, Peacemaking and Peacekeeping' (31 January 1992) UN Doc A/47/277-S/24111 and UNGA, 'Supplement to an Agenda for Peace' (25 January 1995) UN Doc A/50/60-S/1995/1.

40 See: UNSC Res 1265 (17 September 1999) UN Doc S/RES/1265 and UNSC Res 1270 (22 October 1999) UN Doc S/RES/1270. See also: S Rushton, 'The UN Secretary-General and Norm Entrepreneurship: Boutros Boutros-Ghali and Democracy Promotion' 14(1) (2008) GG 95–110.

41 See: UNGA, 'Report of the Secretary-General. Sexual Exploitation and Abuse: Implementing a Zero Tolerance Policy' (15 February 2018) UN Doc A/72/751.

42 F Teson, *A Philosophy of International Law* (Westview 1998) 73.

43 *'Lotus' Case ([France v Turkey])* PCIJ Rep Series A No 10, 18.

44 UN, Eighth Report on State Responsibility, UN Doc A/CN.4/318 and Add.1–4, 2 (1979) Y.B. Int'l L. Comm'n 3 (1980) 36.

the government has 'effective control over the territory and people of the state' and therefore 'possesses the exclusive authority to express the will of the state in its international affairs'.[45] As Chapter 5 will explore, however, where there is a weak or failed state, or competing claims to effective control over certain territories, the matter of who may provide consent becomes less clear.

For peacekeeping, consent is crucial both to distinguish peacekeeping from other forms of intervention, such as peace enforcement, and to provide the peacekeeping intervention with its legality. As Orakhelashvili argues, consent 'is even a factor capable of validating behaviour which would otherwise be illegal'.[46] Within this context, the behaviour which is validated (and would otherwise be illegal) is intervention in the form of UN peacekeeping. Consent is, therefore, 'an inevitable element in the legal basis of peacekeeping forces'.[47] Indeed, as was discussed in the previous chapter, the ICJ noted that state consent and an assertion of state sovereignty are embedded within the principle of non-intervention, in that intervention is only allowable at the request or permission of the host state. It therefore follows that as peacekeeping is a form of collective security intervention (a justified or legitimate intervention under the principle of non-intervention) the elements of consent which are embedded within the principle extend to peacekeeping. Consent is thus a 'legal prerequisite for the entry and presence of a peacekeeping operation within a state and its granting makes Article 2(7) inapplicable'.[48] Again, the overlap or intertwined relationship with the principle of non-intervention is evident. That is, as was discussed in the previous chapter, Article 2(7) of the UN Charter contains the only direct reference to intervention within the Charter, specifically prohibiting states from intervening in a state's domestic jurisdiction.[49] Consent to the presence of a peacekeeping operation therefore prevents peacekeeping from violating Article 2(7) and becoming intervention. It therefore follows that if the element of consent is lost the peacekeeping operation risks becoming illegal intervention, in violation of Article 2(7). Peacekeeping can thus be viewed as interventionist behaviour which would be considered illegal, if not for the validating consent.

This argument begins to blur, however, when considering contemporary peacekeeping operations which utilise Chapter VII. In light of the exception contained within Article 2(7), which states that the provision 'shall not

45 D Whippman, 'Military Intervention, Regional Organisations, and Host-State Consent' in B Kondoch (ed) *International Peacekeeping* (Ashgate 2007) 113–114.

46 Orakhelashvili (n19) 518.

47 ibid.

48 N Tsagourias, 'Consent, Neutrality/Impartiality and the Use of Force in Peacekeeping: Their Constitutional Dimension' (2007) 11(3) JCSL 465–482, 469.

49 Article 2(7) UN Charter.

prejudice the application of enforcement measures under Chapter VII',[50] if Chapter VII is invoked, Article 2(7) is not violated. Therefore, if the Security Council mandates a peacekeeping operation under Chapter VII, it may disregard Article 2(7) and intervene in the domestic affairs of the host state, without its consent. This does not mean that the Council derogates from the norm of non-intervention contained within Article 2(7); rather, in declaring a situation to be a threat or breach of international peace, under Article 39 of Chapter VII, the Council adjudicates the matter to be non-domestic and therefore within the remit of their jurisdiction.[51] As such, if a peacekeeping operation's mandate invokes Chapter VII, as do some contemporary operations such as MONUSCO[52] and MINUSCA,[53] then, in theory, the operation could continue without host state consent, without violating Article 2(7), but would then become peace enforcement, not peacekeeping. The Council's use of the phrase 'Acting under Chapter VII' within peacekeeping mandates, as noted earlier, therefore further muddies the water, blurring the boundaries between peacekeeping and peace enforcement and the legal requirement for host state consent. Despite this, consent is still considered to be 'indispensable' for the deployment of an operation; otherwise a forceful operation would be peace enforcement, not peacekeeping.[54] It is thus the 'primary distinction' between peace enforcement and peacekeeping,[55] thereby playing an important role in establishing the legal basis 'for the emplacement and presence of a peacekeeping force within a state'.[56] Without consent, then, the peacekeeping operation becomes intervention.

From a TWAIL perspective, the inclusion of consent as a principle of peacekeeping could be seen as crucial for maintaining newly independent states' sovereignty and consequently their control over processes or actions within their state.[57] Therefore, both the principle of non-intervention and the principle of consent within peacekeeping protect states' sovereignty, ostensibly providing these Global South states with a shield against hegemonic intervention, in this instance, in the form of UN peacekeeping. However, as this chapter and Chapter 5 will go on to examine, in practice, it is doubtful as

50 ibid.

51 TM Franck, *Fairness in International Law and Institutions* (OUP 1998) 222.

52 UNSC Res 2666 (20 December 2022) UN Doc S/RES/2666.

53 UNSC Res 2659 (14 November 2022) UN Doc S/RES/2659.

54 Orakhelasvili (n19) 519.

55 Interview with Mona Ali Khalil, former Senior Legal Officer of the UN Office of the Legal Counsel, Director of MAK LAW International and an Affiliate of the Harvard Law School Program on International Law and Armed Conflict ('Interviewee 12') (New York (Skype) 5 December 2019) DOI: <http://doi.org/10.17639/nott.7119>.

56 Tsagourias (n48) 469.

57 On sovereignty, see: S N'zatioula Grovogui, *Sovereigns, Quasi Sovereigns and Africans: Race and Self-Determination in International Law* (Minnesota University Press 1996).

to how much these concepts can be used by the Global South to advance their own interests. Indeed, as TWAIL scholars such as Anghie argue, sovereignty, in particular, is 'a flexible instrument that readily lends itself to the powerful imperatives of the civilising mission' and is thus a Euro-centric concept.[58] As will be explored, similar arguments can also be made about the concept of peacekeeping and by extension the principle of consent.

Regardless, in line with the non-intervention rhetoric at the time of peacekeeping's conception, Hammarskjöld included the prerequisite of host state consent within peacekeeping's legal framework, also drawing a distinction between operations mandated by the General Assembly and actions taken by the Security Council under Chapter VII[59] – again highlighting the Charter-basis arguments previously discussed. Operations of 'Forces' mandated by the General Assembly were said to have required host state consent in order to be 'stationed or operate on the territory of a given country'.[60] Hammarskjöld then went on to note that this did not exclude the possibility of the Council establishing 'such a Force within the wider margins provided under Chapter VII'.[61] This suggests that consent is either not necessary or was less important for peacekeeping operations mandated under Chapter VII, thereby placing a question mark over the principle of consent and its ability to limit peacekeeping as a form of intervention. However, Hammarskjöld refused to expand upon this, arguing that it was not 'necessary to elaborate this point further, since no use of the Force under Chapter VII' 'has been envisaged'.[62] At the point in which peacekeeping was created and institutionalised, its creators did therefore not envisage it to be a forceful, potentially interventionist tool, highlighting how far peacekeeping has since evolved, with contemporary operations perhaps going beyond the concept of peacekeeping and breaching the intervention line, as will be explored in the subsequent chapters.

De Jure v De Facto

Whilst it is well-established, then, that consent is essential for the creation and deployment of a peacekeeping operation, what is less clear is the role and legal necessity of continuing consent throughout the duration of the operation's deployment. That is, whether a withdrawal of consent results in the operation having to exit the country immediately or whether it is only to exit at the end of its mandate period, if consent is still withdrawn. A distinction can, again, be drawn here between operations depending on

58 A Anghie, 'Finding the Peripheries: Sovereignty and Colonialism in Nineteenth Century International Law' (1999) 40(1) HarvIntlLJ 1–71, 71.
59 Summary Study (n5) paras 167, 177, 179–180.
60 ibid, para 5.
61 ibid, paras 179–180.
62 ibid.

their Charter basis. For the traditional model of peacekeeping operations, deployed under Chapter VI, consent must be maintained in order for the operation to remain deployed.[63] If consent is withdrawn then the operation must exit the host state, as occurred with UNEF in 1967 when Egypt revoked its consent.[64] Similarly, when Croatia and Rwanda withdrew their consent to UNPROFOR[65] and UNAMIR,[66] respectively, the UN operation was either replaced by a smaller operation[67] or removed from the country completely.[68]

For Chapter VII operations, however, it appears that once an operation has been consensually deployed, host state consent becomes important for the operational or practical effectiveness of the mission, rather than a legal requirement for its continued presence.[69] Put differently, if the host state effectively withdraws their consent, this does not necessarily result in the operation having to exit nor does it turn the peacekeeping operation into an illegal intervention, as it was initially deployed with consent. As the former Head of the Peacekeeping Department in the Office of Legal Counsel (UNOLC), Mona Ali Khalil, noted, a host state can maintain consent but withdraw effective consent.[70] That is, there is a '*de jure* consent v *de facto* consent' – 'legally, the *de jure* consent cannot be withdrawn within a mandate, only at the end of it'.[71] Therefore, a host state consents to an operation being deployed but cannot request its withdrawal during the operation's mandate. As Ali Khalil points out, in this instance, at the mandate renewal date, there needs to be 'either a re-definition of the mandate to appease the host and/or some kind of political pressure'; once again it 'comes down, like everything else, to the will of the Council'.[72] Thus, the TWAIL narrative, which was established in the previous chapter, of a hierarchical power structure embed-

63 As occurred with UNEF: UNGA, 'Report of the Secretary-General on the Withdrawal of the United Nations Emergency Force' (26 June 1967) UN Doc A/6730. See: SS Malawer, 'The Withdrawal of UNEF and a New Notion of Consent' (1970) 4(1) CILJ 25–36; JI Garvey, 'United Nations Peacekeeping and Host State Consent' (1970) 64(2) AJIL 241–269; R Higgins, 'A General Assessment of United Nations Peacekeeping' in A Cassese (ed) *United Nations Peacekeeping: Legal Essays* (Springer 1978) 5

64 UNGA Doc A/6730 (n63). See also: R Higgins, *United Nations Peacekeeping: Documents and Commentary. Vol III: Africa* (OUP 1980) 361–362.

65 UNSC Res 743 (21 February 1992) UN Doc S/RES/743. See also: T Tardy, 'United Nations Protection Force (UNPROFOR)' in JA Koops, T Tardy, N MacQueen and PD Williams (eds) *The Oxford Handbook of United Nations Peacekeeping Operations* (OUP 2015) 371–382.

66 UNSC Res 997 (9 June 1995) UN Doc S/RES/997.

67 UNCRO; UNGA-SC, 'Letter dated 12 January 1995 from the Permanent Representative of Croatia to the United Nations addressed to the Secretary-General' (12 January 1995) UN Doc A/50/64 – S/1995/28, 4; UNSC Res 981 (31 March 1995) S/RES/981.

68 As was the case with UNAMIR in Rwanda.

69 Tsagourias (n48).

70 Interviewee 12, Mona Ali Khalil (n55).

71 ibid.

72 ibid.

ded within the UN system can be applied. That is, if peacekeeping operations are beholden to the veto-wielding P5 of the Security Council, then this once again reinforces the patterns of dominance and subordination which TWAIL seeks to highlight and counteract.[73] Furthermore, the inability of the host state to eject a Chapter VII peacekeeping operation from its territory during its mandate period supports the previously made argument that the principle of consent may not be a shield for protecting the Global South host states and their ability to control actions within their state. Rather, it could be viewed as a 'flexible instrument', like sovereignty, which lends itself to the dominant, hegemonic powers, in particular the P5, and their agendas.[74]

However, whilst maintaining consent throughout the operation's deployment may not be legally necessary, it does remain important. As will be demonstrated in Chapter 5's examination of consent in practice, 'without host government consent, there is very little you can do'.[75] That is, although consent may only be legally required for deployment, once within the country it is still required, practically, to allow the operation to function. This issue has been recognised in key peacekeeping documents such as the *Capstone* doctrine which notes that whilst a host state may initially consent to the deployment of the operation, it may 'subsequently seek to restrict the operation's freedom of action, resulting in a *de facto* withdrawal of consent'.[76] *Capstone* states that this challenges the rationale for the peacekeeping operation and would alter the international community's approach to supporting the peace process. The maintenance of relations with the host state is therefore essential, and as *Capstone* notes, a UN peacekeeping operation 'must work continuously to ensure that it does not lose the consent of the main parties'.[77]

Furthermore, subsequent peacekeeping studies have found that an 'absence of genuine host-state consent represents one of the greatest threats to the success of modern peacekeeping missions'.[78] Indeed, a Senior Political Officer within the UN Department of Peace Operations (DPO) noted that 'even the most "dysfunctional state" still has multiple tools at its disposal to basically bring the mission to its knees or stop it from carrying out its basic

73 See, for example: M Mutua, 'Savages, Victims, and Saviors: The Metaphor of Human Rights' (2001) 42(1) HarvIntlLJ 201–245; JT Gathii, 'International Law and Eurocentricity' (1998) 9 EJIL 184–211 and BS Chimni, 'Third World Approaches to International Law: A Manifesto' (2006) 8 ICLR 3–27.

74 A Anghie, *Imperialism, Sovereignty and the Making of International Law* (CUP 2007).

75 Interview 16 (n33).

76 UN, *United Nations Peacekeeping Operations: Principles and Guidelines* ('Capstone Doctrine') (DPKO 2008) 32.

77 ibid, 33.

78 S Sebastián and A Gorur, 'UN Peacekeeping & Host-State Consent: How Missions Navigate Relationships with Governments' (Stimson Centre March 2018) 5.

functions'.[79] Obtaining and then maintaining host state consent is therefore 'an absolute must'.[80] As such, strategies may be devised in order to manage deteriorating consent and establish shared expectations.[81] This may primarily be undertaken by the Secretary-General and, by extension, the Special Representative of the Secretary-General (SRSG), who play a key role in the interpretation and application of the principle of consent. Indeed, it is the role of the Secretary-General to work with member states to ensure host state consent is maintained or, if withdrawn, to apply political pressure to ensure it is retained by the mandate renewal. Furthermore, from a TWAIL perspective, it could be viewed as an example of the SG engaging in the dynamic of difference and reducing the apparent gap between the dominant UN and the 'other' host state, through the peacekeeping operation. Similarly, within the field, it is the SRSG who has to maintain relationships between the peacekeeping force and the host state and, thus, maintain consent.[82] It could be argued, then, that this, in itself, is coercive action designed to alter the state and thus a form of intervention. It could be viewed as diplomatic or political intervention as UN personnel are applying pressure or attempting to persuade the host state to change their opinion on the presence of an external, dominant entity – the UN peacekeeping operation – being deployed within their state. Thus, as will be explored in detail in Chapter 5, in this instance, peacekeeping arguably crosses the divide and becomes intervention, thereby contravening the principle of non-intervention.

The Dividing Line?

The principle of consent within peacekeeping is perhaps the most crucial of the three fundamental principles, as it acts as a thin red boundary line between peacekeeping and peace enforcement or intervention. However, where consent is dubious or withdrawn during the mandate period, then the line between peacekeeping and intervention becomes blurred. Maintaining consent is therefore essential for a peacekeeping operation, as is evidenced by the efforts which the United Nations goes to in order to repair relationships with the host state. Whilst this could, again, in itself be viewed as intervention, it signals the importance of the principle of consent for maintaining peacekeeping's non-interventionist status. Indeed, as a Senior Political Officer in the UN Secretariat noted, 'no matter what the mandate says', there is no real prospect of the United Nations 'charging off and doing its own military

79 Interview 16 (n33).
80 ibid.
81 I Johnstone, 'Managing Consent in Contemporary Peacekeeping Operations' (2011) 18(2) IntPeacekeep 168–182.
82 See: Karlsrud (n27).

operations without there being a degree of consent from the Government – so the principles very much apply to peacekeeping'.[83]

The principle of consent therefore forms a central part of peacekeeping's legal framework, demarcating its boundaries and acting as a thin red line between peacekeeping and intervention. It follows, then, that when the principle is expanded, contorted or re-interpreted, this alters peacekeeping's boundaries and, consequently, supports or undermines the principle of non-intervention. This is further compounded by the fact that consent is one-third of the 'Holy Trinity' and as the principles cohabit in a competitive, continuously evolving arena, when there is an alteration or expansion of one, this has a knock-on effect on the others, as the remainder of this chapter and subsequent chapters will highlight.

Impartiality

The second principle in the Holy Trinity, impartiality, is often considered to be the 'lifeblood of peacekeeping', providing it with its distinctiveness.[84] Whilst consent is concerned specifically with the host state and establishes the dividing line between peacekeeping and peace enforcement, or intervention, impartiality is focused on the peacekeepers and their behaviour. It requires peacekeepers to be unbiased in their dealings with the parties to the conflict and in the execution of their mandate.[85] This is not, however, the same as neutrality, despite the often confused and inconsistent use of both terms by UN personnel.[86] Whilst neutrality 'refers to the character of a peacekeeping operation', impartiality 'is an operational term and refers to the conduct of the operation'.[87] That is, peacekeeping operations should not hold any prejudices against parties to the conflict, nor should they influence events within the host state.[88] More broadly, for the principle of non-intervention, in theory, impartiality acts as somewhat of a barrier or protective bubble for the internal affairs of the host state; again, a red boundary line around peacekeeping.

However, the difficulty with the principle of impartiality is that it is an 'elusive goal';[89] whilst it is widely recognised as a necessary norm or princi-

83 Interviewee 16 (n33) 51.

84 A James, *Britain and the Congo Crisis 1960–1963* (Macmillan 1996) 211.

85 Capstone (n76).

86 D Donald, 'Neutrality, Impartiality and UN Peacekeeping at the Beginning of the 21st Century' (2002) 9(4) IntPeacekeep 21–38, 24–26.

87 Tsagourias (n48) 478.

88 Summary Study (n5) 8–10; S/RES/743 (n118) 10.

89 DN Gibbs, 'The United Nations, International Peacekeeping and the Question of "Impartiality": Revising the Congo Operation of 1960' (2000) 38(3) JModAfrStud 359–382, 359.

ple, it is unclear what it actually means. The concept itself is not a given, it is a claim and, as such, is disputable.[90] This, in turn, leads to questions about the legal basis or legal validity of the principle, with some debating whether it amounts to a 'general principle of law' in the sense of Article 38(1)(c) of the ICJ Statute or whether it gains legal effect through, for example, a binding Security Council resolution or the UN Charter.[91] For peacekeeping, then, the principle of impartiality still forms a part of its legal framework but could, perhaps, be viewed as a principle which is not as robust as the other two principles.

Evolution

As with the other principles and norms of peacekeeping, the application or understanding of impartiality in practice has evolved over time, in line with changes to peacekeeping and interventionist practices. The concept of impartiality stems from a 'particularly rigid interpretation' of the UN Charter, specifically Article 2(7) which, as previously discussed, prohibits the United Nations from intervening in national matters, except when acting under Chapter VII.[92] Spijker suggests that Article 2(7) should therefore be read as a 'warning to all domestic governments' that the United Nations is not created to resolve their internal issues for them.[93] The principle of impartiality thereby supports the principle of non-intervention as it flows directly from the prohibition on intervention in domestic affairs in Article 2(7). Furthermore, 'the idea that the UN could act impartially' is also found in Article 40 of Chapter VII of the UN Charter,[94] which provides that the provisional measures which the Council may authorise 'shall be without prejudice to the rights, claims or position of the parties concerned'.[95] It is based upon these notions that Hammarskjöld included impartiality as a fundamental principle of peacekeeping.[96]

Initially, however, impartiality was not defined or made explicit; instead impartiality within these operations was predominantly found or maintained through the composition of the force, as the permanent members (P5) of the

90 See: E Paddon Rhoads, *Taking Sides in Peacekeeping: Impartiality and the Future of the United Nations* (OUP 2016).
91 K Macak, 'A Matter of Principle(s): The Legal Effect of Impartiality and Neutrality on States as Humanitarian Actors' (2015) 97(897/898) IRRC 157–181.
92 O Spijkers, 'The Evolution of United Nations Peacekeeping in the Congo' (2015) 19(1–2) IntPeacekeep 88–117, 91.
93 ibid.
94 J Boulden, 'Mandates Matter: An Exploration of Impartiality in United Nations Operations' (2005) 11 GG 147–160, 148.
95 Article 40, UN Charter.
96 Summary Study (n5).

Council or interested parties were excluded from providing troops.[97] From a TWAIL perspective, this application of impartiality could be viewed as both a challenge to and a maintenance of the imbalance of powers within the United Nations and the dominance of the hegemonic states which Chapter 2 outlined. On the one hand, it could be viewed as a challenge to hegemony as it places a limitation on the dominant states of the Security Council, preventing them from contributing troops to the operation and thus removing their ability to potential intervene or alter the operation, via its troops, in the field to promote their interests and agendas. By extension, this restriction on the P5 to physically intervene in the host state could also be viewed as further reinforcement for the principle of non-intervention, as Chapter 2 highlighted how these power dynamics also animate intervention, with the principle vulnerable to being used by the dominant states. Therefore, prohibiting the P5 from contributing troops could be seen as limiting the risk of the principle of non-intervention being contorted or expanded by these powers in practice. However, on the other hand, this limitation on the P5 does not negate the fact that the Council is the organ which sets the peacekeeping agenda, producing the peacekeeping operation's mandate.[98] Therefore, whilst the P5 have historically not contributed troops (a tradition that is now changing with China's increasing contribution[99]), they have ultimate control over deciding when and how the other states' troops are deployed and what tasks they undertake during this time. In essence, then, as the majority of troop-contributing nations today are from the Global South,[100] the application of impartiality in this manner maintains the dominant-subordinate divide as the dominant P5 states set the peacekeeping agenda, with the subordinate Global South implementing it.[101] That is, the dominant states control the direction of peacekeeping, whilst displacing 'the military, political and strategic risks and personnel costs of labour-intensive peacekeeping onto the poorer and weaker states of the Global South'.[102] This, in turn, has also had a practical effect on

97 This was a particular request by President Nasser of Egypt before the deployment of UNEF, see: B Urquhart, *A Life in Peace and War* (WW Norton 1987) 132–133.

98 See: P Wallensteen and P Johansson, 'The UN Security Council: Decisions and Actions' in S von Einsiedel, DM Malone and B Stagno Ugarte (eds) *The UN Security Council in the 21st Century* (Lynne Rienner 2015) 27–56.

99 CJ Fung, 'China's Small Steps into UN Peacekeeping Are Adding up' (24 May 2023, IPI Global Observatory) <https://theglobalobservatory.org/2023/05/chinas-small-steps-into-un-peacekeeping-are-adding-up/>.

100 UN Peacekeeping, 'Troop and Police Contributors Data' <https://peacekeeping.un.org/en/troop-and-police-contributors>.

101 As of August 2023, the top five contributing states were Bangladesh, Nepal, India, Rwanda and Pakistan, ibid.

102 P Cunliffe, 'The Politics of Global Governance in UN Peacekeeping' (2009) 16(3) IntPeacekeep 323–336, 324.

peacekeeping, as subsequent chapters will explore, with some debating how this affects the 'quality' of peacekeeping.[103]

Furthermore, highlighting how the 'normative composition' of peacekeeping operations is 're-balanced each time',[104] impartiality has differed depending on what model of peacekeeping the operation adopts. Hammarskjöld argued that the use of force in non-Chapter VII operations must be 'impartial, in the sense that it does not serve as a means to force settlement, in the interests of one party, of political conflicts or legal issues recognised as controversial'.[105] For traditional peacekeeping operations, such as UNEF, impartiality therefore meant being passive, with peacekeepers obliged to 'maintain normal relations with a party whose behaviour was being censured by most of the international community'.[106] Thus, peacekeepers were essentially a referee, overseeing the implementation of agreements and restricted by the parties, the modest mandates and the dynamics of the Cold War. As such, it was arguably easier for peacekeepers to maintain impartiality as the tasks which they were required to undertake were relatively simple, monitoring and observation tasks, in less complex or less volatile post-conflict settings. For the principle of non-intervention, then, impartiality, in this instance, supported the principle as it limited peacekeeper's activities, thereby limiting peacekeeping's interventionist nature.

However, this changed as peacekeeping evolved, in line with changing conflict dynamics. As the previous chapter outlined, as the global order and international relations evolved, so too did interventionist practice, including peacekeeping. For impartiality, a reimagining of the concept was required as peacekeeping moved to a robust model and began to undertake joint operations with the host state forces. These joint operations have included activities such as capacity building, justice reform and military operations, with peacekeepers involved in planning, logistical support and/or the execution of the operation.[107] As such, it is questionable how these joint operations can be reconciled with the principle of impartiality and, beyond this, the

103 See: J Levin, J MacKay and A Nasirzadeh, 'Selectorate Theory and the Democratic Peacekeeping Hypothesis: Evidence from Fiji and Bangladesh' (2015) 23(1) IntPeacekeep 107–132; F Haas and N Ansorg, 'Better Peacekeepers, Better Protection? Troop Quality of United Nations Peace Operations and Violence Against Civilians' (2018) 55(6) JPeaceRes 742–758.

104 Karlsrud (n27) 527.

105 Summary Study (n5).

106 M Goulding, 'The Evolution of United Nations Peacekeeping' (1993) 69(3) IntAff 451–464, 455.

107 See, for example: S/RES/1925 (n18) which mandated MONUSCO to support the DRC Government in strengthening the capacity of the judicial institutions; UN Peacekeeping, 'MONUSCO Plans to Boost the Operational Capacity of the FARDC against the ADF Rebels' (25 October 2020) <https://peacekeeping.un.org/en/beni-monusco-plans-to-boost-operational-capacity-of-fardc-against-adf-rebels>.

principle of non-intervention. Indeed, when initially shaping peacekeeping, Hammarskjöld explicitly stated that UN operations 'must be separate and distinct from activities by any national authorities'.[108] Joint operations therefore contravene this traditional understanding of impartiality; however, the same cannot be said for the post-Cold War, expanded interpretation of impartiality. It has been argued that joint operations are not 'necessarily a violation of the impartiality principle' as 'you can still be impartial' and undertake such operations.[109] In particular, one senior political advisor noted that 'it's pretty obvious now, the interpretation of the principles has evolved over time' so that 'it's very clear that impartiality doesn't mean neutrality'.[110] Therefore, 'the fact that you're impartial doesn't prevent you from taking action to neutralise or to diminish the ability of those actors to derail a peace process or a political process'.[111] Indeed, for the fulfilment of tasks such as the protection of civilians, which permits an extensive level of force, impartiality is, again, considered to be maintained as the Council mandates permit force to be used against any actor which poses a threat to civilians, thereby including both state and non-state actors.[112] However, impartiality becomes dubious when a peacekeeping operation becomes engaged in joint operations, particularly military endeavours. That is, it becomes 'harder to sustain the notion of impartiality of the UN mission, if its military component is engaged in military assistance to one of the parties to the conflict'.[113] The notion of impartiality 'can be respected, however, while the civilian component is assisting the government in other mandated activities such as judicial sector reform and human rights reform'.[114] The expansion of impartiality to include joint operations, then, is not a violation of the principle but simply an evolution, yet it remains questionable how far the principle can evolve before it is no longer a legal principle and is simply practice. Similarly, it could be argued that this expansion of the principle of impartiality to include joint operations undermines the principle of non-intervention as it presents an opportunity for the peacekeeping operation to coerce the host state government in situations involving military, political and humanitarian matters and also reduces the

108 UNSC 'Report of the Secretary-General' (18 July 1960) UN Doc S/4389, 5.

109 Interview with Independent Expert and Former UN Political Adviser ('Interviewee 8') (New York, 26 November 2019) DOI: <http://doi.org/10.17639/nott.7119> 45.

110 Interviewee 16 (n33) 44.

111 ibid.

112 See: F Blyth and P Cammaert, 'Using Force to Protect Civilians in United Nations Peacekeeping Operations' in H Willmot, R Mamiya, S Sheeran and M Weller (eds) *Protection of Civilians* (OUP 2016); M Ali Khalil, 'Legal Aspects of the Use of Force by United Nations Peacekeepers for the Protection of Civilians' in H Willmot, R Mamiya, S Sheeran and M Weller (eds) *Protection of Civilians* (OUP 2016).

113 Interviewee 12 (n55).

114 ibid, 45.

likelihood of peacekeepers being even-handed in protecting civilians. Thus, it is possible to view the joint operations as a potential form of intervention – a matter which will be discussed in further detail in Chapter 5.

Impartial Complicity

Closer cooperation with the host state also raises further implications, beyond a potential expansion or contravention of the principle of impartiality. In particular, a deeper military involvement has resulted in legal and practical implications, such as the potential invocation of international humanitarian law and the possible complicity of the United Nations in violations of international law.[115] The latter issue, in particular, has proved to be most problematic, leading to the United Nations attempting to create safety nets or assurances, in order to distance itself from such acts and thereby maintain the United Nations' legitimacy, credibility and impartiality. Of these initiatives, the most significant has been the United Nations' Human Rights Due Diligence Policy (HRDDP), which requires the United Nations to assess whether their partners comply with international humanitarian law, human rights and refugee law before joint operations commence.[116] The policy began as a conditionality policy, specific to the Congo, before being expanded to the HRDDP and made applicable to all UN missions, offices, agencies, funds and programmes which deal with non-UN forces. According to senior UN personnel, 'there was a sense of urgency, that we could no longer support operations that inflicted harm on civilians' and 'ultimately, we needed to apply that same policy across the board'.[117] The policy therefore demonstrates how interpretations of the principles within the field can result in a bottom-up change to the overall peacekeeping frameworks.

Indeed, as a result of the interpretation of the principle in the Congo, in late 2010 the UN Policy Committee decided that the conditionality policy 'should apply globally and system-wide, and launched an internal inter-agency process', led by the Department of Peacekeeping Operations and the Office of the High Commissioner for Human Rights, 'to work on the development of a new policy'.[118] From this, the UN Human Rights Due Diligence

115 UNSG, 'Secretary-General Bulletin: Observance by United Nations Forces of International Humanitarian Law' (6 August 1999) UN Doc ST/SGB/1999/13.

116 UNGA-SC, 'Human Rights Due Diligence Policy' (5 March 2013) UN Doc A/67/775-S/2013/110 ('HRDDP').

117 Interview with Senior UN DPO Personnel, Policy, Evaluation and Training Division ('Interviewee 10') (New York, 3 December 2019) DOI: <http://doi.org/10.17639/nott.7119> pg 47.

118 J Labbé and A Boutellis, 'Peace Operations by Proxy: Implications for Humanitarian Action of UN Peacekeeping Partnerships with Non-UN Security Forces' (2013) 95(891/892) IRRC 539–559, 554–555.

Policy (HRDDP) was developed and officially adopted as an internal policy in July 2011[119] before being made public in March 2013.[120] For some, it can be viewed as a 'faithful implementation of existing legal obligations of the UN' and a procedural mechanism which requires a balancing act between not contributing to violations of international law and the need to fulfil the goals of the operation.[121] Indeed, as Mona Ali Khalil, a former Senior Legal Officer of the UN Office of Legal Counsel (UNOLC), noted, the full and prompt implementation of the HRDDP has been impeded by 'the constant fear that the host government will stop cooperating with the UN mission altogether and/or ask the UN mission to leave its country'.[122] Ali Khalil advises, however, that the proper implementation of the HRDPP is not only 'the right thing', it is also 'the practical thing' because 'if you lose your moral credibility, it will inevitably undermine your operational effectiveness'.[123]

The HRDDP thus highlights both the nuances within the principle of impartiality and the interconnectedness of the fundamental principles. That is, placing strict conditions on the host state in order to maintain impartiality may have a negative impact on relations with the state and therefore the principle of consent. Similarly, as was argued in relation to the maintenance of consent, it may also be possible to view the HRDDP as coercive action designed to influence change in the host state, as the United Nations is exerting pressure on the government to make alterations in order to meet their standards or agenda. More specifically, the peacekeeping operation is coercing the host state government to make changes to their national armed forces by presenting them with an ultimatum – make the proposed changes or the United Nations will withdraw its support. Thus, the HRDDP could be viewed as a form of political or diplomatic intervention. In addition, applying a TWAIL lens, regardless of the well-intentioned motives of the HRDDP, as was seen in Chapter 2's discussion of humanitarian-based interventions, the standards of behaviour and human rights values which underpin the policy are, ultimately, based on Western-centric ideals. Therefore, as occurred with the principle of non-intervention, the dominance of the hegemonic powers is, again, subtly reinforced within the concept of peacekeeping through the HRDDP.

In a similar vein, some have critiqued the policy for serving 'the more limited purpose of shielding the UN mission from accusations of complicity in war crimes', rather than significantly reducing the occurrence of crimes

119 UNSG, Decision No 2011/18 (13 July 2011).
120 HRDDP (n116).
121 HP Aust, 'The UN Human Rights Due Diligence Policy: An Effective Mechanism against Complicity of Peacekeeping Forces?' (2015) 20(1) JCSL 61–73.
122 Interviewee 12 (n55).
123 ibid.

by the host state forces.[124] Indeed, a former military commander within MONUSCO noted that they did not understand why the United Nations 'should be extremely strict in conditioning [their] support' as they 'have these conditions on the table' but then 'continue to play with the people who are the real sponsors of instability'.[125] They argue that 'it's a total contradiction'; 'you cannot blame this general or these people who are corrupt'; instead 'it is a collective responsibility'.[126] As Chapter 5 will explore, then, the implementation of the HRDDP can present numerous issues, not least its seemingly selective application which, applying a TWAIL lens, could be viewed as another example of a concept being wielded as a tool by the dominant powers to protect their interests – as previously noted for the concept of sovereignty and the principle of consent. That is, it could be argued that the HRDDP is predominantly used by the United Nations as a form of protection from implication in violations of international law, rather than as a tool to protect peoples of the Global South state from such violations. Put differently, as former UN personnel have noted, the policy does little to alter the human rights situation within the host state;[127] rather, it attempts to remove a select few personnel from the host state's armed forces, whilst acting as a shield for the United Nations against accusations of complicity. It is arguable, then, that a shrinking of peacekeeping's boundaries and a move back to a traditional model of peacekeeping through a re-interpretation of the principles and a reduction in an operation's mandated tasks is more preferable.

An Elusive Goal?

An exploration of the evolution of impartiality also highlights how there is a subjective element to impartiality and, within peacekeeping, this is two pronged. Firstly, for the peacekeeping operation and the United Nations, impartiality is based on the fundamental values of the United Nations, which were formulated predominantly by hegemonic powers. As seen in Chapter 2, applying a TWAIL lens highlights how the United Nations was created with very little involvement from the Global South; hence the values promulgated within the UN Charter and which underpin the organisation are based on standards set by the dominant powers, in particular the P5 within the

124 T Vircoulon, 'After MONUC, Should MONUSCO Continue to Support Congolese Military Campaigns?' (Crisis Group, 19 July 2010) <https://www.crisisgroup.org/africa/central-africa/chad/after-monuc-should-monusco-continue-support-congolese-military-campaigns>.

125 Interview with Former Senior Military Commander ('Interviewee 11') (New York (Skype) 3 December 2019) DOI: <http://doi.org/10.17639/nott.7119> pg 47.

126 ibid.

127 ibid.

Security Council.[128] It therefore follows that if the understanding of impartiality within peacekeeping is based upon these values and standards then they are based upon the values and interests of the hegemonic powers. This then leads to the second level of understanding of impartiality: that there is perhaps a presumption that all peacekeepers subscribe to these 'universal' values and, therefore, neutrally apply this understanding of the principle of impartiality in practice.[129] However, peacekeepers will undoubtedly bring with them values from their home country and their own personal beliefs.[130] Indeed, numerous studies have been conducted on the psychology of peacekeepers, particularly in the post-Cold War era as the increase in multi-dimensional operations places different demands on peacekeeper's behaviour and ethos, in comparison to the traditional models of peacekeeping.[131] That is, multi-dimensional peacekeeping operations require peacekeepers to make decisions about who is right and wrong and to act accordingly.[132] The differing approaches to this are revealed in practice in, for example, the varying appetites to engage in conflict to protect civilians[133] and the sexual exploitation and abuse of civilians by peacekeepers.[134] This raises two key issues with the principle of impartiality. First, it highlights how there is a distinction or disconnect within impartiality between the broader understanding of what impartiality is within peacekeeping and what it means in practice. At the Security Council, mandating level, impartiality is a concept based on the values of the United Nations, which establishes the requirement for peacekeepers to be unbiased and unprejudiced in their dealings with parties to the conflict and execution of the mandate. However, in reality, when carrying out the mandate, it appears that an application of impartiality carries with it the subjective beliefs of the individual peacekeepers. Therefore, it is the individual and their Troop Contributing Nation (TCN) commanders who ultimately interpret what it means to be impartial and then act accordingly.

128 See, for example: Mutua (n73); M Mazower, *No Enchanted Palace: The End of Empire and the Ideological Origins of the United Nations* (PUP 2009).

129 Such as: UN Peacekeeping, 'Ten Rules Codes of Personal Conduct for Blue Helmets' and 'No Excuse' cards, see: UN Peacekeeping, 'Standards of Conduct' <https://peacekeeping.un.org/en/standards-of-conduct>.

130 See: PA Poole and TW Britt, *The Psychology of the Peacekeeper: Lessons from the Field* (Praeger 2003).

131 HJ Langholtz, 'The Psychology of Peacekeeping: Genesis, Ethos, and Application' (1998) 4(3) PeaceConflJPP 217–236.

132 See: Paddon Rhoads (n90).

133 Interview with Former MONUSCO Military Personnel ('Interviewee 4') (Shrivenham, UK, 28 October 2019) DOI: <http://doi.org/10.17639/nott.7119>.

134 See, for example: BBC News, 'DR Congo: UN Peacekeepers Face Fresh Sexual Abuse Claims' (*BBC News*, 28 April 2017) <https://www.bbc.co.uk/news/world-africa-39745357>; for current data see: UN Conduct in Field Missions, 'Sexual Exploitation and Abuse: Table of Allegations' <https://conduct.unmissions.org/table-of-allegations>.

From this stems the second issue – that it is then these individuals who are ultimately determining peacekeeping actions and, therefore, in essence, the interventionist nature of the peacekeeping operation. Put differently, it could be argued that if the decision to use force to protect civilians falls to individuals or groups of peacekeepers, then whether or not they act then determines both the interpretation of impartiality and the extent to which the operation is interventionist.

The contemporary, expanded version of the principle of impartiality, then, renders the very concept of impartiality even more dubious and unattainable. If impartiality is taken to be an 'elusive goal', then joint endeavours which are undertaken in contemporary multi-dimensional operations seemingly push this goal further away. Furthermore, as will be explored in the Chapter 5, this expanded interpretation and application of impartiality have numerous problematic implications such as a risk to peacekeeper's safety, UN complicity in violations of international law and the operation's potential engagement as a party to the conflict. Arguably, on these occasions, it places the United Nations in a very grey area, where peacekeeping could perhaps be viewed as intervention in all but name. Undertaking military operations alongside state forces or engaging in capacity-building activities could, thus, all be viewed as coercive action designed to alter the state and, therefore, intervention. Despite this, the operation seemingly retains its non-interventionist status here, not by the principle of impartiality, but by the single thread of host state consent. Indeed, the consent of the state, as explored in the previous section, appears to be key in preventing the peacekeeping operation from becoming both peace enforcement and intervention. As will be explored in subsequent chapters, there may be a need for a reimagining or clarifying of the concept of impartiality in order to re-establish its relevance and position as a legal principle within contemporary, multidimensional operations, which have expanded the principle to its very limits, if not beyond.

Limited Use of Force

As with the other principles, traditionally, the principle of non-use of force was interpreted narrowly to mean force only in self-defence. Peacekeepers therefore had a 'right' to use force in response to an armed attack upon themselves or attempts to make them withdraw from their positions.[135] Again, within his Summary Study, Hammarskjöld set out the principle of non-use of force, explicitly noting that it should be 'exercised under strictly defined conditions'.[136] Whilst Hammarskjöld did not expand upon the 'certain cases'

135 Summary Study (n5) 70, 179.
136 ibid.

in which self-defence may be used, it was made clear that peacekeepers were not permitted to take the initiative or proactively use force.[137] The traditional peacekeeping operations therefore followed this narrow concept of self-defence, based on the inherent right of self-defence of an individual.[138] The exception to this, however, was ONUC. As will be explored in the Chapter 5, ONUC used a significant level of force and is considered to be the first 'case of a transition from peacekeeping to peace-enforcement'.[139] Whilst ONUC therefore greatly expanded the principle of non-use of force, this can be viewed as somewhat of an anomaly for that period, with the United Nations quickly retreating back to the traditional, passive operations. However, despite this retreat, the precedent had been set, with the possibility of force beyond self-defence no longer improbable. Similarly, it could also be argued that for the principle of non-intervention, this expansion of the use of force created a similar precedent within the principle, creating the possibility for peacekeeping's interventionist nature to be expanded, thereby undermining the principle of non-intervention.

Indeed, Hammarskjöld's successors began to gradually include a creeping expansion of the concept of self-defence, through their interpretations of the norm. In a report on the United Nations' operation in Cyprus, Secretary-General U Thant broadened self-defence to include defence 'necessary in the discharge of its function' and the defence of 'UN posts, premises and vehicles' and 'other personnel under attack'.[140] UNSG Waldheim then extended the definition of self-defence to include 'resistance to attempts by forceful means to prevent it [the force] from discharging its duties under the mandate of the Security Council'.[141] Thus, Waldheim established the broader concept of self-defence which still exists today – defence of the self, the mission and its components and the mandate. Whilst the Security Council has upheld the UN mission's inherent right of self-defence, that right 'has been interpreted broadly to include not only defence of the personnel, premises, property and freedom of movement of the UN operation but also defence of the mandate itself'.[142] By expanding the latter concept to include any impediment to the fulfilment of the mandate, some have rendered the concept of self-defence 'meaningless'.[143] By extension, it could then be argued that it has also had the same effect on the principle of non-use of force and, therefore, the boundaries of peacekeeping and non-intervention. That is, the broadened

137 ibid.

138 See: T Findlay, *The Use of Force in UN Peace Operations* (OUP 2002) 20–49.

139 Goulding (n106) 453.

140 UNSC, 'Note by the Secretary-General' (11 April 1964) UN Doc S/5653, 10, 16–19.

141 UNSC, 'Report of the Secretary-General on the Implementation of Security Council Resolution 340' (27 October 1973) UN Doc S/11052/Rev.1, para 4.

142 Interviewee 12 (n55).

143 ibid.

concept of self-defence creates numerous potential opportunities for the use of force, thereby potentially expanding peacekeeping's boundaries, taking it closer to intervention and simultaneously constricting the principle of non-intervention.

Robust or Enforcement?

The second most notable shift in the principle of non-use of force came with the move to robust peacekeeping which emerged in the late 1990s in response to the United Nations' failures to prevent mass atrocities.[144] As outlined in the previous chapter, this marked somewhat of a tipping point for attitudes towards intervention, whereby the hesitancy within peacekeeping after ONUC began to change. This shift 'began with norm entrepreneurs advocating Chapter VII to protect civilians in conflict'.[145] Indeed, the then-Secretary-General, Kofi Annan, building upon this, commissioned the Brahimi Report,[146] which aimed to 'improve the creaking peacekeeping function whose credibility had suffered greatly in the mid-1990s'.[147] Annan sought to challenge those 'who clung to a vision of the UN Charter that, in their view, said that the use of force was unacceptable', arguing that protagonists of conflict must be confronted and stopped 'through force if necessary'.[148] As such, the Brahimi Report expanded the use of self-defence within peacekeeping from defence of the individual to defence of the mission. It also introduced the concept of 'robust peacekeeping', whereby peacekeepers could use force to defend both the mission's components and the operation's mandate.[149] In recognition of the potential implications of this increased level of force, Annan also issued an SG Bulletin on the observance by UN forces of international humanitarian law (IHL).[150] This concept of robust peacekeeping was then further developed by Annan's successor, Ban Ki Moon, with the *Capstone Doctrine* defining it as peacekeeping which involved the use of force at the tactical level, whilst peace enforcement involved the use of force at the strategic level.[151] This was further reiterated by the Special Committee on Peacekeeping Operations (C-34) who vehemently argued that robust

144 T Tardy, 'A Critique of Robust Peacekeeping in Contemporary Operations' (2011) 18(2) IntPeacekeep 152–167.
145 LM Howard and AK Dayal, 'The Use of Force in UN Peacekeeping' (2018) 72 IntOrgan 71–103, 72.
146 UNGA, 'Report of the Panel on United Nations Peace Operations' ('Brahimi Report') (21 August 2000) UN Doc A/55/305-S/2000/809.
147 ND White, 'Peace Operations' in V Chetail (ed) *Post-Conflict Peacebuilding: A Lexicon* (OUP 2010) 215.
148 K Annan, *Interventions: A Life in War and Peace* (Penguin 2013) 78–79.
149 Brahimi Report (n146).
150 SG Bulletin on IHL (n115).
151 Capstone (n76).

peacekeeping is 'not peace enforcement', reiterating the strategic and tactical distinction.[152] It could be argued, then, that Annan's acknowledgement of the potential triggering of IHL and Ban Ki Moon's distinction of robust peacekeeping and peace enforcement indicate that this expansion took the principle of non-use of force much closer to the intervention line. Thus, whilst this broad authorisation to use force goes beyond the traditional or reasonable concept of self-defence, thereby moving peacekeeping 'into the realms of peace enforcement',[153] a slim line can seemingly be drawn between these robust peacekeeping operations and peace enforcement. Indeed, the 'dividing line between peace enforcement and peacekeeping operations with coercive components is very fine'.[154] It is arguable, then, that the Secretary-Generals recognised that robust peacekeeping could potentially go beyond the boundaries of peacekeeping and therefore attempted to clarify the concept and to set some form of boundary.

However, this boundary between peacekeeping and peace enforcement grew even thinner in the early 2010s, when the principle of non-use of force was expanded even further. During this period, the concept of robust peacekeeping widened to include terms such as 'stabilisation' and a greater emphasis on the protection of civilians (PoC), in what some refer to as 'peace-enforcement mandates'.[155] From 2013, peacekeeping operations in the Central African Republic and Mali were given mandates to 'stabilise' territory,[156] whilst the Force Intervention Brigade (FIB) was launched in the DRC as part of MONUSCO to use 'all necessary means' to 'neutralise' and 'disarm' armed groups in 'targeted offensive operations'.[157] In this latter operation, the concept of robust peacekeeping was expanded even further as the FIB clearly designated an enemy and 'purposefully did not treat all parties equally'[158] – all of which have been identified as hallmarks of peace enforcement. Robust peacekeeping, then, has a 'clearly interventionist quality',[159] arguably because of the element of coercion contained within the broad interpretation of non-use of force and self-defence. As such, robust peacekeeping takes peacekeeping into the realm of peace enforcement which,

152 UNGA Special Committee on Peacekeeping Operations (C34), 'Draft DPKO/DFS Concept Note' (February 2010 Substantive Session) 3.

153 C Henderson, *The Use of Force and International Law* (CUP 2018) 193.

154 Tsagourias (n48) 472.

155 J Karlsrud, 'The UN at War: Examining the Consequences of Peace-Enforcement Mandates for the UN Peacekeeping Operation in the CAR, the DRC and Mali' (2015) 36(1) TWQ 40–54.

156 See: CAR UNSC Res 2149 (10 April 2014) UN Doc S/RES/2149; Mali UNSC Res 2100 (25 April 2013) UN Doc S/RES/2100

157 UNSC Res 2098 (28 March 2013) UN Doc S/RES/2098.

158 Henderson (n153) 194.

159 Gibbs (n89) 360.

in turn, takes peacekeeping much closer to the intervention line. However, it could be said that this undermines but ultimately does not contravene the principle of non-intervention on the basis that it was initially deployed with host state consent. Again, then, as with impartiality, consent seemingly saves the principle of non-use of force from becoming intervention when it is interpreted broadly.

Regardless, UN peacekeeping operations have continued to adopt a much more robust posture which was optimised in the 2017 'Cruz Report', directed by Secretary-General Antonio Guterres.[160] Within this, it was argued that 'the era of "Chapter VI-style" peacekeeping is over' and both the United Nations and troop- or police-contributing nations needed to 'change their mindsets, take risks and show a willingness to face these new challenges', rather than be 'gripped by a "Chapter VI Syndrome"'.[161] Indeed, military personal within MONUSCO's Force component note that the recommendations from the Cruz Report are used as guidelines for the mission's operational planning.[162] This posture and discourse could therefore be viewed as broadening the principle of non-use of force to its limits, once again taking it much closer to peace enforcement and the intervention line, thus simultaneously undermining the principle of non-intervention. In particular, the pressure on peacekeepers to adopt a more forceful stance invokes a much stronger interventionist rhetoric within peacekeeping and creates the possibility for the peacekeeping operation to become a form of armed intervention. That is, it takes peacekeeping much closer to being perceived as 'an intervention which uses force',[163] which, as seen in the previous chapter, was identified by the ICJ as one of the most obvious forms of prohibited intervention.

This insistence on the need to take more forceful risks, from a TWAIL perspective, could also be perceived as being uncomfortably similar to colonial civilising missions, whereby force was often used by external actors to effect change in the host state and fulfil its mission which, in turn, reinforced the colonial patterns of domination and subordination.[164] In a similar vein, then, as peacekeeping operations have a mandate designed to make alterations within the host state, albeit with consent, the use of heightened levels of force

160 CA Dos Santos Cruz, WR Phillips, S Cusimano, 'Improving Security of United Nations Peacekeepers: We Need to Change the Way We Are Doing Business' ('Santos Cruz Report') (19 December 2017) <https://peacekeeping.un.org/sites/default/files/improving_security_of_united_nations_peacekeepers_report.pdf>.

161 ibid, Executive Summary.

162 Interview with Senior MONUSCO Military Personnel ('Interviewee 17') (Skype, 9 February 2020) DOI: <http://doi.org/10.17639/nott.7119>.

163 *Case Concerning Military and Paramilitary Activities in and against Nicaragua (Nicaragua v United States of America)* [1986] ICJ Rep 14, para 205.

164 Such as the *Force Publique* in the Congo, see: D Van Reybrouck, *Congo: The Epic History of a People* (Fourth Estate 2015).

to fulfil these tasks may be viewed as reminiscent of colonial practices. Again, underlining arguments made in the previous chapter, particularly by TWAIL scholars such as Anghie,[165] that colonialism animates international law and contemporary practices, including peacekeeping, may perpetuate colonial dichotomies and practices. Indeed, robust peacekeeping has proved problematic for many in the Global South, with the Non-Aligned Movement, in particular, criticising it for its lack of clarity, calling into question its underlying assumptions, such as the notion that more robustness leads to greater effectiveness.[166] This, in turn, raises questions about the logistical or practical problems which robust peacekeeping presents. As Sloan argues, the United Nations is 'fundamentally ill-suited to undertake militarised peacekeeping'.[167] This is evident in the numerous criticisms which UN peacekeeping operations have faced in recent years for failing to fulfil tasks.[168] Similarly, this expanded use of force also triggers concerns about the invocation of IHL, the safety of peacekeepers, the perception of the operation and the reliance on peacekeeping operations to exercise force – all matters which will be explored in detail in the subsequent sections.

As a result, given robust peacekeeping's expansion of the principle of non-use of force, potential unintended consequences and impingement of the thin red line between peacekeeping and intervention, it is questionable: 'all necessary means' to what ends?[169] It could be argued that the negatives of the turn to robust peacekeeping far outweigh any positives; therefore, the necessity of this expanded use of force and the turn to robust peacekeeping is debatable. Indeed, this continued expansion of peacekeeping's robust mandates is said to be 'in danger of getting "out of its depth" and biting off more than it can, or indeed, should, chew'.[170] Thus, there should arguably be a limit to how far the principle of non-use of force, along with the other fundamental principles, can be expanded and contorted before they no longer remain relevant to peacekeeping. As such, it is proposed that a contracting of peacekeeping's boundaries, through a move back towards a more traditional model of

165 Anghie (n74).

166 C De Coning, A Stensland and T Tardy, 'Beyond the "New Horizon": A Seminar on the Future Challenges of UN Peacekeeping' (NUPI 2010) 19.

167 J Sloan, *The Militarisation of Peacekeeping in the Twenty-First Century* (Hart Publishing 2011) 282.

168 See: R Gowan, 'The Peacekeeping Quagmire' (2015) 16(2) GeorgeJIntAff 31–38; T Oladipo, 'The UN's Peacekeeping Nightmare in Africa' (*BBC News*, 5 January 2017) <https://www.bbc.co.uk/news/world-africa-38372614>. EM Lederer, 'UN Peacekeeping on 75th Anniversary: Successes, Failures and Challenges ahead in a Divided World' (*The Independent*, 25 May 2023) <https://www.independent.co.uk/news/ap-liberia-yugoslavia-cambodia-rwanda-b2345471.html>.

169 CT Hunt, 'All Necessary Means to What Ends? The Unintended Consequences of the "Robust Turn" in UN Peace Operations' (2016) 24(1) IntPeacekeep 108–131.

170 Henderson (n153) 200.

peacekeeping and a narrower interpretation of the principles, is preferable. Once again, this, in turn, would have implications for the principle of non-intervention as, if the peacekeeping principles are broadened almost to their limits (as the use of force is at times), then this erodes the boundary between peacekeeping and intervention, thereby undermining or even contravening the principle of non-intervention.

Conclusions: Peacekeeping as Intervention?

Whilst peacekeeping does not possess an articulated legal framework, as this chapter has explored, the three fundamental principles, together with the normative framework which will be explored in the following chapter, form a complex peacekeeping framework. This chapter has demonstrated how the fundamental principles (consent, impartiality and limited use of force) have continually evolved and been re-interpreted, typically, in line with the fluctuating interventionist practices or global trends which were highlighted in Chapter 2. That is, when there has been strong non-intervention rhetoric, such as during decolonisation, the principles have been interpreted narrowly, limiting their scope. Conversely, when there has been increased support for intervention, as occurred in the post-Cold War era, the principles have been interpreted more broadly, thereby expanding the concepts.

Peacekeeping's legal framework could therefore be imagined as a red elastic band that can continually expand and contract depending on how the principles are reimagined. The legal framework is therefore fluid which, in turn, means that the boundary between peacekeeping and intervention is also fluid. As this chapter has explored, where the principles are interpreted narrowly (typically within a traditional peacekeeping operation) then the boundaries of peacekeeping are limited and so too is peacekeeping's interventionist potential. However, when they are interpreted broadly, as with many contemporary multi-dimensional operations, the boundaries are significantly stretched, often to their very limits, if not beyond, thereby undermining or potentially contravening the principle of non-intervention. It could therefore be argued that there must be a limit to how far these concepts evolve before they are no longer peacekeeping principles, acting as a barrier between peacekeeping and intervention, but, instead, become intervention. At this point, it is proposed that a shrinking of peacekeeping's boundaries, through a narrower interpretation and application of the principles, would help to solidify the line between peacekeeping and intervention and maintain the principles' relevance.

Furthermore, this chapter has also highlighted how the unequal power dynamics and colonial legacies which were identified within the principle of non-intervention in Chapter 2 also exist within peacekeeping, particularly through the inherent imbalance within the Security Council, creating continual examples of Anghie's dynamic of difference. Peacekeeping's frameworks and an application of these frameworks can therefore, at times, be seen to reinforce or recreate the colonial dichotomies of domination and subordination, particularly where there is an element of coercion or peacekeeping is taken closer to the intervention line. This, again, underlines the argument that many features of both international law and international institutions or legal systems 'acknowledge and reinforce the substantial power differentials between [their] participants'.[171] This, in turn, leads back to the notion that international law is based on 'fictions' of state equality and state consent[172] which leads to the more general debate over whether international law is truly international.[173] Therefore, as was seen with the principle of non-intervention in Chapter 2, the influence of colonialism and the persistent power differentials have also permeated the concept of peacekeeping – a theme which the subsequent chapters will continue to explore.

Whilst this chapter has explored peacekeeping's legal framework, which lies at the heart of peacekeeping, the subsequent chapter will examine the norms of democracy promotion, protection of civilians and prohibition of sexual exploitation and abuse forming peacekeeping's broader normative framework, which surrounds the legal framework. These frameworks, as the subsequent chapter will highlight, do not exist in isolation but, rather, at times overlap with some of the norms possessing legal underpinnings which introduces elements of international law into peacekeeping's legal framework. The principles and norms thus rarely live harmoniously and instead 'coexist in a competitive arena' with the normative composition of a peacekeeping operation being 're-balanced each time'.[174] The following chapter will therefore explore peacekeeping's normative framework, its overlap with the legal framework and its relationship with the principle of non-intervention.

References

Anghie A, 'Finding the Peripheries: Sovereignty and Colonialism in Nineteenth Century International Law' (1999) 40(1) HarvIntlLJ 1–71

Anghie A, *Imperialism, Sovereignty and the Making of International Law* (CUP 2007)

Ali Khalil M, 'Legal Aspects of the Use of Force by United Nations Peacekeepers for the Protection of Civilians' in H Willmot, R Mamiya, S Sheeran and M Weller (eds) *Protection of Civilians* (OUP 2016)

Annan K, *Interventions: A Life in War and Peace* (Penguin 2013)

171 H Charlesworth, 'International Legal Encounters with Democracy' (2017) 8(6) GlobalPolicy 34–43, 34.

172 G Simpson, 'Imagined Consent: Democratic Liberalism in International Legal Theory' (1994) 15 AYIL 103–128.

173 L Eslava and S Pahuja, 'Between Resistance and Reform: TWAIL and the Universality of International Law' (2011) 3(1) TradeL&Dev 103–130.

174 Karlsrud (n27) 527.

Aust HP, 'The UN Human Rights Due Diligence Policy: An Effective Mechanism against Complicity of Peacekeeping Forces?' (2015) 20(1) JCSL 61–73
Autesserre S, *The Frontlines of Peace: An Insider's Guide to Changing the World* (OUP 2021)
BBC News, 'DR Congo: UN Peacekeepers Face Fresh Sexual Abuse Claims' (*BBC News*, 28 April 2017) <https://www.bbc.co.uk/news/world-africa-39745357>
Bellamy AJ and P Williams, *Understanding Peacekeeping* (2nd edn, Polity Press 2010)
Blyth F and P Cammaert, 'Using Force to Protect Civilians in United Nations Peacekeeping Operations' in H Willmot, R Mamiya, S Sheeran and M Weller (eds) *Protection of Civilians* (OUP 2016)
Boulden J, 'Mandates Matter: An Exploration of Impartiality in United Nations Operations' (2005) 11 GG 147–160
Bowman EH and JE Fanning, 'The Logistics Problems of a UN Military Force' (1963) 17(2) IntOrg 355–376
Case Concerning Military and Paramilitary Activities in and Against Nicaragua (Nicaragua v United States of America) [1986] ICJ Rep 14
Certain Expenses of the United Nations (Article 17, Paragraph 2 of the Charter) (Advisory Opinion) [1962] ICJ Rep 151
Charlesworth H, 'International Legal Encounters with Democracy' (2017) 8(6) GlobalPolicy 34–43
Charter of the United Nations (24 October 1945)
Chimni BS, 'Third World Approaches to International Law: A Manifesto' (2006) 8 ICLR 3–27
Ciobanu D, 'The Power of the Security Council to Organize Peacekeeping Operations' in A Cassese (ed) *United Nations Peacekeeping: Legal Essays* (Springer 1978)
Coleman JL, KE Himma and SJ Shapiro, *The Oxford Handbook of Jurisprudence and Philosophy of Law* (OUP 2004)
Cunliffe P, 'The Politics of Global Governance in UN Peacekeeping' (2009) 16(3) IntPeacekeep 323–336
De Coning C, 'Mediation and Peacebuilding: SRSGs and DSRSGs in Integrated Missions' (2010) 16(2) GG 281–299
De Coning C, A Stensland, T Tardy, 'Beyond the "New Horizon": A Seminar on the Future Challenges of UN Peacekeeping' (NUPI 2010)
De Wet E, *The Chapter VII Powers of the United Nations Security Council* (Hart Publishing 2004)
Donald D, 'Neutrality, Impartiality and UN Peacekeeping at the Beginning of the 21st Century' (2002) 9(4) IntPeacekeep 21–38
Dos Santos Cruz CA, WR Phillips, S Cusimano, 'Improving Security of United Nations Peacekeepers: We Need To Change The Way We Are Doing Business' ("Santos Cruz Report") (19 December 2017) <https://peacekeeping.un.org/sites/default/files/improving_security_of_united_nations_peacekeepers_report.pdf>
Doyle MW and N Sambanis, 'Peacekeeping Operations' in TG Weiss and S Daws (eds) *The Oxford Handbook on the United Nations* (OUP 2007)
Eslava L and S Pahuja, 'Between Resistance and Reform: TWAIL and the Universality of International Law' (2011) 3(1) TradeL&Dev 103–130
Findlay T, *The Use of Force in UN Peace Operations* (OUP 2002)
Franck TM, *Fairness in International Law and Institutions* (OUP 1998)
Fukuyama F, *The End of History and the Last Man* (Penguin 2020)

Fung CJ, 'China's Small Steps into UN Peacekeeping Are Adding Up' (IPI Global Observatory, 24 May 2023) <https://theglobalobservatory.org/2023/05/chinas-small-steps-into-un-peacekeeping-are-adding-up/>

Garvey JI, 'United Nations Peacekeeping and Host State Consent' (1970) 64(2) AJIL 241–269

Gathii JT, 'International Law and Eurocentricity' (1998) 9 EJIL 184–211

Gibbs DN, 'The United Nations, International Peacekeeping and the Question of "Impartiality": Revising the Congo Operation of 1960' (2000) 38(3) JModAfrStud 359–382

Goulding M, 'The Evolution of United Nations Peacekeeping' (1993) 69(3) IntAff 451–464

Gowan R, 'The Peacekeeping Quagmire' (2015) 16(2) GeorgeJIntAff 31–38

Haas F and N Ansorg, 'Better Peacekeepers, Better Protection? Troop Quality of United Nations Peace Operations and Violence Against Civilians' (2018) 55(6) JPeaceRes 742–758

Henderson C, *The Use of Force and International Law* (CUP 2018)

Higgins R, 'A General Assessment of United Nations Peacekeeping' in A Cassese (ed) *United Nations Peacekeeping: Legal Essays* (Springer 1978)

Higgins R, *United Nations Peacekeeping: Documents and Commentary. Vol III: Africa* (OUP 1980)

Hillen III, 'UN Collective Security: Chapter Six and a Half' (1994) 24(1) Parameters 27–37

Howard LM and AK Dayal, 'The Use of Force in UN Peacekeeping' (2018) 72 IntOrgan 71–103

Hunt CT, 'All Necessary Means to What Ends? The Unintended Consequences of the "Robust Turn" in UN Peace Operations' (2016) 24(1) IntPeacekeep 108–131

Interview with Former MONUSCO Military Personnel ('Interviewee 4') (Shrivenham, UK, 28 October 2019) DOI: <http://doi.org/10.17639/nott.7119>

Interview with Independent Expert and Former UN Political Adviser ('Interviewee 8') (New York, 26 November 2019) DOI: <http://doi.org/10.17639/nott.7119>

Interview with Senior UN DPO Personnel, Policy, Evaluation and Training Division ('Interviewee 10') (New York, 3 December 2019) DOI: <http://doi.org/10.17639/nott.7119>

Interview with Former Senior Military Commander ('Interviewee 11') (New York (Skype) 3 December 2019) DOI: <http://doi.org/10.17639/nott.7119>

Interview with Mona Ali Khalil, former Senior Legal Officer of the UN Office of the Legal Counsel, Director of MAK LAW International and an Affiliate of the Harvard Law School Program on International Law and Armed Conflict ('Interviewee 12') (New York (Skype) 5 December 2019) DOI: <http://doi.org/10.17639/nott.7119>

Interview with Senior Political Affairs Officer, UN DPO ('Interviewee 16') (New York, 10 December 2019) DOI: <http://doi.org/10.17639/nott.7119>

Interview with Senior MONUSCO Military Personnel ('Interviewee 17') (Skype, 9 February 2020) DOI: <http://doi.org/10.17639/nott.7119>

James A, *Britain and the Congo Crisis 1960–1963* (Macmillan 1996)

Johnstone I, 'The Secretary-General as Norm Entrepreneur' in S Chesterman (ed) *Secretary or General? The UN Secretary-General in World Politics* (CUP 2007)

Johnstone I, 'Managing Consent in Contemporary Peacekeeping Operations' (2011) 18(2) IntPeacekeep 168–182

Karlsrud J, 'Special Representatives of the Secretary-General as Norm Arbitrators? Understanding Bottom-up Authority in UN Peacekeeping' (2013) 19(4) GG 525–544

Karlsrud J, 'The UN at War: Examining the Consequences of Peace-Enforcement Mandates for the UN Peacekeeping Operation in the CAR, the DRC and Mali' (2015) 36(1) TWQ 40–54

Karlsrud J, 'United Nations Stabilization Operations: Chapter VII and a Half' (2019) 18(5) Ethnopolitics 494–50

Kelsen H, *The Law of the United Nations: A Critical Analysis of its Fundamental Problems* (Frederick A Praeger 1964)

Kille KJ, 'Moral Authority and the UN Secretary-General's Ethical Framework' in KJ Kille (ed) *The UN Secretary General and Moral Authority: Ethics and Religion in International Leadership* (GUP 2007)

Labbé J and A Boutellis, 'Peace Operations by Proxy: Implications for Humanitarian action of UN Peacekeeping Partnerships with Non-UN Security Forces' (2013) 95(891/892) IRRC 539–559

Labuda PI, 'United Nations Peacekeeping as Intervention by Invitation: Host State Consent and the Use of Force in Security Council-Mandated Stabilisation Operations' (2020) JUFIL 1–37

Langholtz HJ, 'The Psychology of Peacekeeping: Genesis, Ethos, and Application' (1998) 4(3) PeaceConflJPP 217–236

Lederer EM, 'UN Peacekeeping on 75th Anniversary: Successes, Failures and Challenges Ahead in a Divided World' (*The Independent*, 25 May 2023) <https://www.independent.co.uk/news/ap-liberia-yugoslavia-cambodia-rwanda-b2345471.html>

Levin J, J MacKay and A Nasirzadeh, 'Selectorate Theory and the Democratic Peacekeeping Hypothesis: Evidence From Fiji and Bangladesh' (2015) 23(1) IntPeacekeep 107–132

Lie T, *In the Cause of Peace: Seven Years with the United Nations* (Macmillan Co 1954).

'Lotus' Case ([France v Turkey]) PCIJ Rep Series A No 10

Macak K, 'A Matter of Principle(s): The Legal Effect of Impartiality and Neutrality on States as Humanitarian Actors' (2015) 97(897/898) IRRC 157–181

Malawer SS, 'The Withdrawal of UNEF and a New Notion of Consent' (1970) 4(1) CILJ 25–36

Mazower M, *No Enchanted Palace: The End of Empire and the Ideological Origins of the United Nations* (PUP 2009)

Mickelson K, 'Rhetoric and Rage: Third World Voices in International Legal Discourse' (2011) 16(2) WisIntlLJ 353–419

Mutua M, 'Savages, Victims, and Saviors: The Metaphor of Human Rights' (2001) 42(1) HarvIntlLJ 201–245

N'zatioula Grovogui S, *Sovereigns, Quasi Sovereigns and Africans: Race and Self-Determination in International Law* (Minnesota University Press 1996)

Oladipo T, 'The UN's Peacekeeping Nightmare in Africa' (*BBC News*, 5 January 2017) <https://www.bbc.co.uk/news/world-africa-38372614>

Orakhelashvili A, 'The Legal Basis of the United Nations Peace-Keeping Operations' (2003) 43 VaJIL 485–524

Paddon Rhoads E, *Taking Sides in Peacekeeping: Impartiality and the Future of the United Nations* (OUP 2016)

Poole PA and TW Britt, *The Psychology of the Peacekeeper: Lessons from the Field* (Praeger 2003)

Ravndal EJ, '"A Force for Peace": Expanding the Role of the UN Secretary-General Under Trygve Lie, 1946–1953' 23(3) (2017) GG 443–459

Report of the United Nations Preparatory Commission, December 23, 1945 (HM Stationary Office, London, 1946)

Rushton S, 'The UN Secretary-General and Norm Entrepreneurship: Boutros Boutros-Ghali and Democracy Promotion' 14(1) (2008) GG 95–110

Schachter O, 'Dag Hammarskjold and the Relation of Law to Politics' (1962) 56(1) AJIL 1–8

Schachter O, 'The Uses of Law in International Peacekeeping' (1964) 50(6) VLR 1096–1114

Sebastián S and A Gorur, 'UN Peacekeeping & Host-State Consent: How Missions Navigate Relationships with Governments' (Stimson Centre, March 2018)

Simma B et al, *The Charter of the United Nations: A Commentary* (2nd edn, OUP 2002)

Simpson G, 'Imagined Consent: Democratic Liberalism in International Legal Theory' (1994) 15 AYIL 103–128

Sloan J, *The Militarisation of Peacekeeping in the Twenty-First Century* (Hart Publishing 2011)

Spijkers O, 'The Evolution of United Nations Peacekeeping in the Congo' (2015) 19(1–2) IntPeacekeep 88–117

Tardy T, 'A Critique of Robust Peacekeeping in Contemporary Operations' (2011) 18(2) IntPeacekeep 152–167

Tardy T, 'United Nations Protection Force (UNPROFOR)' in JA Koops, T Tardy, N MacQueen and PD Williams (eds) *The Oxford Handbook of United Nations Peacekeeping Operations* (OUP 2015)

Teson F, *A Philosophy of International Law* (Westview 1998)

Tsagourias N, 'Consent, Neutrality/Impartiality and the Use of Force in Peacekeeping: Their Constitutional Dimension' (2007) 11(3) JCSL 465–482

Tsagourias N and ND White, *Collective Security Theory, Law and Practice* (CUP 2013)

UN, *United Nations Peacekeeping Operations: Principles and Guidelines* ('Capstone Doctrine') (DPKO 2008)

UN, Eighth Report on State Responsibility, UN Doc A/CN.4/318 and Add.1-4, 2 (1979) Y.B. Int'l L. Comm'n 3 (1980)

UN Conduct in Field Missions, 'Sexual Exploitation and Abuse: Table of Allegations' <https://conduct.unmissions.org/table-of-allegations>

UNGA, 'Summary Study' A/3943 (9 October 1958) UN Doc A/3943

UNGA (15th Session, 882nd Plenary Meeting) (3 October 1960) UN Doc A/PV.882

UNGA, 'Report of the Secretary-General on the Withdrawal of the United Nations Emergency Force' (26 June 1967) UN Doc A/6730

UNGA, 'Report of the Secretary-General: An Agenda for Peace: Preventive, Diplomacy, Peacemaking and Peacekeeping' (31 January 1992) UN Doc A/47/277-S/24111

UNGA, 'Report of the Panel on United Nations Peace Operations' ("Brahimi Report") (21 August 2000) UN Doc A/55/305-S/2000/809

UNGA, 'Report of the Secretary-General: Sexual Exploitation and Abuse: Implementing a Zero Tolerance Policy' (15 February 2018) UN Doc A/72/751

UNGA, 'Supplement to An Agenda for Peace' (25 January 1995) UN Doc A/50/60-S/1995/1
UNGA Res 377 (V) (3 November 1950)
UNGA Res 997 (ES-I) (2 November 1956)
UNGA Res 998 (ES-I) (4 November 1956)
UNGA Res 1000 (ES-I) (5 November 1956)
UNGA Res 1474 (ES-IV) (20 September 1960)
UNGA-SC, 'Letter Dated 12 January 1995 from the Permanent Representative of Croatia to the United Nations addressed to the Secretary-General' (12 January 1995) UN Doc A/50/64 – S/1995/28
UNGA-SC, 'Human Rights Due Diligence Policy' (5 March 2013) UN Doc A/67/775-S/2013/110
UNGA Special Committee on Peacekeeping Operations (C34), 'Draft DPKO/DFS Concept Note' (February 2010 Substantive Session)
UN Peacekeeping, 'Role of the General Assembly' <https://peacekeeping.un.org/en/role-of-general-assembly>
UN Peacekeeping, 'Troop and Police Contributors Data' <https://peacekeeping.un.org/en/troop-and-police-contributors>
UN Peacekeeping, 'Ten Rules Codes of Personal Conduct for Blue Helmets' and "No Excuse" cards, see: UN Peacekeeping, "Standards of Conduct"' <https://peacekeeping.un.org/en/standards-of-conduct>
UN Peacekeeping, 'MONUSCO Plans to Boost the Operational Capacity of the FARDC Against the ADF Rebels' (25 October 2020) <https://peacekeeping.un.org/en/beni-monusco-plans-to-boost-operational-capacity-of-fardc-against-adf-rebels>
UNSC, 'Note by the Secretary-General' (11 April 1964) UN Doc S/5653
UNSC Record, 'Annual Report from 16 July 1958 to 15 July 1959' (13 July 1960) UN Doc S/4381
UNSC, 'Report of the Secretary-General on the Implementation of Security Council Resolution 340' (27 October 1973) UN Doc S/11052/Rev.1
UNSC Res 143 (14 July 1960) UN Doc S/RES/143
UNSC Res 186 (4 March 1964) UN Doc S/RES/186
UNSC Res 743 (21 February 1992) UN Doc S/RES/743
UNSC Res 981 (31 March 1995) S/RES/981
UNSC Res 997 (9 June 1995) UN Doc S/RES/997
UNSC Res 1265 (17 September 1999) UN Doc S/RES/1265
UNSC Res 1270 (22 October 1999) UN Doc S/RES/1270
UNSC Res 1279 (30 November 1999) UN Doc S/RES/1279
UNSC Res 1925 (28 May 2010) UN Doc S/RES/1925
UNSC Res 2098 (28 March 2013) UN Doc S/RES/2098
UNSC Res 2100 (25 April 2013) UN Doc S/RES/2100
UNSC Res 2149 (10 April 2014) UN Doc S/RES/2149
UNSC Res 2502 (19 December 2019) UN Doc S/RES/2502
UNSC Res 2659 (14 November 2022) UN Doc S/RES/2659
UNSC Res 2666 (20 December 2022) UN Doc S/RES/2666
UNSC, 'Report of the Secretary-General' (18 July 1960) UN Doc S/4389
UNSC Verbatim Record (13/14 July 1960) UN Doc S/PV.873
UNSC Verbatim Record (25 October 1973) UN Doc S/PV.1750

UNSG, 'Address by Secretary-General Dag Hammarskjöld at University of California Convocation, Berkeley' (13 May 1954) Press Release SG/382

UNSG, 'Secretary-General Bulletin: Observance by United Nations Forces of International Humanitarian Law' (6 August 1999) UN Doc ST/SGB/1999/13

UNSG, Decision No 2011/18 (13 July 2011).

Urquhart B, *Hammarskjöld* (Alfred A Knopf 1972)

Urquhart B, *A Life in Peace and War* (WW Norton 1987)

Van Reybrouck D, *Congo: The Epic History of a People* (Fourth Estate 2015)

Vircoulon T, 'After MONUC, Should MONUSCO Continue to Support Congolese Military Campaigns?' (*Crisis Group*, 19 July 2010) <https://www.crisisgroup.org/africa/central-africa/chad/after-monuc-should-monusco-continue-support-congolese-military-campaigns>

Wallensteen P and P Johansson, 'The UN Security Council: Decisions and Actions' in S von Einsiedel, DM Malone and B Stagno Ugarte (eds) *The UN Security Council in the 21st Century* (Lynne Rienner 2015)

Whippman D, 'Military Intervention, Regional Organisations, and Host-State Consent' in B Kondoch (ed) *International Peacekeeping* (Ashgate 2007)

White ND, 'The UN Charter and Peacekeeping Forces: Constitutional Issues' (1996) 3(4) IntPeacekeep 43–63

White ND, 'Peace Operations' in V Chetail (ed) *Post-Conflict Peacebuilding: A Lexicon* (OUP 2010)

White ND, 'Peacekeeping Doctrine: An Autonomous Legal Order?' (2019) 88(1) NJIL 86–110

Whittle D, 'The Limits of Legality and the United Nations Security Council: Applying the Extra-Legal Measures Model to Chapter VII Action' (2015) 26(3) EJIL 671–698

Chapter 4

Peacekeeping – An Expanding Normative Framework

An Expanding Normative Framework

The 'Holy Trinity' of principles, buttressed by policy developments such as the *Capstone Doctrine* and *Brahimi Report*, form a general legal framework for UN peacekeeping, albeit one which is constantly stretched, re-interpreted and, on occasions, pushed to its limits. This framework surrounds peacekeeping like a red elastic band, forming an invisible boundary line between peacekeeping and intervention which contracts and retracts as peacekeeping continually evolves and the principles and norms are re-interpreted within each peacekeeping operation. If the fundamental principles are viewed as the core of peacekeeping, the closest peacekeeping has to a beating legal heart, then the norms of peacekeeping – such as democracy promotion, protection of civilians and the prohibition of sexual exploitation and abuse – are the ribcage which surrounds peacekeeping's heart. That is, these norms – which may have commonalities with principles of law but are, ultimately, not underpinned by law and therefore do not amount to legal principles[1] – form part of a wider normative framework which the legal framework sits within. Together, the two distinct but occasionally overlapping frameworks form part of peacekeeping's overall framework, providing somewhat of a guidance for UN peacekeeping.

Whilst there are other norms within peacekeeping, such as promoting gender equality and protecting human rights, the book will focus on the above three norms as they, firstly, reflect some of the main justifications or motivations for contemporary interventions, which Chapter 2 explored: namely, humanitarian or security-based interventions. Secondly, they are three norms which have been most prevalent within peacekeeping operations, particularly within the United Nations' operations in the DRC – the case study for this book. This chapter will examine how, as with the fundamental principles,

1 On legal normativity, see generally: JL Coleman, KE Himma and SJ Shapiro, *The Oxford Handbook of Jurisprudence and Philosophy of Law* (OUP 2004).

DOI: 10.4324/9781003371649-4

these norms are interpreted and applied, altering peacekeeping's frameworks and the thin, elastic, red boundary line between peacekeeping and intervention. It will argue that a narrow interpretation of these norms constricts peacekeeping's normative framework, thereby reinforcing the principle of non-intervention; whereas a broad interpretation expands the frameworks, consequently undermining and potentially contravening the principle of non-intervention.

Through this exploration of peacekeeping's frameworks, it will also highlight two key issues– firstly, that the principles and norms do not exist harmoniously and, secondly, that the UN Secretary-General plays a key role in introducing and developing peacekeeping norms. Whilst it is well-established that peacekeeping operates (or should operate) according to the three fundamental principles and other important norms, these are rarely found to coexist harmoniously and consistently. Rather, these norms 'exist in a competitive arena' and, within the context of a peacekeeping operation, 'the normative composition is re-balanced each time'.[2] For each peacekeeping operation, these norms are re-interpreted, re-defined or re-actualised to meet the realities on the ground, the demands of the Security Council mandate and the resources provided for the operation. Indeed, there is an ongoing battle about what peacekeeping ought to be and do[3] and, as such, practices and normative reasonings which underpin these are significant when tracing how the norms of peacekeeping operations 'wax and wane'.[4] Therefore, as interventionist rhetoric was found in Chapter 2 to have waxed and waned (often in direct correlation with the hegemonic powers' agendas), the same can also be said for peacekeeping's norms and frameworks. From a TWAIL perspective, then, similar arguments can be made about how the re-balancing of norms and this battle between what peacekeeping is or ought to be, is, like the principle of non-intervention, set within the dynamics of the hegemonic powers' agendas. Just as Chapter 2 identified how elements of the principle of non-intervention (such as contemporary justifications for intervention) are based on Western values and standards, the same arguments can be made about the norms of peacekeeping, as this chapter will explore. In particular, Chapter 2 identified the inherent power imbalances within the UN Security Council and how this could influence the shaping of laws, norms and practices, such as the principle of non-intervention. As the Security Council plays a key role in peacekeeping, again, the same arguments made about the principle of non-intervention -= the powers of the veto-wielding P5 and the prevalence of hegemony – can be extended and applied to peacekeeping.

2 J Karlsrud, 'Special Representatives of the Secretary-General as Norm Arbitrators? Understanding Bottom-up Authority in UN Peacekeeping' (2013) 19(4) GG 525–544, 527.

3 AJ Bellamy and P Williams, *Understanding Peacekeeping* (2nd ed, Polity Press 2010).

4 Karlsrud (n2) 527.

Furthermore, the Secretary-General, as a 'norm entrepreneur' and 'commander in chief' of UN peacekeeping plays a significant part in developing and shaping peacekeeping, including creating, institutionalising and interpreting norms within peacekeeping.[5] This also includes coordinating the establishment of a force, reporting to the Security Council on its progress[6] and exercising command and control over the operation.[7] Within the field, the office of the Secretary-General is embodied in the Special Representative of the Secretary-General (SRSG) who is head of each peacekeeping operation. Operating under the authority of the Security Council mandate and the SG, the SRSGs have significant discretion on the trajectory of the operation and the implementation of the mandate.[8] Indeed, the priorities and success of a peacekeeping operation can differ greatly, depending on the background or orientation of the SRSG, as 'each SRSG has a different vision of what the mission would be like'.[9] The norm entrepreneurship of the office of the SG therefore adds a further nuance to our understanding of peacekeeping's legal and normative frameworks and amplifies the interventionist potential of peacekeeping operations. That is, the ability of the SG and their office to mould peacekeeping means that they are, consequently, able to shape the principle of non-intervention, depending on how they choose to interpret mandates and conduct peacekeeping operations. However, this is not necessarily a negative. Indeed, from a TWAIL perspective, it could be argued that the ability of the SG and SRSG to potentially shape peacekeeping presents an opportunity to amplify the Third World voice, challenge the hegemonic powers within the Security Council and create the space for a more bottom-up or people-centred approach to peacekeeping.[10] As the SRSG, in particular, has the power and influence to 'muster and align' the resources of agencies, donors and countries to support peacebuilding efforts,[11] then it follows that through the SRSG, Global South states may lobby or petition for their

5 I Johnstone, 'The Secretary-General as Norm Entrepreneur' in S Chesterman (ed) *Secretary or General? The UN Secretary-General in World Politics* (CUP 2007) 123–138.

6 The first Secretary-General, Trygve Lie, set a precedent by using the report as an opportunity to outline his reactions to events and to record the successes and failures of the organisation, thus creating the space for the SG to act as a norm entrepreneur, highlight specific issues or promote their agendas. See: T Lie, *In the Cause of Peace: Seven Years with the United Nations* (Macmillan Co 1954).

7 Article 98, UN Charter.

8 See: C De Coning, 'Mediation and Peacebuilding: SRSGs and DSRSGs in Integrated Missions' (2010) 16(2) GG 281–299.

9 Interview with Independent Expert and Former UN Political Adviser ('Interviewee 8') (New York, 26 November 2019) DOI: <http://doi.org/10.17639/nott.7119> pg 13.

10 F Carver, 'Peacekeeping Desperately Needs a New Model, and a People-Centred Approach Could Work' (Pass Blue, 4 September 2022) <https://www.passblue.com/2022/09/04/peacekeeping-desperately-needs-a-new-model-and-a-people-centered-approach-could-work/>.

11 De Coning (n8).

interests and agendas within a given context. Further, it is not only states that could lobby the SRSG but individuals and local, regional or national actors within the host state. Given the SRSG's unique position within the field, if the SRSG adopts an adaptive leadership approach and engages with these actors, including steering the operation towards supporting grassroots or local initiatives to promote peace, then this expands the Global South voice within peacekeeping and moves peacekeeping towards a more bottom-up, people-centred approach as opposed to a top-down, outsider-led approach which, for some, is the key to creating sustainable peace.[12] Indeed at various points throughout this book, it will be highlighted when a people-centred, bottom-up approach would be desirable to both move peacekeeping away from the intervention line and to amplify peacekeeping's effectiveness.

Democracy Promotion

Based on the age-old notion that 'democracies do not wage war on each other', international law and international institutions have been developed 'so as to reinforce democratic governance'.[13] For peacekeeping, this has resulted in peacekeeping operations undertaking democracy promotion – tasks embedded within the operation's mandate to support the furtherance of democracy within the host state. After a growing consensus for 'democratic governance',[14] in 1989, the Security Council, following reports from Secretaries-General Kurt Waldheim[15] and Javier Perez de Cuellar,[16] established the United Nations Transition Assistance Group (UNTAG) to help supervise the electoral process in Namibia.[17] This marked the first occasion in which UN peacekeeping engaged in democratisation tasks. The norm then became formally introduced into UN peacekeeping and peacebuilding in the early 1990s, in line with the rise of democratisation within international law in the post-Cold War era and the shift in interventionist practice as was noted

12 See: S Autesserre, *The Frontlines of Peace: An Insider's Guide to Changing the World* (OUP 2021); F Carver, 'Linked up Peacekeeping' (Protection Approaches, July 2022) <https://protectionapproaches.org/linked-up-peacekeeping>; C de Coning, J Karlsrud, P Troost, 'Towards More People-Centric Peace Operations: From "Extension of State Authority" to "Strengthening Inclusive State-Society Relations"' (2015) 4(1), 49 Stability: International Journal of Security & Development 1–13.

13 J Crawford, 'Democracy and International Law' (1993) 64(1) BYIL 113–133.

14 See: R Mani and J Krause, 'Democratic Governance' in V Chetail (ed) *Post-Conflict Peacebuilding: A Lexicon* (OUP 2010) 105–122.

15 UNSC, 'Secretary-Report, Proposals for Namibia. Supplement for April, May and June 1978' (10 April 1978) UN Doc S/12636.

16 UNSC, 'Further Report of the Secretary-General Concerning the Question of Namibia' (23 January 1989) UN Doc S/20412.

17 UNTAG recommended in: UNSC Res 435 (29 September 1978) UN Doc S/RES/435 and eventually established in UNSC Res 629 (16 January 1989) UN Doc S/RES/629.

in Chapter 2.[18] In his inaugural speech as Secretary-General, Boutros-Ghali stressed the importance of the 'United Nations role in strengthening fundamental freedoms and democratic institutions' and noted that 'if there is no development without democracy, there can also be no democracy without development'.[19] Boutros-Ghali viewed the end of the Cold War as presenting a historic opportunity for changing the world and the nature of international affairs and introduced both the concept of democracy and the term peacebuilding into UN terminology and practice.[20] In *An Agenda for Peace* Boutros-Ghali institutionalised the norm of democracy promotion, arguing that there was 'an obvious connection between democratic practices ... and the achievement of true peace and security'.[21] Therefore, the introduction of the principle within UN peacekeeping was evidently premised on the theory of liberal democratic peace that democracies do not go to war with one another and, as such, 'liberalism is rationalised and presented as the only form of political rationality capable of meeting the challenges of the modern world'.[22]

Civilising Mission?

This presumption that liberal democracy is the most ideal form of governance and the inclusion of democracy promotion within peacekeeping therefore raise numerous issues. Firstly, for the principle of non-intervention, the inclusion of the norm has the potential to undermine the principle of non-intervention as it expands peacekeeping's normative framework by broadening the tasks which a peacekeeping operation is required to undertake. That is, as seen in previous chapters, as peacekeeping evolved from traditional to multi-dimensional operations, their mandates and operational tasks grew, consequently expanding both peacekeeping's boundaries and its interventionist potential. In particular, whereas the traditional model of peacekeeping focused on conflict or post-conflict management, the inclusion of democracy promotion pushed peacekeeping into the realm of statebuilding.[23]

18 See: Crawford (n13) and H Charlesworth, 'Democracy and International Law' in H Charlesworth (ed) *Recueil des Cours 371: Collected Courses of the Hague Academy of International Law 2014* (Brill 2015) 43–152.
19 UNGA (46th Session, 59th Meeting) (5 December 1991) UN Doc A/46/PV.59, 16.
20 ibid.
21 UNGA, 'Report of the Secretary-General. An Agenda for Peace: Preventive, Diplomacy, Peacemaking and Peacekeeping' (31 January 1992) UN Doc A/47/277-S/24111 and UNGA, 'Supplement to an Agenda for Peace' (25 January 1995) UN Doc A/50/60-S/1995/1.
22 M Mazower, *Governing the World: The History of an Idea, 1815 to the Present* (Penguin 2012) 11–12.
23 See: KZ Marten, *Enforcing the Peace: Learning from the Imperial Past* (Columbia University Press 2004).

Furthermore, for many peacekeeping operations, establishing or supporting democracy is a key part of the exit strategy and a criterion for measuring the success of the operation; an operation may only be considered a 'success' and therefore leave the host state if a sufficient level of democratic governance is established.[24] As such, it could be argued that democracy promotion, in this instance, is a form of intervention as it invokes an element of coercion as it is, essentially, an implicit ultimatum – the host state must establish a system of democratic governance, which meets the standards of the external actor, before the actor withdraws from their territory. In essence, the norm of democracy promotion could be viewed, then, as a form of coercive action designed to influence change or alter the host state and, thus, intervention or, more specifically, political intervention.

From a TWAIL perspective, democracy promotion could also be viewed as problematic as it invokes notions of 'civilisation' and is based on Western standards and values. That is, the very concepts of sovereignty and statehood, for TWAIL scholars, are deeply rooted in colonial standards and were crafted 'without pre-colonial Africa in mind'.[25] Therefore, the Global South, when gaining independence, subscribed to an international legal system which they played no part in creating, and it is arguable that the same arguments could also be made for democracy promotion. It is indisputable that 'civilisation', in particular, played an important role in shaping international law, particularly through colonial intervention during the Age of Empire, as the previous chapter demonstrated. Whilst this narrow concept of 'civilisation' ended in the new post-1945 world order, if 'civilisation' is instead considered as an argumentative pattern, 'one that constantly oscillates' between the two interconnected logics of 'conditional inclusion and perpetual exclusion or deferral of inclusion', then 'civilisation' persists.[26] As TWAIL scholars, such as Anghie and Tzouvala, have argued, the concept of 'civilisation' remains and has simply been reinvented in, for example, the 'war on terror'[27] or global capitalist expansion.[28] It could similarly be argued that 'civilisation' is also replicated in democratisation and, more specifically, the norm of democracy promotion within UN peacekeeping operations as it invokes the same notions of inclusion and exclusion. Indeed, it is 'regarded as axiomatic in the western world that the most civilised form of government' is the 'western form of democracy'.[29] As such, non-democratic states are seemingly viewed by the

24 See: B Heldt and P Wallensteen, *Peacekeeping Operations: Global Patterns of Intervention and Success, 1948–2004* (3rd ed, Folke Bernadotte Academy Publications 2007).
25 M Mutua, 'Why Redraw the Map of Africa: A Moral and Legal Inquiry' (1995) 16(4) MichJIntL 1113–1176, 1120.
26 N Tzouvala, *Capitalism as Civilisation: A History of International Law* (CUP 2020) 5.
27 A Anghie, *Imperialism, Sovereignty and the Making of International Law* (CUP 2007).
28 Tzouvala (n26).
29 BK Nehru, 'Western Democracy and the Third World' (1979) 1(2) TWQ 53–70, 53.

West as adopting a less civilised form of governance or, in other words, as uncivilised. Similar to the discussion on humanitarian-based interventions in Chapter 2, democracy, like human rights, is therefore a concept based on Western ideals which are devoid of the input of the Third World and are 'essentially infinite' and highly ambiguous.[30]

Whilst the United Nations is said to have recognised this Western-centric nature of democracy, reflected in its un-willingness 'to develop a substantive notion of democracy',[31] the concept has still been promoted within the UN system, not least through its inclusion in peacekeeping mandates. Furthermore, given that the United Nations is dominated by hegemonic powers (as was laid out in Chapter 2), the presumption of democracy as the most ideal form of governance has prevailed and has filtered into UN peacekeeping through the inclusion of the norm of democracy promotion. It appears that this has then been somewhat accepted by both the host state and those within the Council who seek to counter Western democracy promotion,[32] because of the consensual nature of peacekeeping. Therefore, because a peacekeeping operation is deployed with the host state's consent, it follows that they consent to the operation's mandate and the tasks contained within it, including democracy promotion. However, as previously noted, in practice a distinction can be drawn between *de jure* consent (consent to the deployment of the operation which cannot be withdrawn) and *de facto* consent (consent to tasks or changes during the mandate period). As will be discussed in later chapters, it then becomes debatable as to how much the host state consents to the democracy promotion tasks in reality and to what extent they are able to voluntarily accept or reject such endeavours.

Regardless of this debate, the argument remains that the pattern of 'civilisation' – conditional inclusion versus exclusion or deferral – is found within UN peacekeeping, in this instance when the host state is required to adopt a democratic system, under the supervision of a peacekeeping operation. The dominant actor thereby requires the subordinate Global South state to conform to their standards, often despite the fact that democracy may neither answer the latter's needs nor be in line 'with their native traditional pattern of the exercise of governmental authority'.[33] As a result, these peacekeeping operations become comparable with colonial civilising missions, as they invoke similar patterns of domination, subordination and conformity to hegemonic standards, which is legitimised by international law. Indeed,

30 M Mutua, 'The Ideology of Human Rights' (1996) 36 VaJIntl 589–658, 593.

31 H Charlesworth, 'International Legal Encounters with Democracy' (2017) 8(6) GlobalPolicy 34–43, 36.

32 Russia and China, see: A Kendall-Taylor and D Shullman, 'How Russia and China Undermine Democracy' (*Foreign Affairs*, 2 October 2018) <https://www.foreignaffairs.com/articles/china/2018-10-02/how-russia-and-china-undermine-democracy>.

33 Charlesworth (n18) 57.

for some TWAIL scholars, the United Nations' shaping of post-conflict states through constitutional support, such as democracy promotion, 'serves as a classic instance' of the 'imperial project at work'.[34]

Moreover, it could be further argued that this is, again, a replication of Anghie's dynamic of difference, as previously noted. Here, a gap between two cultures is identified (non-democratic system) with the dominant actor (the UN peacekeeping operation) seeking to close that gap by altering or normalising (democratising) the 'other' (the host state). This simultaneously justifies intervention for, in theory, an indefinite period of time as (notwithstanding host state consent to mandate renewals) it is the hegemonic power that determines the standard which must be met and, therefore, whether the gap has been closed, with the subordinate 'other' having acquired a sufficient level of democratisation. Again, as was previously noted, this altering of the 'other' includes an element of coercion – an implication that a certain standard of democratisation is a pre-requisite for the withdrawal of an operation – resulting in peacekeeping amounting to a form of political intervention.

A Pipedream?

The inclusion of democracy promotion within peacekeeping's normative framework, then, raises questions about the apparent presumption that the Western-centric notion of democracy is the most desired form of governance and one which is necessary for achieving peace. This becomes even more problematic given that its inclusion expands peacekeeping's boundaries and the interventionist potential of a peacekeeping operation, thereby taking peacekeeping closer to the intervention line, simultaneously undermining the principle of non-intervention.

Nevertheless, following its introduction, subsequent Secretaries-General have continued to emphasise the importance of democracy,[35] and the Security Council has routinely mandated its operations to include democratisation tasks.[36] These have taken numerous forms, such as providing technical assistance, monitoring and observing elections and ensuring security to allow for the organisation of elections.[37] More broadly, it has also included the development of bureaucracies and administrations, justice and

34 V Sripati, 'The United Nation's Role in Post-Conflict Constitution-Making Processes: TWAIL Insights' (2008) 10(4) ICLR 411–420, 420.

35 K Annan, 'Democracy as an International Issue' (2002) 8(2) GG 135–142; UNGA, 'Report of the Secretary-General: In Larger Freedom: Towards Security, Development and Human Rights for All' (21 March 2005) UN Doc A/59/2005.

36 Such as in Haiti: UNSC Res 2313 (13 October 2016) UN Doc S/RES/2313; and Mali: UNSC Res 2100 (25 April 2013) UN Doc S/RES/2100.

37 See: Mani and Krause (n14).

the rule of law and security sector reform.[38] Therefore, as peacekeeping has evolved into robust, multi-dimensional peacekeeping operations, its democratisation tasks have simultaneously expanded.[39] As such, elections and election support have now become a key part of many peacekeeping operations.[40] As noted earlier, then, this inclusion of democratisation within UN peacekeeping signalled a shift of focus from one of peacebuilding and securing a peaceful post-conflict environment to one of statebuilding[41] – a task which some argue should not be undertaken by UN peacekeeping as it is a very poor tool for achieving such aims.[42] Indeed, senior personnel within the UN Secretariat suggest that 'a serious question which needs to be asked' is how realistic or helpful it is 'to expect a peacekeeping operation, that operates on the basis of consent, impartiality, to essentially play the role of an arbiter in an electoral process'.[43] On this basis, an argument can, again, be made for shrinking peacekeeping operations and returning to a more traditional model, with a narrower interpretation and application of peacekeeping norms, as was suggested for some of the legal principles in the previous chapter.

Similarly, for some, it is questionable whether 'turning a peacekeeping operation into a tool for democracy promotion' is a true reflection or expression of the Council's will and their main aim of addressing threats to international peace and security.[44] As Marten argues, 'the notion of imposing liberal democracy abroad is a pipedream' and peacekeepers should therefore limit their goals to providing stability, rather than trying to transform societies.[45] It could therefore be argued that in addition to the problem of whether democracy should be imposed as the desired or preferable form of governance, there is a second notable problem of whether democratisation by UN peacekeepers is both appropriate and logistically possible and, if so, how it is to be quantified.

That is, it is unclear what the benchmark is for 'successful' democracy or democratic elections and what it means for a peacekeeping operation if

38 ibid.

39 See, for example, the UN's peacekeeping operations in Liberia (UNSC Res 866 (22 September 1993) UN Doc S/RES/866 and UNSC Res 1020 (10 November 1995) UN Doc S/RES/1020) and Democratic Republic of the Congo (UNSC Res 1291 (24 February 2000) UN Doc S/RES/1291).

40 See: H Fjelde and HM Smidt, 'Protesting the Vote? Peacekeeping Presence and the Risk of Electoral Violence' (2022) 52(3) British Journal of Political Science 1113–1132.

41 B Reilly, 'Elections in Post-Conflict Societies' in E Newman and R Rich (eds) *The UN Role in Promoting Democracy: Between Ideals and Reality* (UN University Press 2004) 188.

42 Interviewee 8 (n9).

43 Interview with Senior Political Affairs Officer, UN DPO ('Interviewee 16') (New York, 10 December 2019) DOI: <http://doi.org/10.17639/nott.7119> pg 3.

44 ibid.

45 Marten (n23) 155.

these elections are not 'successful'.[46] For example, as will be explored in later chapters, the elections which UN peacekeepers have supported in the DRC have been highly controversial, with numerous allegations of corruption and election fraud.[47] This then exemplifies the argument made by some TWAIL scholars that 'international law does not take global democracy seriously' as it imposes certain obligations on states (such as the need to hold democratic elections) but does not hold them responsible for any further deepening or development of the concept.[48] It appears that simply obtaining the level of 'democratic state' or fulfilling the basic requirements of holding elections suffices for meeting the international community's standards imposed to transform the non-democratic state. In a similar vein, the United Nations' emphasis on democracy is perhaps somewhat ironic, given that the organ which sets the peacekeeping mandate, and thus the democracy promotion tasks, is the Security Council. As seen in Chapter 2, the Council is highly undemocratic, given the disproportionate amount of power which the permanent five members hold; therefore, there is, once again, somewhat of a disconnect between rhetoric and practice – the United Nations promotes democracy yet is dominated by an extremely undemocratic organ.

The norm of democracy promotion within UN peacekeeping therefore continues to highlight the same patterns of domination and subordination and the furtherance of hegemonic ideals and agendas, as was seen in the development of the principle of non-intervention in Chapter 2. This then supports the notion that many features of both international law and international institutions or legal systems 'acknowledge and reinforce the substantial power differentials between its participants'.[49] Furthermore, applying a TWAIL lens to the concept of democracy and its inclusion within peacekeeping also highlights how democracy is based upon ideals and standards (specifically Western ideals), thereby lacking any legal underpinning beyond the Security Council mandate. As such, it is a norm, rather than a legal principle, thereby contributing to peacekeeping's normative, but not legal, framework. For the principle of non-intervention, the norm of democracy promotion is also problematic as its ambiguous nature expands peacekeeping's red boundary line, permitting a peacekeeping operation to undertake ill-defined and potentially limitless interventionist activities, under the justification of

46 B Heldt, 'Peacekeeping Operations and Transitions to Democracy' in H Fjelde and K Höglund (eds) *Building Peace, Creating Conflict* (Nordic Academic Press 2011) 47–71

47 J Burke, 'Congo Election Runner-up Rejects Tshisekedi Victory as "Electoral Coup"' (*The Guardian*, 10 January 2019) <https://www.theguardian.com/world/2019/jan/10/congo-election-felix-tshisekedi-declared-winner-in-contentious-result>.

48 BS Chimni, 'International Institutions Today: An Imperial Global State in the Making' (2004) 15(1) EJIL 1–37, 8.

49 Charlesworth (n31) 34.

democracy promotion which, in turn, severely undermines and potentially contravenes, at times, the principle of non-intervention.

The Protection of Civilians

Unlike the norm of democracy promotion, the protection of civilians (PoC) has much clearer legal underpinnings in international humanitarian and human rights law.[50] Indeed, it is argued that UN peacekeeping operations are obliged to comply with human rights standards and prevent or halt violations of human rights, regardless of whether the operation has a PoC mandate.[51] PoC therefore invokes or reflects some principles and obligations under international law, such as compliance with international humanitarian law when engaged in armed conflict.[52] As such, whilst PoC primarily forms a key part of peacekeeping's broader normative framework, it could also be said to contribute to peacekeeping's legal framework, where it leads to a peacekeeping operation invoking these elements of international law.

Of the three 'new' norms explored within this book, it is also the most interventionist as it has now evolved to permit a substantial, seemingly endless level of force in order to protect civilians, thereby expanding the legal and normative boundaries surrounding peacekeeping and, by extension, contracting the principle of non-intervention. Described by former Secretary-General Ban Ki Moon as a 'defining purpose of the UN in the twenty-first century',[53] PoC has become a centre of gravity for peacekeeping operations with over 95% of peacekeepers now mandated to protect civilians.[54] This has arisen through a rapid expansion of the concept over the past 20 years, with noticeable changes almost every 5 years as pressure to ensure peacekeepers protect civilians has increased.[55]

The United Nations' first involvement in the protection of civilians within a peacekeeping operation can be traced back to the United Nations' Operation in the Congo (ONUC) in 1960. Whilst ONUC did not have a PoC mandate

50 Geneva Convention Relative to the Protection of Civilian Persons in Time of War (Fourth Geneva Convention) (12 August 1949) (75 UNTS 287); JM Henckaerts and L Doswald-Beck, *Customary International Humanitarian Law. Volume 1: Rules* (CUP 2005) Rules 87–195, pp299–379.

51 A Clapham, 'Protection of Civilians under International Human Rights Law' in H Willmot, R Mamiya, S Sheeran and M Weller (eds) *Protection of Civilians* (OUP 2016) 141–159.

52 UNSG, 'Secretary-General Bulletin: Observance by United Nations Forces of International Humanitarian Law' (6 August 1999) UN Doc ST/SGB/1999/13.

53 UN News, 'Responsibility to Protect: Ban Urges Action to Make UN-Backed Tool "A Living Reality"' (*UN News*, 18 January 2012) <https://news.un.org/en/story/2012/01/400702>.

54 UN Peacekeeping, 'Protecting Civilians' <https://peacekeeping.un.org/en/protecting-civilians>.

55 See: A Gilder, 'The UN and the Protection of Civilians: Sustaining the Momentum' (2023) 28 JCSL 1–32.

from the Security Council,[56] an Operational Directive permitted the peacekeepers to afford 'where feasible ... every protection' to 'unarmed groups' who may be subjected to violence, 'using armed force if necessary'.[57] For some, this has been read to include the protection of civilians and should be marked as the start of the United Nations' foray into such operations. Indeed, Mona Ali Khalil, argues that this was the first PoC mandate, 'not by virtue of the design of the mandate' but on the basis of the then-SG, Hammarskjöld's announcement that he would be reading the mandate as allowing ONUC 'to have the authority to step in to save civilian lives'.[58] Whilst there was 'of course' some objection from members of the Council, 'his interpretation of ONUC's mandate prevailed'.[59] In the early 1990s, the United Nations more firmly began to experiment with the concept of protection of civilians with the UN protection forces in the Former Yugoslavia.[60] These were tasked with an indirect PoC focusing on humanitarian space and access and protection of safe areas.[61]

Following this, the UNSC authorised a specific PoC mandate for the peacekeeping operation in Sierra Leone in 1999.[62] It was at this point that the Council began to insert the language of 'imminent threat' into mandates, stating that peacekeepers were to protect civilians who were 'under imminent threat of physical violence'.[63] This introduction of PoC reflected the shifting attitudes towards intervention, as was seen in Chapter 2, with member states believing that they had a responsibility to prevent or stop the failures of the 1990s (such as the Rwandan genocide) from occurring again.[64] When opening a debate on the introduction of PoC, UNSG Annan noted that 'enforcement action is a difficult step' which often goes against political or other interests, but these interests are superseded by 'universal values', and PoC is one such value.[65] Annan therefore introduced and interpreted the norm of PoC

56 See the Security Council Resolutions on PoC: UNSC Res 1265 (17 September 1999) UN Doc S/RES/1265 and UNSC Res 1270 (22 October 1999) UN Doc S/RES/1270.

57 Operations Directive No 8 (untitled), February 1961, UN Archives DAG/13/1.6.5.0.0; Operations Directives August 1960–January 1964, Box 3, pp2–3.

58 Interview with Mona Ali Khalil, former Senior Legal Officer of the UN Office of the Legal Counsel, Director of MAK LAW International and an Affiliate of the Harvard Law School Program on International Law and Armed Conflict ('Interviewee 12') (New York (Skype) 5 December 2019) DOI: <http://doi.org/10.17639/nott.7119>.

59 ibid.

60 See: UNSC Res 743 (21 February 1992) UN Doc S/RES/743.

61 See: UNSC Res 770 (13 August 1992) UN Doc S/RES/770; UNSC Res 836 (4 June 1993) UN Doc S/RES/836.

62 S/RES/1270 (n56).

63 ibid.

64 UNGA-SC, 'Report of the Secretary-General: The Causes of Conflict and the Promotion of Durable Peace and Sustainable Development in Africa' (13 April 1998) UN Doc A/52/871-S/1998/318.

65 UNSC (54th Year, 4046th Meeting) (16 September 1999) UN Doc S/PV/4046, 4.

both within UN peacekeeping and the UN system more broadly, recognising that it was a form of intervention but justifying it on a moral or humanitarian basis. Again, similarities can be drawn here with the humanitarian-based interventions which were discussed in Chapter 2. Indeed, Annan's advocating for PoC, along with the concept of responsibility to protect (R2P), became known as the 'Kofi Doctrine' – a belief that state sovereignty could no longer be a shield against UN intervention on behalf of 'we, the peoples'.[66] This ambiguously broadened the scope of UN peacekeeping operations by creating a further task within peacekeeping mandates that provided yet another justification for intervention.[67] If it was acknowledged that the norms of PoC and R2P required the relinquishing of an element of sovereignty then, by corollary, it can be implied that there is also a sacrifice or constriction of the principle of non-intervention. This then undermines the principle, particularly as the concept of PoC is ill-defined and, as it is continually evolving, is potentially normatively limitless; thus, in theory, the interventionist nature of the peacekeeping operation in this regard is also limitless. As was seen with the norm of democracy promotion, questions then arise as to how far this norm can be expanded before it crosses the intervention line.

This broadening of peacekeeping's boundaries becomes even more problematic when it is combined with forceful rhetoric (such as Annan's acknowledgement of the need for 'enforcement action'[68]) or uncertainty about the level of force which could or should be used by peacekeepers in order to fulfil this task. This was particularly the case with the United Nations' operation in Sierra Leone, which led to debates in the Security Council that highlighted the differing approaches to intervention amongst the permanent members and exemplified the hegemonic political dynamics within the Council which Chapter 2 outlined. On the one hand, the UK, fully endorsing the inclusion of PoC in peacekeeping operations, argued that the Council 'should not shy away' from 'more robust mandates if a force needs to act in enforcement mode' to, for example, protect civilians.[69] Conversely, whilst China equally supported the protection of civilians, recognising that the Council had an 'unshirkable duty' in maintaining international peace and security, rather than supporting the use of force for peacekeepers, it emphasised the need

66 See: K Annan, *Interventions: A Life in War and Peace* (Penguin 2013) and J Cooper Ramo, 'The Five Virtues of Kofi Annan' (*Time*, 4 Sept 2000) <http://content.time.com/time/world/article/0,8599,2056090,00.html>.

67 See, the first thematic resolution on PoC: S/RES/1265 (n56) and subsequent resolutions, such as UNSC Res 1296 (19 April 2000) UN Doc S/RES/1296; UNSC Res 1502 (26 August 2003) UN Doc S/RES/1502; UNSC Res 1894 (11 November 2009) UN Doc S/RES/1894; UNSC Res 2475 (20 June 2019) UN Doc S/RES/2475; UNSC Res 2573 (27 April 2021) UN Doc S/RES/2573.

68 S/PV/4046, 4.

69 ibid, 17.

for PoC to cut across the political, humanitarian, development and assistance fields.[70] It thereby argued that the fundamental way to protect civilians is to 'effectively prevent and do away with conflict' and that the issue of PoC should be 'more appropriately and more thoroughly deliberated' in the General Assembly.[71] This therefore highlights, not only the differing approaches to intervention within the Security Council but, more broadly, how the norm of PoC exposes the same patterns of subordination and domination that Chapter 2 identified within the principle of non-intervention.

It is also, like democracy promotion and humanitarian-based interventions, a norm which is based upon Western values and standards, again, reinforcing patterns of domination and subordination both within international law and international relations. Applying a TWAIL lens, then, the UK's rhetoric of robust intervention could be viewed as promoting a Global North agenda, as the invocation of force and emphasis on the Security Council as the primary decision maker reinforces the dominance of the Council and therefore the hegemonic powers. On the other hand, the arguments put forward by China, that the norm of PoC should be debated and decided upon within the General Assembly, challenges this dominance as all member states could participate in moulding the concept of PoC, rather than simply the dominant actors within the Security Council.[72] From a TWAIL perspective, this latter proposal is therefore vital as it offers a counter to hegemony and allows the Global South to play a role in shaping international law and restructuring the international system.[73] Furthermore, for the principle of non-intervention, it would also limit the concept of PoC, demarcating boundaries for the norm and thereby limiting the interventionist potential of PoC and, by extension, the peacekeeping operation.

Forceful Protection

Despite these initial debates on the normative and practical boundaries of PoC, the concept rapidly evolved, with five subsequent operations mandated to protect civilians.[74] There remained, however, a troubling lack of

70 ibid, 21.
71 ibid.
72 See the Security Council Resolutions on PoC (n56 and n67).
73 M Mutua, 'Critical Race Theory and International Law: The View of an Insider-Outsider' (2000) 45(5) VillLRev 841–854, 852; JT Gathii, 'A Critical Appraisal of the International Legal Tradition of Taslim Olawale Elias' (2008) 21(2) LJIL 317–349.
74 DRC: S/RES/1291 (n39) para 8 and later UNSC Res 1925 (28 May 2010) UN Doc S/RES/1925, paras 11 and 12(a); Liberia: UNSC Res 1509 (19 September 2003) UN Doc S/RES/1509 para 3(j); Cote d'Ivoire: UNSC Res 1528 (27 February 2004) UN Doc S/RES/1528 para 6(i); Haiti: UNSC Res 1542 (30 A1291pril 2004) UN Doc S/RES/1542 para 7(i)(f); South Sudan: UNSC Res 1996 (9 July 2011) UN Doc S/RES/1996 para 3(b).

operational guidance as to how these mandates should be implemented, leading to 'widely varying interpretations' by senior mission leadership in the field and a failure to meaningfully implement the mandates.[75] Once again, this undermined the principle of non-intervention as the ambiguity of the norm of PoC created unclear boundaries for peacekeeping and, consequently, uncertainty over its interventionist potential.

It is also during this period of the early 2000s, as was seen in Chapter 2, that peacekeeping began to shift towards 'robust peacekeeping' which had a direct impact on the implementation of PoC, given that PoC and the use of force are often entwined.[76] The language within mandates therefore began to change, with the use of force to protect civilians becoming more acceptable. In particular, the Brahimi Report noted that 'there are situations in which peacekeepers not only should have the right, but are morally obliged to use force'.[77] This shift towards the inclusion of PoC in peacekeeping operations became institutionalised and professionalised within peacekeeping during the late 2000s as the Security Council began to mandate PoC as a priority task for many operations,[78] with the UN Department of Peacekeeping (DPKO) and the Department of Field Support (DFS) examining the operation of the concept in order to guide mandate implementation.[79] This expansion of the use of force in order to protect civilians and PoC as a priority task became further problematic in 2013 when the Security Council expanded the norm even further with the introduction of the Force Intervention Brigade (FIB) in the DRC – an issue which will be discussed in Chapters 5 and 6. The FIB, deployed alongside MONUSCO, was tasked, amongst other things, to 'ensure … effective protection of civilians under imminent threat of physical violence'.[80] Whilst this may not, initially, appear to differ greatly from other PoC mandates, the FIB was unique as it was authorised to undertake 'targeted offensive operations' to 'neutralise' armed groups, thereby permit-

75 H Willmot and S Sheeran, 'The Protection of Civilians Mandate in UN Peacekeeping Operations: Reconciling Protection Concepts and Practices' (2013) 95(891/892) IRRC 517–538, 521–522.

76 See, for example: M Ali Khalil, 'Legal Aspects of the Use of Force by United Nations Peacekeepers for the Protection of Civilians' in H Willmot, R Mamiya, S Sheeran and M Weller (eds) *Protection of Civilians* (OUP 2016).

77 UNGA, 'Report of the Panel on United Nations Peace Operations' ('Brahimi Report') (21 August 2000) UN Doc A/55/305-S/2000/809.

78 UNAMID (UNSC Res 1769 (31 July 2007) UN Doc S/RES/1769 para 15(a)(ii)); MONUC (UNSC Res 1856 (22 December 2008) UN Doc S/RES/1856 paras 3 and 6); MINURCAT (UNSC Res 1778 (25 September 2007) UN Doc S/RES/1778); UNMISS (UNSC Res 2057 (5 July 2012) UN Doc S/RES/2057).

79 UN DPKO/DFS, 'Draft Operational Concept on the Protection of Civilians in United Nations Peacekeeping Operations' (2010) <http://www.peacekeeping.org.uk/wp-content/uploads/2013/02/100129-DPKO-DFS-POC-Operational-Concept.pdf>.

80 UNSC Res 2098 (28 March 2013) UN Doc S/RES/2098, operative para 11(a)(i).

ting a significant level of force.[81] This force, in turn, could be used to protect civilians, marking a robust, protective modality which was a first for both peacekeeping and PoC. The FIB was then later encompassed within the general mandate of MONUSCO, which was similarly authorised to use force to protect civilians. Indeed, it is now common for the Security Council to act under Chapter VII of the UN Charter, permitting peacekeepers to 'use all necessary means', including the use of force, to 'protect civilians',[82] with its operations in Mali, Central African Republic and DRC, for example, all containing robust PoC mandates.[83] As previously noted, this then causes confusion over the peacekeeping operation's Charter basis and the practical implications of this (such as how much force is permissible), thereby again blurring the boundaries between peacekeeping and peace enforcement and the non-intervention line.

It could therefore be argued that the norm of PoC creates a double-edged expansion within peacekeeping's frameworks, consequently constricting the boundaries of the principle of non-intervention. Firstly, as it became a firmly established norm of peacekeeping, it created a further justification for intervention – similar to the development of the norm of democracy promotion – thereby expanding peacekeeping's normative framework and simultaneously constricting the principle of non-intervention. Secondly, it also had the effect of expanding peacekeeping's legal framework as it broadened the principle of limited use of force by permitting force to be used to protect civilians, given that force was permitted in defence of the mandate and PoC was now a mandated task. The potential for force to be used in fulfilment of this task thus appears limitless, again expanding peacekeeping's boundaries and undermining the principle of non-intervention.

A Priority for Whom?

In addition to the overlap with the use of force and the unclear normative and conceptual boundaries of PoC, its evolution into a priority task for peacekeepers is also questionable on two further grounds. Firstly, the very concept of PoC – to protect all civilians – is an impossible task for any actor, not least a UN peacekeeping operation with limited capabilities. Whilst peacekeepers may be able to 'mitigate harm', it is argued that 'you will always have shortcomings and the idea that you won't is illusory'.[84] It has therefore been

81 S/RES/1925 (n74).

82 See, for example: UNSC Res 2556 (18 December 2020) UN Doc S/RES/2556.

83 UNSC Res 2480 (28 June 2019) UN Doc S/RES/2480; UNSC Res 2499 (15 November 2019) UN Doc S/RES/2499; S/RES/2556 (ibid).

84 Interview with Senior Human Rights Officer in the Office of the UN High Commissioner of Human Rights ('Interviewee 13') (New York, 6 December 2019) DOI: <http://doi.org/10.17639/nott.7119> pg 59.

suggested that a mitigation, rather than a protection, framework would be preferable as peacekeepers simply 'can't protect'.[85]

This then leads to the second issue – whether the protection of civilians should even be a task for peacekeeping at all or whether it should be the primary responsibility of the host state and/or other actors within the state.[86] This is not to say that peacekeepers should not protect civilians but that protection efforts should ultimately be undertaken by the host government and its forces. As with the norm of democracy promotion, this would therefore require a narrower interpretation of peacekeeping's normative framework and thus a move back to a more traditional model of peacekeeping which does not include tasks such as PoC. Indeed, some UN personnel working with the field argue that the protection of civilians should be removed as a task, especially a priority task, for peacekeeping operations as it should, instead, be undertaken by national actors, with support from other international entities, if necessary, such as the UN country team.[87] This could be a desirable move as, for some PoC mandated peacekeeping operations, their prioritisation and development of PoC tools has created a reliance on the UN operation both by local communities and the host state.[88] As Chapter 6 will explore, this reliance has been particularly problematic for MONUSCO, with a strategic review noting that MONUSCO had worked 'to perfect its own system, strategies and tools' for PoC but had simultaneously 'tended to diminish the primary role of State authorities in assuming their protection responsibilities'.[89] There is a risk, then, that the host state may become reliant on a peacekeeping operation to protect civilians, rather than fulfilling the task itself, which, in turn, raises numerous issues.

First, given the temporary nature of peacekeeping, as 'you will be gone tomorrow', a peacekeeper 'cannot be part of a lasting solution'.[90] Therefore, PoC tools developed and implemented by UN peacekeeping operations, whilst admirable and necessary, may not create sustainable protection. As such, the emphasis must be on national or local ownership, with the operation aiding this and 'creating an enabling environment'.[91] Second, it arguably

85 ibid, 73.
86 See: PI Labuda, 'With or against the State? Reconciling the Protection of Civilians and Host-State Support in UN Peacekeeping' (IPI 2020).
87 Interview with Personnel in MONUSCO's Stabilisation Support Unit ('Interviewee 19') (Skype, 21 February 2020). DOI: <http://doi.org/10.17639/nott.7119>.
88 J Reynaert, 'MONUC/MONUSCO and Civilian Protection in the Kivus' (IPIS 2010).
89 UNSC, 'Transitioning from Stabilization to Peace: An Independent Strategic Review of MONUSCO' ('Strategic Review') (25 October 2019) UN Doc S/2019/842, para 77.
90 Interview with Former Senior Military Commander ('Interviewee 11') (New York (Skype) 3 December 2019) DOI: <http://doi.org/10.17639/nott.7119> pg 7.
91 See: J Russo and R Mamiya, 'The Primacy of Politics and the Protection of Civilians in UN Peacekeeping' (IPI 2022).

increases the interventionist nature of the peacekeeping operation as it is, in essence, undertaking the role of the state in this area. In this instance, then, if the host state is willing to accept the United Nations undertaking this protectorate role, it could be viewed not as intervention in the form of coercive action but, rather, intervention by invitation. That is, it could be likened to the joint operations that were discussed in Chapter 2, which some argue are a form of intervention by invitation because they are 'a function of the host state's consent' for UN intervention.[92] If PoC is to be viewed as a task which falls within a state's national jurisdiction, then, if it is established that the host state actively encourages or explicitly consents to a peacekeeping operation undertaking PoC activities, this could also be viewed as a form of intervention by invitation. This, in turn, presents a third issue with the norm of PoC – the creation of the image of the United Nations and its peacekeeping operations as 'the saviour', which 'would be able to bring protection to every corner of the country'.[93] From a TWAIL perspective, it could be argued that this idea of the United Nations as the protector or guardian of civilians is synonymous with the civilising mission and the colonial dichotomies of a 'civilised' external actor, enlightening and 'civilising' the subordinate 'other'. Indeed, it has been noted that it is a 'very convenient approach' to have the United Nations in charge of protecting and to default 'on a very inadequate organisation, an outlet to protect', resulting in 'basically substituting to regalian powers that the state cannot implement'.[94]

The inclusion of PoC as a priority task for peacekeepers may therefore be seen as not only expanding peacekeeping's interventionist nature but as, again, reinforcing the patterns of domination and subordination which have been prevalent throughout the development of the principle of non-intervention and, now, the evolution of peacekeeping. Furthermore, whilst PoC predominantly contributes to peacekeeping's normative framework, its impact on legal principles, such as the use of force, and its potential invocation of international law obligations, such as IHL, result in the norm also contributing to peacekeeping's legal framework. As was discussed with the other principles and norms, the impact or effect the norm then has on peacekeeping's boundaries and the principle of non-intervention is dependent on how it is interpreted and applied. That is, if PoC is interpreted narrowly, it constricts the red elastic boundary line around peacekeeping, consequently reinforcing the principle of non-intervention. On the other hand, if PoC is broadly interpreted and applied, as it is when mandated as a priority task, then this significantly expands peacekeeping's boundaries, permitting potentially limitless intervention and thereby undermining the principle of non-intervention.

92 Labuda (n86).
93 Interviewee 13 (n84) 73.
94 ibid.

Prohibition of Sexual Exploitation and Abuse

As with the norm of protection of civilians, the prohibition of sexual exploitation and abuse (SEA) by peacekeepers can also be said to have clear legal underpinnings in international humanitarian, criminal and human rights law. For example, within IHL, rape and sexual violence is prohibited in both international and non-international armed conflicts,[95] whilst international criminal law lists rape and other forms of sexual violence as a crime against humanity.[96] Therefore, as with PoC, whilst the prohibition of SEA predominantly contributes to peacekeeping's normative framework, it also makes a subsidiary contribution to peacekeeping's legal framework.

The norm of prohibition of SEA, however, differs slightly from the other two norms discussed within this chapter. Firstly, whereas democracy promotion and PoC could be generally viewed as positive or proactive norms that focus on altering the state, the prohibition of SEA is concerned with preventing certain acts committed by peacekeepers and therefore attempts to effect change within the peacekeeping operation itself, rather than the state. Secondly, as a result of the controversy of SEA by UN peacekeepers, the norm has been relatively slow to develop, due to a mix of the United Nations' 'gross institutional failure' to handle allegations[97] and member states' reluctance to prosecute its own troops when they have committed such acts. This then leads to a culture of impunity and a stagnating norm, with slow progress made in addressing SEA – something which has not occurred with the other two norms, given their rapid expansion in a relatively short timeframe. In relation to the principle of non-intervention, the prohibition of SEA, as a peacekeeping norm, again differs from the other norms as it is not, in itself, interventionist. Rather, it is attempting to prevent a form of intervention – SEA – and, as such, may be viewed as a norm which reinforces the principle of non-intervention as it attempts to limit peacekeeping's boundaries.

One Case Too Many

As with peacekeeping's other norms, the prohibition of sexual exploitation and abuse emerged within UN peacekeeping in the 1990s when, as Chapter 2

95 Protocol Additional to the Geneva Conventions of 12 August 1949 relating to the Protection of Victims of International Armed Conflicts (Protocol I) (6 June 1977) and relating to the Protection of Victims of Non-International Armed Conflicts (Protocol II) (8 June 1977).

96 Article 7(1)(g) Rome Statute of the International Criminal Court (last amended 2010) (17 July 1998). See also: Articles 8(2)(b)(xxii) violation in IAC and 8(e)(vi) violation in NIAC. For the first definition of sexual violence, see: *Prosecutor v Akayesu* (Judgment) ICTR-96-4-T (2 September 1998).

97 'Panel Slams UN for "Gross Institutional Failure" to Act on CAR Child Sex Allegations' (17 December 2015) <https://www.dw.com/en/panel-slams-un-for-gross-institutional-failure-to-act-on-car-child-sex-allegations/a-18925783>.

discussed, the eroding of the Cold War paralysis led to a revival of UN peacekeeping. In particular, it developed after numerous allegations of misconduct by UN peacekeepers, particularly in Cambodia and Bosnia, with UN personnel accused of involvement in the use of prostitutes,[98] trafficking and forced sex work.[99] Initially, there was a reluctance by the United Nations 'to recognise the direct and indirect involvement of peacekeepers in trafficking' and other acts of SEA.[100] The first attempt to address the issue was noted in Secretary-General Kofi Annan's 1999 bulletin on the 'Observance by UN Forces of International Humanitarian Law'[101] – again highlighting the norm's legal underpinnings. This was then followed by investigations of the UN High Commission for Refugees (UNHCR) and the Office of Internal Oversight Services (OIOS)[102] and a further bulletin in 2003, this time specifically addressing SEA by clearly defining and elaborating on prohibited acts and identifying the roles and responsibilities of relevant actors.[103] This included member states which were tasked with undertaking criminal prosecutions in their domestic jurisdictions, if a proper investigation amounted to evidence supporting an allegation of SEA. Again, within this bulletin, reference was made to the 1999 SG bulletin on IHL, noting that operations under 'UN command and control are prohibited from committing acts of sexual exploitation and sexual abuse' and 'have a particular duty of care towards women and children', pursuant to section 7 of the 1999 Bulletin,[104] thus, again reinforcing the norm's legal underpinnings.

Annan then followed this initial bulletin with a commissioned report in 2005, after acknowledging that the procedures in place 'were manifestly inadequate and that a fundamental change in approach was needed'.[105] The Zeid

98 The number of prostitutes within Cambodia rose from 6,000 before the mission to more than 25,000 in 1993. See: S Whitworth, *Men, Militarism and UN Peacekeeping* (Lynne Rienner 2004) 67–68.

99 The issue of SEA in Cambodia was further compounded by the shipping of an additional 800,000 condoms to the country to prevent the spread of HIV and other STIs. See: O Simic, *Regulation of Sexual Conduct in UN Peacekeeping Operations* (Springer 2012) 41. See also: K Bolkovac, *The Whistleblower* (Palgrave 2011); J Murray, 'Who Will Police the Peace-Builders? The Failure to Establish Accountability for the Participation of United Nations Civilian Police in the Trafficking of Women in Post-Conflict Bosnia and Herzegovina' (2003) 34(2) ColumHRLR 475–528, 492–493.

100 ibid, Simic, 42.

101 UNSG Bulletin (n52).

102 UNGA, 'Investigation into Sexual Exploitation of Refugees by Aid Workers in West Africa' (11 October 2002) UN Doc A/57/465; UNGA Res 57/306 (22 May 2003) UN Doc A/RES/57/306.

103 UNSG, 'Secretary-General Bulletin: Special Measures for Protection for Sexual Exploitation and Abuse' (9 October 2003) UN Doc ST/SGB/2003/13, sections 1–4.

104 ibid, 2.2.

105 UNGA, 'A Comprehensive Strategy to Eliminate Future Sexual Exploitation and Abuse in United Nations Peacekeeping Operations' ('Zeid Report') (24 March 2005) UN Doc A/59/710, 1.

Report, for the first time, provided a comprehensive strategy to eliminate SEA in peacekeeping operations.[106] This included establishing independent investigative teams, curfew setting and establishing clear lines of communication to allow for local populations to report allegations.[107] These could therefore be viewed as boundary setting initiatives, particularly the imposition of a curfew, as they restricted peacekeepers behaviour and reaffirmed peacekeeping's boundaries, thereby reinforcing the principle of non-intervention. The Zeid Report also acknowledged that the decision to prosecute peacekeepers was left to the troop-contributing nation and was, therefore, a sovereign decision. This then highlights two key problems within the norm of SEA. Firstly, this early formulation of the norm was reactive instead of proactive; that is, it focused upon how to address allegations after conduct had occurred, rather than attempting to prevent the conduct. Secondly, it was (and remains) based on a reliance on the troop-contributing country (TCC) to prosecute their troops if they commit SEA whilst acting as a UN peacekeeper.[108] Thus, the norm is beholden to member states' sovereignty, which has led to a culture of impunity as states have been reluctant to prosecute their own troops, as will be further explored later in this section and in subsequent chapters.

UNSG Annan's 'zero tolerance policy'[109] was further developed by his successors, such as UNSG Ban Ki Moon, who also issued a bulletin addressing SEA, expanding the norm further by including the prohibition of discrimination, sexual harassment and the abuse of authority within the Secretariat.[110] Ban Ki Moon then commissioned a report from the 'High Level Panel on Peace Operations' (HIPPO Report) in 2014, which undertook an extensive analysis of the challenges facing peacekeeping.[111] The HIPPO Report concluded that, despite the introduction of the norm prohibiting SEA and the 'persuasive rhetoric', the United Nations was still not putting the norm of zero tolerance policy into practice.[112] The report therefore recommended, amongst other things, that states, particularly TCCs, 'immediately and vigorously investigate and prosecute all credible allega-

106 ibid.
107 ibid.
108 Per UN Model Status of Forces Agreement (SOFA) peacekeeping troops are under the exclusive authority of their home country, not the UN.
109 UN News, 'Annan Further Enhances "Zero Tolerance" of Sexual Abuse by UN Peacekeepers' (*UN News*, 13 October 2006) <https://news.un.org/en/story/2006/10/196122-annan-further-enhances-zero-tolerance-sexual-abuse-un-peacekeepers>.
110 UNSG, 'Secretary-General Bulletin: Prohibition of Discrimination, Harassment, Including Sexual Harassment and Abuse of Authority' (11 February 2008) UN Doc ST/SGB/2008/5.
111 UNGA-SC, 'Report of the High-Level Independent Panel on Peace Operations' ("HIPPO Report") (17 June 2015) UN Doc A/70/95-S/2015/446.
112 ibid, 80.

tions'.[113] SG Ban Ki Moon then reiterated this in a report on implementing these recommendations, when he also noted that 'a single substantiated case of [SEA] involving UN personnel is one case too many'.[114] This was then buttressed by a Security Council resolution in 2016 which reaffirmed its support for the United Nations' zero tolerance policy and endorsed the Secretary-General's decision to repatriate units which had committed SEA and requested the SG to replace any military or police units whose troop- or police-contributing country had not investigated allegations.[115] Whilst the endorsement of the Council could be viewed as greater support for the norm, again, the interpretation of the norm during this period was limited to reacting to SEA, as opposed to prevention, and was dependent on member states' complicity.

More recently, this approach has also been taken by the current Secretary-General, Antonio Guterres, who launched a high-level task force to prevent and respond to SEA,[116] along with a 'Zero Tolerance', four-pronged strategy.[117] At a similar time, documents such as the 'Military Aide Memoire' which outlined guidance for Commanders on measures to combat SEA in UN military were published to complement relevant training prior to and during deployment to peacekeeping operations.[118] This Zero Tolerance strategy again aimed to prioritise the rights of victims, end impunity through strengthened reporting and investigations, engage with civil society and improve strategic communication,[119] thus building upon the same normative frameworks which his predecessors had set. However, Guterres also broadened the norm slightly, re-interpreting it to include a 'Clear Check' system

113 ibid, 86, paras 284–285.

114 UNGA, 'Report of the Secretary-General: Special Measures for Protection from Sexual Exploitation and Sexual Abuse' (16 February 2016) UN Doc A/70/729, 1; UNGA-SC, 'The Future of United Nations Peace Operations: Implementation of the Recommendations of the High-Level Independent Panel on Peace Operations' (2 September 2015) UN Doc A/70/357-S/2015/682.

115 UNSC Res 2272 (11 March 2016) UN Doc S/RES/2272, 1–2.

116 UN Peacekeeping, 'The Secretary-General Announces Task Force on UN Response to Sexual Exploitation and Abuse' (6 January 2017) <https://peacekeeping.un.org/en/secretary-general-announces-task-force-un-response-to-sexual-exploitation-and-abuse>.

117 See: UNGA, 'Report of the Secretary-General: Special Measures for Protection from Sexual Exploitation and Abuse: A New Approach' (15 May 2017) UN Doc A/71/818 and A/71/818/Corr 1. See also update on the strategy: UNGA, 'Report of the Secretary General: Special Measures for Protection from Sexual Exploitation and Abuse' (20 March 2018) UN Doc A/72/751 and A/72/751/Corr.1.

118 UN Peacekeeping, 'The Military Aide Memoire: United Nations Measures against Sexual Exploitation and Abuse' (October 2017) <https://resourcehub01.blob.core.windows.net/$web/PK%20Training/Materials/000%20References/016-1%20The%20Military%20Aide%20Memoire%20United%20Nations%20Measures%20against%20Sexual%20Exploitation%20and%20Abuse.pdf>.

119 UNGA, UN Doc A/71/818 (n121).

which prevented UN staff who had been dismissed for SEA allegations from being re-employed.[120] This developed the norm to be more proactive than it previously had been, by attempting to prevent or mitigate the risk of SEA occurring within peacekeeping operations.

For peacekeeping's legal and normative frameworks, then, the prohibition of SEA has added to these frameworks but, unlike the previous two norms, it has not expanded peacekeeping's interventionist boundaries but, rather, has attempted to limit peacekeeper's behaviour and therefore the operation's interventionist nature. As such, it has reinforced, rather than undermined, the principle of non-intervention. The norm is therefore somewhat unique in that whereas a broadening of the other two norms would expand peacekeeping's boundaries and its interventionist potential, consequently constricting the principle of non-intervention, an expansion of the prohibition of SEA would have the opposite effect. That is, an expansion of the norm would constrict peacekeeping's boundaries by restricting peacekeepers' behaviour, and therefore an operation's interventionist potential, whilst simultaneously reinforcing the principle of non-intervention.

Reverse Intervention

When considering the norm's relationship with the principle of non-intervention, it could be argued that, in essence, the norm of prohibition of SEA can be viewed as a form of intervention in reverse. That is, it is not the norm itself which is a form of intervention but, rather, it is the act (SEA) which it aims to prohibit that is the intervention. By extension, it could also be argued that the slow development of the norm could be seen to be a form of indirect intervention as member states' reluctance or slow progress in taking significant action to prevent it occurring is enabling this intervention. Indeed, despite the development of the norm, SEA remains the most problematic issue within UN peacekeeping,[121] with the operational initiatives such as the pre-deployment training and 'no excuse cards' found to be significantly lacking.[122] Furthermore, highlighting how peacekeeping's normative framework can overlap with its legal framework, some have argued that the involvement of peacekeepers in SEA is politically advantageous to warring parties in the host state, providing them with financial and

120 See: UN Clear Check, 'The UN Efforts to Combat SEA/Sexual Harassment' (21 May 2021) <https://unsceb.org/sites/default/files/2021-05/2021%20-%20Briefing%20Note%20on%20Clear%20Check.pdf>.

121 For current reports, see: UN Conduct in Field Missions, 'Sexual Exploitation and Abuse: Table of Allegations' <https://conduct.unmissions.org/table-of-allegations>.

122 See: ICAI, 'Sexual Exploitation and Abuse by International Peacekeepers' (ICAI September 2020) <https://icai.independent.gov.uk/wp-content/uploads/ICAI-SEA-Review.pdf>.

propagandist benefits and thereby breaching the United Nations' principle of impartiality.[123] Stemming from this there are then what could be categorised as three main problems with (or related to) the norm of prohibition which hinders its evolution, its sufficient implementation to adequately address or eradicate SEA and its support of the principle of non-intervention.

Firstly, despite the development of mechanisms for reporting allegations, including a more open dialogue with civilians, many victims are still reluctant to report SEA for numerous reasons, including a fear of retaliation by the perpetrator[124] or stigmatisation and ostracism from their families and communities.[125] This then links with the second notable problem – the power differentials between these vulnerable people and the UN peacekeepers deployed to protect them within volatile post-conflict environments. This occurs, in particular, in the form of gendered power relations, whereby peacekeepers who are trained as combat military men may have social practices towards local women and girls which 'flow from military-masculine identities constructed around the notion of the inferior feminine "other"'.[126] Indeed, research has found that peacekeeping operations with a higher proportion of female peacekeepers and personnel, from TCCs with better records of gender equality, have lower levels of SEA allegations.[127] This suggests that gender parity may go some way in reducing SEA but, ultimately, would not address the root cause.[128] Similarly, as peacekeeping operations are composed of peacekeepers from a vast array of countries, there are numerous cultural attitudes within the TCCs with differing rules, for example, on the age of consent and the legality of prostitution.[129] This therefore creates cultural variance within peacekeeping operations which has been identified as problematic by representatives of major international humanitarian organisations who note that, 'some troops come in, much more kind of focused, willing to engage and at least try to fulfil the mandate', whilst others 'have no interest or no appetite to

123 K Grady, 'Sexual Exploitation and Abuse by UN Peacekeepers: A Threat to Impartiality' (2010) 17(2) IntPeace 215–228.

124 S Lee and S Bartels, '"They Put a Few Coins in Your Hand to Drop a Baby in You": Study of Peacekeeper-Fathered Children in Haiti' (2019) 27(2) IntPeacekeep 177–209.

125 C Csáky, 'No One to Turn to: The Under-Reporting of Child Sexual Exploitation and Abuse by Aid Workers and Peacekeepers' (Save the Children 2008) 12–13.

126 P Higate, 'Peacekeepers, Masculinities, and Sexual Exploitation' (2007) 10(1) MenMasculin 99–119, 101. See also: L Howard, *Power in Peacekeeping* (CUP 2019).

127 S Karim and K Beardsley, 'Explaining Sexual Exploitation and Abuse in Peacekeeping Missions: The Role of Female Peacekeepers and Gender Equality in Contributing Countries' (2016) 53(1) JPeaceResearch 100–115.

128 ibid.

129 C van der Mark, 'Sexual Exploitation and Abuse by UN Peacekeepers: Why the Problem Continues to Persist' (PeaceWomen 2012) 37–38.

engage into an environment that is often alien to them'.[130] As such, these latter troops 'make sure they are safe' and then 'you see quite absurd kind of stuff in many of these peacekeeping operations, which is quite discouraging'.[131] The norm of prohibition of SEA therefore struggles to impose a normative standard on culturally and sociologically diverse peacekeepers, in order to prohibit the intervention of peacekeepers through SEA.

This then leads to the third significant problem within SEA – impunity. As previously noted, when an allegation of SEA has been substantiated it is left to the home state (TCC) to prosecute their peacekeepers,[132] which has proved to be 'exceedingly rare'.[133] Whilst peacekeepers enjoy functional immunity when acting within their UN role,[134] in theory, civilian peacekeepers who are accused of SEA are acting outside of their official functions and therefore should be prosecuted by local authorities, whilst military peacekeepers who commit SEA ought to be prosecuted by their home state (the TCC).[135] However, again, the problem is one of implementation, particularly for acts committed by military peacekeepers as they remain under the command and control of their host state, which has a Memorandum of Understanding with the United Nations, and it is therefore the TCC which is solely responsible for peacekeepers' accountability.[136] This practice is also enshrined within legal instruments such as the Status of Force Agreement (SOFA) which provides that any criminal prosecutions of peacekeepers must be with the TCC, not the host state, thereby protecting peacekeepers by granting them immunity from prosecutions by the host state.[137] As such, the complex legal and normative rules surrounding peacekeepers' immunity, combined with a reluctance by member states to prosecute, perhaps based on either a lack of resources or

130 Interview with Senior DRC/Great Lakes Coordinator from International Organisation ('Interviewee 2') (Geneva, 12 November 2018) DOI: <http://doi.org/10.17639/nott.7119> pg 23.
131 ibid.
132 See: Z Deen-Racsmány, 'The Relevance of Disciplinary Authority and Criminal Jurisdiction to Locating Effective Control under the ARIO' (2016) 13(2) IOLR 341–378.
133 K Jennings, 'The Immunity Dilemma: Peacekeepers' Crimes and the UN's Response' (E-International Relations 18 September 2017) <https://www.e-ir.info/2017/09/18/the-immunity-dilemma-peacekeepers-crimes-and-the-uns-response/>.
134 Convention on the Privileges and Immunities of the United Nations (CPIUN) (1946–1947) 1 UNTS, 15.
135 See: R Freedman, 'UNaccountable: A New Approach to Peacekeepers and Sexual Abuse' (2018) 29(3) EJIL 961–985, 963.
136 See: Z Deen-Racsmány, 'The Amended UN Model Memorandum of Understanding: A New Incentive for States to Discipline and Prosecute Members of National Peacekeeping Contingents?' (2011) 16(2) JCSL 321–355.
137 See: R Burke, 'Status of Forces Deployed on UN Peacekeeping Operations: Jurisdictional Immunity' (2011) 16(1) JCSL 63–104.

a desire to maintain their reputation and TCC status, has led to a culture of impunity in relation to SEA.[138]

As TWAIL scholar Chimni has noted, the lack of institutional and individual responsibility means that the United Nations represents 'the rule of nobody', whereby 'a myriad small decisions are taken and interpretations advanced for which no one in particular is responsible'.[139] This is particularly the case for SEA by peacekeepers, where 'the commitment to accountability by TCC and member states is not where it needs to be'; 'there is still resistance to having adequate accountability' from these actors and 'as long as that is the case, the UN will only be able to do so much'.[140] The interpretation and applications of the norm of prohibition of SEA therefore present a relatively weak contribution to both the normative and legal frameworks surrounding peacekeeping. That is, there is the potential for these accountability rules to be established as part of the legal and normative frameworks but only if member states are willing to apply them. In other words, there is the shadow of a framework or boundary line established here but it is not fully realised because of member states' resistance to holding their own troops accountable. For the principle of non-intervention, this treads a fine line between supporting and undermining the principle – the more peacekeepers are held accountable, the stronger the legal and normative frameworks on accountability within peacekeeping become and therefore the greater the support for the principle of non-intervention. On the other hand, the less willing states are to apply these rules, the weaker peacekeeping's frameworks in this area become, with a risk that this impunity would undermine the principle of non-intervention.

Furthermore, from a TWAIL perspective, this could be viewed as another replication of the continual colonial power dynamics of domination and subordination, which is recreated here on two levels. The very act of a peacekeeper committing SEA is arguably an example of a dominant external actor (peacekeepers) exploiting their position to the detriment of the vulnerable subordinate other (local populations), whilst member states' reluctance and the United Nations' inability to prosecute such acts could also be viewed as an example of domination and subordination, with the hegemonic powers unwilling or unable to support the subordinate victims. Indeed, it could be argued further that this exploitation of the Global South peoples by the external actor is reminiscent of the colonial civilising missions and the abuses which were perpetuated during this time.[141] Further, the complex accountability rules and the inability

138 Freedman (n135) 969–974.

139 Chimni (n48) 22.

140 Interviewee 13 (n84) 75.

141 See for example: D Van Reybrouck, *Congo: The Epic History of a People* (Fourth Estate 2015).

of the United Nations to hold peacekeepers liable are what TWAIL scholars would perceive as international law's complicity in the 'repression and silencing of non-European and other peoples'.[142] That is, the structure of the United Nations and the rules on accountability effectively shield those peacekeepers who commit offensives and, by extension, their TCC, at the expense of the victims. In other words, international law protects the hegemonic powers and TCCs from the Global South whilst silencing the Global South victims of SEA. Indeed, some senior personnel within the UN Secretariat believe that there is a lot more which the United Nations could be doing to counter this, arguing that 'we could escalate the pressure quite significantly, we could be more public about it, alternatively we could repatriate it'.[143] In particular, they note that the Secretary-General has the prerogative to do this 'but the backlash he would receive in return would be severe'.[144] Once again, then, the deeply entrenched political power dynamics within the UN system, which were explored in Chapter 2, reappear here, with the United Nations beholden to the member states in somewhat of a deadlock which, ultimately, results in the oppression of peoples of the Global South. However, in somewhat of a softening of this, in 2016 the Security Council granted the Secretary-General the right to repatriate peacekeeper units if the TCC failed to prosecute alleged perpetrators of SEA within six months.[145] Whilst this goes some way in clarifying and reinforcing the SG's authority, targeting 'the part of the accountability chain that the Secretariat cannot' and adding 'new impetus and political support' to the United Nations' ongoing agenda on SEA, there still remain doubts about the operationalisation and practical feasibility of repatriation.[146]

The norm of prohibition of SEA, then, has the potential to significantly contribute to peacekeeping's normative and legal frameworks and, consequently, reinforce the principle of non-intervention. However, its contribution is limited by member states' reluctance to fully embrace the norm and hold peacekeepers accountable. When this is compared with the rapid expansion of the other two norms explored within this book, it, again, highlights the perpetual power dynamics that are embedded within both the United Nations and international law which were first highlighted in Chapter 2. That is, it appears that the norms of democracy promotion and PoC align with the dominant states' interests and agenda and, therefore, have been

142 JT Gathii, 'Twenty-Second Annual Grotius Lecture: The Promise of International Law: A Third World View' (2021) 114 ASILProc 165–187, 182.

143 Interview with Senior UN DPO Personnel, Policy, Evaluation and Training Division ('Interviewee 10') (New York, 3 December 2019) <http://doi.org/10.17639/nott.7119> pg 74.

144 ibid.

145 S/RES/2272 (n115).

146 J Whalan, 'Dealing with Disgrace: Addressing Sexual Exploitation and Abuse in UN Peacekeeping' (IPI 2017).

developed quite rapidly. On the other hand, the norm of prohibition of SEA has not advanced at the same pace, perhaps because it could potentially challenge the dominant powers and TCCs if their peacekeepers are accused of committing SEA. Thus, the agenda of the hegemonic powers has prevailed at the expense, on occasions, of the Global South.

The norm of prohibition of SEA has therefore provided a thin contribution to peacekeeping's normative framework, with a subsidiary contribution to peacekeeping's legal framework through its potential to invoke laws on accountability, potential overlap with the principle of impartiality and, as noted earlier, its underpinning in IHL and ICL. This, in turn, both supports and undermines the principle of non-intervention, as the inclusion of the norm within peacekeeping's frameworks reinforces non-intervention, yet, at the same time, states' reluctance to support the norm does little to prevent SEA, thereby undermining the principle.

Conclusions: Peacekeeping as Intervention?

Whilst peacekeeping does not possess an articulated legal or normative framework, as this chapter and the previous chapter have explored, there exist principles and norms which, together, form a complex peacekeeping framework. On the one hand, the fundamental principles of consent, impartiality and limited use of force constitute peacekeeping's legal framework, which lies at the heart of peacekeeping. And on the other hand, the norms of democracy promotion, protection of civilians and prohibition of sexual exploitation and abuse form peacekeeping's broader normative framework, which surrounds the legal framework. As has been seen within this chapter, however, these frameworks do not exist in isolation but, rather, at times, overlap with the norms of PoC and prohibition of SEA possessing legal underpinnings which introduces elements of international law into peacekeeping's legal framework.

Furthermore, as Chapters 3 and 4 have highlighted, these principles and norms rarely live harmoniously and instead 'coexist in a competitive arena' with the normative composition of a peacekeeping operation being 're-balanced each time'.[147] There is therefore, again, a degree of overlap between the principles and norms with an interpretation of one norm impacting the composition of another norm or principle – such as PoC and the use of force or the prohibition of SEA and impartiality. Indeed, this chapter has demonstrated how these norms have continually evolved and been re-interpreted, typically, in line with the fluctuating interventionist practices or global trends which were highlighted in Chapter 2. That is, when there has been strong non-intervention rhetoric, such as during decolonisation, the principle and norms have been interpreted narrowly, limiting their scope. Conversely,

147 Karlsrud (n2) 527.

when there has been increased support for intervention, as occurred in the post-Cold War era, the norms have been interpreted more broadly, thereby expanding the concepts.

Peacekeeping's legal and normative frameworks could therefore be imagined as red elastic bands that can continually expand and contract depending on how the principles and norms are reimagined. The frameworks are thus fluid which, in turn, means that the boundary between peacekeeping and intervention is also fluid; indeed, the chapter has demonstrated how differing interpretations and applications of the norms may result in peacekeeping becoming, on occasions, a form of intervention, that is, a form of coercive action designed to influence change or alter the host state – such as when peacekeeping operations undertake extensive democracy promotion tasks or apply the HRDDP, placing ultimatums on the state to alter their armed forces. As this chapter has explored, where the concepts are interpreted narrowly (typically within a traditional peacekeeping operation) then the boundaries of peacekeeping are limited and so too is peacekeeping's interventionist potential. However, when they are interpreted broadly, as with many contemporary multi-dimensional operations, the boundaries are significantly stretched, often to their very limits, if not beyond, thereby undermining or potentially contravening the principle of non-intervention. It could therefore be argued that there must be a limit to how far these concepts evolve before they are no longer peacekeeping principles or norms, acting as a barrier between peacekeeping and intervention, but, instead, become intervention in themselves. Indeed, at various points throughout this chapter it has been argued that some norms could be interpreted more narrowly, thereby shrinking peacekeeping's boundaries. For this to occur it would require a move away from the large multi-dimensional operation towards the more traditional model – a matter which will be explored in further detail in the subsequent chapters.

Furthermore, this chapter has also highlighted how the unequal power dynamics and colonial legacies which were identified within the principle of non-intervention in Chapter 2 also exist within peacekeeping, particularly through the inherent imbalance within the Security Council, creating continual examples of Anghie's dynamic of difference. Peacekeeping's frameworks and an application of these frameworks can therefore, at times, be seen to reinforce or recreate the colonial dichotomies of domination and subordination, particularly where there is an element of coercion or peacekeeping is taken closer to the intervention line. This, again, underlines the argument that many features of both international law and international institutions or legal systems 'acknowledge and reinforce the substantial power differentials between [their] participants'.[148] This, in turn, leads back to the notion that international

148 Charlesworth (n31) 34.

law is based on 'fictions' of state equality and state consent[149] which leads to the more general debate over whether international law is truly international.[150] Therefore, as was seen with the principle of non-intervention in Chapter 2, the influence of colonialism and the persistent power differentials have also permeated the concept of peacekeeping.

If the contents of this book can be imagined as a three-tiered pyramid, then, whilst Chapter 2 explored the top of this pyramid – the principle of non-intervention – the third and fourth chapters have explored the second layer – the most prevalent form of intervention today, peacekeeping. Having now established the legal and normative frameworks which demarcate peacekeeping's boundary line, Chapters 5 and 6 will take this further by exploring the third and final layer to the pyramid – peacekeeping in practice. Building upon these explorations of non-intervention and peacekeeping, the subsequent chapters will examine how peacekeeping's principles and norms have been interpreted and applied in the United Nations' peacekeeping operations in the DRC, as this has been one of the United Nations' most long-lasting operations. Thus, the analysis of peacekeeping's relationship with the principle of non-intervention will be taken deeper, with the aim of ascertaining specific incidences in which an interpretation or application of the norms and principles may contract or expand peacekeeping's boundaries and therefore support or undermine the principle of non-intervention.

References

——, 'Panel Slams UN for "Gross Institutional Failure" To Act on CAR Child Sex Allegations' (17 December 2015) <https://www.dw.com/en/panel-slams-un-for-gross-institutional-failure-to-act-on-car-child-sex-allegations/a-18925783>

Ali Khalil M, 'Legal Aspects of the Use of Force by United Nations Peacekeepers for the Protection of Civilians' in H Willmot, R Mamiya, S Sheeran and M Weller (eds) *Protection of Civilians* (OUP 2016)

Anghie A, *Imperialism, Sovereignty and the Making of International Law* (CUP 2007)

Annan K, 'Democracy as an International Issue' (2002) 8(2) GG 135–142

Annan K, *Interventions: A Life in War and Peace* (Penguin 2013)

Bolkovac K, *The Whistleblower* (Palgrave 2011)

Burke, 'Status of Forces Deployed on UN Peacekeeping Operations: Jurisdictional Immunity' (2011) 16(1) JCSL 63–104

Burke J, 'Congo Election Runner-Up Rejects Tshisekedi Victory as "Electoral Coup"' (*The Guardian*, 10 January 2019) <https://www.theguardian.com/world/2019/jan/10/congo-election-felix-tshisekedi-declared-winner-in-contentious-result>

149 G Simpson, 'Imagined Consent: Democratic Liberalism in International Legal Theory' (1994) 15 AYIL 103–128.

150 L Eslava and S Pahuja, 'Between Resistance and Reform: TWAIL and the Universality of International Law' (2011) 3(1) TradeL&Dev 103–130.

Carver F, 'Linked Up Peacekeeping' (*Protection Approaches*, July 2022) <https://protectionapproaches.org/linked-up-peacekeeping>

Carver F, 'Peacekeeping Desperately Needs a New Model, and a People-Centred Approach Could Work' (*Pass Blue*, 4 September 2022) <https://www.passblue.com/2022/09/04/peacekeeping-desperately-needs-a-new-model-and-a-people-centered-approach-could-work/>

Charlesworth H, 'Democracy and International Law' in H Charlesworth (ed) *Recueil des Cours 371: Collected Courses of the Hague Academy of International Law 2014* (Brill 2015)

Charlesworth H, 'International Legal Encounters with Democracy' (2017) 8(6) GlobalPolicy 34–43

Chimni BS, 'International Institutions Today: An Imperial Global State in the Making' (2004) 15(1) EJIL 1–37

Clapham A, 'Protection of Civilians under International Human Rights Law' in H Willmot, R Mamiya, S Sheeran and M Weller (eds) *Protection of Civilians* (OUP 2016)

Convention on the Privileges and Immunities of the United Nations (CPIUN) (1946–1947) 1 UNTS

Cooper Ramo J, 'The Five Virtues of Kofi Annan' (*Time*, 4 September 2000) <http://content.time.com/time/world/article/0,8599,2056090,00.html>

Crawford J, 'Democracy and International Law' (1993) 64(1) BYIL 113–133

Csáky C, *No One to Turn To: The Under-Reporting of Child Sexual Exploitation and Abuse by Aid Workers and Peacekeepers* (Save the Children 2008)

de Coning C, Karlsrud J, Troost P, 'Towards More People-Centric Peace Operations: From "Extension of State Authority" to "Strengthening Inclusive State-Society Relations"' (2015) 4(1):49 Stability: International Journal of Security & Development 1–13

Deen-Racsmány Z, 'The Amended UN Model Memorandum of Understanding: A New Incentive for States to Discipline and Prosecute Members of National Peacekeeping Contingents?' (2011) 16(2) JCSL 321–355

Deen-Racsmány Z, 'The Relevance of Disciplinary Authority and Criminal Jurisdiction to Locating Effective Control under the ARIO' (2016) 13(2) IOLR 341–378

Eslava L and Pahuja S, 'Between Resistance and Reform: TWAIL and the Universality of International Law' (2011) 3(1) TradeL&Dev 103–130

Fjelde H and Smidt HM, 'Protesting the Vote? Peacekeeping Presence and the Risk of Electoral Violence' (2022) 52(3) British Journl of Political Science 1113–1132

Freedman R, 'UNaccountable: A New Approach to Peacekeepers and Sexual Abuse' (2018) 29(3) EJIL 961–985

Gathii JT, 'A Critical Appraisal of the International Legal Tradition of Taslim Olawale Elias' (2008) 21(2) LJIL 317–349

Gathii JT, 'Twenty-Second Annual Grotius Lecture: The Promise of International Law: A Third World View' (2021) 114 ASILProc 165–187

Geneva Convention Relative to the Protection of Civilian Persons in Time of War (Fourth Geneva Convention) (12 August 1949) (75 UNTS 287)

Gilder A, 'The UN and the Protection of Civilians: Sustaining the Momentum' (2023) 28 JCSL 1–32

Grady K, 'Sexual Exploitation and Abuse by UN Peacekeepers: A Threat to Impartiality' (2010) 17(2) IntPeace 215–228

Heldt B, 'Peacekeeping Operations and Transitions to Democracy' in H Fjelde and K Höglund (eds) *Building Peace, Creating Conflict* (Nordic Academic Press 2011)

Heldt B and Wallensteen P, *Peacekeeping Operations: Global Patterns of Intervention and Success, 1948–2004* (3rd edn, Folke Bernadotte Academy Publications 2007)

Henckaerts JM and Doswald-Beck L, *Customary International Humanitarian Law. Volume 1: Rules* (CUP 2005) Rules 87–195

Higate P, 'Peacekeepers, Masculinities, and Sexual Exploitation' (2007) 10(1) MenMasculin 99–119

Howard L, *Power in Peacekeeping* (CUP 2019)

ICAI, 'Sexual Exploitation and Abuse by International Peacekeepers' (ICAI, September 2020) <https://icai.independent.gov.uk/wp-content/uploads/ICAI-SEA-Review.pdf>

Interview with Senior DRC/Great Lakes Coordinator from International Organisation ('Interviewee 2') (Geneva, 12 November 2018) DOI: <http://doi.org/10.17639/nott.7119>

Interview with Independent Expert and Former UN Political Adviser ('Interviewee 8') (New York, 26 November 2019) DOI: <http://doi.org/10.17639/nott.7119>

Interview with Senior UN DPO Personnel, Policy, Evaluation and Training Division ('Interviewee 10') (New York, 3 December 2019) DOI: <http://doi.org/10.17639/nott.7119>

Interview with Former Senior Military Commander ('Interviewee 11') (New York (Skype) 3 December 2019) DOI: <http://doi.org/10.17639/nott.7119>

Interview with Mona Ali Khalil, former Senior Legal Officer of the UN Office of the Legal Counsel, Director of MAK LAW International and an Affiliate of the Harvard Law School Program on International Law and Armed Conflict ('Interviewee 12') (New York (Skype) 5 December 2019) DOI: <http://doi.org/10.17639/nott.7119>

Interview with Senior Human Rights Officer in the Office of the UN High Commissioner of Human Rights ('Interviewee 13') (New York, 6 December 2019) DOI: <http://doi.org/10.17639/nott.7119>

Interview with Senior Political Affairs Officer, UN DPO ('Interviewee 16') (New York, 10 December 2019) DOI: <http://doi.org/10.17639/nott.7119>

Interview with Personnel in MONUSCO's Stabilisation Support Unit ('Interviewee 19') (Skype, 21 February 2020) DOI: <http://doi.org/10.17639/nott.7119>

Jennings K, 'The Immunity Dilemma: Peacekeepers' Crimes and the UN's Response' (*E-International Relations*, 18 September 2017) <https://www.e-ir.info/2017/09/18/the-immunity-dilemma-peacekeepers-crimes-and-the-uns-response/>

Karim S and Beardsley K, 'Explaining Sexual Exploitation and Abuse in Peacekeeping Missions: The Role of Female Peacekeepers and Gender Equality in Contributing Countries' (2016) 53(1) JPeaceResearch 100–115

Kendall-Taylor A and Shullman D, 'How Russia and China Undermine Democracy' (*Foreign Affairs*, 2 October 2018) <https://www.foreignaffairs.com/articles/china/2018-10-02/how-russia-and-china-undermine-democracy>

Labuda PI, 'With or Against the State? Reconciling the Protection of Civilians and Host-State Support in UN Peacekeeping' (IPI 2020)

Lee S and Bartels S, 'They Put a Few Coins in Your Hand to Drop a Baby in You' Study of Peacekeeper-Fathered Children in Haiti' (2019) 27(2) IntPeacekeep 177–209

Mani R and Krause J, 'Democratic Governance' in V Chetail (ed) *Post-Conflict Peacebuilding: A Lexicon* (OUP 2010)

Marten KZ, *Enforcing the Peace: Learning From the Imperial Past* (Columbia University Press 2004)

Mazower M, *Governing the World: The History of an Idea, 1815 to the Present* (Penguin 2012)

Murray J, 'Who Will Police the Peace-Builders? The Failure to Establish Accountability for the Participation of United Nations Civilian Police in the Trafficking of Women in Post-Conflict Bosnia and Herzegovina' (2003) 34(2) ColumHRLR 475–528

Mutua M, 'Why Redraw the Map of Africa: A Moral and Legal Inquiry' (1995) 16(4) MichJIntL 1113–1176

Mutua M, 'The Ideology of Human Rights' (1996) 36 VaJIntl 589–658

Mutua M, 'Critical Race Theory and International Law: The View of an Insider-Outsider' (2000) 45(5) VillLRev 841–854

Nehru BK, 'Western Democracy and the Third World' (1979) 1(2) TWQ 53–70

Operations Directive No 8 (untitled), February 1961, UN Archives DAG/13/1.6.5.0.0 Operations Directives August 1960–January 1964, Box 3

Prosecutor v Akayesu (Judgment) ICTR-96-4-T (2 September 1998)

Protocol Additional to the Geneva Conventions of 12 August 1949 Protection of Victims of International Armed Conflicts (Protocol I) (6 June 1977) and Protection of Victims of Non-International Armed Conflicts (Protocol II) (8 June 1977)

Reilly B, 'Elections in Post-Conflict Societies' in E Newman and R Rich (eds) *The UN Role in Promoting Democracy: Between Ideals and Reality* (UN University Press 2004)

Reynaert J, 'MONUC/MONUSCO and Civilian Protection in the Kivus' (IPIS 2010)

Rome Statute of the International Criminal Court (last amended 2010) (17 July 1998)

Russo J and Mamiya R, *The Primacy of Politics and the Protection of Civilians in UN Peacekeeping* (IPI 2022)

Simic O, *Regulation of Sexual Conduct in UN Peacekeeping Operations* (Springer 2012)

Simpson G, 'Imagined Consent: Democratic Liberalism in International Legal Theory' (1994) 15 AYIL 103–128

Sripati V, 'The United Nation's Role in Post-Conflict Constitution-Making Processes: TWAIL Insights' (2008) 10(4) ICLR 411–420

Tzouvala N, *Capitalism as Civilisation: A History of International Law* (CUP 2020)

UN Clear Check, 'The UN Efforts to Combat SEA/Sexual Harassment' (21 May 2021) <https://unsceb.org/sites/default/files/2021-05/2021%20-%20Briefing%20Note%20on%20Clear%20Check.pdf>

UN Conduct in Field Missions, 'Sexual Exploitation and Abuse: Table of Allegations' <https://conduct.unmissions.org/table-of-allegations>

UN DPKO/DFS, 'Draft Operational Concept on the Protection of Civilians in United Nations Peacekeeping Operations' (2010) <http://www.peacekeeping.org.uk/wp-content/uploads/2013/02/100129-DPKO-DFS-POC-Operational-Concept.pdf>

UN News, 'Annan Further Enhances "Zero Tolerance" of Sexual Abuse by UN Peacekeepers' (*UN News*, 13 October 2006) <https://news.un.org/en/story/2006/10/196122-annan-further-enhances-zero-tolerance-sexual-abuse-un-peacekeepers>

UN News, 'Responsibility to Protect: Ban Urges Action to Make UN-backed Tool "A Living Reality"' (*UN News*, 18 January 2012) <https://news.un.org/en/story/2012/01/400702>

UN Peacekeeping, 'Conduct in UN Field Missions: Training' <https://conduct.unmissions.org/prevention-training>

UN Peacekeeping, 'Protecting Civilians' <https://peacekeeping.un.org/en/protecting-civilians>

UN Peacekeeping, 'The Secretary-General Announces Task Force on UN Response to Sexual Exploitation and Abuse' (6 Jan 2017) <https://peacekeeping.un.org/en/secretary-general-announces-task-force-un-response-to-sexual-exploitation-and-abuse>

UN Peacekeeping, 'The Military Aide Memoire: United Nations Measures against Sexual Exploitation and Abuse' (October 2017) <https://resourcehub01.blob.core.windows.net/$web/PK%20Training/Materials/000%20References/016-1%20The%20Military%20Aide%20Memoire%20United%20Nations%20Measures%20against%20Sexual%20Exploitation%20and%20Abuse.pdf>.

UN Sexual Exploitation and Abuse, 'No Excuse Card' <http://dag.un.org/bitstream/handle/11176/400598/2-No-excuse-card-2pages-EN-Form.pdf?sequence=9&isAllowed=y>

UNGA (46th Session, 59th Meeting) (5 December 1991) UN Doc A/46/PV.59

UNGA, 'Report of the Secretary-General: An Agenda for Peace: Preventive, Diplomacy, Peacemaking and Peacekeeping' (31 January 1992) UN Doc A/47/277-S/24111 and UNGA, 'Supplement to An Agenda for Peace' (25 January 1995) UN Doc A/50/60-S/1995/1

UNGA, 'Report of the Panel on United Nations Peace Operations' ("Brahimi Report") (21 August 2000) UN Doc A/55/305-S/2000/809

UNGA, 'Investigation into Sexual Exploitation of Refugees by Aid Workers in West Africa' (11 October 2002) UN Doc A/57/465

UNGA, 'Report of the Secretary-General: In Larger Freedom: Towards Security, Development and Human Rights for All' (21 March 2005) UN Doc A/59/2005

UNGA, 'A Comprehensive Strategy to Eliminate Future Sexual Exploitation and Abuse in United Nations Peacekeeping Operations' ("Zeid Report") (24 March 2005) UN Doc A/59/710

UNGA, 'Report of the Secretary-General: Special Measures for Protection from Sexual Exploitation and Sexual Abuse' (16 February 2016) UN Doc A/70/729

UNGA, 'Report of the Secretary-General: Special Measures for Protection from Sexual Exploitation and Abuse: A New Approach' (15 May 2017) UN Doc A/71/818 and A/71/818/Corr 1

UNGA, 'Report of the Secretary General: Special Measures for Protection from Sexual Exploitation and Abuse' (20 March 2018) UN Doc A/72/751 and A/72/751/Corr.1

UNGA Res 57/306 (22 May 2003) UN Doc A/RES/57/306

UNGA-SC, 'Report of the Secretary-General: The Causes of Conflict and the Promotion of Durable Peace and Sustainable Development in Africa' (13 April 1998) UN Doc A/52/871-S/1998/318

UNGA-SC, 'Report of the High-level Independent Panel on Peace Operations' ("HIPPO Report") (17 June 2015) UN Doc A/70/95-S/2015/446

UNGA-SC, 'The Future of United Nations Peace Operations: Implementation of the Recommendations of the High-Level Independent Panel on Peace Operations' (2 September 2015) UN Doc A/70/357-S/2015/682

UNSC, 'Secretary-Report, Proposals for Namibia: Supplement for April, May and June 1978' (10 April 1978) UN Doc S/12636

UNSC, 'Further Report of the Secretary-General Concerning the Question of Namibia' (23 January 1989) UN Doc S/20412

UNSC (54th Year, 4046th Meeting) (16 September 1999) UN Doc S/PV/4046
UNSC, 'Transitioning from Stabilization to Peace: An Independent Strategic Review of MONUSCO' ("Strategic Review") (25 October 2019) UN Doc S/2019/842
UNSC Res 435 (29 September 1978) UN Doc S/RES/435
UNSC Res 629 (16 January 1989) UN Doc S/RES/629
UNSC Res 743 (21 February 1992) UN Doc S/RES/743
UNSC Res 770 (13 August 1992) UN Doc S/RES/770
UNSC Res 836 (4 June 1993) UN Doc S/RES/836
UNSC Res 866 (22 September 1993) UN Doc S/RES/866
UNSC Res 1020 (10 November 1995) UN Doc S/RES/1020
UNSC Res 1265 (17 September 1999) UN Doc S/RES/1265
UNSC Res 1270 (22 October 1999) UN Doc S/RES/1270
UNSC Res 1291 (24 February 2000) UN Doc S/RES/1291
UNSC Res 1296 (19 April 2000) UN Doc S/RES/1296
UNSC Res 1502 (26 August 2003) UN Doc S/RES/1502
UNSC Res 1509 (19 September 2003) UN Doc S/RES/1509
UNSC Res 1528 (27 February 2004) UN Doc S/RES/1528
UNSC Res 1542 (30 April 2004) UN Doc S/RES/1542
UNSC Res 1769 (31 July 2007) UN Doc S/RES/1769
UNSC Res 1778 (25 September 2007) UN Doc S/RES/1778
UNSC Res 1856 (22 December 2008) UN Doc S/RES/1856
UNSC Res 1894 (11 November 2009) UN Doc S/RES/1894
UNSC Res 1925 (28 May 2010) UN Doc S/RES/1925
UNSC Res 1996 (9 July 2011) UN Doc S/RES/1996
UNSC Res 2057 (5 July 2012) UN Doc S/RES/2057
UNSC Res 2098 (28 March 2013) UN Doc S/RES/2098
UNSC Res 2272 (11 March 2016) UN Doc S/RES/2272
UNSC Res 2313 (13 October 2016) UN Doc S/RES/2313
UNSC Res 2475 (20 June 2019) UN Doc S/RES/2475
UNSC Res 2480 (28 June 2019) UN Doc S/RES/2480
UNSC Res 2499 (15 November 2019) UN Doc S/RES/2499
UNSC Res 2556 (18 December 2020) UN Doc S/RES/2556
UNSC Res 2573 (27 April 2021) UN Doc S/RES/2573
UNSG, 'Secretary-General Bulletin: Observance by United Nations Forces of International Humanitarian Law' (6 August 1999) UN Doc ST/SGB/1999/13
UNSG, 'Secretary-General Bulletin: Special Measures for Protection for Sexual Exploitation and Abuse' (9 October 2003) UN Doc ST/SGB/2003/13
UNSG, 'Secretary-General Bulletin: Prohibition of Discrimination, Harassment, including Sexual Harassment and Abuse of Authority' (11 February 2008) UN Doc ST/SGB/2008/5
Van Der Mark C, *Sexual Exploitation and Abuse by UN Peacekeepers – Why the Problem Continues to Persist* (PeaceWomen 2012)
Van Reybrouck D, *Congo: The Epic History of a People* (Fourth Estate 2015)
Whalan J, *Dealing with Disgrace: Addressing Sexual Exploitation and Abuse in UN Peacekeeping* (IPI 2017)
Whitworth S, *Men, Militarism and UN Peacekeeping* (Lynne Rienner 2004)
Willmot H and Sheeran S, 'The Protection of Civilians Mandate in UN Peacekeeping Operations: Reconciling Protection Concepts and Practices' (2013) 95(891/892) IRRC 517–538

Chapter 5

Peacekeeping's Legal Framework in Practice

The United Nations' Peacekeeping Laboratory

It has been said that 'the fortune of peacekeeping would rise and fall in the Congo'.[1] Indeed, the Democratic Republic of the Congo (DRC) is often referred to as a laboratory or 'furnace [for] the evolution of peacekeeping'[2] – providing the 'biggest theatre'[3] in which new policies have developed. With three operations deployed in 1960, 1999 and 2010, the Congo operations provide excellent case studies for examining the peacekeeping frameworks in practice.

The start of the United Nations' peacekeeping endeavours in the DRC began in 1960 when the *Opération des Nations Unies au Congo* (ONUC) was deployed during Africa's decolonisation period, shortly after the country gained independence from Belgium.[4] A mass exodus of Europeans, a breakdown in law and order and a secessionist war in the province of Katanga plunged the Congo into a series of conflicts, dubbed the 'Congo crisis'.[5] As a result, the newly elected Congolese government requested 'UN military assistance', 'to protect the national territory of the Congo', less than two weeks after gaining independence.[6] Whilst ONUC was initially deployed as

1 Interviewee 9 quoting a former head of peacekeeping. Interview with Senior UN DPPA-DPO Personnel ('Interviewee 9') (New York, 27 November 2019) DOI: <http://doi.org/10.17639/nott.7119> pg 36.

2 Interview with Mona Ali Khalil, former Senior Legal Officer of the UN Office of the Legal Counsel, Director of MAK LAW International and an Affiliate of the Harvard Law School Program on International Law and Armed Conflict ('Interviewee 12') (New York (Skype) 5 December 2019) DOI: <http://doi.org/10.17639/nott.7119> pg 36.

3 Interview with Former MONUSCO Military Personnel ('Interviewee 4') (Shrivenham, UK, 28 October 2019) DOI: <http://doi.org/10.17639/nott.7119> pg 36.

4 UNSC Res 143 (14 July 1960) UN Doc S/RES/143.

5 Within the UN debates on the situation in the DRC was referred to as the 'Congo crisis', see: UNGA (15th Session, 912th Plenary Meeting) (8 November 1960) UN Doc A/PV.912.

6 UNSC, 'Cable dated 12 July 1960 from the President of the Republic of the Congo and Supreme Commander of the National Army and the Prime Minister and the Minister of National Defense addressed to the Secretary-General of the United Nations' (13 July 1960) UN Doc S/4382.

DOI: 10.4324/9781003371649-5

a traditional, passive peacekeeping operation, it quickly evolved to use an unprecedented level of force, in both strategy and tactics, making it 'indistinguishable from a standard military campaign'.[7] The operation was eventually considered a success when it assisted in the prevention of the Katangan secession, subsequently withdrawing in 1964.

In the years that followed, the Congo endured a 32-year dictatorship and 2 major armed conflicts, including 'Africa's World War', which led to the return of the United Nations in 1999 to oversee the signing of the Lusaka Ceasefire Agreement.[8] Initially, as with ONUC, the *Mission de L'Organisation des Nations Unies en République Démocratique du Congo* (MONUC) was a relatively simple, traditional Chapter VI peacekeeping mission composed of 500 military observers tasked with overseeing the fulfilment of the peace agreement.[9] However, with persistent conflict and cycles of violence, the operation rapidly evolved into a much more robust, multi-dimensional operation, eventually changing its name to the *Mission de L'Organisation des Nations Unies pour la Stabilisation en République Démocratique du Congo* (MONUSCO) in 2010, to recognise the new inclusion of the 'stabilisation' element.[10]

The evolution of the United Nations' operations in the Congo has therefore mirrored the cyclical evolution of the principle of non-intervention, which was outlined in Chapter 2, with MONUSCO evolving during intervention's shift from a military to security approach. Since then, MONUSCO became the United Nations' largest peacekeeping operation to date, totalling over 20,000 personnel at its peak.[11] In an attempt to adapt to changing conflict dynamics and demands from the Security Council, the Congolese government and regional actors, the operation has continually reinvented itself. Most notably, in 2013 the Security Council mandated the operation to include a 'Force Intervention Brigade', authorised to undertake 'targeted offensive operations' to 'neutralise' armed groups, in cooperation or through

7 T Findlay, *The Use of Force in UN Peace Operations* (OUP 2002) 51.

8 UNSC, 'Ceasefire Agreement' ('Lusaka Ceasefire') (23 July 1999) UN Doc S/1999/815; G Prunier, *Africa's World War: Congo, the Rwandan Genocide, and the Making of a Continental Catastrophe* (Oxford University Press 2011).

9 UNSC Res 1234 (9 April 1999) UN Doc S/RES/1234; UNSC Res 1258 (6 August 1999) UN Doc S/RES/1258; UNSC Res 1273 (5 November 1999) UN Doc S/RES/1273; UNSC Res 1279 (30 November 1999) UN Doc S/RES/1279; UNSC Res 1291 (24 February 2000) UN Doc S/RES/1291.

10 On stabilisation, see: A Gilder, *Stabilization and Human Security in UN Peace Operations* (Routledge 2022); C de Coning and C Aoi, 'Conclusion: Towards a United Nations Stabilization Doctrine: Stabilization as an Emerging UN Practice' in C de Coning, C Aoi and J Karlsrud (eds) *UN Peacekeeping Doctrine in a New Era Adapting to Stabilisation, Protection and New Threats* (Routledge 2017) 288–310; A Boutellis, 'Can the UN Stabilize Mali? Towards a UN Stabilization Doctrine?' (2015) 4(1) Stability 1–16.

11 MONUSCO's current personnel total (as of August 2023) is 17,753. See: UN Peacekeeping, 'MONUSCO Fact Sheet' <https://peacekeeping.un.org/en/mission/monusco>.

joint operations with the Congolese armed forces.[12] In addition to a significant military presence, the operation also has large civilian and police components, thereby differing greatly from ONUC's predominantly military force.[13] Together, the components have undertaken numerous mandated tasks such as the overseeing of three democratic elections in 2006, 2011 and 2018 (with questionable success);[14] responding to public health emergencies (including Ebola outbreaks and the COVID-19 pandemic) and preventing or deterring armed groups and local militias, particularly within the east of the country.[15] As of 2023, MONUSCO is now part-way through its exit strategy,[16] presenting future opportunities to review how the withdrawal of peacekeepers impacts the peacekeeping frameworks.

Armed with Legal Principles

Peacekeeping in the DRC therefore offers a wealth of examples of various aspects of peacekeeping, not least how the three fundamental principles have been interpreted and applied. As Spijker notes, when the United Nations first entered the Congo in the early 1960s it was equipped 'not with heavy arms but with legal principles'.[17] However, as this chapter will demonstrate, when tracking the evolution of the principles in practice, it is clear to see that the same could not be said for today's robust, multi-functional peacekeeping operations. Whilst many within the Secretariat maintain that the traditional peacekeeping principles are still relevant,[18] it is undeniable that they have been expanded and contorted, at times almost beyond recognition, to adapt to conditions in the field and, in part, to reflect the interventionist rhetoric or trends which were outlined in Chapter 2. As such, these re-interpretations could be said to expand the scope of peacekeeping as a form of intervention, consequently contracting the principle of non-intervention. That is, as Chapter 3 highlighted, when the principles are interpreted narrowly then peacekeeping's boundaries are limited and so too is peacekeeping's interventionist potential. However, when they are interpreted broadly, as with the United Nations' operations in the Congo, the boundaries are signifi-

12 UNSC Res 2098 (28 March 2013) UN Doc S/RES/2098.
13 See MONUSCO facts and figures (n11).
14 ibid.
15 See: UNSC Res 2666 (20 December 2022) UN Doc S/RES/2666.
16 ibid, UNSC, 'New Strategy for Mission Withdrawal: 8778th Meeting' (7 December 2020) UN Doc SC/14374.
17 O Spijkers, 'The Evolution of United Nations Peacekeeping in the Congo' (2015) 19(1–2) IntPeacekeep 88–117, 89.
18 See Interviewee 12 (n2) and Interviewee 16: Interview with Senior Political Affairs Officer, UN DPO ('Interviewee 16') (New York, 10 December 2019) DOI: <http://doi.org/10.17639/nott.7119> pg 42.

cantly expanded, often to their limits, thereby undermining the principle of non-intervention.

An examination of peacekeeping within the DRC also highlights how the functioning of the peacekeeping operations in practice may also create an additional layer of interpretation of the principles of peacekeeping and, thus, potentially broaden its interventionist scope.[19] That is, once the Security Council has interpreted the peacekeeping principles and created the mandate, there is a splintering as is this is then re-interpreted and re-actualised in the field by the SRSG and senior leadership within the operation. This may, in practice, result in differing approaches on how to implement the mandate, particularly between the civilian and military components, thereby resulting in differing interpretations of the fundamental principles which are embedded within the SC mandate. For example, within MONUSCO, the day to day planning and general guidance is one which is led by a civilian strategy 'and the military con-ops are supposed to be embedded in the mission concept and follow the civilian led SC mandate'.[20] However, there are often difficulties in coordination and communication between these components with MONUSCO struggling 'enormously, as most missions do, to integrate the military within the broader kind of multi-dimensional mission structure'.[21] In particular, the exclusion of civilians from operational planning has been a recurring source of contention for civilian staff,[22] whilst military personnel argue that secrecy of operations is a necessity and was 'one of the conditions of success of the FARDC against M23'.[23] It could therefore be argued that each interpretation of the mandate creates a further nuance within the concept of peacekeeping and, consequently, the principle of non-intervention. That is, each re-interpretation creates a new mark within the red boundary line around peacekeeping and, if repeated, may build up to create a permanent opening, resulting in an expansion of this boundary line and therefore an expansion of peacekeeping and its interventionist potential.

This chapter will therefore examine how ONUC, MONUC and MONUSCO have interpreted and applied the fundamental principles and

19 On the civil-military structure of peacekeeping, see: UN DPKO, 'Civil-Military Coordination Policy' (9 September 2002) <https://www.refworld.org/pdfid/451ba7624.pdf>; UN, 'Civil-Military Coordination Specialized Training Materials (UN-CIMIC STM)' (UN DPO-DFS, 2004) <http://repository.un.org/bitstream/handle/11176/89582/STM%20UNCIMIC.pdf?sequence=1&isAllowed=y>.

20 Interview with Independent Expert and Former UN Political Adviser ('Interviewee 8') (New York, 26 November 2019) DOI: <http://doi.org/10.17639/nott.7119> pg 25.

21 Interview with Senior UN DPO Personnel, Policy, Evaluation and Training Division ('Interviewee 10') (New York, 3 December 2019) DOI: <http://doi.org/10.17639/nott.7119> pg 66.

22 Interviewee 8 (n20) pg 25.

23 Interview with Former Senior Military Commander ('Interviewee 11') (New York (Skype) 3 December 2019) DOI: <http://doi.org/10.17639/nott.7119> pg 26.

how this, in turn, has altered the fluid, red elastic boundary line which surrounds peacekeeping. Building upon the analysis of the previous two chapters it will also continue to apply a TWAIL lens to demonstrate how the inequalities and power disparities embedded within the peacekeeping frameworks may transpire in practice. Taking each of the fundamental legal principles in turn – consent, impartiality and limited use of force – the chapter will take the analysis from Chapter 3 deeper by exploring specific examples of how these principles are interpreted and applied in practice and how this, in turn, impacts both peacekeeping's frameworks and the principle of non-intervention.

Consent

As Chapter 3 established, the principle of consent is a cornerstone for peacekeeping, creating a distinction between peacekeeping and peace enforcement and validating what would otherwise be illegal intervention. Therefore, consent, as was seen at numerous points throughout Chapter 3, prevents peacekeeping from becoming intervention. Despite its importance for peacekeeping operations in the DRC, numerous issues have arisen in regards to the principle of consent which highlights the more general problems outlined in Chapter 3. These issues can be loosely categorised into two themes: consent from whom and consent for what. Firstly, at times, the Congo has lacked a clear government or leader, had competing claims for territorial control and has been referred to as a failed state, making it unclear who can or should provide consent.[24] Secondly, throughout the United Nations' 60-year relationship with the DRC, relations between the organisation and the country's political leadership have frequently broken down. This has ranged from veiled threats and criticisms of the operation to explicit statements requesting that the UN operation withdraw from the country. On these occasions, consent has effectively been withdrawn, yet the operation has remained. This calls into question the maintenance of host state consent and whether the host is simply consenting to the deployment of the operation and is not legally required to consent to any changes – substantial, strategic or tactical – once the operation is deployed. If the host state is therefore unable to consent to significant changes to the operation or unable to eject a peacekeeping operation from its territory until the end of its mandate, it is arguable that this may amount to coercive action designed to alter the state and thus intervention and, consequently, a violation of the principle of non-intervention.

24 See: W Reno, 'Congo: From State Collapse to "Absolutism", to State Failure' (2006) 27(1) TWQ 43–56, 47.

Obtaining Consent

After the Congo gained independence and the 'Congo crisis' ensued, the newly independent Congolese government telegrammed the then-Secretary-General, Dag Hammarskjöld, requesting the 'dispatch by the United Nations of military assistance' to protect their territory against 'the present external aggression' which was a 'threat to world peace' and a 'conspiracy' to perpetuate the 'colonialist regime'.[25] Therefore, for ONUC, host state consent was clearly established as there had been an explicit request from the president and prime minister of the Congo and thus explicit consent for UN intervention. There was therefore no violation of the principle of non-intervention through ONUC's deployment, but the context and nature of the Congolese request highlight broader issues within international law at that time, as explored in the previous chapters.

Firstly, the deployment of the peacekeeping operation was, again, somewhat of an ironic use of intervention to counter intervention, as seen in Chapter 2, with the United States' imperial intervention to counter European intervention in the colonial era. Secondly, the nature of the Congo's request for assistance was both a first for UN peacekeeping and, applying a TWAIL lens, demonstrated the significant power differentials which existed during that period and the beginning of the shift from a dominant Global North to a rising Global South – which Chapter 2 noted was also a tipping point for the principle of non-intervention. That is, at the time the Congolese government made their request, they were not yet a member state of the United Nations[26] and therefore brought their complaint to the Secretary-General, rather than the Security Council. The Congo's lack of member status also meant that, despite gaining independence, they had no power or voice within the UN system, arguably leaving them in a vulnerable position for the first few weeks of ONUC's deployment. Indeed, within General Assembly debates it was Congo's former colonial power, Belgium, that was consulted on matters relating to the Congo, thus, from a TWAIL perspective, maintaining the colonial-colonised dichotomy and paternalistic power imbalances.[27] It could also be viewed as another example of Anghie's dynamic of difference with the dominant actors (the United Nations and Belgium) identifying and seeking to bridge the gap between themselves and the 'others' (Congo).

However, despite the Congolese government having no formal voice within the General Assembly before and shortly after ONUC's deployment, it intuitively manipulated the Cold War dynamics to successfully obtain UN

25 S/4382 (n6).

26 UNGA Res 1480 (XV) (20 September 1960) UN Doc GA/RES/1480 (XV); UNGA, 'Resolutions Adopted by the General Assembly During its Fifteenth Session' (20 September–20 December 1960) 15th Session, UN Doc Supp No 16 (A/4684) 64.

27 ibid, A/4684.

support and exercise a degree of influence, culminating in the deployment of ONUC.[28] In particular, after Hammarskjöld acceded to the Congolese request and brought the matter before the Security Council, the Congolese government threatened to 'appeal to the Bandung Treaty Powers' – a 'euphemism for Chinese "volunteers"'[29] – should there be a delay in UN assistance.[30] As Draper noted at the time, 'in terms of *realpolitik*', this was 'the most telling and operative part' of the Congolese telegrams.[31] This manipulation of the Cold War dynamics and politics of the P5 by the Congolese therefore demonstrates the ability of the host state to influence external intervention even when they possess little formal power. Thus, as will be explored later in this section, even when a state appears to be unable to alter the peacekeeping operation, it still has a broad range of tactics or tools which it can use to influence an operation. For the principle of non-intervention, this suggests that even when peacekeeping appears to enter the realm of intervention, becoming coercive action designed to influence change in the host state, the host may still be able to counter this potential intervention, thereby reinforcing the principle of non-intervention. From a TWAIL perspective, this could also be viewed as an example of the Global South exercising their voice and using international law and institutions to challenge the dominance of the hegemonic powers.[32] This example, in particular, epitomises the changing nature of international relations during this period, which Chapter 2 explored. That is, it demonstrates the rise of the Global South, through the General Assembly, which provided smaller, newly independent states with equal voting power and a platform to express their interests and defend their sovereignty, often through an application of the principle of non-intervention.

MONUC and MONUSCO

For the United Nations' later missions in the DRC, MONUC and MONUSCO, the attainment of host state consent has also proved to be complex. Following the traditional model of peacekeeping, MONUC was deployed after the signing of the Lusaka Ceasefire agreement as a simple monitor and observe mission.[33] However, the Security Council resolution which established MONUC

28 S/RES/143 (n4).
29 TM Franck, 'United Nations Law in Africa: The Congo Operation as a Case Study' (1962) 27(4) *L&ContemProb* 632–652, 634.
30 UNGA, 'Annual Report of the Secretary-General on the Work of the Organisation' (16 June 1960–15 June 1961) UN Doc A/4800. See also: UN Doc S/4382 (n6) 2.
31 GIAD Draper, 'The Legal Limitations upon the Employment of Weapons by the United Nations Force in the Congo' (1963) 12(2) ICLQ 387–413, 389.
32 See: G Abi-Saab, 'The Third World Intellectual in Praxis: Confrontation, Participation, or Operation behind Enemy Lines' (2016) 37(11) TWQ 1957–1971.
33 S/RES/1279 (n9).

made no reference to host state consent; instead it referred to the agreement and noted the role that it requested the United Nations to play 'in the implementation of the ceasefire'.[34] Within the Lusaka Agreement, the signatory parties, which included the DRC, agreed that the UN Security Council 'acting under Chapter VII of the UN Charter' shall be 'requested to constitute, facilitate and deploy an appropriate peacekeeping force in the DRC to ensure implementation' of the agreement.[35] It therefore appears that host state consent was granted for the deployment of MONUC through the Lusaka Agreement, thereby an indirect or implied consent. Whilst this could perhaps bring the operation closer to violating the principle of non-intervention, as Sloan notes, instead of referring to consent, the resolutions reaffirmed 'the sovereignty, territorial integrity and political independence' of the DRC.[36] Thus, in emphasising sovereignty and territorial integrity, which are a corollary of non-intervention, it appears that the Council did not perceive MONUC to be intervention and, therefore, their interpretation of the principle of consent here reinforced the principle of non-intervention. This was compounded by repeated assurances from the Congolese government, which the Council took as evidence of their support for the deployment of MONUC and therefore implied consent.[37] The Council's recognition of the Congo's support could also reflect the Council's awareness that the host state was in a position to reject any changes to the mandate which were not based within the mandatory provisions of Chapter VII.[38] As will be discussed later in this section, this then leads to the importance of maintaining host state consent and whether the host state can or should consent to changes in the mandate.

For MONUSCO, as it was a continuation of MONUC, consent for deployment was not legally required. However, what remains unclear is whether the Congolese government had to (and did) consent to significant changes, namely the re-naming and evolution of the mission to include a stabilisation element. If there was no consent, then it could be argued that the operation's sole legal basis became Chapter VII, thus taking the operation across the line into intervention. Indeed, the United Nations essentially ignored the host state requests during this period and continued with the stabilisation agenda, which could arguably be perceived as coercive action to alter the host state and, thereby, intervention. In the months leading up to MONUC's evolution into MONUSCO, the DRC's president, Kabila, repeatedly

34 ibid.

35 Lusaka Ceasefire (n8) para 11 (a).

36 J Sloan, *The Militarisation of Peacekeeping in the Twenty-First Century* (Hart Publishing 2011).

37 UNSC Res 1332 (14 December 2000) UN Doc S/RES/1332. UNSC Res 1341 (22 February 2001) UN Doc S/RES/1341.

38 J Sloan (n36).

demanded that the United Nations withdraw from the Congo.[39] In late 2009, shortly after the Security Council had renewed MONUC's mandate, Kabila requested a detailed draw-down plan for the operation by 30 June 2010.[40] Again, in February 2010, three months before the Security Council authorised MONUSCO, Kabila officially asked the Under-Secretary General for Peacekeeping Operations, Alain Le Roy, to ensure the removal of MONUC by mid- to late 2011, with the first draw-down to take place around June 2010 to coincide with the 50th anniversary of Congo's independence.[41] At this point, it could be argued that consent to the operation had been revoked, yet the United Nations remained in the DRC, authorising MONUC's evolution to MONUSCO, which Le Roy argued demonstrated 'a new phase in the Congo'.[42] In order to seemingly placate Congolese concerns, the Council did, however, also authorise the withdrawal of up to 2,000 personnel by 30 June 2010,[43] but no further plans were made to withdraw the operation in 2011, as Kabila had requested. In essence, then, the host state was arguably ignored by both the United Nations and the peacekeeping operation, with the external actors continuing to pursue their agenda, regardless of the express desires of the host state. It appears that in this instance, peacekeeping expanded beyond its boundaries, becoming intervention and therefore undermining the principle of non-intervention. Further, from a TWAIL perspective, this could also be viewed as a replication of the dichotomies of the colonial civilising mission, with the enlightened, external, hegemonic power pursuing their agenda and essentially dictating to the subordinate 'other'.

This, again, highlights the precarious interpretations of the principle of consent and raises questions as to whether host state consent is only required for deployment, with the retraction of consent during the operation having little legal or practical effect – a matter which will be explored in subsequent sections. It could also be argued that, more broadly, through a TWAIL lens, this again reflects the long-standing power differentials within interventionist practice which were outlined in Chapter 2, with the Congo (a Global South state) still struggling to assert its voice against the United Nations (an

39 T Vircoulon, 'After MONUC, Should MONUSCO Continue to Support Congolese Military Campaigns?' (Crisis Group, 19 July 2010) <https://www.crisisgroup.org/africa/central-africa/chad/after-monuc-should-monusco-continue-support-congolese-military-campaigns>.

40 Oxford Analytica, 'Congo-Kinshasa: MONUC Exit Is Probable, but Premature' (*Oxford Analytica*, 1 April 2010) <https://reliefweb.int/report/democratic-republic-congo/congo-kinshasa-monuc-exit-probable-premature>.

41 UN News, 'First Set of UN Troops Could Leave DR Congo by June Says Peacekeeping Chief' (*UN News*, 5 March 2010) <https://news.un.org/en/story/2010/03/331642-first-set-un-troops-could-leave-dr-congo-june-says-peacekeeping-chief>.

42 News Wires, 'UN to Withdraw up to 2000 Troops from DR Congo' (*France 24*, 28 May 2010) <https://www.france24.com/en/20100528-un-withdraw-2000-troops-dr-congo-monuc>.

43 UNSC Res 1925 (28 May 2010) UN Doc S/RES/1925, 3.

organisation led by dominant powers), as it did during ONUC's deployment. Indeed, these typical interventionist positions played out in the Security Council, underlining the inherent hierarchy within the organ and the differing approaches to intervention amongst the P5, which have also been outlined in previous chapters. Whilst the United States and France pushed for MONUC to remain in the DRC, with the former stating that MONUC was needed for the protection of civilians and security sector reform, China took the opposite view.[44] A usual proponent of non-intervention, China argued that the Congo could not have a new beginning whilst MONUC was deployed, stating that it fully supported Kabila's desire 'to fly his own wings'.[45] This latter phrase, in particular, demonstrates that the peacekeeping operation was seen as an unwelcome restriction or limitation on the host state's sovereignty and, therefore, coercive action amounting to intervention.

Consent from Whom?

A further issue which has arisen in the United Nations' operations in the Congo is who is entitled to provide consent, the answer to which has the potential to broaden the principle of consent, as the greater the number of actors who are able to provide consent, the broader the principle and therefore the broader the peacekeeping frameworks. Whilst consent is typically attributable to the state,[46] within the DRC there have been numerous competing claims for power within certain areas, which challenges the government's exclusive control of the whole territory. This, in turn, calls into question whether non-state actors could or should also provide consent to the peacekeeping operation. Where the state's capacity to govern has withered (such as in the east of the country), non-state actors, including armed groups, traditional leaders, churches and civil society groups, have competed to fill these gaps, resulting in Congolese society developing 'new forms of social organisation ... to compensate for the overwhelming failures of the post-colonial nation-state'.[47] The 'effective control' doctrine could therefore be applied to ascertain whether or not these non-state actors have exercised 'effective control' over certain parts of the Congo and, as such, should be required to provide consent to the presence of the UN peacekeeping operation in those areas.

44 Closed-door Security Council meeting, quoted in: Congo Research Group, 'The Future of MONUC (and Debt Relief)' (*CRG*, 18 March 2010) <http://congoresearchgroup.org/future-of-monuc-and-debt-relief/>.

45 ibid.

46 UN, Eighth Report on State Responsibility, Document A/CN.4/318 and Add.1-4, 2 (1979) Y.B. Int'l L. Comm'n 3 (1980), 36.

47 T Trefon, *Reinventing Order in the Congo: How People Respond to State Failure in Kinshasa* (Zed Books 2004) 2.

Similar to the principle of non-intervention, the effective control doctrine is an ill-defined concept within international law, with no definite source; it is instead pieced together through international treaties, regulations and case law.[48] Determining whether an actor possesses authority within a territory generally involves three factors. Firstly, Article 42 of the Hague Regulations states that territory is occupied when it is 'actually placed under the authority of the hostile army' and where 'authority has been established and can be exercised'.[49] Secondly, the Fourth Geneva Convention notes that the occupying power 'exercises the functions of the government in such territory'[50] and thirdly, in international case law it was found that the occupier's authority is 'to the exclusion of the established government'.[51] It could be argued that, at certain points within the DRC's history, these three elements are satisfied, most notably during the 1960 Katangan secession and, more recently, in Eastern Congo where there are a significant number of armed groups.

Taking the first of these examples, shortly before ONUC's deployment, the authorities in the South East province of Katanga declared its independence from the rest of Congo. The sizeable province operated independently from the rest of the Congolese territory, with its own leadership (Moise Tshombé) and infrastructure, and was vehemently at odds with the Congolese government which explicitly requested UN assistance in preventing the secession.[52] It could therefore be argued that Tshombé and his party had effective control of Katanga as authority had been established and exercised, with the secession leaders exercising the functions of the government in that area, at the exclusion of the established government. As such, it is debatable whether Tshombé's party should have provided consent for the deployment of UN troops within Katanga. For the United Nations, this was a problematic issue as obtaining the Katangan leadership's consent would have gone against the Congolese government's request and could have been interpreted as *de facto* recognition of the secession's authority. This would have constituted engagement in the matter of Katanga's independence and,

48 See, for example, the two control tests (strict control or agency test and the effective control test) set out in *Nicaragua* which help to determine the attribution of international responsibility to states for conduct of other actors or individuals. *Case Concerning Military and Paramilitary Activities in and against Nicaragua (Nicaragua v United States of America)* [1986] ICJ Rep 14.

49 Article 42, Hague Convention (II) with Respect to the Laws and Customs of War on Land and Its Annex: Regulations Concerning the Laws and Customs of War on Land (29 July 1899) and Hague Convention (IV) Respecting the Laws and Customs of War on Land and Its Annex: Regulations Concerning the Laws and Customs of War on Land (18 October 1907).

50 Geneva Convention Relative to the Protection of Civilian Persons in Time of War (Fourth Geneva Convention) (12 August 1949) (75 UNTS 287), Article 6.

51 *Hostage Case, United States v List (Wilhelm) and ors* (Trial Judgment) (1950) 11 TWC 757.

52 S/4382 (n6); S/RES/143 (n4); UNSC Res 145 (22 July 1960) UN Doc S/RES/145.

as such, 'an illegal interference in the domestic affairs' of the Congo[53] – an issue which will be discussed further in this chapter's section on impartiality. However, by not obtaining consent from the Katangan authorities, there was arguably a risk that the presence of peacekeepers could have been an illegal intervention, instead of a consensual peacekeeping intervention. This notion is perhaps supported by the fact that Hammarskjöld initially refused to permit the deployment of UN peacekeepers into Katanga, fearing that it may have been viewed as an occupying force.[54] As such, it could be argued that Hammarskjöld's interpretation of the principle of consent required consent from Katanga, resulting in a clash between the fundamental principles of consent and impartiality. That is, to acknowledge consent was needed from Katanga would be to recognise their authority, thus breaching the United Nations' impartiality by engaging in internal affairs and going against the explicit instructions of the Congolese government. On the other hand, to not obtain consent from Katanga would have maintained the United Nations' impartiality but potentially risked amounting to intervention if Katanga established it had effective control, as it appears to have had. Whilst Hammarskjöld initially delayed deployment into Katanga, ultimately, the United Nations did not perceive a need to obtain their consent as troops were deployed in the area in late 1960, with the Security Council stating that it 'strongly deprecates the secessionist activities illegally carried out by the provincial administration of Katanga'.[55] As such, the United Nations evidently viewed the Congo as a whole, and therefore deploying into Katanga was neither coercion nor intervention. The Katangan secession therefore exemplifies both the key role which the SG may play in interpreting peacekeeping norms and how an interpretation of these principles has a direct impact on the interventionist nature of peacekeeping and, consequently, on the principle of non-intervention. It also highlights how, as the previous chapters have discussed, the fundamental norms do not co-exist harmoniously and have to be interpreted or adapted in order to live together, with the interpretation or application of one principle potentially impacting the others. Again, this highlights the argument established in Chapters 3 and 4 – that peacekeeping's frameworks are fluid, with the boundaries constantly expanding and contracting depending on how the principles and norms are interpreted and applied in the field. This, in turn, has the potential to blur the boundaries between peacekeeping and intervention, with an expanded or unclear reading of a principle having the potential to undermine the principle of non-intervention.

53 N Tsagourias, 'Consent, Neutrality/Impartiality and the Use of Force in Peacekeeping: Their Constitutional Dimension' (2007) 11(3) JCSL 465–482, 475.

54 R Bunche, *An American Odyssey* (WW Norton & Company 1998) 130.

55 UNSC Res 169 (24 November 1961) UN Doc S/RES/169, 1.

Similarly, for the later operations of MONUC and MONUSCO, if the effective control doctrine is applied, an argument could, again, be made for the need to obtain consent from regional or local authorities, particularly those in the east of the country where there is little state penetration.[56] The size of Western Europe, the Congo spans multiple times zones and has hundreds of ethnic groups and languages, with 'distinct political-economic structures and regional orientations' and a vast number of political parties and, 'more importantly, contains numerous competing power networks'.[57] In particular, 'the national elites' power base does not critically depend on formal control over the East.'[58] That is, the government has little authority or presence in the East of Congo and, as such, derives most of its income and influence from other parts of the country. This is in part due to the political exclusion or narrow power base which President Mobutu adopted during the 1970s in the midst of his dictatorship.[59] This led to decentralised nodes of power which were not directly dependent on the 'closed networks of presidential patronage'.[60] More recently, during Kabila (Jnr)'s regime, the 'presidential patronage network's' control 'remained patchy'; thus, its power did not reach to all corners of the national territory and the same can be said of the current regime under Tshisekedi.[61] The central government's penetration is therefore highly uneven and is sometimes contested, with local actors continuing to 'exercise influence over the lower echelons of the territorial administration and parts of security agencies'.[62] This is further complicated by the involvement or interventions of neighbouring states, particularly Rwanda and Uganda, which have repeatedly supported armed groups in Eastern Congo to influence change within the DRC or further their interests, including the exploitation of natural resources.[63]

56 See, for example, the 2013 Special Report of the Secretary-General, which notes that the Congolese government has 'limited ability to exert full authority over its territory and to provide basic services and security and security to the population'. UNSC, 'Special Report of the Secretary-General on the DRC and the Great Lakes Region' (27 February 2013) UN Doc S/2013/119, para 9.

57 J Verweijen, 'Stable Instability: Political Settlements and Armed Groups in the Congo' (Rift Valley Institute 2016) 14.

58 ibid.

59 See: W Reno, *Warlord Politics and African States* (Lynne Rienner 1998).

60 Verweijen (n57) 17.

61 ibid, 32.

62 ibid.

63 See: *Case concerning Armed Activities on the Territory of the Congo (Democratic Republic of the Congo v Uganda)* Judgment of 19 December [2005] ICJ Rep 168; H Tamm, 'Status Competition in Africa: Explaining the Rwandan-Ugandan Clashes in the Democratic Republic of Congo' (2019) 118(472) AfrAff 509–530; Human Rights Watch, 'Uganda in Eastern DRC: Fueling Political and Ethnic Strife' (HRW, 1 March 2001) <https://www.hrw.org/report/2001/03/01/uganda-eastern-drc/fueling-politcal-and-ethnic-strife>.

Within the East of Congo, then, it could be argued that where authority is established and exercised by non-state actors, at the exclusion of the government, then these actors have effective control and, therefore, should consent to the presence of UN peacekeeping in their territory. However, whilst this argument may be compelling in theory, in practice it is unlikely to be as persuasive. As Roth notes, for 'local impositions', it may be more preferable to engage in 'plausibly democratic or constitutional solutions to recognition contests'.[64] Therefore, rather than seeking to obtain formal consent from local or regional authorities for its presence in those areas, the peacekeeping operation would do better to engage with these leaders to ensure better cooperation and increased implementation of initiatives, as seen, for example, with the Stabilisation Support Unit in Eastern Congo which works collaboratively with numerous actors, including local leadership.[65]

Whilst the interpretation of the principle of consent, in this instance, may not expand or alter peacekeeping's frameworks to any great extent, what this example arguably highlights is how peacekeeping and, similarly, peacebuilding focus on the state, adopting a top-down, state-centric approach, rather than a bottom-up, grassroots-led approach, which some argue may be more beneficial for creating and sustaining long-term peace.[66] From a TWAIL perspective, such an approach could also render peacekeeping less interventionist as it would magnify the voice of the Global South peoples, thereby challenging the dominant powers' narrative and agendas. A recommendation stemming from this examination of the application of the principles of peacekeeping could therefore be for a more bottom-up or people-centred approach to implementing peacekeeping frameworks – a suggestion which will be explored at various points throughout the remaining chapters.

Consent for Deployment

Once consent has been obtained, two further interconnected issues have arisen within the United Nations' peacekeeping operations in the DRC, which were noted in Chapter 3 as nuances that have emerged within the principle of consent. The first issue is the scope of the host state consent, that is, whether it has consented only to the deployment of the operation or if this extends to any changes made to the operation whilst it is deployed. The second issue is the maintenance of consent and its impact on the operation, including whether a withdrawal of consent requires the peacekeepers to also withdraw.

64 B Roth, 'Secessions, Coups and the International Rule of Law: Assessing the Decline of the Effective Control Doctrine' (2010) 11 MelbJIntlL 393–440, 395.

65 MONUSCO, 'Stabilisation Support Unit' <https://monusco.unmissions.org/en/stabilization-support-unit>.

66 S Autesserre, *The Frontlines of Peace* (CUP 2010).

Prior to ONUC's deployment, the United Nations' first peacekeeping endeavour – UNEF – was created through the recommendatory powers of the General Assembly in its 'Uniting for Peace' resolution.[67] As such, whilst the GA was 'enabled to *establish* the force with the consent' of troop-contributing countries, 'it could not request for force to be *stationed* or *operate* on the territory of a given country' without the host state's consent.[68] UNEF's presence was therefore 'consensual or contractual', with host state consent required for any changes or decisions within the operation, such as the composition and stationing of the force.[69] However, ONUC was authorised by the Security Council, not the General Assembly, and, therefore, was 'not based on contract but on legislation'.[70] Under Chapter VII of the UN Charter, the powers which the Council may exercise in response to threats or breaches of peace and acts of aggression are not recommendations but rather are compulsory on member states.[71] Indeed, when mandating ONUC, the Council 'affirmed that its decisions were mandatory under Chapter VII of the Charter',[72] not by express reference to Chapter VII but by calling upon member states 'in accordance with Articles 25 and 49 of the Charter to accept and carry out the decisions of the Security Council'.[73] This was also reiterated by Hammarskjöld who noted that member states were legally bound to accept and carry out Security Council decisions and was later reaffirmed by the ICJ who stated that decisions of the Council, whether taken within Chapter VI or Chapter VII, are binding on member states under the terms of Article 25.[74]

ONUC's deployment has therefore been described as a 'legislative intervention', in comparison to UNEF's contractual intervention, with two key consequences.[75] Firstly, ONUC could be 'altered legislatively', whereas 'a contract can only be altered by the consent of the parties'.[76] Secondly, it could not be terminated, as a consensual relationship could, by the withdrawal of host state consent.[77] Therefore, throughout ONUC's deployment, SG Hammarskjöld made numerous changes to the operation, without host state consent. This

67 UNGA Res 377 (V) (3 November 1950) UN Doc A/RES/377(V).

68 UNGA, 'Second and Final Report of the Secretary General on the Plan for an Emergency International United Nations Force' (6 November 1956) UN Doc A/3302, 4.

69 Franck (n29) 638–639.

70 ibid, 639.

71 Article 25, Charter of the United Nations (24 October 1945) ('UN Charter').

72 EM Miller, 'Legal Aspects of United Nations Action in Congo' (1961) 55(1) AJIL 1–28, 15.

73 UNSC Res 146 (9 August 1960) UN Doc S/RES/146, para 5.

74 *Certain Expenses of the United Nations (Article 17, Paragraph 2 of the Charter)* (Advisory Opinion) [1962] ICJ Rep 151; *Legal Consequences for States of the Continued Presence of South Africa in Namibia (South West Africa) notwithstanding Security Council Resolution 276* (Advisory Opinion) [1971] ICJ Rep 16.

75 Franck (n29) 638–640.

76 ibid, 639.

77 ibid.

included establishing 'neutral' zones for political refugees[78] and authorising ONUC to exercise force against the government to protect the territorial immunity of the Ghanaian Embassy and to defend ONUC's control of the port of Matadi,[79] which was authorised by the Security Council having previously been recommended by the General Assembly.[80] As Franck notes, 'the consent of the Congolese authorities was never regarded' by any member state, except perhaps France, 'as a prerequisite to altering the nature of the intervention'.[81] Indeed, the Security Council's second resolution authorised ONUC to restore law and order,[82] 'without further caveat about acting "in consultation with the Government of the Congo"'.[83] Furthermore, Hammarskjöld explicitly reminded the Congolese that the relation between themselves and the United Nations was 'not merely a contractual relationship in which the Republic can impose its conditions as a host state'.[84] Rather, it was 'a relationship governed by mandatory decisions of the Security Council' and therefore no government could 'by unilateral action' determine how measures taken by the Council, within this context, should be carried out.[85] Therefore, as explored in the previous chapter, it appears that host state consent is only legally necessary for the deployment of a Security Council-mandated operation and not for any subsequent changes. Put differently, the host state cannot determine when an operation's deployment is to end or decide when specific Council measures should be terminated, nor could it determine how the mandated tasks are to be implemented.[86] Whilst there may be an anomaly within this argument, as ONUC was, at one point, mandated by the GA when the Council was deadlocked,[87] the Assembly extended ONUC's powers but did not create any significant, new tasks beyond what the Council had already created, thereby maintaining the 'legislative' characterisation.[88] Regardless, the invocation of language such as 'mandatory decisions' of the Council and the express stipulation that the host state cannot, unilaterally, alter these Council measures could be viewed as coercive action. That is, as Chapter 2 set out, if coercive action is understood as activities which override the element of voluntariness then, arguably, this is one such example, as the host state is unable to

78 Annual Report (n30) 7, 35.
79 Annual Report (n30) 24, 37–39.
80 UNGA Res 1671 (XVI) (18 December 1961) UN Doc S/RES/1671/XVI; S/RES/169 (n55).
81 Franck (n29) 641.
82 S/RES/145 (n55).
83 Franck (n29) 641.
84 UNSC, 'Exchange of Correspondence between the Secretary-General and the President of the Republic of the Congo Concerning Matadi' (30 March 1961) UN Doc S/4775, 3.
85 ibid.
86 Miller (n72) 15.
87 UNGA Res 1474 (ES-IV) (20 September 1960) UN Doc A/RES/1474(ES-IV).
88 B Oswald, H Durham and A Bates, *Documents on the Law of UN Peace Operations* (OUP 2010) 22.

voluntarily alter or reject changes to the 'mandatory' Security Council decisions. As such, when a peacekeeping operation is undertaking mandated tasks that the host state may wish to challenge, but cannot, then this could amount to intervention and therefore an expansion of peacekeeping's legal framework and a violation of the principle of non-intervention.

For the United Nations' subsequent operations in the Congo, as these were all mandated by the Security Council, it is arguable that the ONUC approach extends and, consequently, these are also legislative interventions. Therefore, the host state is, again, not legally required to consent to any changes to the operation, once it is deployed, as evidenced in the previous section of this chapter when consent was not needed or obtained for MONUC's stabilisation evolution into MONUSCO. Similarly, consent was not provided when the Security Council authorised the deployment of the Force Intervention Brigade (FIB)[89] – a unique, forceful unit authorised to undertake unprecedented levels of force in tactical operations.[90] For both these substantial changes, it is arguable that, whilst not legally necessary under the UN Charter, consent should have been obtained, particularly for the introduction of the FIB, based on the novelty of the concept and to ensure the peacekeeping force complied with international law and did not violate the norm of non-intervention. Although it could be counter-argued that there was no need to obtain explicit consent for the FIB, given the regional involvement in its creation and because the Congolese government was said to have manipulated the situation to ensure the Brigade was created,[91] its impact on the principles of peacekeeping remains. That is, it could be argued that the FIB created a new expansion of peacekeeping and the fundamental principles and subsequently constricted the principle of non-intervention. In other words, it created a new hole or exception within the red boundary line that demarcates both peacekeeping and non-intervention. As such, it is arguable that such a novel development should have required the explicit consent of the host state. Whilst it could, again, be argued that consent was implicit, based on the government's agreement to undertake joint operations with the FIB,[92] the fact remains that the FIB broadened peacekeeping's boundaries, bringing it closer to crossing the threshold into intervention.

89 UNSC, '"Intervention Brigade" Authorised' (28 March 2013) Meetings Coverage SC/10964.

90 S/RES/2098 (n12).

91 K Berwouts, 'DRC/North Kivu: Waiting for the Intervention Brigade' (*African Arguments*, 22 July 2003) <https://africanarguments.org/2013/07/22/drc-north-kivu-waiting-for-the-intervention-brigade-by-kris-berwouts/>.

92 See: PI Labuda, 'United Nations Peacekeeping as Intervention by Invitation: Host State Consent and the Use of Force in Security Council-Mandated Stabilisation Operations' (2020) JUFIL 1–37; D Olivier, 'The FIB Goes to War' (*African Defence Review*, 29 August 2013) <https://www.africandefence.net/the-fib-goes-to-war/> and UNSC, 'Final Report of the Group of Experts on the DRC' (23 January 2014) UN Doc S/2014/42.

Again, it could also be argued that, from a TWAIL perspective, these substantial alterations, taken without explicit host state consent, reflect the power differentials between the host state and the peacekeeping operation. That is, it could be said that once that element of sovereignty is forgone, and the United Nations has been allowed to enter the host state, the operation, in essence, retains that part of the sovereignty, using it to make key decisions about the functioning of the operation within the host's territory. Indeed, this could, again, be viewed as another example of Anghie's dynamic of difference with the dominant United Nations (in particular the mandating Security Council) identifying a gap between themselves and the subordinate 'other' (the host state) and then seeking to reduce that gap by mandating specific tasks which the peacekeeping operation must undertake.

Maintaining or Coercing Consent?

Although a peacekeeping operation still retains its legality, then, the lack of consent to substantial changes takes the operation much closer to the intervention boundary line, as it is possible to view these changes as forms of coercive action undertaken by the peacekeeping operation/UN to alter the host state – as occurred, for example, throughout ONUC's deployment, with the shift from MONUC to MONUSCO and with the creation of the FIB. This then leads to the second key issue – the maintenance of host state consent throughout the operations deployment – and the distinction between *de jure* and *de facto* consent in practice, which was set out in Chapter 3. Within the DRC, on numerous occasions the Congolese government has withdrawn effective consent and has acted to thwart the activities of the peacekeeping operations. In these instances, *de jure* consent is maintained, as this 'cannot be withdrawn within a mandate', but *de facto* the host government can rescind its effective cooperation.[93] Sustaining consent, in such instances, becomes a political issue, with 'either a re-definition of the mandate to appease the host government and/or some kind of political pressure' to get the host state to agree to the extension of the operation's mandate.[94]

For ONUC, difficulties arose almost immediately between the United Nations/ONUC and the newly formed Congolese government which were exacerbated by both the decolonisation period and Cold War dynamics which were explored in Chapter 2. Indeed, Congo's first prime minister, Lumumba, chose to turn to the Soviet Union for assistance after relations with the West broke down, resulting in a tense relationship between Lumumba and

93 Interviewee 12 (n2).
94 ibid.

the then Secretary-General, Hammarskjöld.[95] Whilst the government had requested UN support, it was initially very hostile towards ONUC and 'every Congolese political faction considered ONUC the enemy'.[96] Even when ONUC was viewed more favourably, Congo's political leaders 'change[d] their views as often as their suits'.[97] Lumumba, in particular, severely criticised the operation, arguing that it was not doing enough to prevent the Katangan secession.[98] Again, as previously noted, whilst this did not deter Hammarskjöld or his successor, U Thant, from implementing the Security Council mandates as they wished (underlining that this could be deemed to be coercive action and therefore intervention), it created an undesirable tension between the operation and the government. From a TWAIL perspective, this also highlights, again, the remnants of the colonial dynamics which still lingered throughout decolonisation, as was seen in Chapter 2. In particular, Chapter 2 noted how Lumumba's relationship with the United Nations and the Western states could be viewed as an example of a 'Northern subversive strategy' designed to undo regimes which were not favourable to Western hegemonic states.[99]

Furthermore, as ONUC became increasingly forceful, the loss of consent – both from the host state and other dominant armed actors in the territory – placed individual peacekeepers at risk. As Hatto notes, ONUC demonstrates that if some non-state groups withdraw their consent to the United Nations' presence, then the safety of UN peacekeepers may be at risk.[100] This arguably demonstrates that whilst *de facto* or effective consent may not be legally necessary, it is evidently important for the operational success and the safety of the peacekeepers. This highlights the importance of maintaining host state consent throughout deployment and perhaps demonstrates a more practical nuance within peacekeeping's legal framework. That is, the practicalities or realities of peacekeeping in the field may often underpin or buttress the legal principles in some form of an indirect, bottom-up approach which, ultimately, seemingly emphasises the importance and relevance of peacekeeping's principles, particularly the principle of host state consent.

95 See: A O'Malley, '"What an Awful Body the UN Have Become!!" Anglo-American-UN Relations During the Congo Crisis, February–December 1961' (2016) 14(1) JTransStud 26–46, 31.

96 WJ Durch, 'The UN Operation in the Congo: 1960–1964' in WJ Durch (ed) *The Evolution of UN Peacekeeping: Case Studies and Comparative Analysis* (St Martin's Press 1993) 315–352, 345.

97 ibid, 333.

98 B Urquhart, 'Character Sketches: Patrice Lumumba' <https://news.un.org/en/spotlight/patrice-lumumba-brian-urquhart>.

99 BS Chimni, 'Third World Approaches to International Law: A Manifesto' (2006) 8 ICLR 3–27, 6.

100 R Hatto, 'From Peacekeeping to Peacebuilding: The Evolution of the Role of the United Nations in Peace Operations' (2013) 95(891/892) IRRC 495–515, 498.

Despite these potential lessons which could have been taken from ONUC, similar tensions have persisted in the United Nations' later operations. Initially, when the United Nations re-entered the Congo with MONUC, there were few tensions between the host and the operation. This was perhaps due to the fact that it was a difficult transition period, with a weak government, and there was, therefore, an element of reliance on MONUC for ensuring the implementation of the Lusaka Agreement and ending the conflict. This reliance by weak transitional governments is said to lead to the tolerance of a more significant level of intervention as the host government becomes reliant on the United Nations for security and development assistance.[101] Arguably, this was reflected in MONUC's generally positive relationship with the Congolese government within the first few years of its deployment. However, as is typical with transition governments, as they become stronger, they are less interested in a significant military presence and interference in government practices.[102] Indeed, the tipping point for the Congolese state appears to have been the 2006 elections – the first 'democratic' elections since the country gained independence in 1960. Following this, MONUC/MONUSCO has had a tumultuous relationship with the Congolese government, in particular Kabila, who, when asked about the peacekeeping operation, said it was 'a love-hate relationship'.[103] Whilst noting that both MONUSCO and the Congo were in the same boat – if one succeeded, so did the other – Kabila argued that was a difference in interpretations of 'success', with the operation focusing on 'elections and human rights' whilst the state viewed a reduction in armed groups and a population living in 'total harmony' to be the markers of success.[104] This view of the United Nations has driven repeated calls for the operation's exit. As previously noted, in 2009–2010, prior to MONUC's evolution into MONUSCO, Kabila repeatedly called for the United Nations' departure, which he continued to reiterate throughout his tenure.[105] Most notably, in 2018, when the country prepared to hold further elections, Kabila once again demanded UN withdrawal, arguing that their presence had now been 'largely mitigated'.[106] However, it has been suggested that Kabila knew that these attempts to 'get rid' of MONUSCO would be 'very risky' as 'he could risk his own power by putting so much pressure' on the United Nations

101 I Johnstone, 'Managing Consent in Contemporary Peacekeeping Operations' (2011) 18(2) IntPeacekeep 168–182, 174–175.

102 ibid.

103 Foreign Affairs, 'Big Man in Congo: A Conversation with Joseph Kabila' (*Foreign Affairs*, 14 December 2018) <https://www.foreignaffairs.com/interviews/2018-12-14/big-man-congo>.

104 ibid.

105 UN News (n41).

106 UNGA Plenary (73rd Session, 6th & 7th Meetings) (25 September 2018) UN Doc GA/12062.

to withdraw.[107] Instead, Kabila is said to have 'lived with them [MONUSCO] and used them to get rid of this own opponents', such as Jean Pierre Bemba.[108] This, again, highlights, how the UN peacekeeping operation can, at times, be considered to be a form of coercive action designed to alter the host state (and therefore intervention) as the host state's clear rejections of the operation and withdrawal of effective consent are, in essence, ineffective. In other words, there is a loss of the element of voluntariness here as the host state cannot eject the operation or challenge its tasks during the mandate period. Furthermore, the remarks by Kabila, in particular the statement made about differing interpretations of success, typify the TWAIL arguments which have been made throughout the previous chapters, concerning the hegemonic ideals and standards which are embedded within peacekeeping and international law. Indeed, there is a clear divide here, with the Global South state (the Congolese government) seeking to challenge the dominant powers' (UN) agenda yet unable to because of the 'legalised hierarchy' which the United Nations is predicated upon.[109] This could again be viewed, then, as another example of international law acknowledging and reinforcing 'substantial power differentials between its participants'[110] as peacekeeping's frameworks and the composition of the United Nations uphold the mandatory decisions of the Security Council, thereby maintaining the dominance of the Council and, in particular, the permanent five members.

Making Sense of Consent in the DRC

The United Nations' endeavours in the Congo demonstrate the nuances within the principle of consent and, as was seen in Chapter 3, the role of consent in acting as the thin red boundary line between peacekeeping and intervention. In particular, the United Nations' experience in the Congo highlights how consent may only be legally required for the deployment of a Security Council-mandated peacekeeping operation but seemingly still needs to be maintained throughout deployment, firstly, to a certain degree for the functioning of the operation and, secondly, to prevent the operation from treading or even crossing the interventionist line. As this section has outlined, maintaining host state consent has been crucial when trying to implement a mandate as there is 'little you can do' without the host's consent.[111] Indeed,

107 Interview with Congolese Independent Expert ('Interviewee 5') (Oxford, UK, 29 October 2019) DOI: <http://doi.org/10.17639/nott.7119> pg 6.

108 ibid.

109 G Simpson, *Great Powers and Outlaw States: Unequal Sovereignty in the International Legal Order* (CUP 2004) 170–171.

110 H Charlesworth, 'International Legal Encounters with Democracy' (2017) 8(6) Global Policy 34–43, 34.

111 Interviewee 16 (n18).

the Effectiveness of Peace Operations Network has argued that a main strategic constraint of MONUSCO has been the degree to which cooperation with the host state has diminished over the years.[112] It noted that many interlocutors have observed that MONUSCO 'has been working with a government that does not want it to be there'.[113] For some in the Department of Peace Operations (DPO), this has been a source of frustration as they recognise the somewhat improved relationship with the new president, Tshisekedi, and note, with regret, 'all those years we spent knocking our head, trying to work with Kabila and his obstinacy'.[114] However, others who have worked in the mission in the field argue very differently, noting that the Force component, for example, still has a great deal of operational freedom, even when lacking host state consent or support.[115] This suggests that there may perhaps be a gap between the legal, political and conceptual understanding of the principle of consent in UN headquarters and the operational realities in the mission headquarters, suggesting a need for an increase in dialogue between the different UN personnel to ensure a unified understanding of the principle and how it should best be interpreted and applied within peacekeeping.

Overall, as previously noted, maintaining consent can become a political issue, requiring changes to the mandate to appease the host or some form of political pressure on the host government. However, as was seen in Chapter 3, exerting some form of pressure on the host state to maintain its consent to the operation, in itself, could be perceived as a form of coercive action to influence change in the state and, therefore, intervention. Again, this leads us back to the persistent power differentials within both peacekeeping and international relations more broadly, which a TWAIL lens highlights and which, in turn, influence the interpretation and application of the fundamental principles of peacekeeping.

Indeed, it could be argued that the disregard or seeming manipulation of host state consent expands peacekeeping's legal framework as a significant amount of emphasis is placed upon the host state's initial consent to deployment, which then permits an operation to undertake numerous actions or changes once within the host state. As such, this broader interpretation of the principle expands peacekeeping's frameworks, similarly expanding peacekeeping's red boundary line and thereby undermining or, at times, contravening the principle of non-intervention, as the Congo examples illustrate. Once again, as Chapter 3 noted, the principle of consent ultimately prevents the deployment or presence of the peacekeeping operation from crossing

112 Effectiveness of Peace Operations Network, 'Assessing the Effectiveness of the United Nations Mission in the DRC/MONUC-MONUSCO' (NUPI 2019) 18–19, 120–121.

113 ibid.

114 Interviewee 9 (n1) 6.

115 Contrast, Interviewee 16 (n18) and Interviewee 11 (n23).

peacekeeping's boundary line and becoming intervention. However, it could be argued that when relations between the operation and the host government break down and consent is effectively withdrawn, then the specific actions of the operation during this time (such as MONUC's shift to MONUSCO) could be viewed as a form of intervention. This therefore, again, demonstrates the fluidity of peacekeeping's boundaries and frameworks and the blurring of the boundary between peacekeeping and intervention.

Impartiality

As with the principle of consent, the interpretation and application of the principle of impartiality in the United Nations' operations in the Congo have also presented numerous issues. This section will explore two of these – joint operations with the Congolese armed forces (FARDC) and the United Nations' human rights due diligence policy (HRDDP) – which were outlined in Chapter 2. Whilst there are numerous other examples throughout the United Nations' history in the Congo which could highlight the application of impartiality (such as ONUC's involvement in the Katanga secession and MONUC and MONUSCO's capacity building or justice reform)[116] joint military operations are perhaps the most illustrative example. Through an examination of these, the broader issues with the principle of impartiality will be highlighted. The first of these is the difficulty in fulfilling a complex mandate or host state requests and remaining impartial. The second is the risks of conducting joint operations to the perception of the operation by locals, armed groups and other actors, and the third is the United Nations' potential implication in violations of international law by host state actors. This section will explore, then, how these issues, which arise from a broader interpretation of impartiality, have expanded peacekeeping's frameworks and, consequently, undermine the principle of non-intervention. This section will therefore question whether there must be limits to this evolution in order for impartiality to remain a legal principle, rather than simply a reflection of practice, and for it to regain peacekeeping's interventionist boundaries.

Joint Operations with the FARDC

As was seen in Chapter 3, the authorisation of joint operations between the host state and peacekeeping operation was a significant evolution both within UN peacekeeping and, specifically, within peacekeeping in the DRC. In the United Nations' first operation in the Congo, Hammarskjöld explicitly stated that the authority granted to ONUC could not be exercised 'either

116 CIVIC, 'Enabling Support by Mitigating Risk' (CIVIC, June 2020) <https://civiliansinconflict.org/publications/policy/enabling-support-by-mitigating-risk/>.

in competition with the representatives of the host government or in cooperation with them in any joint operation'.[117] Evidently, then, Hammarskjöld perceived joint ventures to be beyond the remit of peacekeeping, thereby narrowly interpreting the principle of impartiality and constricting peacekeeping's frameworks in this instance. This, in turn, supported the principle of non-intervention and reflected the general non-interventionist rhetoric at that time. However, 40 years later, as the United Nations returned to the Congo, the principle of impartiality was interpreted much more broadly when joint operations became a part of MONUC's mandate almost immediately.[118] In line with the United Nations' move to robust peacekeeping and the new concept of impartiality, which was discussed in the previous chapter, MONUC was soon tasked with protecting civilians and working in cooperation with the host state.

Partnership

MONUC first began to work closely with the Congolese state during 'phase II' of its deployment when the operation's size and tasks were expanded.[119] The Security Council tasked MONUC with establishing a joint structure with the Congolese Joint Military Commission, which was created under the Lusaka Ceasefire Agreement, to 'ensure close coordination' during MONUC's deployment.[120] This then led to numerous joint operations and increased cooperation, with 'co-signed orders' between the Congolese government and MONUSCO at the strategic, operational and higher levels of the military.[121] In particular, co-signed orders between MONUSCO and the FARDC began at the brigade and sector levels in South Kivu, Ituri and North Kivu, with the endorsement of senior military in Kinshasa.[122] A former Deputy-Force Commander within MONUC/MONUSCO noted that 'in terms of interaction and joint planning, lots of things had been done and where possible'.[123] Evidently, then, the newer concept of impartiality was interpreted and applied quite broadly within the Congo, almost instantaneously, and this continued, seemingly expanding even further as the operation became more robust and began to shift from MONUC to MONUSCO, with a larger, more complex mandate. For peacekeeping's frameworks, then, this broader interpretation of impartiality arguably expanded peacekeeping's boundary line, thereby taking the operation much closer to the intervention line and undermining

117 UNSC, 'Report of the Secretary General' (18 July 1960) UN Doc S/4389, 5.
118 S/RES/1291 (n9).
119 ibid, para 6, page 3.
120 ibid.
121 Interviewee 11 (n23) 45.
122 ibid.
123 ibid.

the principle of non-intervention. Once again, the differing interpretations of impartiality from ONUC to MONUC mirrored the shift from non-intervention to interventionist rhetoric that was seen throughout the development of the principle of non-intervention in Chapter 2.

From late 2008 onwards, MONUC was also increasingly mandated to support FARDC operations against armed groups as part of the former's protection of civilian tasks. Between 2008 and 2010, 'the Mission's mandate evolved significantly' and 'an increasingly comprehensive approach to the provision of support to FARDC was developed'.[124] During this period, one of the most notable joint operations was *Kimia II*, launched by the FARDC in 2009 in the East of Congo and supported by MONUC.[125] The aim of this operation was to forcibly disarm a Rwandan Hutu armed group, the Democratic Forces for the Liberation of Rwanda (FDLR), which had been present in the DRC since the Rwandan genocide.[126] The launching of *Kimia II* came after the DRC's joint operation (*Umoja Wetu*)[127] with Rwandan military forces, following a shift in political alliances between the DRC and Rwanda in January 2009. This marked a dramatic change in what had been an extremely turbulent relationship and was aimed at bringing peace and security to the region. The operation was therefore highly politicised and involved complex, historical regional matters, rather than simply the internal affairs of the Congo. This arguably raises two key, interconnected problems for the United Nations, which have reoccurred, in varying degrees, throughout MONUC/MONUSCO's other joint operations with the Congolese government.

Firstly, it seemingly draws the United Nations into, not only the internal affairs of the Congo, but also regional matters, thereby calling into question the United Nations' impartiality and, in turn, taking the operation closer to intervention. That is, whilst the rhetoric of impartiality remained within MONUC's mandate, supporting the host state in conducting operations against specific actors placed the United Nations against these actors (or other parties to the conflict), thereby potentially jeopardising the United Nations' impartiality. Indeed, the UN Special Rapporteur on Extrajudicial Executions argued that 'the Security Council's mandate [had] transformed MONUC into a party to the conflict in the Kivus',[128] thus breaching impartiality and

124 L Zerrougui, 'Strengthening the Rule of Law and Protection of Civilians in the Democratic Republic of the Congo' (*UN Chronicle*, August 2018) <https://www.un.org/en/chronicle/article/strengthening-rule-law-and-protection-civilians-democratic-republic-congo>.

125 UNSC, 'Fourth Special Report of the Secretary-General on the United Nations Organization Mission in the Democratic Republic of the Congo' (21 November 2008) UN Doc S/2008/728, 3.

126 See: UNSC, 'Final Report of the Group of Experts on the Democratic Republic of the Congo' (12 December 2008) UN Doc S/2008/773, paras 69–113.

127 See: S Schulman and F Rusagara, 'Umoja Wetu: A Photo Essay' (2009) 154(2) RUSIJ 90–97.

128 S/2008/773 (n126).

potentially triggering international humanitarian law.[129] Again, this demonstrates how peacekeeping's frameworks are fluid, with the principles overlapping and often invoking other elements of international law, such as IHL, thereby contributing to peacekeeping's legal framework.

This broad interpretation and application of the principle of impartiality also has further practical consequences in relation to the perception of the operation and, potentially, the safety of peacekeepers. Given the complex history of the Congo and the Great Lakes region, support for these operations runs 'the risk of partiality' because of the organisation of rebel armed groups along ethnic lines.[130] In particular, MONUC-supported FARDC operations, such as *Kimia II*, were heavily influenced by the Tutsi-based rebel group CNDP which was 'increasingly resented by other local communities'.[131] This resulted in other Congolese armed groups forging alliances with the FDLR (the group which the joint operation was targeting) in order to protect their community interests.[132] A former MONUC senior military leader noted that the Force therefore had to deal with 'competing priorities' – the mandate, the support of the Congolese army and then attacks because of this support.[133] Indeed, they state that the attack on the Force in Semiliki 'was precisely because we [were] supporting the Congolese army'.[134] An expansive interpretation of impartiality therefore also risks peacekeepers' safety by embroiling them in conflict and presenting them as a target.[135]

Implications

This then leads to the second notable problem which the United Nations has faced when conducting joint operations with the Congolese armed forces – the potential implications for the United Nations if any negative conduct occurs during the operation. As seen in Chapter 3, joint operations not only stretch the principle of impartiality but also potentially implicate the United Nations in any violations or crimes committed by the host state forces whether before, during or after the joint operation. Indeed, *Kimia II* was severely criticised for failing 'miserably to root out the militias', for committing violations of international law and for aggravating 'an already

129 UNSG, 'Secretary-General's Bulletin: Observance by United Nations Forces of International Humanitarian Law' (6 August 1999) UN Doc ST/SGB/1999/13.

130 Vircoulon (n39).

131 ibid.

132 ibid.

133 Interviewee 9 (n1) 50.

134 ibid.

135 See: J Verweijen, 'Strange Battlefield Fellows: The Diagonal Interoperability between Blue Helmets and the Congolese Army' (2017) 24(3) IntPeacekeep 363–387.

devastating humanitarian crisis'.[136] It was further found that 'the human cost of the operations ha[d] been high due to the abuses perpetrated against civilian populations' by FARDC troops, FDLR and RUD-Urunana reprisal attacks and by Mai-Mai groups.[137] In particular, during the operation, former rebels of the political armed group CNDP,[138] who had been integrated into the FARDC, were found to have committed rapes and killings of civilians.[139] It is estimated that more than 1,400 civilians had been killed – half by the FDLR and half by Congolese and Rwandan armed forces and allied militia – with 7,500 women raped and 900,000 forced to flee their homes.[140] The Secretary-General later acknowledged these allegations, noting that 'some components of the United Nations system called for an immediate end to *Kimia II* and for the withdrawal of MONUC support for FARDC'.[141] Indeed, the UN Special Rapporteur on Extrajudicial Executions described the military operations as 'a disaster', with Operation *Kimia II* 'producing catastrophic results', and noted that in many areas the FARDC 'posed the greatest direct risk to security'.[142] Again, it is difficult to see how the United Nations could maintain its impartiality and, more broadly, the credibility of the organisation when it was supporting operations and forces that committed such acts. It also demonstrates how, in practice, there are differing understandings within the United Nations (both in the Secretariat and the operation) of what is an appropriate interpretation of the principle of impartiality, highlighting how, as Chapters 3 and 4 noted, the 'normative composition' of peacekeeping operations is 're-balanced each time'.[143] As such, it could be argued that this again exemplifies how peacekeeping's frameworks are continually contorted, re-interpreted and re-applied, thereby leaving the boundary between

136 D Steingberg, 'UN Must Stop Backing Congo's Disastrous Operation against Marauding Rebel Militias' (International Crisis Group, 30 November 2009) <https://www.crisisgroup.org/africa/central-africa/democratic-republic-congo/un-must-stop-backing-congos-disastrous-operation-against-marauding-rebel-militias>.

137 UNSC, 'Final Report of the Group of Experts on the Democratic Republic of the Congo' (23 November 2009) UN Doc S/2009/603, 8.

138 *Congrès National pour la Défense du Peuple*, led by Laurent Nkunda.

139 Human Rights Watch, 'DRC: Events of 2008' (HRW 2008) <https://www.hrw.org/world-report/2009/country-chapters/democratic-republic-congo>.

140 Human Rights Watch, 'You Will Be Punished: Attacks on Civilians in Eastern Congo' (HRW 2009) <https://www.hrw.org/sites/default/files/reports/drc1209webwcover2.pdf>.

141 UNSC, 'Thirtieth Report of the Secretary-General on the United Nations Organisation Mission in the Democratic Republic of the Congo' (4 December 2009) UN Doc S/2009/623, para 9.

142 P Alston, 'Press Statement by Professor Philip Alston, UN Special Rapporteur on Extrajudicial Executions. Mission to the DR Congo' (15 October 2009) <https://reliefweb.int/report/democratic-republic-congo/press-statement-professor-philip-alston-un-special-rapporteur>.

143 J Karlsrud, 'Special Representatives of the Secretary-General as Norm Arbitrators? Understanding Bottom-up Authority in UN Peacekeeping' (2013) 19(4) GG 525–544, 527.

peacekeeping and intervention uncertain and, thus, undermining the principle of non-intervention.

Furthermore, the Congolese military leadership also presented numerous problems for the United Nations and its maintenance of impartiality. The Congolese army commander, Major General Dieudonné Amuli Bahigwa, appointed a newly made general, former CNDP leader Bosco Ntaganda, as his effective deputy commander. At the time, Ntaganda was wanted on an arrest warrant issued by the International Criminal Court (ICC) for alleged war crimes and crimes against humanity[144] – a matter which the Congolese government was said to be aware of.[145] Nevertheless, rather than arrest Ntaganda, as they were legally obliged to do given they were a party to the ICC, the government removed Ntaganda's name from the official organisational structure of the *Kimia II* operation.[146] Then, in a letter to MONUC's head of mission, the Congolese Minister of Defence explicitly stated that Ntaganda was not playing a role in *Kimia II*.[147] However, it was later found that Ntaganda had played an important role in the operation, acting as the *de facto* deputy commander and overseeing the integration of CNDP soldiers into the FARDC.[148] MONUC had therefore, unknowingly, conducted a joint operation with a former rebel leader who was accused of gross violations of international law and who would later lead a mutiny to form the rebel group, M23.[149] M23 then went on to terrorise Eastern Congo, performing summary executions, rapes and forced recruitment of children, culminating in the group capturing the city of Goma and the United Nations subsequently launching the Force Intervention Brigade, specifically to target the M23 armed group.[150] Whilst the M23 were thought to have been defeated in 2013, in October 2021 the armed group re-emerged, continuing its insurgent campaign in Eastern Congo, with similar offences committed, leading to the deployment of an East African Community (EAC) force.[151]

During the *Kimia II* operation, MONUC and, consequently, the United Nations were therefore at risk of being complicit in the crimes committed

144 *The Prosecutor v Bosco Ntaganda* (Judgment) ICC-01/04-02/06 (8 July 2019).

145 HRW (n139).

146 ibid.

147 UNSC, 'Twenty-Eighth Report of the Secretary-General on the United Nations Organization Mission to the Democratic Republic of Congo' (20 June 2009) UN Doc S/2009/335, para 3.

148 HRW (n140) 43–44.

149 See: Al Jazeera, 'Q&A: Who Are DR Congo's M23 Rebels?' (*AL Jazeera*, 5 Nov 2013) <https://www.aljazeera.com/news/africa/2013/08/201382411593336904.html>.

150 See for example: Human Rights Watch, 'DR Congo: M23 Rebels Kill, Rape Civilians' (*Human Rights Watch*, 22 July 2013) <https://www.hrw.org/news/2013/07/22/dr-congo-m23-rebels-kill-rape-civilians>.

151 See: France24, 'East African Leaders Agree to Extend Troop Deployment in Eastern DR Congo' (France 24, 1 June 2023) <https://www.france24.com/en/africa/20230601-east-african-leaders-agree-to-extend-troop-deployment-in-eastern-dr-congo>.

by the FARDC thereby potentially breaching the principle of impartiality. Moreover, this could also be viewed as an example of the host state still exercising its sovereignty in the presence of an external actor. That is, as was noted within the principle of consent, whilst the host state may not be able to force a withdrawal of an operation during the mandate period, it has various tools at its disposal which permits it to still exercise its sovereign rights (here to determine the composition of its national armed forces), even when it has forgone an element of sovereignty to the peacekeeping operation. In this instance, the state still deployed people to its armed forces as it wished and simply withheld or altered information it then gave to the United Nations.

Despite this incident, MONUC and MONUSCO continued to work alongside the Congolese armed forces. On 1 January 2010, MONUC began a new phase of joint military operations with the FARDC, against the FDLR, known as *Amani Leo*.[152] The purpose of this operation was similar to that of *Kimia II* – to protect civilians, to prevent armed groups, such as the FDLR, from re-gaining territory and to 'create conditions for stabilisation and re-establishment of State authority'.[153] However, there was one noticeable difference with this operation in comparison to previous joint ventures – for *Amani Leo*, MONUC began to condition its support to specific FARDC units, based on human rights vetting.[154] Both the FARDC and MONUC military commands agreed to numerous measures such as the deployment of Military Police at the battalion level 'to prevent and sanction violations of human rights, international humanitarian and refugee law by their own forces'.[155] These conditions embedded within the operational directive of *Amani Leo* arguably demonstrate the lessons which the United Nations had learned from *Kimia II*, that is, the need to include conditions and precautions to limit or prevent violations and UN complicity. Thus, a conditionality policy was born, which, for peacekeeping's frameworks, could be viewed as an attempt to retract the boundaries of impartiality and counter the potential complicity of the United Nations in violations of international law. The conditionality policy could be viewed, then, as another reimagining of the principle of impartiality and, perhaps, an implicit recognition that the broadening of impartiality to include joint operations had been taken too far. In other words, the elastic band of peacekeeping's boundaries had been stretched to

152 MONUC, 'DR Congo: Peacekeepers Plan Operation Amani Leo with FARDC in North Kivu' (*MONUC*, 19 Jan 2010) <https://reliefweb.int/report/democratic-republic-congo/dr-congo-peacekeepers-plan-operation-amani-leo-fardc-north-kivu>.

153 MONUC, 'MONUC Outlines Cooperation with FARDC in Operation Amani Leo' (*MONUC*, 5 March 2010) <https://monuc.unmissions.org/en/monuc-outlines-cooperation-fardc-operation-amani-leo>.

154 Global Security, 'National Committee for the Defense of the People (CNDP)' <https://www.globalsecurity.org/military/world/para/cndp.htm>.

155 MONUC (n152).

its limits and the conditionality policy was an attempt to retract this boundary, shrinking peacekeeping's frameworks, reducing peacekeeping's scope and bringing it away from the interventionist line.

From 'Conditionality' to 'Due Diligence'

The consequences stemming from MONUC's joint operations with the FARDC therefore led to the development of a conditionality policy. In particular, it arose as a direct response to the Kiwanja massacre in 2008 where an estimated 150 people were killed, half a mile away from MONUSCO peacekeepers.[156] As such, the United Nations was criticised for 'the lack of response and some of the joint support and joint operations that were supposed to go into the FARDC'.[157] Whilst the Security Council had noted, within MONUC's mandate, that joint operations were to be undertaken 'in accordance with international humanitarian, human rights and refugee law', this was evidently not enough.[158] MONUC officials, including the protection advisor under the Deputy SRSG, 'who was detailing with OCHA and the protection cluster', therefore began to draft a 'non-paper on the conditionality' on how they should engage and the criteria for determining who they could and could not work with.[159] This emphasises the key role of the office of the SRSG/SG in interpreting norms and shaping peacekeeping, in this instance, motivated by the concerns over the FARDC's behaviour and the possibility of the United Nations being complicit in that behaviour when they provided support or directly engaged in joint operations.[160] However, despite this clear need for steps to be taken, the conditionality policy was said to be a 'very sensitive topic' with some of the senior leadership concerned about the political partnership with the Congolese government and the difficulty in carrying this message to the government and national counterparts.[161] Indeed, to place conditions on MONUC support would be to place pressure on an already precarious relationship and could have risked losing the operation's relationship with the host state and, consequently, host state consent.[162] Again, this

156 Human Rights Watch, 'Killings in Kiwanja: The UN's Inability to Protect Civilians' (HRW, 11 December 2018) <https://www.hrw.org/report/2008/12/11/killings-kiwanja/uns-inability-protect-civilians>.

157 Interview with Senior Human Rights Officer in the Office of the UN High Commissioner of Human Rights ('Interviewee 13') (New York, 6 December 2019) DOI: <http://doi.org/10.17639/nott.7119>.

158 UNSC Res 1856 (22 December 2008) UN Doc S/RES/1856, para 3(g).

159 Interviewee 13 (n157).

160 'Leaked Memo: MONUC-Draft Policy on Conditionality of Support to the FARDC' (12 October 2009) <http://www.innercitypress.com/OLA1MONUC101209.pdf>.

161 Interviewee 13 (n157).

162 See: S Sebastián and A Gorur, 'UN Peacekeeping & Host-State Consent: How Missions Navigate Relationships with Governments' (Stimson Centre March 2018).

could be viewed as another example of how the fundamental principles exist in a competitive overlapping arena. That is, withdrawing the boundaries of impartiality here by placing conditions on the host state had the potential of impacting the United Nations' relationship with the host government and consequently impacting the principle of consent. Similarly, as Chapter 3 discussed, conditioning support could also be viewed as coercive action designed to influence the state and therefore intervention, as the United Nations may be deemed to be exerting pressure on the government to make alterations to their armed forces, in order to meet both the United Nations' standards and basic international laws. Furthermore, from a TWAIL perspective, regardless of the good intentions of the policy, as was also seen in Chapter 3, it could be viewed as another example of dominant powers' standards and ideals being imposed on the Global South.

MONUC was therefore placed in a difficult position, with political officers within the Secretariat concerned about this relationship and arguing that as they had a Security Council mandate, they had no choice but to support the Congolese armed forces.[163] On the other hand, legal officers within the operation recognised that the mandate did not absolve peacekeepers, or the United Nations, from its international obligations 'in terms of IHL and human rights'.[164] Indeed, the concept did not gain traction until an Office of Legal Affairs (OLA) opinion, which stated the United Nations' legal responsibilities, including individual legal responsibility for Force Commanders or SRSGs, 'if a peacekeeping operation is either aiding and abetting or being complicit to international crimes'.[165] In an internal memorandum the OLA stated that if MONUC had reason to believe that the FARDC were committing violations of international law, they 'may not lawfully continue to support that operation, but must cease its participation in it completely'.[166] MONUC could therefore 'not lawfully provide logistic or "service" support to any FARDC operation' if it had reason to 'believe that the FARDC units' were involved in such violations.[167] The OLA argued that this was on the basis of the United Nations' obligations under 'customary international law and from the Charter to uphold, promote and encourage respect for human rights, international humanitarian law and refugee law'.[168] The OLA therefore justified the conditionality policy on the basis of peacekeeper's obligations

163 Interviewee 13 (n157).
164 ibid.
165 ibid, 46.
166 *New York Times*, 'Confidential Note from the UN Office of Legal Affairs to Mr. Le Roy, Head of the Department of Peacekeeping Operations: MONUC-Operation Kimia 2' (1 April 2009) <https://www.nytimes.com/interactive/projects/documents/united-nations-correspondence-on-peacekeeping-in-the-democratic-republic-of-the-congo#p=1>.
167 ibid.
168 ibid.

under international law, rather than as a necessity for the maintenance of the principle of impartiality. This further contributed to peacekeeping's legal framework by reaffirming the potential application of these broader areas of international law.

Following this, the policy was then implemented into MONUC's practice, under the leadership of the then-Deputy SRSG for the Rule of Law (and later SRSG for MONUSCO) Leila Zerrougui.[169] This highlighted the important role which senior leadership, particularly within the office of the SG/SRSG, have in acting as norm entrepreneurs and shaping the peacekeeping operation as, in quite an irregular fashion, the first occasion in which MONUC suspended support for a Congolese operation 'defied all procedure because it was done in a very kind of executive fashion'.[170] That is, the current Under-Secretary General for Peace Operations, Jean-Pierre Lacroix, in a press conference in the Congo, 'on the spot' said that 'he would suspend support' for a Congolese battalion which had had been accused of crimes.[171] The policy was then officially endorsed by the Security Council in MONUC's mandate in 2009 where it stated that MONUC support for an FARDC-led military operation was 'strictly conditioned on FARDC's compliance' with IHL, human rights and refugee law.[172] The Council stressed that MONUC and FARDC cooperation should be conducted on the basis of joint planning, with MONUC interceding with the FARDC command 'if elements of a FARDC unit receiving MONUC's support are suspected of having committed grave violations of such laws'.[173] The inclusion of conditionality within MONUC's Security Council mandate was therefore important as it removed the previous caveat argument made by some political officers who argued that support had to be maintained, regardless of any violations, because it was within MONUC's mandate.[174]

The conditionality policy, or the roots of the HRDDP, therefore began as a very Congo-specific policy, focused on addressing UN complicity and, by extension, arguably restricting or regaining an element of the expanded principle of impartiality. However, it was soon recognised that this was an issue which was not Congo specific. According to senior UN personnel, 'there was a sense of urgency, that we could no longer support operations that inflicted harm on civilians' and 'ultimately, we needed to apply that same policy across the board'.[175] As explored in Chapter 3, this then led to the development of

169 Interviewee 13 (n157). See also: CIVIC (n116).
170 ibid.
171 ibid.
172 UNSC Res 1906 (23 December 2009) UN Doc S/RES/1906 para 22.
173 ibid.
174 Interviewee 13 (n157).
175 Interviewee 10 (n21).

the HRDDP which was adopted as an internal policy in July 2011[176] before being made public in March 2013.[177] This then takes us to the most infamous joint venture to be launched in the DRC – the Force Intervention Brigade – which was deployed, perhaps not so coincidentally, at a similar time to the publication of the HRDDP.

The FIB: An African Solution?

The FIB was deployed as a separate offensive combat unit within the Force Component of MONUSCO in March 2013.[178] The FIB was originally composed of 3,069 soldiers and was mandated to carry out 'targeted offensive operations' either unilaterally or jointly with the Congolese Armed Forces, FARDC.[179] Such operations were to be carried out 'in a robust, highly mobile and versatile manner', with the aim of preventing the expansion of armed groups, neutralising these groups and disarming them.[180] Again, the objective of the FIB, to target armed groups in the East, was similar to the previous joint operations MONUC/MONUSCO had undertaken with the FARDC. In particular, the FIB was deployed to target the Mouvement du 23 mars (M23) which had emerged out of former CNDP rebels that had been recruited into the FARDC but later mutinied, denouncing their conditions within the Congolese armed forces and accusing the government of insufficiently committing to the peace agreement.[181] Whilst the Brigade is most often discussed in relation to the use of force, it also significantly expanded the principle of impartiality, arguably in three main ways: its invocation of regional interests and interventions; its specific targeting mandate; and the subsequent perception it created of the United Nations.

Firstly, the way in which the Brigade materialised greatly differed in comparison to the previous joint operations, in that it emerged as an idea amongst external states. The concept was initially conceived at the International Conference of the Great Lakes (ICGLR) and was supported by the South African Development Community (SADC).[182] As the M23 pursued its strategy in the summer of 2012, the African Union and the ICGLR proposed the

176 UN Secretary General, Decision No 2011/18, 13 July 2011. See also: HP Aust, 'The UN Human Rights Due Diligence Policy: An Effective Mechanism against Complicity of Peacekeeping Forces?' (2015) 20(1) JCSL 61–73.

177 UNGA-SC, 'Human Rights Due Diligence Policy' (5 March 2013) UN Doc A/67/775-S/2013/110.

178 S/RES/2098 (n14).

179 ibid.

180 S/RES/2098 (n12) para 12.

181 UNSC, 'Report of the Secretary General on the UN Organisation Stabilisation Mission in the Democratic Republic of the Congo' (23 May 2012) UN Doc S/2012/355.

182 See: UN Doc S/2013/119 (n56); UNSC, 'Statement by the Presidential of the Security Council' (19 October 2012) UN Doc S/PRST/2012/22, 2.

establishment of a neutral international force to 'eradicate existing armed groups'[183] and sent a team of representatives to meet with MONUSCO personnel 'to see what could be done'.[184] Whilst the concept of a Brigade had 'clearly garnered some support from Kinshasa and other parts of the region', 'it was quite clear that this neutral force was always going to lack the means to be deployed'.[185] In particular, it is said that the Security Council, 'as is still the case, didn't want to finance [as occurred] in Somalia, a new African force'.[186] Instead, the Council requested that the Secretary-General report on options for MONUSCO,[187] leading to a UN Military Advisor meeting with the Chairs of SADC and ICGLR to discuss harmonising the regional and UN initiatives.[188] The FIB could therefore be viewed as a replication of some of the interventionist practices discussed in earlier chapters. In particular, it could be viewed as a form of collective security or multilateral intervention, whereby a group of states have identified a problem within another state and agreed to collectively act in an attempt to remedy this problem, all the while under the auspices of the United Nations.

Moreover, it could also be viewed as a form of regional intervention and, for some, was 'a move for African solutions to African problems',[189] which, as seen in Chapter 2, is more preferable, from a TWAIL perspective, than imported, foreign solutions.[190] Indeed, the force was composed of troops from South Africa, Tanzania and Malawi[191] and is said to have been 'a successful attempt of African solutions to claim, take and keep ownership of the African conflict – which Congo is'.[192] Furthermore, the FIB was launched alongside a regional political agreement – the 'Peace, Security and Cooperation (PSC) Framework' – which outlined 'key action at the national, regional and

183 Declaration of the Heads of State and Government of the Member States of the ICGLR at the Fourth Ordinary Summit and Special Session on Sexual and Gender Based Violence, Kampala (15–16 December 2011) para 1 <https://www.icglr-rtf.org/publication/view/kampala-declaration-2011/>; Declaration of the Heads of State and Government of the Member States of the ICGLR on the Security Situation in Eastern DRC – Extraordinary summit, Addis Ababa (15 July 2012) preamble and para 4.

184 Interviewee 9 (n1).

185 ibid.

186 ibid.

187 UNSC Res 2076 (20 November 2012) UN Doc S/RES/2076, preamble, para 9.

188 UNSC, 'Letter Dated 27 November 2012 from the Secretary-General Addressed to the President of the Security Council' (27 November 2012) UN Doc S/2013/876.

189 Interviewee 11 (n23) 56.

190 A Mazuri, *Towards a Pax Africana: A Study of Ideology and Ambition* (University of Chicago 1967) 203.

191 Declaration of the Heads of State and Government of the Member States of the International Conference of the Great Lakes Region on the Security Situation in Eastern DRC – 5th Extraordinary Summit, Kampala (24 November 2012) paras 10–12.

192 Interview with Independent Expert ('Interviewee 3') (Skype, 10 December 2018) DOI: <http://doi.org/10.17639/nott.7119>.

international levels required to end the recurring cycles of violence' in Eastern DRC.[193] The framework has since proved to be most useful in weakening some of Congo's long-standing rebel groups, the FDLR and ADF,[194] and contributing to the (temporary) defeat of M23. The benefits of the framework have therefore 'outlasted the benefits of the intervention brigade but, of course, one is more spectacular than the other'.[195] For the Congo, in particular, the FIB also put pressure on Rwanda, which had intervened extensively in the DRC for many years, 'not to intervene and not to provide covert support to the M23'.[196] Therefore, 'what happened around the FIB' is said to have been a 'game changer', as 'the Congolese FARDC was suddenly able to overcome the boogeyman of Rwanda'.[197] The FIB thus played a key role in Congo's attempts to rid itself of historical, regional or neighbouring intervention.

Again, this creates an interesting dynamic which has been previously discussed. That is, it highlights the shift in interventionist practices in the modern era, the move to regional intervention or, specifically in this case, 'African solutions to African problems' which, whilst still intervention, is seemingly more palatable. Indeed, as the M23 re-emerged in 2021, the regional organisation EAC deployed troops to Eastern DRC in 2022/2023, firstly with a contingent of Kenyan soldiers, followed by Burundian, Ugandan and South Sudanese contingents.[198] Similar to the FIB, this has been linked to a political process but whereas the FIB was not adequately linked to the PSC Framework, the EAC is leading on both the political dialogue and the military action, with EAC members reiterating their commitment to a political process, acknowledging that there cannot be a purely military solution.[199] There is therefore greater Global South ownership and less UN involvement, highlighting both the shift in intervention practices and the development of regional organisations and interventions.

However, whilst this form of intervention does break away from Anghie's dynamic of difference and the practice of the hegemonic powers intervening

193 UNSC, 'Special Report of the Secretary-General on the Democratic Republic of the Congo and the Great Lakes Region' (27 February 2003) UN Doc S/2013/119, 7.

194 *UN News*, 'Five Years On' (*UN News*, 28 Feb 2018) <https://ungreatlakes.unmissions.org/five-years-progress-has-been-made-implementation-peace-security-and-cooperation-framework-drc-and>; UN Office of the Special Envoy for the Great Lakes Region, 'Joint Press Release on the Peace, Security and Cooperation Framework, JPR21' (27 February 2018) <https://ungreatlakes.unmissions.org/five-years-peace-security-and-cooperation-framework-drc-and-region-remains-central-achieving-lasting>.

195 Interviewee 9 (n1) 55.

196 Interviewee 9 (n1) 65.

197 ibid.

198 France24 (n151).

199 J Russo, 'The East African Community Steps into the Crisis in the DRC. Will It Help?' (IPI 12 December 2022) <https://theglobalobservatory.org/2022/12/east-african-community-crisis-drc/>.

to offer solutions or close the gap with the Global South, it is not without its problems. As was noted in earlier chapters, the concept has been used to justify extensive inter-African intervention, which is as 'problematic and riddled with hidden agendas as traditional interventions'.[200] This has particularly been the case in the Congo with its complex relationships with Rwanda and Uganda and, more specifically, for the FIB, with the allegations of sexual exploitation and abuse by FIB troops, mainly from the South African contingent – a matter which will be explored in the subsequent chapter.

FIB Targeting: Evolution or Breach?

The creation of the FIB within this complex mix of regional interventions is therefore a significant expansion of the principle of impartiality, which consequently expands peacekeeping's frameworks, potentially undermining the principle of non-intervention. Similarly, the second way in which the FIB expanded impartiality, potentially even breaching the principle, is through its use of targeting. That is, the Security Council mandated the FIB to go beyond the usual peacekeeping powers of using force in defence or reaction to threats, to using force to target specific named actors, thereby seemingly contravening the principle of impartiality and severely undermining, if not violating, the principle of non-intervention.

This therefore raises the question – is the FIB's ability to target named actors another evolution of the principle of impartiality or is it a violation of the principle? For the framework brigade or regular troops in MONUSCO, the Security Council had authorised them to 'take all necessary measures' to protect the mission, mandate and civilians from threats of violence from 'any of the parties engaged in the conflict'.[201] Therefore, as a former UN senior legal officer notes, if and when government troops 'were to attack or pose a threat to civilians, as they often have done, MONUSCO would have a duty under the PoC mandate to neutralise that threat'.[202] As such, 'impartiality is arguably intact in the PoC mandate, as long as the mandate is implemented regardless of the source of the threat'.[203] However, the FIB's mandate differs from this and is said to be 'biased in every aspect'[204] as, on top of the PoC mandate, it permits the FIB to take the initiative and identify, track down and engage with specific armed groups.[205] Mona Ali Khalil argues that

200 C Ero, 'The Problems with "African Solutions"' (*International Crisis Group*, 2 December 2013) <https://www.crisisgroup.org/africa/problems-african-solutions>.

201 See for example: S/RES/2098 (n12) para 12(a)(i).

202 Interviewee 12 (n2).

203 ibid.

204 L Müller, 'The Force Intervention Brigade: United Nations Forces beyond the Fine Line between Peacekeeping and Peace Enforcement' (2015) 20(3) JCSL 359–380, 366.

205 S/RES/2098 (n12).

'MONUSCO's impartiality became problematic when its peacekeepers were mandated to engage in hostilities with named actors' – as such, 'it [the FIB's military action] is no longer in response to an actual attack or imminent threat but rather because of the non-state party to the conflict being named or designated as a target', thus 'destroying impartiality'.[206] As one senior UN human rights advisor noted, it 'puts us completely on one side because you've got a defined enemy'.[207] The Brigade is therefore said to be 'actively engaged in favour of one party to an ongoing armed conflict, disregarding the peacekeeping principles'.[208] It could therefore be argued that the FIB's ability to undertake targeting cannot be viewed as an evolution of the principle of impartiality and is, instead, a breach of the principle, consequently taking peacekeeping beyond its demarcated boundaries and into the realm of intervention.

Indeed, senior personnel involved in the FIB's creation noted that 'very few of us thought that the Council would actually agree to everything we was asking for because we was asking for extraordinary powers, powers that had not been granted to any UN entity before', such as the ability to undertake targeted offensive operations.[209] Thus, it could be argued that there was an awareness that the FIB would greatly expand, or even breach, some of the fundamental principles of peacekeeping, but this was disregarded. This appears to stem from the rationale that 'if we stick only to the principles, if we have a very low reading of what peacekeeping can and cannot do, we are going to have a lot of failures'.[210] This implies that peacekeeping's principles and, therefore, its legal frameworks are malleable and should be expanded and contorted to suit the needs on the ground. This, from a TWAIL perspective, could be viewed as problematic as it renders peacekeeping open to being used by the hegemonic powers, particularly the dominant states in the Security Council, as a tool to further their interests and agenda – as was discussed in Chapters 2 and 3. Further, it is even more problematic for the relevance of the peacekeeping principles and the clarity of peacekeeping's frameworks or boundaries and for the principle of non-intervention as the fluctuating or potentially limitless expanding of peacekeeping's frameworks undermines the principle of non-intervention.

Distinguishing 'Blue' and 'Black' Helmets

This then leads to the third noticeable issue with the inclusion of the FIB, which is the numerous practical consequences which arise from a Brigade

206 ibid.
207 Interviewee 13 (n157) 59.
208 Müller (n204) 360.
209 Interviewee 9 (n1) 60.
210 Interviewee 11 (n23) 43.

that is mandated to target and neutralise specific armed groups.[211] In particular, it creates the perception, for both local communities and armed groups, that all peacekeepers are combatants in the conflict and therefore a target, placing peacekeepers at risk. Indeed, it has been noted that the greatest 'challenge' which MONUSCO has faced is the difficulty of distinguishing between 'blue UN and black UN'.[212] That is, within a peacekeeping operation, 'you cannot have a physical separation between those who [are] going to go on the offensive and those who are going to go in the protection' or another component; 'it doesn't work like that, it's overlapping'.[213] Therefore, it is difficult to distinguish between the civilian or general framework peacekeepers (the 'blue UN') and the military or FIB ('black UN'). The lack of a clear distinction could therefore result in all elements of the operation being associated with the FIB. For civilians or local communities this may create a disconnect between the United Nations and the local population – an issue which will be explored in the subsequent chapter when examining the protection of civilians. For armed groups, there is a risk that they may perceive all UN personnel or any organisation associated with the United Nations as adversaries – as has occurred with international humanitarian organisations in the Congo, which have been targeted by armed groups or connected to peacekeepers' misconduct.[214] Furthermore, the UN Country Team and UN Office for the Coordination of Humanitarian Affairs (OCHA)[215] have often been confused or associated with the UN peacekeeping operation. As former senior OCHA personnel have noted, during MONUC's deployment, when 'the mission started to be part of the conflict', 'there was one contingent particularly, from a country I'm not going to cite, that was heavily engaged in the fight, together with the government'.[216] As such, the United Nations was perceived as supporting the government. This proved to be 'extremely difficult' for OCHA personnel as 'we were in rebel territory', and it became 'extremely dangerous for some of our staff' at times.[217] Whilst the 'peacekeepers had the "black logo" and OCHA had "the blue logo" … who knows that'.[218] Again, this

211 See, for example: DM Tull, 'The Limits and Unintended Consequences of UN Peace Enforcement: The Force Intervention Brigade in the DR Congo' (2017) 25(2) IntPeacekeep 167–190.

212 Interviewee 5 (n107).

213 Interviewee 11 (n23) 57.

214 Interview with Senior DRC/Great Lakes Coordinator from International Organisation ('Interviewee 2') (Geneva, 12 November 2018) DOI: <http://doi.org/10.17639/nott.7119>.

215 See: UN Country Team <https://drcongo.un.org> and OCHA <https://www.unocha.org/drc>.

216 Interview with Senior UNDP Personnel, formerly OCHA ('Interviewee 1') (Geneva, 20 November 2018) DOI: <http://doi.org/10.17639/nott.7119> pg 53.

217 ibid.

218 ibid.

highlights the practical implications[219] or consequences of a broad interpretation of impartiality and, arguably, the need for the United Nations to regain some element of impartiality, through a return to a narrower interpretation of impartiality. In other words, there is a need to not repeat the FIB in any other future peacekeeping operations.

Partially Impartial

Despite the numerous problems which MONUC and MONUSCO have encountered when undertaking joint operations, they have continued to be conducted. However, the practice has now evolved to include policy innovations, such as the HRDDP, which attempts to address some of the challenges.[220] Indeed, it is said that MONUSCO is 'probably the mission that invests the most resources into the implementation of the HRDDP'.[221] There are therefore various examples in which MONUSCO has supported FARDC operations but has later withdrawn its support due to the host state's behaviour, perhaps the most infamous of which is Operation *Sukola I* and the 'Red Generals'.[222] The operation was, again, aimed at neutralising the armed group, FDLR, in Eastern Congo, and initial operational planning included the full support of MONUSCO.[223] However, during the planning, it transpired that the head of the operation (General Bruno Mandevu) and the commander of North Kivu, the region where the operation was to be conducted (General Fall Sikabwe), had poor human rights records.[224] Applying the HRDDP, MONUSCO refused to support the operation unless the two generals were removed, but the Congolese government refused to accede to the United Nations' ultimatum. The government spokesman, Lambert Mende, stated that it was a 'sovereign decision' and the Congo was 'not under anyone's supervision'[225] – language which, from a TWAIL perspective, highlights the ever-present power divide and desire of Global South states to challenge hegemonic power. Consequently, the government ignored the

219 See also: J Labbé and A Boutellis, 'Peace Operations by Proxy: Implications for Humanitarian Action of UN Peacekeeping Partnerships with Non-UN Security Forces' (2013) 95(891/892) IRRC 539–559.

220 HRDDP (n177).

221 Interviewee 10 (n21) 48.

222 UNSC, 'Midterm Report of the Group of Experts on the Democratic Republic of the Congo' (16 October 2015) UN Doc S/2015/797.

223 ibid, 8.

224 M Nichols, 'UN to Congo: Remove Generals Accused of Abuses or Lose Support' (*Reuters*, 4 February 2015) <https://www.reuters.com/article/us-congodemocratic-un/u-n-to-congo-remove-generals-accused-of-abuses-or-lose-support-idUSKBN0L823120150204>.

225 The East African, 'DR Congo Rejects UN Ultimatum to Sack Tainted Generals' (*The East African*, 6 February 2015) <https://www.theeastafrican.co.ke/news/ea/DR-Congo-rejects-UN-ultimatum-to-sack-tainted-generals/4552908-2615116-j6p131/index.html>.

United Nations' deadline and instead unilaterally announced that it would be launching the operation without UN troops and with the two generals still leading the offensive.[226] It is argued that the UN therefore put themselves in an 'awkward position', by placing themselves 'at loggerheads' with the Congolese government because it was obvious that the condition – removing the two generals – was never going to be met.[227] The United Nations was 'essentially paralysed' and 'all of that contributed to what, overtime, came to be a reduction in the effectiveness' of the FIB.[228] Indeed, it is frequently noted that after the FIB's initial success in neutralising the M23, it has been unable to replicate this level of effectiveness, for numerous reasons.[229] Following the Red Generals predicament, then, it has been suggested that instead of a 'red flag strategy', a 'mitigation strategy' would have been better.[230] That is, the United Nations could have noted their concerns and found mitigating circumstances or alternative conditions, without demanding the generals be removed.[231] In doing this, it would arguably have prevented the United Nations from becoming complicit in violations of international law and still maintained relations with the host state, thereby not jeopardising the host's cooperation or consent. This would also remove the potentially coercive ultimatum – to remove specific members of the national armed forces – thereby reducing the potential for the peacekeeping operation to be deemed to be an intervention.

The implementation of the HRDDP in the case of the Red Generals and its impact on the principles of impartiality and consent once again highlight how the fundamental principles cohabit in a competitive arena, with an expansion of one having an impact on another. More importantly, it also reinforces the argument made in Chapter 3 – that the HRDDP, regardless of the seemingly well-intentioned motivations underpinning it, may be viewed as coercive action designed to influence change in the host state. This is based on the fact that it attempts to coerce the host state into making changes to its national armed forces, threatening to withdraw support if the conditions are not, thereby impacting on the state's self-determination and sovereignty. Indeed, the Congolese government explicitly recognised that the composition of its national armed forces was a 'sovereign decision' and refused to comply with the United Nations' request, supporting the argument that the imposition of conditions is a form of coercive action and, therefore, intervention. Once again, from a TWAIL perspective it also demonstrates the patterns of

226 ibid.
227 Interviewee 9 (n1).
228 ibid, 49.
229 EPON (n112).
230 Interviewee 8 (n20 48.
231 Interviewee 9 (n1) 49.

domination and subordination which still linger within the United Nations and presents another example of a peacekeeping policy which is based on the dominant powers' standards and ideals.

This then leads back to the main concern of this broadening of impartiality – whether it amounts to a violation or simply an evolution of the principle and, by extension, whether it merely takes peacekeeping closer to intervention or if it amounts to a contravention of the principle of non-intervention. Whilst the previous chapter noted that the broadening of impartiality to include joint operations is not a violation of the principle of impartiality but simply an evolution, it remains questionable how far it can evolve before it is no longer a legal principle and is simply practice. That is, the initial joint operations between MONUC and the FARDC could be viewed as an evolution, as they entailed joint planning with co-signed orders and, more crucially, were initially conceived in the Lusaka Ceasefire Agreement, which the Congolese host state signed.[232] Therefore, joint operations in this instance could be viewed as a voluntary decision by the host state, as they had willingly agreed to them when signing the Lusaka Agreement. Although a TWAIL critique would perhaps argue that it is questionable what choice the Congo had in signing the agreement and would recognise the significant involvement of the dominant powers in crafting and implementing the agreement,[233] the fact remains that the Congolese host state undertook joint planning and led the operations, with MONUC's support.

For the later joint operations, including the FIB, it could be argued that the interpretation and application of impartiality has gone beyond an evolution and has instead breached the principle of impartiality and, similarly, the principle of non-intervention. This is based upon the fact that these newer operations may result in an application of the HRDDP which imposes on the state's sovereign rights, such as the creation and composition of their armed forces and the mode of activity or operations conducted by these armed forces. As has been noted throughout this chapter and in Chapter 3, an application of the HRDDP could therefore be viewed as coercive action when a joint operation is paused or the peacekeeping operation threatens to withdraw support until the host state implements the former's proposed changes. Thus, in this instance, there is a coercive impact on the host state's sovereign rights, in particular, the structure of their armed forces, thereby amounting to intervention. In a similar vein, the FIB's ability to target specific actors within the host state's territory could also be viewed as a breach, rather than an evolution of

232 Lusaka Agreement (n8).

233 See: Crisis Group, 'The Agreement on a Cease-Fire in the Democratic Republic of Congo' (ICG Democratic Republic of Congo Report No 5, 20 August 1999); E Rogier, 'The Inter-Congolese Dialogue: A Critical Overview' in M Malan and JP Gomes, *Challenges of Peace Implementation: The UN Mission in the Democratic Republic of the Congo* (ISS, 2004) 29.

the principle of impartiality, and, by extension, a breach of non-intervention. That is, as has been noted, targeting is difficult to reconcile with the notion of impartiality and, furthermore, impinges upon the Congolese state's sovereign rights, such as decisions on its national security or, to a certain degree, the state's right to declare war, particularly when the armed groups which the FIB is targeting are supported by neighbouring states, such as Rwanda and Uganda. Thus, the interpretation and application of impartiality here, again, amount to a violation of the principles of impartiality and non-intervention. Even when the choice of target in these operations is selected by the host state, it is arguable that an element of coercion still exists, in part based upon the fact that the FIB is a creation of the Security Council and, therefore, as previously outlined, is a mandatory decision or measure, thus again removing an element of voluntariness and invoking coercive, compulsory language. In this instance, then, the FIB could be viewed as engaging in coercive action which amounts to political or military intervention, particularly as determining which actors to target could, effectively, influence a change in the Congo's relations with its neighbours. Thus, again, this broader interpretation and application of the principle of impartiality, as evidenced in the creation of the FIB, embroil the United Nations in sovereign matters, resulting in the United Nations attempting to coerce change in the host state and, thus, amounting to intervention.

It could be argued, then, that the interpretation and application of the principle of impartiality within the United Nations' operations in the Congo have broadened peacekeeping's frameworks beyond an acceptable limit, consequently severely undermining and, at times, contravening the principle of non-intervention. However, it is arguable that despite this, the operation, as a whole, seemingly retains its non-interventionist status by a single thread – host state consent. That is, the consent of the state to the deployment of the operation, as explored in the previous section, is key to preventing the peacekeeping operation from becoming both peace enforcement and intervention. Therefore, whilst some of MONUSCO's practices may amount to intervention, it does not contravene the principle of non-intervention as the operation is acting under the umbrella of host state consent (*de jure* consent) – albeit, at times, this consent may be effectively withdrawn. Furthermore, it could also be argued that this expansion of the principle of impartiality to include joint operations is not a violation of the principle of non-intervention as it is, instead, an intervention by invitation.[234] As was seen in Chapter 2, it has been argued that whilst peacekeepers are authorised to conduct joint operations with host state forces, the Council cannot mandate the host to conduct such operations. Therefore, where a host state plans and conducts joint operations, this should instead be viewed as 'a function of the host state's consent'

234 Labuda (n92).

for UN intervention and therefore an invitation to intervention.[235] From this angle, then, this broader interpretation of impartiality to include joint operations is, perhaps, best viewed as a significant expansion of the peacekeeping frameworks and, therefore, a challenge to but not a violation of the principle of non-intervention.

Limited Use of Force

A sense of déjà vu emerges when examining the United Nations' use of force in the DRC. Each time a peacekeeping operation has entered the country, it has done so tentatively or passively but has then rapidly evolved to a robust, highly forceful operation in an attempt to counter the complexities in the field. As with the previous two principles, the evolution of the principle of non-use of force from narrow to broad can be seen in the United Nations' peacekeeping endeavours in the Congo. Again, this brings with it a plethora of issues, some of which overlap or impact with the other two principles, demonstrating, once more, the inextricable links between the fundamental principles and their competitive existence. Furthermore, where an expansive use of force has been adopted, it too has seemingly broadened the boundaries of peacekeeping, thereby constricting the boundaries of the principle of non-intervention. Similar questions once again emerge as to how far the principle of non-use of force can be expanded before it becomes something else entirely; that is, how robust can peacekeeping be, before it becomes peace enforcement or intervention? Is there a limit to its expansion or is it, like the principle of impartiality, saved by the single thread of (precarious) host state consent?

Rapid Evolution

For ONUC, following the traditional model of passive peacekeeping, the Security Council initially adhered to a strict application of non-use of force.[236] ONUC was limited to using force only in response to threats or attacks or to apprehend criminals, and to set up check points or post guard positions to prevent disorder, for example, at airports, rail stations and roads.[237] These positions were also only established if required to implement the necessary functions within the agreement with the Congolese government,[238] thus suggesting that, perhaps in these early stages, host state consent may have been

235 ibid, 3.
236 S/RES/143 (n4) 2.
237 S/4775 (n84); UNSC (15th year, 896th meeting) (9–10 September 1960) UN Doc S/PV/896, 14–30.
238 ibid.

needed for operational changes to the mission. More importantly, for the principle of non-use of force, Hammarskjöld emphasised that 'the basic element involved is clearly the prohibition against any initiative in the use of armed force'.[239] This was then reiterated in operational directives (rules of engagement) where it was stated that for the 'use of arms', 'on no account are weapons to be used unless in cases of great and sudden emergency and for the purpose of self-defence'.[240] Even in self-defence, it was noted that firing 'should be resorted to only in extreme instances'.[241] Similarly, for the 'protection of internal security', it was further stated that ONUC 'should exhaust all possible peaceful means of keeping order before any resort to force'.[242] When interpreting these mandates and directives in the field, the then-SRSG, Ralph Bunche, stressed the use of force only in self-defence, referring to ONUC as a 'peace force, not a fighting force', and noting that ONUC was there 'to do harm to no one, if it can be avoided'.[243] Evidently, as was seen with the principle of impartiality, Hammarskjöld and senior leadership within ONUC initially took a very narrow reading of the principles, limiting its use of force and espousing strong non-interventionist rhetoric. This therefore highlights, again, how the office of the SG acts as a norm entrepreneur and reflects how peacekeeping evolved in line with the patterns of intervention which Chapter 2 explored. In this instance, the narrow interpretation of force mirrored the non-interventionist rhetoric that was espoused during that time as newly independent states were emerging through decolonisation.

However, despite this strong non-interventionist, limited use of force discourse, the United Nations' approach quickly changed as tensions in the Congo grew. Indeed, whilst reiterating minimal force, in private correspondence to Hammarskjöld, Bunche discussed the potential need for ONUC to employ force 'with [a] liberal interpretation of [the] self-defence principle' in certain areas of the Congo.[244] Following the assassination of Lumumba, the death of Hammarskjöld and growing conflict, the Security Council took a much more proactive approach to the use of force. The primary objective of ONUC shifted from taking the 'necessary steps' to support the withdrawal of foreign troops and maintain law and order, to taking 'vigorous action', including 'the use of the requisite measure of force, if necessary'.[245]

239 S/4389 (n117) 5.
240 Quoted in: UNSC, 'Observations by the Special Representative of the Secretary-General in the Republic of the Congo on the Memorandum by Major-General HT Alexander (S/4445, Annex II)' (21 August 1960) UN Doc S/4451, 2.
241 ibid.
242 ibid.
243 ibid.
244 Quoted in: B Urquhart (n98) 329.
245 S/RES/169 (n55) 4.

Under these mandates, ONUC launched numerous forceful and, at times, highly controversial operations, such as Operation Morthor which resulted in hundreds of casualties and led to internal disputes over whether the SG had authorised the SRSG to take military action.[246] Furthermore, within this expansion of the use of force, in its final military endeavour (*Operation Grandslam*) ONUC used airpower for the first time in UN history.[247] In an attempt to end the Katangan secession, Swedish jets neutralised Katanga's air force in a coordinated attack with ONUC's ground force, eventually ending the secession.[248] ONUC's unique use of airpower further expanded the interpretation of the principle of non-use of force and set a precedent which has now resulted in attack helicopters and drones becoming an important strategic, military component of peacekeeping operations[249] – demonstrating how the Congo has, at times, shaped UN peacekeeping in somewhat of a bottom-up approach.

This rapid expansion of the principle therefore demonstrates the fluidity of peacekeeping's frameworks and epitomises a recurring dichotomy within peacekeeping and the interpretation and application of the fundamental principles, which is the clash between theory and practice or a battle between idealism and pragmatism. That is, whilst UN peacekeeping was conceived in order to be a passive, monitoring tool, in reality, in order to achieve its aim of maintaining international peace and security, it has had to mould, adapt and evolve beyond these initial conceptions – as has already been seen with the other two fundamental principles. Therefore, it could be said that whilst a certain position or desire is postulated, in practice this may not occur. This is a difficulty which persists today, with current MONUSCO military personnel noting that there is an 'absolute tension' between the idealism and universalism of rights and responsibilities, which is translated into the mandate, and the difficulties peacekeepers face when trying to apply that criterion.[250] Thus, the 'idealist position' of, for example, limited use of force 'is right but the pragmatic position is what happens'.[251] It could be further argued that this spotlights a broader issue of the approach peacekeeping takes to

246 See: Findlay (n7) 75–76; S Collins, 'Letters Show O'Brien Had UN Authority for Actions in Katanga' (*The Irish Times*, 31 November 2018) <https://www.irishtimes.com/news/politics/letters-show-o-brien-had-un-authority-for-actions-in-katanga-1.3695184>; M Kennedy and A Magennis, *Ireland, the United Nations and the Congo* (Four Courts Press 2014).

247 W Dorn, 'The UN's First "Air Force": Peacekeepers in Combat, Congo 1960–64' (2013) 77(4) JMilHist 1399–1425, 1399.

248 ibid.

249 See for example: T Piiparinen, 'Beyond the Technological Turn: Reconsidering the Significance of the Intervention Brigade and Peacekeeping Drones for UN Conflict Management' (2015) 21(1) GG 141–160.

250 Interview with Senior MONUSCO Military Personnel ('Interviewee 17') (Skype, 9 February 2020) DOI: <http://doi.org/10.17639/nott.7119>.

251 ibid.

post-conflict states which is, applying a TWAIL lens, seemingly based upon the dominant powers' standards and ideals, with a lack of consideration for the complexities of the Global South state. Put simply, peacekeeping operations and their mandates could be viewed as an example of an oversimplified 'Western' answer to a very complex, misunderstood problem.[252]

Nowhere is this dichotomy more evident than with ONUC and its rapid evolution of the non-use of force which was repeated when the United Nations returned to the Congo in August 1999 with MONUC. Similar to ONUC's deployment, as previously noted, MONUC was deployed as a traditional, passive operation of 90 military personnel, designed to monitor and observe the Lusaka Ceasefire Agreement,[253] and was not authorised to use force beyond self-defence. Thus, the principle of non-use of force was narrowly interpreted.[254] However, as with ONUC, within one year of deployment the operation rapidly and forcefully expanded, with a 'second phase' of deployment in February 2000, raising the troop ceiling to 500 observers and 5,537 military personnel[255] – a significant increase from the initial deployment. This expansion coincided with the United Nations' shift to robust peacekeeping and the publication of the Brahimi Report, which expanded the use of force from individual self-defence to defence of the mission.[256] As was seen in Chapters 2 and 3, through robust peacekeeping, peacekeepers were now permitted to use force to defend themselves, the mission's components and the mandate. Thus, as was seen in the previous chapter, the principle of non-use of force was notably expanded, resulting in a simultaneous expansion of peacekeeping's frameworks and boundaries, which, in turn, began to undermine the principle of non-intervention.

For MONUC, this robustness was reflected in its Security Council mandate which, for the first time, expressly stated that it was 'acting under Chapter VII', permitting MONUC to 'take the necessary action', as it deemed 'within its capabilities' to protect UN personnel, facilities and equipment and to protect civilians 'under imminent threat of physical violence'.[257] Therefore, again, the United Nations, upon returning to the Congo, rapidly expanded its interpretation and application of the principle of non-use force. However, on this occasion, whilst ONUC had uniquely expanded on its own accord, MONUC's broader application of the use of force was in keeping with the general consensus within peacekeeping at that time. Within the DRC, the

252 W Easterly, *The White Man's Burden* (OUP 2006) 9.

253 S/RES/1258 (n9).

254 S/RES/1234 (n9).

255 S/RES/1291 (n9).

256 UNGA, 'Report of the Panel on United Nations Peace Operations' ('Brahimi Report') (21 August 2000) UN Doc A/55/305-S/2000/809, paras 48–51. UNGA, 'Report of the Special Committee on Peacekeeping Operations' (28 March 2003) UN Doc A/57/767, para 46.

257 S/RES/1291 (n9) 8.

principle was then evolved further in 2002 following another increase in troops to 8,700 personnel.[258] On this occasion, the Council endorsed an SG proposal for a revised concept of operations[259] which called for the significant strengthening of MONUC through the creation of a 'forward force' composed of 'two robust task forces' in order to support the disarmament, demobilisation and repatriation (DDR) of foreign armed groups.[260] Within this mandate, however, the Council simply 'endorsed' the proposal and did not explicitly invoke Chapter VII or permit the operation to 'take all necessary measures' when conducting these duties. It is therefore suggested that this 'leads to the conclusion that this was not an authorisation to use force beyond self-defence'.[261] Whilst this may be true, it could be argued that the increased military presence and the introduction of 'robust' task forces all create the impression of a much more robust, forceful operation. That is, it may not have broadened the use of force beyond self-defence but it arguably could still be viewed as a subtle, vertical expansion of the principle or, at the very least, a clarification of the newer concept of self-defence, as it permitted force during the fulfilment of a mandate task – DDR.

Indeed, further nuances within the norm of non-use of force emerged through MONUC when, in 2003, following a Secretary-General recommendation,[262] its use of force was notably expanded with the introduction of a 'Interim Emergency Multinational Force' (IEMF).[263] This temporary French-led force was deployed in Bunia for four months and was authorised to undertake 'all necessary measures' to fulfil its mandate.[264] Most notably, the aim of this force, which later became the EU-led *Operation Artemis*,[265] was 'to contribute to the stabilization of the security conditions'.[266] The language within the mandates was therefore, again, robust but now also included the term 'stabilisation',[267] which could likewise be perceived as a creeping expansion or experiment of this broadened principle of non-use force and, thus, an expansion of peacekeeping's legal framework. As a result, these subtle developments – force to

258 UNSC Res 1445 (4 December 2002) UN Doc S/RES/1445 10.

259 ibid, 10.

260 UNSC, 'Special Report of the Secretary-General on the United Nations Organization Mission in the Democratic Republic of the Congo' (10 September 2002) UN Doc S/2002/1005, paras 48–54.

261 Sloan (n36).

262 UNSC, 'Letter Dated 15 May 2003 from the Secretary-General Addressed to the President of the Security Council' (28 May 2003) UN Doc S/2003/574.

263 UNSC Res 1484 (30 May 2003) UN Doc S/RES/1484.

264 ibid.

265 S Ulriksen, C Gourlay and C Mace, 'Operation Artemis: The Shape of Things to Come?' (2004) 11(3) IntPeacekeep 508–525.

266 ibid, 1.

267 See: A Gilder, 'The Effect of "Stabilization" in the Mandates and Practice of UN Peace Operations' (2019) 66 NILR 47–73.

fulfil DDR tasks, the IEMF and the introduction of stabilisation – could all be seen as undermining the principle of non-intervention as they broaden the principle of non-use of force and permit the peacekeeping operation to engage in further activities which creep closer to the intervention boundary line. That is, these activities are proactive (in comparison to the traditional concept of reactive force in self-defence) and relate to matters which fall within the scope of the host state's sovereignty, such as domestic and foreign policies, territorial integrity and state authority, with the ill-defined notion of 'stabilisation', in particular, engaged in institution building. As such, the peacekeeping operation's use of force here could be viewed as coercive action designed to influence change in these areas of the host state, thereby amounting to intervention. Even if, at this point, the activities fall short of this threshold and do not amount to intervention or a violation of the principle of non-intervention, they are, at the very least, a notable expansion of peacekeeping's frameworks and, therefore, expand the red boundary line surrounding peacekeeping, consequently contracting the boundaries of non-intervention.

This broadening of the principle of non-use of force also blurs the boundaries between peacekeeping and peace enforcement. Indeed, for some, ONUC's robust military activities, in particular *Operation Morthor*, 'marked a temporary lapse of ONUC from peacekeeping into peace enforcement'.[268] As the former Under-Secretary for Peacekeeping, Marrack Goulding, noted, ONUC was the first 'case of a transition from peacekeeping to peace enforcement'.[269] However, the ICJ in *Expenses* found differently, highlighting that the force was directed at non-state actors, rather than the state, noting that ONUC was not 'coercive or enforcement action' and was commenced 'at the request, or with the consent' of the host state.[270] This statement from the ICJ suggests, then, that ONUC was not intervention as it was supported by host state consent and was not coercive action directed at the state. Therefore, as with the principle of impartiality, even if the principle of non-use of force is interpreted broadly, the existence of host state consent, again, means that the operation is consensual peacekeeping and thus not peace enforcement or in violation of the principle of non-intervention.

Despite this, an argument can still be made as to how far these principles are able to expand before they stretch peacekeeping's boundaries to its limits and take it across the line into intervention. Indeed, for MONUC's deployment, the then-Secretary-General, Kofi Annan, later noted that 'a firm military intervention, of the kind that went beyond the impartial peacekeeping' that had previously been implemented, was necessary to create stability in

268 Findlay (n7) 75.
269 M Goulding, 'The Evolution of United Nations Peacekeeping' (1993) 69(3) IntAff 451–464, 453.
270 *Certain Expenses* (n74) 164.

the East of Congo.[271] Arguably, this could be interpreted as both a disregard for the fundamental principles or, again, a battle of idealism versus pragmatism, with the latter prevailing. By extension, it may then be argued that this indicates that MONUC, in practice, went beyond (and was intended to go beyond) peacekeeping, potentially crossing the line into intervention. However, again, it is seemingly the element of consent which hangs as a single thread, holding the peacekeeping operation back from violating the principle of non-intervention.

An Extension of the State?

This precarious expansion of non-use of force in the Congo began to peak from 2003 to 2006 when the country underwent a transition period, holding its first democratic elections since its independence. During this time, MONUC's troop capacity significantly increased again,[272] and it was authorised to use 'all necessary means' to complete its mandated tasks, which began to include both PoC and election support.[273] For example, it was able to use force to 'deter any foreign or Congolese armed group from attempting to use force to threaten the political process'[274] and to assist in the 'establishment of a secure and peaceful environment for the holding of free and transparent elections'.[275] In a similar vein, the Security Council again authorised the deployment of a temporary, EU-led force – EUFOR – to 'support MONUC to stabilise the situation' and contribute to the protection of civilians.[276] Once again, then, the Council had authorised a smaller, temporary force and invoked the language of 'stabilisation' which resulted in some of the most robust and forceful peacekeeping action in the United Nations' history.[277] In particular, the term 'stabilisation' was included in the operation's name in 2010 with the shift from MONUC to MONUSCO,[278] which further militarised the operation, permitting an increased level of force to fulfil a broad range of tasks in order to create stability.[279]

271 K Annan, *Interventions: A Life in War and Peace* (Penguin 2013) 117.
272 UNSC Res 1493 (28 July 2003) UN Doc S/RES/1493.
273 UNSC Res 1565 (1 October 2004) UN Doc S/RES/1565, 4(b).
274 UNSC Res 1649 (21 December 2005) UN Doc S/RES/1649.
275 UNSC Res 1756 (15 May 2007) UN Doc S/RES/1756, para 3(e).
276 UNSC Res 1671 (25 April 2006) UN Doc S/RES/1671, 2, 8.
277 See: T Tardy, 'The European Union and UN Peace Operations: What Global-Regional Peace and Security Partnership?' in C de Coning and M Peter (eds) *United Nations Peace Operations in a Changing Global Order* (Palgrave Macmillan 2019) and A Mattelaer, 'EUFOR RDC and the Development of the ESDP' (2007) 60(3) StudDip 73–89.
278 S/RES/1925 (n43).
279 See: C de Coning, 'Implications of Stabilisation Mandates for the Use of Force in Peace Operations' in P Nadin, *The Use of Force in UN Peacekeeping* (Routledge 2018); D Curran and CT Hunt, 'Stabilization at the Expense of Peacebuilding in UN Peacekeeping Operations' (2020) 26(1) GG 46–68.

Furthermore, the inclusion of protection of civilians within MONUC's mandate again reflected the broader peacekeeping and intervention agenda, as seen in Chapters 2 and 3. It also marked the beginning of MONUC/MONUSCO's engagement with PoC, which eventually became (and remains) a priority task for the operation.[280] Whilst this will be discussed in greater detail in the subsequent chapter, for the principle of non-use of force, the inclusion of PoC expanded the principle as peacekeepers were permitted to use force in defence of themselves, the mission components and the mandate – which now included the extremely ambiguous task of acting to protect civilians from threats of violence.[281] Thus, it could be argued that the potential for force to be used, under the justification of PoC, became, essentially, limitless. Moreover, this, again, highlights how peacekeeping's principles and norms cohabit in a competitive arena, constantly being reimagined and altered in reaction to a re-interpretation or application of its counterparts. Indeed, whilst the task of PoC is 'supposed to be implemented neutrally and impartially', that is, against both state and non-state actors, within the Congo, it is usually only implemented against the latter.[282] As such, when exercising force against non-state actors, to protect civilians from attacks, MONUC/MONUSCO, like ONUC, has 'ended up fighting on the government's side'.[283] As was seen within the impartiality section, this then raises issues relating to the risks for peacekeepers, the perception by armed groups of the peacekeepers as legitimate targets and the potential triggering of international humanitarian law. Moreover, it arguably also places the peacekeeping operation in the unusual position of essentially becoming (or being perceived to be) an extensive of the host state armed forces, as its selective use of force almost exclusively against armed groups, in essence, results in the eradication of the state's enemies or opponents – an issue which also occurs with the FIB and its targeting mandate.

Neutralising State Opponents

The introduction of the FIB in 2013 therefore marked another significant expansion or evolution of the principle of non-use of force within the Congo, specifically through its ability to launch 'targeted offensive operations' to 'neutralise' armed groups.[284] Indeed, by its own admission, the United

280 See, for example: UNSC Res 1592 (30 March 2005) UN Doc S/RES/1592; S/RES/1856 (n158); UNSC Res 2502 (19 December 2019) UN Doc S/RES/2502; UNSC Res 2556 (18 December 2020) UN Doc S/RES/2556; UNSC Res 2612 (20 December 2021) UN Doc S/RES/2612; S/RES/2666 (n15).

281 ibid.

282 C Henderson, *The Use of Force and International Law* (CUP 2018) 186.

283 ND White, 'Peacekeeping or War-Fighting?' in ND White and C Henderson, *Research Handbook on International Conflict and Security Law* (Edward Elgar 2013) 582.

284 S/RES/2098 (n12) para 9.

Nations labelled the FIB 'the first ever offensive combat force' in UN peacekeeping.[285] Whilst this had the potential to mark a new era for robust peacekeeping, the Security Council mandate explicitly stated that it was created 'on an exceptional basis and without setting a precedent', and it was perhaps best viewed as a temporary expansion of the principle of non-use of force.[286]

Whilst the level of force which the FIB is permitted to use is seemingly no different from the level of force which the rest of the framework brigade are authorised to use under MONUSCO's PoC mandate,[287] the difference (and therefore the expansion to the non-use of force principle) lies in the way in which this use of force may be triggered or used. Under any PoC mandate, force is authorised against 'any individual or group that commits physical violence against civilians or threatens to do so'.[288] Thus, regardless of whether the perpetrator is a state or non-state actor, the source of the threat is 'a legitimate target'.[289] Within the FIB's mandate, however, 'the M23 is, named in the resolution as the target, regardless of whether they're physically attacking civilians or jeopardising the safety of civilians in any particular moment'.[290] It is this – the specific, explicit targeting of one of the parties to the conflict – which is 'the new, dynamic, tectonic shift in the mandate',[291] not the fact that the FIB is using robust force, which was already authorised in MONUSCO's PoC mandate. The targeting of specific actors then, as with the principle of impartiality, is also extremely problematic for the principle of non-use of force and expands peacekeeping's frameworks to its limits, taking peacekeeping much closer to the intervention line, potentially violating the principle of non-intervention, if such force is used.

However, whilst this remains true, it has been noted that the FIB 'did not actually need to invoke the offensive nature of the force' because 'the M23 did something incredibly stupid' and attacked the United Nations.[292] Therefore, the FIB's actions against the M23 were not 'an offensive operation, it was always a self-defence'.[293] As a former MONUSCO military commander noted, by attacking the United Nations, the M23 'gave us the obvious reasons to intervene, we had to stop the threat, we had to stop the source of

285 UN Press Release, 'Intervention Brigade Authorized as Security Council Grants Mandate Renewal for United Nations Mission in Democratic Republic of Congo' (SC/10964, 28 March 2013).
286 S/RES/2098 (n12) para 9.
287 S/RES/2502 (n280).
288 Interviewee 12 (n2).
289 ibid.
290 ibid.
291 ibid.
292 Interviewee 9 (n1) See also: UNSC, 'Report of the Secretary-General on MONUSCO' (17 December 2013) UN Doc S/2013/757; UNSC, 'Report of the Secretary-General on MONUSCO' (30 June 2014) UN Doc S/2014/450, paras 28, 53.
293 Interviewee 9 (n1)

what was killing civilians' and 'we were able to fire without causing civilian casualty'.[294] Thus, whilst the FIB had a more expanded version of the use of force, it Instead relied upon the broader, self-defence interpretation of force, acting in defence of itself and civilians.[295] As such, it can be argued that this expansion of the principle of non-use of force is only an expansion in theory and not, yet, in practice. Therefore, it could be seen as undermining but not yet violating the principle of non-intervention.

Similarly, the inclusion of the ill-defined term 'neutralising' also expands the principle of non-use of force, taking peacekeeping much closer to coercive, enforcement action. Indeed, the neutralising of armed groups 'is seen by most people [within the "broader peacekeeping community"] as the crossing of a line that is very problematic for a peacekeeping operation', which was demonstrated by the 'FIB experience, post-M23'.[296] Again, this neutralisation of specific targets is also where there is an overlap with the principle of impartiality, as previously discussed, as the choice of actor to target has implications for the United Nations' partiality and the perception of the United Nations. Again, the selection of targets also potentially renders the operation vulnerable to being used by the state to eradicate its enemies. Thus, in these instances where MONUSCO is mandated to support the state in neutralising armed groups, the peacekeeping operation could be viewed as an extension of the state. Indeed, these 'neutralisation' efforts, which are designed to establish security and stability in certain areas of the Congo, form part of MONUSCO's broader stabilisation-related activities which, some have argued, result in MONUSCO 'entering into a form of mutual symbiosis with the state'.[297] That is, in these contexts, such as when MONUSCO has supported the state in neutralising the ADF armed group, 'the UN is an extension and amplification of the state, increasing its monopolising potential in the security realm, helping it to eradicate enemies' and boosting the state's capacity to deliver basic services to the population.[298]

This, again, is difficult to reconcile with peacekeeping's fundamental principles and, by extension, the principle of non-intervention and creates the perception of the United Nations as undertaking a 'parastatal role',[299] with over 60% of the population viewing the operation's partnership with the

294 Interviewee 11 (n23).

295 On the FIB and IHL, see: B Sonczyk, 'The Protection of the Intervention Brigade under Article 8(2)(e)(iii) of the Rome Statute of the International Criminal Court' (2015) 13 QILZoom-in 13, 25–40.

296 Interviewee 10 (n21) 62.

297 AC Day and CT Hunt, 'UN Stabilisation Operations and the Problem of Non-Linear Change: A Relational Approach to Intervening in Governance Ecosystems' (2020) 9(1) Stability 1–23, 14.

298 ibid.

299 ibid.

Congolese army negatively.[300] Thus, if the operation is seemingly undertaking functions of the state or acting alongside the host in the execution of these sovereign functions, this could, again, be viewed as a form of intervention but, arguably, one which undermines but does not violate the principle of non-intervention. This is because, when the operation undertakes these tasks in joint operations or in cooperation with the host state, it could be viewed as another form of intervention by invitation. If the state is willing to accept the United Nations undertaking this more forceful role, it could be viewed as intervention by invitation as the same arguments which have been made earlier and in Chapter 3 regarding joint operations could be applied here, with this being viewed as 'a function of the host state's consent'.[301]

Moreover, the targeting and neutralising mandate also has an effect on the legal character of the operation and the risk to peacekeepers. As Mona Ali Khalil notes, 'to the extent that the FIB was an integral part of MONUSCO, the FIB mandate resulted in MONUSCO being deemed a party to the conflict – not just the FIB'.[302] As a result, if and when the FIB is engaged in forceful action and therefore a party to the conflict, international humanitarian law is triggered,[303] thus, again, contributing to the legal frameworks surrounding peacekeeping. Further, whilst Müller argues that this 'intensified role of the UN as an enforcement actor' was 'not prepared by an assessment and adjustment of the rules and principles applicable to UN missions',[304] interviews conducted throughout this research suggest this might not be entirely accurate. Indeed, this was a matter which was considered by the creators of the Brigade, who contemplated the potential scenarios or implications of the FIB using force against the M23.[305] This included debating whether 'if you stop being a peacekeeper and you become subject to the laws of war, does that make the Secretary-General, as a sort of Commander in Chief of the Intervention Brigade, a legitimate target?'[306] It could therefore be argued that there was a recognition of the legal and practical implications of the Brigade but this seemingly did not outweigh the apparent need for the FIB.[307] As such, even though the legal implications were considered and the mandate was 'couched in all sorts of caveated language about "without prejudice to the principles of peacekeeping"', it is 'a sort of conscious departure' from the

300 Congo Research Group, 'Impasse in the Congo: What Do the People Think? Results from a National Public Opinion Poll' (Investigative Report No2, NYU, October 2016) <http://congoresearchgroup.org/wp-content/uploads/2016/10/Final-Poll-CRG-BERCI.pdf>.

301 Labuda (n92).

302 Interviewee 12 (n2).

303 UNSG Bulletin (n129).

304 Müller (n204) 360.

305 Interviewee 9 (n1).

306 ibid, 42.

307 See: SC/10964 (n89).

fundamental principles, particularly the non-use of force.[308] The inclusion of the FIB within MONUSCO therefore expanded the principle of non-use of force by permitting the use of targeting and had the consequential effect of changing 'the nature of the mission' as 'it really transforms peace operations into targets and legitimate targets'.[309] FIB troops thus have a 'double status of combatants and of protected persons',[310] creating a further nuance within the principle of non-use of force and placing the operation closer to the intervention line. Indeed, it has been argued that the United Nations understood the FIB to be a peace enforcement mission rather than a peacekeeping mission because it not only uses robust force, it also takes it further into offensive action.[311] Therefore, as the peacekeeping operation crosses the line into combat, it must also cross the line into intervention, making the action one of enforcement, not peacekeeping. Once more then, the introduction of the FIB significantly expanded peacekeeping's frameworks, blurring the boundaries between peacekeeping and intervention and thereby noticeably undermining the principle of non-intervention.

Force-Less Force

It is clear to see that the United Nations' peacekeeping operations within the Congo have taken a very broad interpretation and application of the principle of non-use of force, thus significantly expanding peacekeeping's frameworks and blurring its boundaries. At times, this has been in keeping with the general consensus on the use of force and interventionist rhetoric, as was outlined in Chapters 2 and 3, such as the shift to robust peacekeeping. At other times, the operation has taken the initiative and expanded the principle specifically within the Congo (e.g. ONUC during decolonisation and the FIB). This, once again, demonstrates how peacekeeping's principles and norms are reimagined or re-interpreted for each peacekeeping operation, emphasising the fluidity of the principles and the peacekeeping frameworks. It also highlights the use of the Congo as a peacekeeping laboratory, often led by the SRSG and senior leadership, and the reputation which MONUC/MONUSCO has gained for being an innovative mission.[312]

However, throughout this expansion, despite the authorisation to use increased levels of force or target/neutralise named actors, this has not always resulted in these powers being used. During MONUC's deployment, despite the high levels of force which the operation was permitted to use under the

308 Interviewee 16 (n18) 51.
309 Interviewee 13 (n157) 59.
310 Müller (n204) 360.
311 P Cammaert and F Blyth, 'Issue Brief: The UN Intervention Brigade in the Democratic Republic of the Congo' (IPI 2013).
312 See, for example: Interviewee 10 (n21); Interviewee 9 (n1) 36–38.

broadened concept of self-defence, it was severely criticised for failing to take military action. In particular, it was criticised for failing to prevent armed rebels from taking the city of Bukavu in 2004, despite the presence of 700 MONUC troops authorised to 'use all necessary means'.[313] Similarly, the FIB has also been criticised for failing to act and for having little success after its initial offensive against the M23.[314] Indeed, it is argued that 'the dynamic which was created in the liberation' of the territory which M23 had occupied 'was not used to create a positive move and we [the FIB] started to hesitate'.[315] The FIB's 'success', or lack thereof, was also further magnified in 2021 with the resurgence of M23 in Eastern Congo.[316] Therefore, as senior UN personnel have noted, 'we almost never get into trouble for using too much force, but we always get into trouble when we use insufficient force'.[317] They maintained that they have never had 'a single conversation with any commander or civilian leader in MONUSCO saying "you use too much force"',[318] further arguing that MONUSCO has never received any complaints that they had used disproportionate or unauthorised force from the ICC or Congolese judicial process.[319] In a similar vein, the Cruz Report also criticised the operation for failing to use force, claiming that troop-contributing nations (TCNs) have 'Chapter VI syndrome',[320] thus suggesting that there is, again, a gap between theory and practice. That is, whilst the principle of non-use of force may be expanded in theory, in practice it is not implemented to its fullest extent and, therefore, in reality, peacekeeping's framework or boundaries are not as expansive as they first appear. Regardless, it still indicates a trend towards intervention, with a more aggressive, militarised form of peacekeeping,[321] which, as this chapter has discussed, is problematic because it blurs the boundaries between peacekeeping and intervention. As such, it could once

313 S/RES/1493 (n272); UN News, 'Rebels Take Bukavu in Eastern DR of Congo, Protesters Target UN' (*UN News*, 2 June 2004) <https://news.un.org/en/story/2004/06/105462-rebels-take-bukavu-eastern-dr-congo-protesters-target-un>.

314 A Novosseloff, 'The Effectiveness of the UN Mission in the Democratic Republic of the Congo' (IPI, 19 December 2019) <https://theglobalobservatory.org/2019/12/effectiveness-un-mission-democratic-republic-of-the-congo/>.

315 Interviewee 11 (n23) 63.

316 Russo (n199).

317 Interviewee 9 (n1).

318 ibid.

319 ibid.

320 CA Dos Santos Cruz, WR Phillips, S Cusimano, 'Improving Security of United Nations Peacekeepers: We Need to Change the Way We Are Doing Business' ('Santos Cruz Report') (19 December 2017) <https://peacekeeping.un.org/sites/default/files/improving_security_of_united_nations_peacekeepers_report.pdf>.

321 R Gowan, 'Fighting Words: The Cruz Report Restores a Military Voice to Peacekeeping Debates' (*IPI*, 19 February 2018) <https://theglobalobservatory.org/2018/02/fighting-words-cruz-report-restores-military-voice/>.

again be argued that a shrinking of the peacekeeping frameworks and a move back towards the more traditional model of peacekeeping is desirable for future peacekeeping operations.

A further issue to also consider is the potential reasons for the lack of force, such as the logistics or 'unpreparedness' of operating in terrain as diverse and complex as the Congo (e.g. engaging in jungle warfare),[322] or the political will and interest of the TCN and, by extension, the risk-appetite of their troops within the field.[323] It is frequently noted that some peacekeepers have a low risk appetite as 'TCNs are not prepared for them to die on peacekeeping operations'.[324] Indeed, 'no normal country would send soldiers to do this type of task and under these conditions', as the jungle terrain of the Congo, combined with the unconventional composition of the armed groups, requires 'special forces', as opposed to conspicuous peacekeepers in blue helmets and white vehicles.[325] Therefore, it is very difficult to conduct these types of operations, even for 'a national, very well organised and strictly commanded and controlled, well-trained military'.[326] The difficulties of the operation, combined with the motivations of the TCNs, thus result in a reluctance from peacekeepers. Whilst some troops may be 'much more kind of focused, willing to engage and at least try to fulfil the mandate', others are not willing and able and 'have no interest or an appetite to engage into an environment that is often alien to them'.[327] This therefore may be one contributing factor or explanation for the lack of force used within the Congo, despite the heightened levels of permitted force. It arguably also highlights the inadequacy of peacekeeping as a tool for this these types of activities, which, again, leads back to an overarching debate within peacekeeping, which is whether it should be undertaking enforcement-style tasks at all.[328] As such, if the expanded use of force is not being used in practice, then it follows that there is little need for the broader interpretation of non-use of force and, as such, peacekeeping frameworks should be retracted, with a move back towards less robust peacekeeping. This, in turn, would bring peacekeeping away from the enforcement or intervention boundary line, consequently reducing peacekeeping's interventionist nature and supporting the principle of non-intervention.

322 Novosseloff (n314).
323 Verweijen (n135).
324 Interviewee 4 (n3) 23.
325 Interviewee 13 (n157).
326 ibid.
327 Interviewee 2 (n214) 23.
328 See, for example: T Tardy, 'A Critique of Robust Peacekeeping in Contemporary Peace Operations' (2011) 18(2) IntPeacekeep 152–167; M Peter, 'Between Doctrine and Practice: The UN Peacekeeping Dilemma' (2015) 21(3) GG 351–370.

Furthermore, the Cruz Report's highlighting of a seeming reluctance to execute Chapter VII action could perhaps be viewed as a recognition by some TCNs that such forceful,[329] coercive action goes beyond peacekeeping's remit and is, therefore, illegal intervention. There are, of course, exceptions to these generalisations, as the president of Uruguay vehemently disagreed with robust peacekeeping and the deployment of the FIB, yet still provided troops who, perhaps somewhat ironically, 'did a good job' as they were more familiar with the terrain and style of warfare than other TCNs.[330] It could also, from a TWAIL perspective, be viewed as an unwillingness by the Global South TCNs to carry out the bidding of the hegemonic powers in the Security Council. The levels of force used within peacekeeping operations may therefore be dependent, to a certain extent, on the motivations, interests and non-interventionist views of the TCN. In particular, many of the Global South TCNs (such as countries in the G77 and NAM) are strong supporters of the principle of non-intervention, perhaps offering an explanation for the reluctance to engage in robust force in the host state. This then leads, again, to the importance of the fundamental principles in providing a red boundary line around peacekeeping, consequently preventing it from crossing the line and becoming intervention. Within the Congo, the rapid evolution of force, the introduction of temporary forces and terms such as 'neutralisation' and stabilisation', combined with the broad PoC mandates and the FIB's targeting powers, all expand the principle of non-use force, at times to its limits and even beyond. As was noted with the principle of impartiality, this expansion then has 'a degree of drift, which has knock on effects on the other two' principles,[331] demonstrating the inextricable links between the Holy Trinity and their un-harmonious co-existence. More specifically, it highlights how the peacekeeping operation, again, is reliant on the principle of consent to maintain its peacekeeping status and how the basis of robust joint or jointly planned operations may lie in consent, with these peacekeeping operations therefore better understood as a form of intervention by invitation.[332]

As with the principle of impartiality, questions remain as to how far the principle can be expanded before it is no longer a legal principle of peacekeeping. It appears that the increased levels of force, through the expanded interpretation of self-defence, may remain as they are now common practice throughout most peacekeeping operations.[333] However, what is still questionable is the effect that the FIB and its targeting/neutralising mandate may have

329 Cruz Report (n320).
330 Interviewee 11 (n23) 59.
331 Interviewee 16 (n18) 67.
332 Labuda (n92).
333 Such as in Darfur, CAR, Mali and South Sudan.

on the principle – whether it is simply a temporary or exceptional expansion, or whether it has now set a precedent and has permanently expanded the boundaries of peacekeeping's use of force. For some, it is obvious that 'of course, in legal terms, we now have a precedence, there's no denying it', but it is noted that the 'alignment of stars' which was needed to create the Brigade is hard to replicate.[334] That is, there existed a rare agreement or mutuality of understanding between the Security Council, those in the field and MONUSCO in order to allow for the creation of the Brigade.[335] For others, it is perhaps a welcome relief that a replication of the FIB would be difficult. Whilst it is recognised that the 'FIB had its moment where it was potentially useful', in that it had an important 'political role', namely through having SADC, as a regional entity invested in Congo, ultimately, the FIB is said to be 'flawed and shouldn't be repeated'.[336] Indeed, senior personnel within the United Nations' Policy, Evaluation and Training Division have noted that 'in terms of doctrine and policy development, we have always treated the FIB as a Secretary-General's exception, as does the Council's approach' through, for example, the explicit statement within MONUSCO's resolutions that it does not create a precedent.[337] There was therefore a sense of relief 'from the perspective of people in New York and peacekeeping policy people' who were 'very glad that it hasn't been replicated anywhere else because it is such an exceptional mandate' that runs counter to tried and tested peacekeeping doctrine and principles.[338]

Conclusions: 'Holy Trinity' or 'Holy Principle'?

An exploration of the interpretation and application of peacekeeping's legal framework in the DRC highlights numerous issues with the frameworks in practice. Firstly, this chapter has demonstrated how the fundamental principles which constitute peacekeeping's core legal framework – consent, impartiality and non-use of force – do not exist harmoniously but, instead, overlap and are continually re-interpreted, re-applied and re-balanced through each mandate renewal or significant evolution of the peacekeeping operation. That is, when one of the principles is expanded, or interpreted more broadly, such as when MONUSCO has embarked upon joint operations with the Congolese armed forces, then this has significantly expanded the principles of impartiality and limited use of force and, as such, has required a re-balancing of all of the principles.

334 Interviewee 9 (n1) 65.
335 ibid.
336 Interviewee 8 (n20) 34.
337 Interviewee 10 (n21) 62.
338 ibid.

This, in turn, leads to the second notable issue which is that an expanded interpretation of these principles results in an expanded peacekeeping framework, which then undermines or potentially contravenes the principle of non-intervention. Throughout this chapter, there have been various points throughout ONUC, MONUC and MONUSCO's deployment where it is arguable that peacekeeping has amounted to coercive action to influence change in the host state and, therefore, intervention. Examples of this include ONUC's involvement in the Katanga secession, MONUC's shift to a stabilisation operation, joint operations conducted by both MONUC and MONUSCO and the implementation of the HRDDP. It has been argued that in all of these instances, the peacekeeping operation has engaged in sovereign matters such as the composition of the host state armed forces and diplomatic or policy issues and has attempted to coerce change within these areas, thereby attempting to influence change in the host state and thus amounting to intervention. Similarly, the chapter has also highlighted how, applying a TWAIL lens, these elements of coercion often expose the recurring patterns of dominance, subordination and the furtherance of the dominant powers' ideals and standards – such as the pressure exerted on states to provide consent to a mandate renewal and the imposition of conditions or standards (through the HRDDP) which must be met before joint operations can be undertaken.

The third issue which has then arisen is whether ONUC, MONUC and MONUSCO's re-interpretation of the fundamental principles, and therefore the peacekeeping frameworks, are best viewed as an evolution or a breach of peacekeeping's boundaries and, by extension, whether they undermine or contravene the principle of non-intervention. Again, the question which must be asked is – should there be a limit on how far these principles may evolve? This is a particularly pertinent issue when it comes to the current formation of MONUSCO, which includes the FIB. As this chapter has demonstrated, the FIB has been one of the greatest challenges to the fundamental principles of peacekeeping, significantly blurring the boundaries between peacekeeping and peace enforcement or intervention. It has invoked numerous debates over the legality of the operation, its compatibility with the fundamental principles and its practical effectiveness, including the risk it imposes upon peacekeepers and the potential invocation of international humanitarian law. It has also highlighted the different approaches to intervention, particularly within the Security Council. That is, whilst the UK and France supported the creation of the Brigade, both Russia and China expressed reservations, with Russia emphasising the inclusion of the fundamental principles in the resolution and China stressing the importance of the operation not setting a precedent.[339] Furthermore, the chapter has highlighted how the FIB's mandate to use targeted force to neutralise armed groups is particularly problematic and difficult

339 UNSC (68th year, 6943rd meeting) (28 March 2013) UN Doc S/PV.6943.

to reconcile with the principles of impartiality and limited use of force, thus taking the peacekeeping operation beyond the boundaries of peacekeeping and into the realm of intervention, thereby seemingly violating the principle of non-intervention. However, as has been noted, it appears that for this expansion of MONUSCO to include the FIB and for most other noticeable evolutions throughout MONUC and MONUSCO's history, the operations have been saved from crossing the boundary line and becoming intervention because of the initial host state consent that was given to the deployment of the operations. Therefore, whilst the principles of impartiality and non-use of force may be expanded to their very limits, host state consent acts as a single, thin barrier, preventing the operation from violating these principles and amounting to a violation of the principle of non-intervention. Put differently, the United Nations' peacekeeping operations in the Congo demonstrate how consent is the distinction between peacekeeping and peace enforcement or intervention. It follows, then, that in theory, as a peacekeeping operation is only ever deployed with host state consent, it can continually expand and evolve once in the field, without ever violating the principle of non-intervention, because of this initial consent. This is arguably problematic as it turns the peacekeeping operation into a hybrid peacekeeping-intervention, which is a far cry from the traditional concept of peacekeeping. Indeed, in these instances, it is perhaps best to view the peacekeeping operation not as peacekeeping but as a form of intervention by invitation, 'a function of the host state's consent',[340] as has been argued throughout this chapter, in particular in relation to joint operations.

This deeper level of analysis of peacekeeping's legal frameworks in practice has therefore demonstrated the complex relationship between the fundamental legal principles and the ability of a peacekeeping operation to significantly evolve without, overall, breaching peacekeeping's boundary line and becoming intervention. These evolutions within the operations in the Congo could therefore be seen as, at times, undermining the principle of non-intervention but, ultimately, not violating it because of the principle of consent. Building upon this analysis, the subsequent chapter will examine peacekeeping's normative framework, again providing specific examples of how peacekeeping's norms have been interpreted and applied within the Congo and whether they too support or undermine the principle of non-intervention.

References

Abi-Saab G, 'The Third World Intellectual in Praxis: Confrontation, Participation, or Operation Behind Enemy Lines' (2016) 37(11) TWQ 1957–1971

Al Jazeera, 'Q&A: Who are DR Congo's M23 Rebels?' (*Al Jazeera*, 5 November 2013) <https://www.aljazeera.com/news/africa/2013/08/201382411593336904.html>

340 Labuda (n92).

Alston P, 'Press Statement by Professor Philip Alston, UN Special Rapporteur on Extrajudicial Executions: Mission to the DR Congo' (15 October 2009) <https://reliefweb.int/report/democratic-republic-congo/press-statement-professor-philip-alston-un-special-rapporteur>

Anghie A, *Imperialism, Sovereignty and the Making of International Law* (CUP 2007)

Annan K, *Interventions: A Life in War and Peace* (Penguin 2013)

Aust HP, 'The UN Human Rights Due Diligence Policy: An Effective Mechanism against Complicity of Peacekeeping Forces?' (2015) 20(1) JCSL 61–73

Autesserre S, *The Frontlines of Peace* (CUP 2010)

Berwouts K, 'DRC/North Kivu: Waiting for the Intervention Brigade' (*African Arguments*, 22 July 2003) <https://africanarguments.org/2013/07/22/drc-north-kivu-waiting-for-the-intervention-brigade-by-kris-berwouts/>

Boutellis A, 'Can the UN Stabilize Mali? Towards a UN Stabilization Doctrine?' (2015) 4(1) Stability 1–16

Bunche R, *An American Odyssey* (WW Norton & Company 1998)

de Coning C and Aoi C, 'Conclusion: Towards a United Nations Stabilization Doctrine: Stabilization as an Emerging UN Practice' in C de Coning, C Aoi and J Karlsrud (eds) *UN Peacekeeping Doctrine in a New Era Adapting to Stabilisation, Protection and New Threats* (Routledge 2017)

Cammaert P and Blyth F, *Issue Brief: The UN Intervention Brigade in the Democratic Republic of the Congo* (IPI 2013).

Case Concerning Military and Paramilitary Activities in and Against Nicaragua (Nicaragua v United States of America) [1986] ICJ Rep 14

Case Concerning Armed Activities on the Territory of the Congo (Democratic Republic of the Congo v Uganda) Judgment of 19 December [2005] ICJ Rep 168

Certain Expenses of the United Nations (Article 17, Paragraph 2 of the Charter) (Advisory Opinion) [1962] ICJ Rep 151

Charlesworth H, 'International Legal Encounters with Democracy' (2017) 8(6) GlobalPolicy 34–43

Chimni BS, 'Third World Approaches to International Law: A Manifesto' (2006) 8 ICLR 3–27

CIVIC, 'Enabling Support by Mitigating Risk' (CIVIC, June 2020) <https://civiliansinconflict.org/publications/policy/enabling-support-by-mitigating-risk/>

Collins S, 'Letters Show O'Brien Had UN Authority for Actions in Katanga' (*The Irish Times*, 31 November 2018) <https://www.irishtimes.com/news/politics/letters-show-o-brien-had-un-authority-for-actions-in-katanga-1.3695184>

Congo Research Group, 'Impasse in the Congo: What Do the People Think? Results from a National Public Opinion Poll' (Investigative Report No2, NYU, October 2016) <http://congoresearchgroup.org/wp-content/uploads/2016/10/Final-Poll-CRG-BERCI.pdf>

Congo Research Group, 'The Future of MONUC (And Debt Relief)' (*CRG*, 18 March 2010) <http://congoresearchgroup.org/future-of-monuc-and-debt-relief/>

Crisis Group, 'The Agreement on a Cease-Fire in the Democratic Republic of Congo' (ICG Democratic Republic of Congo Report No 5, 20 August 1999)

Curran D and Hunt CT, 'Stabilization at the Expense of Peacebuilding in UN Peacekeeping Operations' (2020) 26(1) GG 46–68

Day AC and Hunt CT, 'UN Stabilisation Operations and the Problem of Non-Linear Change: A Relational Approach to Intervening in Governance Ecosystems' (2020) 9(1) Stability 1–23

de Coning C, 'Implications of Stabilisation Mandates for the Use of Force in Peace Operations' in P Nadin (ed) *The Use of Force in UN Peacekeeping* (Routledge 2018)

Declaration of the Heads of State and Government of the Member States of the ICGLR at the Fourth Ordinary Summit and Special Session on Sexual and Gender Based Violence, Kampala (15–16 December 2011) para 1 <https://www.icglr-rtf.org/publication/view/kampala-declaration-2011/>

Declaration of the Heads of State and Government of the Member States of the ICGLR on the Security Situation in Eastern DRC – Extraordinary Summit, Addis Ababa (15 July 2012)

Declaration of the Heads of State and Government of the Member States of the International Conference of the Great Lakes Region on the Security Situation in Eastern DRC – 5th Extraordinary Summit, Kampala (24 November 2012)

Dorn W, 'The UN's First "Air Force": Peacekeepers in Combat, Congo 1960–64' (2013) 77(4) JMilHist 1399–1425

Dos Santos Cruz CA, Phillips WR, Cusimano S, 'Improving Security of United Nations Peacekeepers: We Need to Change the Way We Are Doing Business' ("Santos Cruz Report") (19 December 2017) <https://peacekeeping.un.org/sites/default/files/improving_security_of_united_nations_peacekeepers_report.pdf>

Draper GIAD, 'The Legal Limitations upon the Employment of Weapons by the United Nations Force in the Congo' (1963) 12(2) ICLQ 387–413

Durch WJ, 'The UN Operation in the Congo: 1960–1964' in WJ Durch (ed) *The Evolution of UN Peacekeeping: Case Studies and Comparative Analysis* (St Martin's Press 1993)

Easterly W, *The White Man's Burden* (OUP 2006)

Effectiveness of Peace Operations Network, 'Assessing the Effectiveness of the United Nations Mission in the DRC/MONUC-MONUSCO' (NUPI 2019)

Ero C, 'The Problems with "African Solutions"' (*International Crisis Group*, 2 December 2013) <https://www.crisisgroup.org/africa/problems-african-solutions>

Findlay T, *The Use of Force in UN Peace Operations* (OUP 2002)

Foreign Affairs, 'Big Man in Congo: A Conversation with Joseph Kabila' (*Foreign Affairs*, 14 December 2018) <https://www.foreignaffairs.com/interviews/2018-12-14/big-man-congo>

France24, 'East African Leaders Agree to Extend Troop Deployment in Eastern DR Congo' (*France 24*, 1 June 2023) <https://www.france24.com/en/africa/20230601-east-african-leaders-agree-to-extend-troop-deployment-in-eastern-dr-congo>

Franck TM, 'United Nations Law in Africa: The Congo Operation as a Case Study' (1962) 27(4) L&ContemProb 632–652

Geneva Convention Relative to the Protection of Civilian Persons in Time of War (Fourth Geneva Convention) (12 August 1949) (75 UNTS 287)

Gilder A, 'The Effect of "Stabilization" in the Mandates and Practice of UN Peace Operations' (2019) 66 NILR 47–73

Gilder A, *Stabilization and Human Security in UN Peace Operations* (Routledge 2022)

Global Security, 'National Committee for the Defense of the People (CNDP)' <https://www.globalsecurity.org/military/world/para/cndp.htm>

———, 'Leaked Memo: MONUC-draft policy on conditionality of support to the FARDC' (12 October 2009) <http://www.innercitypress.com/OLA1MONUC101209.pdf>

Goulding M, 'The Evolution of United Nations Peacekeeping' (1993) 69(3) IntAff 451–464

Gowan R, 'Fighting Words: The Cruz Report Restores a Military Voice to Peacekeeping Debates' (*IPI*, 19 February 2018) <https://theglobalobservatory.org/2018/02/fighting-words-cruz-report-restores-military-voice/>

Hague Convention (II) with Respect to the Laws and Customs of War on Land and Its Annex: Regulations Concerning the Laws and Customs of War on Land (29 July 1899)

Hague Convention (IV) Respecting the Laws and Customs of War on Land and Its Annex: Regulations Concerning the Laws and Customs of War on Land (18 October 1907)

Hatto R, 'From Peacekeeping to Peacebuilding: The Evolution of the Role of the United Nations in Peace Operations' (2013) 95(891/892) IRRC 495–515

Henderson C, *The Use of Force and International Law* (CUP 2018)

Hostage Case, United States v List (Wilhelm) and ors (Trial Judgment) (1950) 11 TWC 757

Human Rights Watch, 'Uganda in Eastern DRC: Fueling Political and Ethnic Strife' (HRW, 1 March 2001) <https://www.hrw.org/report/2001/03/01/uganda-eastern-drc/fueling-politcal-and-ethnic-strife>

Human Rights Watch, 'DRC: Events of 2008' (HRW 2008) <https://www.hrw.org/world-report/2009/country-chapters/democratic-republic-congo>

Human Rights Watch, 'You Will be Punished: Attacks on Civilians in Eastern Congo' (HRW 2009) <https://www.hrw.org/sites/default/files/reports/drc1209webwcover2.pdf>

Human Rights Watch, 'DR Congo: M23 Rebels Kill, Rape Civilians' (*Human Rights Watch*, 22 July 2013) <https://www.hrw.org/news/2013/07/22/dr-congo-m23-rebels-kill-rape-civilians>

Human Rights Watch, 'Killings in Kiwanja: The UN's Inability to Protect Civilians' (HRW, 11 December 2018) <https://www.hrw.org/report/2008/12/11/killings-kiwanja/uns-inability-protect-civilians>

Interview with Senior UNDP Personnel, Formerly OCHA ('Interviewee 1') (Geneva, 20 November 2018) DOI: <http://doi.org/10.17639/nott.7119>

Interview with Senior DRC/Great Lakes Coordinator from International Organisation ('Interviewee 2') (Geneva, 12 November 2018) DOI: <http://doi.org/10.17639/nott.7119>

Interview with Independent Expert ('Interviewee 3') (Skype, 10 December 2018) DOI: <http://doi.org/10.17639/nott.7119>

Interview with Former MONUSCO Military Personnel ('Interviewee 4') (Shrivenham, 28 October 2019) DOI: <http://doi.org/10.17639/nott.7119>

Interview with Congolese Independent Expert ('Interviewee 5') (Oxford, 29 October 2019) DOI: <http://doi.org/10.17639/nott.7119>

Interview with Independent Expert and Former UN Political Adviser ('Interviewee 8') (New York, 26 November 2019) DOI: <http://doi.org/10.17639/nott.7119>

Interview with Senior UN DPPA-DPO Personnel ('Interviewee 9') (New York, 27 November 2019) DOI: <http://doi.org/10.17639/nott.7119>

Interview with Senior UN DPO Personnel, Policy, Evaluation and Training Division ('Interviewee 10') (New York, 3 December 2019) DOI: <http://doi.org/10.17639/nott.7119>

Interview with Former Senior Military Commander ('Interviewee 11') (New York (Skype) 3 December 2019) DOI: <http://doi.org/10.17639/nott.7119>

Interview with Mona Ali Khalil, former Senior Legal Officer of the UN Office of the Legal Counsel, Director of MAK LAW International and an Affiliate of the Harvard Law School Program on International Law and Armed Conflict ('Interviewee 12') (New York (Skype) 5 December 2019) DOI: <http://doi.org/10.17639/nott.7119>

Interview with Senior Human Rights Officer in the Office of the UN High Commissioner of Human Rights ('Interviewee 13') (New York, 6 December 2019) DOI: <http://doi.org/10.17639/nott.7119>

Interview with Senior Political Affairs Officer, UN DPO ('Interviewee 16') (New York, 10 December 2019) DOI: <http://doi.org/10.17639/nott.7119>

Interview with Senior MONUSCO Military Personnel ('Interviewee 17') (Skype, 9 February 2020) DOI: <http://doi.org/10.17639/nott.7119>

Johnstone I, 'Managing Consent in Contemporary Peacekeeping Operations' (2011) 18(2) IntPeacekeep 168–182

Karlsrud J, 'Special Representatives of the Secretary-General as Norm Arbitrators? Understanding Bottom-up Authority in UN Peacekeeping' (2013) 19(4) GG 525–544

Kennedy M and Magennis A, *Ireland, the United Nations and the Congo* (Four Courts Press 2014)

Labbé J and Boutellis A, 'Peace Operations by Proxy: Implications for Humanitarian Action of UN Peacekeeping Partnerships with Non-UN Security Forces' (2013) 95(891/892) IRRC 539–559

Labuda PI, 'United Nations Peacekeeping as Intervention by Invitation: Host State Consent and the Use of Force in Security Council-Mandated Stabilisation Operations' (2020) JUFIL 1–37

Legal Consequences for States of the Continued Presence of South Africa in Namibia (South West Africa) notwithstanding Security Council Resolution 276 (Advisory Opinion) [1971] ICJ Rep 16

Mattelaer A, 'EUFOR RDC and the Development of the ESDP' (2007) 60(3) StudDip 73–89

Mazuri A, *Towards a Pax Africana: A Study of Ideology and Ambition* (University of Chicago 1967)

Miller EM, 'Legal Aspects of United Nations Action in Congo' (1961) 55(1) AJIL 1–28

MONUC, 'DR Congo: Peacekeepers Plan Operation Amani Leo with FARDC in North Kivu' (*MONUC*, 19 January 2010) <https://reliefweb.int/report/democratic-republic-congo/dr-congo-peacekeepers-plan-operation-amani-leo-fardc-north-kivu>

MONUC, 'MONUC Outlines Cooperation with FARDC in Operation Amani Leo' (*MONUC*, 5 March 2010) <https://monuc.unmissions.org/en/monuc-outlines-cooperation-fardc-operation-amani-leo>

MONUSCO, 'Stabilisation Support Unit' <https://monusco.unmissions.org/en/stabilization-support-unit>

Müller L, 'The Force Intervention Brigade – United Nations Forces Beyond the Fine Line Between Peacekeeping and Peace Enforcement' (2015) 20(3) JCSL 359–380

News Wires, 'UN to Withdraw up to 2000 Troops from DR Congo' (*France 24*, 28 May 2010) <https://www.france24.com/en/20100528-un-withdraw-2000-troops-dr-congo-monuc>

New York Times, 'Confidential note from the UN Office of Legal Affairs to Mr. Le Roy, Head of the Department of Peacekeeping Operations: MONUC-Operation Kimia 2' (1 April 2009) <https://www.nytimes.com/interactive/projects/documents/united-nations-correspondence-on-peacekeeping-in-the-democratic-republic-of-the-congo#p=1>

Nichols M, 'UN to Congo: Remove Generals Accused of Abuses or Lose Support' (*Reuters*, 4 February 2015) <https://www.reuters.com/article/us-congodemocratic-un/u-n-to-congo-remove-generals-accused-of-abuses-or-lose-support-idUSKBN0L823120150204>

Novosseloff A, 'The Effectiveness of the UN Mission in the Democratic Republic of the Congo' (*IPI*, 19 December 2019) <https://theglobalobservatory.org/2019/12/effectiveness-un-mission-democratic-republic-of-the-congo/>

Olivier D, 'The FIB Goes to War' (*African Defence Review*, 29 August 2013) <https://www.africandefence.net/the-fib-goes-to-war/>

O'Malley A, '"What An Awful Body the UN Have Become!!" Anglo-American-UN Relations During the Congo Crisis, February-December 1961' (2016) 14(1) JTransStud 26–46

Oswald B, H. Durham and A Bates, *Documents on The Law of UN Peace Operations* (OUP 2010)

Oxford Analytica, 'Congo-Kinshasa: MONUC Exit is Probable, But Premature' (*Oxford Analytica*, 1 April 2010) <https://reliefweb.int/report/democratic-republic-congo/congo-kinshasa-monuc-exit-probable-premature>

Peter M, 'Between Doctrine and Practice: The UN Peacekeeping Dilemma' (2015) 21(3) GG 351–370

Piiparinen T, 'Beyond the Technological Turn: Reconsidering the Significance of the Intervention Brigade and Peacekeeping Drones for UN Conflict Management' (2015) 21(1) GG 141–160

Prunier G, *Africa's World War: Congo, the Rwandan Genocide, and the Making of a Continental Catastrophe* (Oxford University Press 2011)

Reno W, *Warlord Politics and African States* (Lynne Rienner 1998)

Reno W, 'Congo: From State Collapse to "Absolutism", to State Failure' (2006) 27(1) TWQ 43–56

Rogier E, 'The Inter-Congolese Dialogue: A Critical Overview' in M Malan and JP Gomes (eds) *Challenges of Peace Implementation: The UN Mission in the Democratic Republic of the Congo* (ISS, 2004)

Roth B, 'Secessions, Coups and the International Rule of Law: Assessing the Decline of the Effective Control Doctrine' (2010) 11 MelbJIntlL 393–440

Russo J, 'The East African Community Steps into the Crisis in the DRC. Will It Help?' (*IPI*, 12 December 2022) <https://theglobalobservatory.org/2022/12/east-african-community-crisis-drc/>

Schulman S and Rusagara F, 'Umoja Wetu: A Photo Essay' (2009) 154(2) RUSIJ 90–97

Sebastián S and Gorur A, 'UN Peacekeeping & Host-State Consent: How Missions Navigate Relationships with Governments' (Stimson Centre, March 2018)

Simpson G, *Great Powers and Outlaw States: Unequal Sovereignty in the International Legal Order* (CUP 2004)

Sloan J, *The Militarisation of Peacekeeping in the Twenty-First Century* (Hart Publishing 2011).

Sonczyk B, 'The Protection of the Intervention Brigade Under Article 8(2)(e)(iii) of the Rome Statute of the International Criminal Court' (2015) 13 QILZoom-in 13

Spijkers O, 'The Evolution of United Nations Peacekeeping in the Congo' (2015) 19(1–2) IntPeacekeep 88–117

Steingberg D, 'UN Must Stop Backing Congo's Disastrous Operation Against Marauding Rebel Militias' (International Crisis Group, 30 November 2009) <https://www.crisisgroup.org/africa/central-africa/democratic-republic-congo/un-must-stop-backing-congos-disastrous-operation-against-marauding-rebel-militias>

Tamm H, 'Status Competition in Africa: Explaining the Rwandan-Ugandan Clashes in the Democratic Republic of Congo' (2019) 118(472) AfrAff 509–530

Tardy T, 'A Critique of Robust Peacekeeping in Contemporary Peace Operations' (2011) 18(2) IntPeacekeep 152–167

Tardy T, 'The European Union and UN Peace Operations: What Global-Regional Peace and Security Partnership?' in C de Coning and M Peter (eds) *United Nations Peace Operations in a Changing Global Order* (Palgrave Macmillan 2019)

The East African, 'DR Congo Rejects UN Ultimatum to Sack Tainted Generals' (*The East African*, 6 February 2015) <https://www.theeastafrican.co.ke/news/ea/DR-Congo-rejects-UN-ultimatum-to-sack-tainted-generals/4552908-2615116-j6p131/index.html>

The Prosecutor v Bosco Ntaganda (Judgment) ICC-01/04-02/06 (8 July 2019)

Tsagourias N, 'Consent, Neutrality/Impartiality and the Use of Force in Peacekeeping: Their Constitutional Dimension' (2007) 11(3) JCSL 465–482

Trefon T, *Reinventing Order in the Congo: How People Respond to State Failure in Kinshasa* (Zed Books 2004)

Tull DM, 'The Limits and Unintended Consequences of UN Peace Enforcement: The Force Intervention Brigade in the DR Congo' (2017) 25(2) IntPeacekeep 167–190

Ulriksen S, Gourlay C and Mace C, 'Operation Artemis: The Shape of Things to Come?' (2004) 11(3) IntPeacekeep 508–525

UN, 'Civil-Military Coordination Specialized Training Materials (UN-CIMIC STM)' (UN DPO-DFS, 2004) <http://repository.un.org/bitstream/handle/11176/89582/STM%20UNCIMIC.pdf?sequence=1&isAllowed=y>

UN, Eighth Report on State Responsibility, Document A/CN.4/318 and Add.1-4, 2 (1979) Y.B. Int'l L. Comm'n 3 (1980)

UN Country Team <https://drcongo.un.org> and OCHA <https://www.unocha.org/drc>

UN DPKO, 'Civil-Military Coordination Policy' (9 September 2002) <https://www.refworld.org/pdfid/451ba7624.pdf>

UN News, 'Rebels Take Bukavu in Eastern DR of Congo, Protesters Target UN' (*UN News*, 2 June 2004) <https://news.un.org/en/story/2004/06/105462-rebels-take-bukavu-eastern-dr-congo-protesters-target-un>

UN News, 'First Set of UN Troops Could Leave DR Congo by June Says Peacekeeping Chief' (*UN News*, 5 March 2010) <https://news.un.org/en/story/2010/03/331642-first-set-un-troops-could-leave-dr-congo-june-says-peacekeeping-chief>

UN News, 'Five Years On' (*UN News*, 28 February 2018) <https://ungreatlakes.unmissions.org/five-years-progress-has-been-made-implementation-peace-security-and-cooperation-framework-drc-and>

UN Office of the Special Envoy for the Great Lakes Region, 'Joint Press Release on the Peace, Security and Cooperation Framework, JPR21' (27 February 2018) <https://ungreatlakes.unmissions.org/five-years-peace-security-and-cooperation-framework-drc-and-region-remains-central-achieving-lasting>

UN Peacekeeping, 'MONUSCO Fact Sheet' <https://peacekeeping.un.org/en/mission/monusco>

UN Press Release, 'Intervention Brigade Authorized as Security Council Grants Mandate Renewal for United Nations Mission in Democratic Republic of Congo' (SC/10964, 28 March 2013)

UN Secretary General, Decision No 2011/18, 13 July 2011

UNGA, 'Second and Final Report of the Secretary General on the Plan for an Emergency International United Nations Force' (6 November 1956) UN Doc A/3302

UNGA (15th Session, 912th Plenary Meeting) (8 November 1960) UN Doc A/PV.912

UNGA, 'Resolutions Adopted by the General Assembly During its Fifteenth Session' (20 September–20 December 1960) 15th Session, UN Doc Supp No 16 (A/4684)

UNGA, 'Annual Report of the Secretary-General on the Work of the Organisation' (16 June 1960–15 June 1961) UN Doc A/4800

UNGA, 'Report of the Panel on United Nations Peace Operations' ("Brahimi Report") (21 August 2000) UN Doc A/55/305-S/2000/809

UNGA, 'Report of the Special Committee on Peacekeeping Operations' (28 March 2003) UN Doc A/57/767

UNGA Plenary (73rd Session, 6th & 7th Meetings) (25 September 2018) UN Doc GA/12062

UNGA Res 377 (V) (3 November 1950) UN Doc A/RES/377(V)

UNGA Res 1474 (ES-IV) (20 September 1960) UN Doc A/RES/1474(ES-IV)

UNGA Res 1480 (XV) (20 September 1960) UN Doc GA/RES/1480 (XV)

UNGA Res 1671 (XVI) (18 December 1961) UN Doc S/RES/1671/XVI

UNGA-SC, 'Human Rights Due Diligence Policy' (5 March 2013) UN Doc A/67/775-S/2013/110

UNSC, 'Cable dated 12 July 1960 from the President of the Republic of the Congo and Supreme Commander of the National Army and the Prime Minister and the Minister of National Defense Addressed to the Secretary-General of the United Nations' (13 July 1960) UN Doc S/4382

UNSC, 'Observations by the Special Representative of the Secretary-General in the Republic of the Congo on the Memorandum by Major-General HT Alexander (S/4445, Annex II)' (21 August 1960) UN Doc S/4451

UNSC (15th year, 896th Meeting) (9–10 September 1960) UN Doc S/PV/896

UNSC, 'Report of the Secretary General' (18 July 1960) UN Doc S/4389

UNSC, 'Exchange of Correspondence Between The Secretary-General and the President of the Republic of the Congo Concerning Matadi' (30 March 1961) UN Doc S/4775
UNSC, 'Ceasefire Agreement' ("Lusaka Ceasefire") (23 July 1999) UN Doc S/1999/815
UNSC, 'Special Report of the Secretary-General on the United Nations Organization Mission in the Democratic Republic of the Congo' (10 September 2002) UN Doc S/2002/1005
UNSC, 'Special Report of the Secretary-General on the Democratic Republic of the Congo and the Great Lakes Region' (27 February 2003) UN Doc S/2013/119
UNSC, 'Letter Dated 15 May 2003 from the Secretary-General addressed to the President of the Security Council' (28 May 2003) UN Doc S/2003/574
UNSC, 'Fourth Special Report of the Secretary-General on the United Nations Organization Mission in the Democratic Republic of the Congo' (21 November 2008) UN Doc S/2008/728
UNSC, 'Final Report of the Group of Experts on the Democratic Republic of the Congo' (12 December 2008) UN Doc S/2008/773
UNSC, 'Final Report of the Group of Experts on the Democratic Republic of the Congo' (23 November 2009) UN Doc S/2009/603
UNSC, 'Twenty-Eighth Report of the Secretary-General on the United Nations Organization Mission to the Democratic Republic of Congo' (20 June 2009) UN Doc S/2009/335
UNSC, 'Thirtieth Report of the Secretary-General on the United Nations Organisation Mission in the Democratic Republic of the Congo' (4 December 2009) UN Doc S/2009/623
UNSC, 'Report of the Secretary General on the UN Organisation Stabilisation Mission in the Democratic Republic of the Congo' (23 May 2012) UN Doc S/2012/355
UNSC, 'Statement by the Presidential of the Security Council' (19 October 2012) UN Doc S/PRST/2012/22
UNSC, 'Letter dated 27 November 2012 from the Secretary-General addressed to the President of the Security Council' (27 November 2012) UN Doc S/2013/876
UNSC, 'Special Report of the Secretary-General on the DRC and the Great Lakes Region' (27 February 2013) UN Doc S/2013/119
UNSC, '"Intervention Brigade" Authorised' (28 March 2013) Meetings Coverage SC/10964
UNSC (68th Year, 6943rd Meeting) (28 March 2013) UN Doc S/PV.6943
UNSC, 'Report of the Secretary-General on MONUSCO' (17 December 2013) UN Doc S/2013/757
UNSC, 'Final Report of the Group of Experts on the DRC' (23 January 2014) UN Doc S/2014/42
UNSC, 'Report of the Secretary-General on MONUSCO' (30 June 2014) UN Doc S/2014/450
UNSC, 'Midterm Report of the Group of Experts on the Democratic Republic of the Congo' (16 October 2015) UN Doc S/2015/797
UNSC, 'New Strategy for Mission Withdrawal: 8778th Meeting' (7 December 2020) UN Doc SC/14374
UNSC Res 143 (14 July 1960) UN Doc S/RES/143
UNSC Res 145 (22 July 1960) UN Doc S/RES/145
UNSC Res 146 (9 August 1960) UN Doc S/RES/146

UNSC Res 169 (24 November 1961) UN Doc S/RES/169
UNSC Res 1234 (9 April 1999) UN Doc S/RES/1234
UNSC Res 1258 (6 August 1999) UN Doc S/RES/1258
UNSC Res 1273 (5 November 1999) UN Doc S/RES/1273
UNSC Res 1279 (30 November 1999) UN Doc S/RES/1279
UNSC Res 1291 (24 February 2000) UN Doc S/RES/1291
UNSC Res 1332 (14 December 2000) UN Doc S/RES/1332
UNSC Res 1341 (22 February 2001) UN Doc S/RES/1341
UNSC Res 1445 (4 December 2002) UN Doc S/RES/1445
UNSC Res 1484 (30 May 2003) UN Doc S/RES/1484
UNSC Res 1493 (28 July 2003) UN Doc S/RES/1493
UNSC Res 1565 (1 October 2004) UN Doc S/RES/1565
UNSC Res 1592 (30 March 2005) UN Doc S/RES/1592
UNSC Res 1649 (21 December 2005) UN Doc S/RES/1649
UNSC Res 1671 (25 April 2006) UN Doc S/RES/1671
UNSC Res 1756 (15 May 2007) UN Doc S/RES/1756
UNSC Res 1856 (22 December 2008) UN Doc S/RES/1856
UNSC Res 1925 (28 May 2010) UN Doc S/RES/1925
UNSC Res 2076 (20 November 2012) UN Doc S/RES/2076
UNSC Res 2098 (28 March 2013) UN Doc S/RES/2098
UNSC Res 2502 (19 December 2019) UN Doc S/RES/2502
UNSC Res 2556 (18 December 2020) UN Doc S/RES/2556
UNSC Res 2612 (20 December 2021) UN Doc S/RES/2612
UNSC Res 2666 (20 December 2022) UN Doc S/RES/2666
UNSG, 'Secretary-General's Bulletin: Observance by United Nations Forces of International Humanitarian Law' (6 August 1999) UN Doc ST/SGB/1999/13
Urquhart B, 'Character Sketches: Patrice Lumumba' <https://news.un.org/en/spotlight/patrice-lumumba-brian-urquhart>
Verweijen J, 'Stable Instability: Political Settlements and Armed Groups in the Congo' (Rift Valley Institute 2016)
Verweijen J, 'Strange Battlefield Fellows: The Diagonal Interoperability Between Blue Helmets and the Congolese Army' (2017) 24(3) IntPeacekeep 363–387
Vircoulon T, After MONUC, Should MONUSCO Continue to Support Congolese Military Campaigns?' (Crisis Group, 19 July 2010) <https://www.crisisgroup.org/africa/central-africa/chad/after-monuc-should-monusco-continue-support-congolese-military-campaigns>
White ND, 'Peacekeeping or War-Fighting?' in ND White and C Henderson (eds) *Research Handbook on International Conflict and Security Law* (Edward Elgar 2013)
Zerrougui L, 'Strengthening the Rule of Law and Protection of Civilians in the Democratic Republic of the Congo' (*UN Chronicle*, August 2018) <https://www.un.org/en/chronicle/article/strengthening-rule-law-and-protection-civilians-democratic-republic-congo>

Chapter 6

Peacekeeping's Normative Framework in Practice

Ending Christmas Tree Mandates?

As the previous chapters have explored, peacekeeping's principles and norms 'exist in a competitive arena' with the normative composition rebalanced each time a peacekeeping operation's mandate is interpreted and applied in practice.[1] As noted in Chapter 4, peacekeeping's norms are not required by fundamental rules of international law and are therefore not legal principles. However, the norms do assist in dealing with some of peacekeeping's complex legal questions, such as the responsibilities and liabilities of peacekeepers accused of sexual exploitation and abuse and the applicability of international humanitarian and human rights law.[2] As such, the norms, at times, may have legal underpinnings or may invoke elements of international law thereby providing a subsidiary contribution to peacekeeping's legal framework. Furthermore, because of the degree of overlap, an expansion of these three newer concepts has also had a knock-on effect on the fundamental legal principles. For example, both the protection of civilians and democracy promotion have resulted in increased levels of force being used; therefore, an expansion of these norms may result in a simultaneous expansion or reimagining of the principle of non-use of force. Again, as was discussed in previous chapters, this highlights how peacekeeping's norms exist in a disharmonious, competitive arena, in which they are rebalanced for each peacekeeping operation and, even, each mandate.[3]

Before examining how these norms are interpreted and applied in practice, it needs to be noted how these norms sit within the peacekeeping mandates. That is, as seen in Chapter 3, peacekeeping operations significantly

1 J Karlsrud, 'Special Representatives of the Secretary-General as Norm Arbitrators? Understanding Bottom-up Authority in UN Peacekeeping' (2013) 19(4) GG 525–544, 527.

2 See: ND White, 'Peacekeeping and International Law' in J Koops, N MacQueen, T Tardy and PD Williams (eds) *The Oxford Handbook of United Nations Peacekeeping Operations* (OUP 2016) 43–59.

3 Karlsrud (n1).

DOI: 10.4324/9781003371649-6

expanded after the Cold War resulting in a shift from traditional to multi-dimensional peacekeeping, with normative aspects playing an increasingly important role.[4] The expansion of the peacekeeping mandate – i.e. the tasks which peacekeepers are asked to undertake – has led to contemporary mandates often being referred to as 'Christmas Tree mandates', given the extensive list of activities which the Security Council places upon a mission.[5] For some, these mandates are problematic, particularly in countries such as the DRC, as, once MONUC/MONUSCO was 'no longer helping parties emerging from a conflict [to] implement a peace agreement', it became 'an open ended, ill-defined statebuilding enterprise'.[6] Similarly, others have recognised that it is not just the volume of tasks which is problematic but the many dissimilar tasks, such as security-related tasks (e.g. PoC) and peacebuilding-related tasks (e.g. organising elections), which hinder an operation's ability to meet the expectations set for them by the Security Council.[7]

Moreover, these complex mandates become more problematic when an operation is nearing the end of its deployment. Within the Congo, as a result of MONUSCO's significantly expanded mandates, in 2019/2020 as the operation prepared to leave, senior UN personnel noted that 'we're looking for an exit strategy' and 'we realise "well, there is no exit"'.[8] As this chapter will highlight, one lesson which could be learnt from MONUSCO's experience is that 'the Council should be less ambitious in designing mandates'.[9] Indeed, in a launch of the Action for Peacekeeping initiative, UN Secretary-General Antonio Guterres called for an end to 'Christmas tree' mandates, arguing that 'by attempting too much, we dilute our efforts and weaken our impact'.[10] More recently, in the United Nations' 'New Agenda for Peace', it was recognised that there is a need for 'the Security Council not to burden peace operations with unrealistic mandates', alongside a need for both the Council and the General Assembly to undertake 'a reflection on the limits and future of peacekeeping'.[11] In exploring peacekeeping's normative

4 See: M Bothe, 'UN Peace Operations' in D Fleck (ed) *The Handbook of the Law of Visiting Forces* (2nd ed, OUP 2018) 50–74.

5 UNSC Report, 'Is Christmas Really Over? The Mandating of Peace Operations' (UNSC, 22 February 2019) <https://www.securitycouncilreport.org/atf/cf/%7B65BFCF9B-6D27-4E9C-8CD3-CF6E4FF96FF9%7D/research_report_council_mandating_february_2019.pdf>.

6 Interview with Senior Political Affairs Officer, UN DPO ('Interviewee 16') (New York, 10 December 2019) DOI: <http://doi.org/10.17639/nott.7119> pg 18.

7 RA Blair, J Di Salvatore and HM Smidt, 'When Do UN Peacekeeping Operations Implement Their Mandates?' (2021) 66(3) American Journal of Political Science 664–680.

8 Interviewee 16 (n6).

9 Interview with Independent Expert and Former UN Political Adviser ('Interviewee 8') (New York, 26 November 2019) DOI: <http://doi.org/10.17639/nott.7119> pg 57.

10 UNSC Report (n5).

11 UN, 'Our Common Agenda Policy Brief 9: A New Agenda for Peace' (July 2023) <https://dppa.un.org/en/a-new-agenda-for-peace> 24.

framework in practice, this chapter will therefore highlight instances when there could be a move to a more realistic mandate, through a contracting of the interpretation and application of the peacekeeping norms. More specifically, the chapter will question whether some of the norms within peacekeeping's normative framework – such as democracy promotion and protection of civilians – should remain a part of peacekeeping's frameworks. In other words, the chapter will question whether peacekeeping has now reached the limits of its current evolutionary cycle and, therefore, should begin to retract back to the more traditional model of peacekeeping and away from large, multi-dimensional operations.

Democracy Promotion

As seen in Chapter 4, the norm of democracy promotion within peacekeeping operations, rather than possessing any legal underpinnings, stems from the 'spirit' of the UN Charter ('We the peoples') and international institutions' preference for democratic governance.[12] The complexities of implementing this norm in peacekeeping practice can, again, be found in the United Nations' numerous operations in the Congo.

Since gaining independence, the DRC has held four elections – 1960, 2006, 2011 and 2018 – with varying degrees of success and varying levels of support from UN peacekeeping operations. In what could be viewed as the first application of an informal norm of democracy promotion within UN peacekeeping, ONUC was deployed 'to a country where the institutions of state were collapsing', referred to by some as the first case of 'painting a country blue' – the act of the United Nations taking over administrative functions of a failed state to restore peace and order.[13] One month after gaining independence from Belgium, the Congo held its first free and fair elections in May 1960.[14] However, under-prepared for independence, democracy struggled to take hold and the newly elected prime minister (Lumumba) and president (Kasavubu) requested UN assistance a mere 12 days after gaining independence.[15]

Therefore, whilst the norm of democracy promotion was only formally introduced into peacekeeping's normative framework in the 1990s, operations such as ONUC were engaging with democracy promotion activities, thereby temporarily expanding the normative framework. For example, ONUC undertook statebuilding activities and assumed significant sovereign

12 Charter of the United Nations 'UN Charter' (24 October 1945), preamble.
13 M Goulding, 'The Evolution of United Nations Peacekeeping' (1993) 69(3) IntAff 451–464, 452.
14 See: D Van Reybrouck, *Congo: The Epic History of a People* (Fourth Estate 2015) 227–281.
15 UNSC Res 143 (14 July 1960) UN Doc S/RES/143.

functions by maintaining law and order and establishing a governance system. This could be viewed not only as an expansion of peacekeeping's normative framework, but also as coercive action designed to alter or influence change in the state and thus intervention. It could be deemed to be intervention because of ONUC's attempts to establish democratic governance within a newly independent state which was reliant on the peacekeeping operation, had little choice over the form of governance established and was unable to voluntarily reject ONUC's decisions on law, order and governance. This then presents an overlap with the principle of consent, as discussed in Chapters 3 and 5, and the extent to which a host state may consent to or reject peacekeeping tasks once an operation is deployed. In this instance, it appears that host state consent was irrelevant during ONUC's mandate period for these democracy promotion tasks. Moreover, this initial attempt at democracy promotion within the Congo raises questions as to what establishing democracy means. For the Belgians it meant organising parliamentary elections, to the Afro-Asian and Soviet-bloc states 'it meant liberating the Congo from Belgian colonial control' and for the United States it meant 'ensuring the country not "fall" to a communist dictatorship'.[16] What is noticeable here is that the decision on what democratic governance in the Congo meant was decided, ultimately, by external actors and not the Congolese themselves. It also highlights the differing agendas and approaches to intervention within the international community.

Two further observations can then be drawn from this. Firstly, the involvement of external actors in the internal affairs of the newly independent Congo established a precedent which has led to continual external intervention in relation to Congolese governance, particularly as Congo has been viewed as pivotal in regional and global politics. For example, Congo's neighbours, Rwanda and Uganda, and the Southern African Development Community (SADC) have all shown a particular interest in Congo's leadership, at times supporting or attempting to influence Congolese politics to further their own agendas or protect their interests within the Great Lakes region.[17] Secondly, from a TWAIL perspective, this supports arguments

16 J Dobbins, SG Jones, K Crane, A Rathmell, B Steele, R Teltschik and A Timilsina, *The UN's Role in Nation-Building: From the Congo to Iraq* (RAND Corporation 2005) 5–29, 9.

17 See: SADC Press Release, 'SADC Reiterates Its Position for a Stable and Peaceful DRC' (*SADC*, 29 May 2020) <https://reliefweb.int/report/democratic-republic-congo/sadc-reiterates-its-position-stable-and-peaceful-drc>; H Tamm, 'Status Competition in Africa: Explaining the Rwandan-Ugandan Clashes in the Democratic Republic of Congo' (2019) 118(472) AfrAff 509–530; M Schneider, 'Examining the Role of Rwanda in the DRC Insurgency' (Crisis Group, 19 September 2012) <https://www.crisisgroup.org/africa/central-africa/democratic-republic-congo/examining-role-rwanda-drc-insurgency>; P Fabricius, 'SADC Prepares to Go Back to the Future in Eastern DRC' (ISS, 19 May 2023) <https://issafrica.org/iss-today/sadc-prepares-to-go-back-to-the-future-in-eastern-drc>.

made in Chapter 3 that democracy (and therefore democracy promotion) is a Western-centric notion which perpetuates the colonial dichotomies of 'civilised' and 'uncivilised', reinforcing patterns of domination and subordination.[18] Indeed, the differing views on how ONUC should interpret and apply the norm of democracy promotion in the Congo arguably reflects how this is a 'classic instance' of the 'imperial project at work', with the dominant external actors determining how the subordinate host state should be governed.[19] This is reinforced by the fact that there was an apparent lack of host state consent to these peacekeeping tasks, in part due to the instability and lack of infrastructure in Congo's initial few months of independence. Furthermore, it could also be viewed as another example of Anghie's dynamic of difference, with the dominant actor (ONUC and member states) identifying a gap between themselves and the Congolese host state (a lack of democratic governance) and then seeking to bridge that gap by altering or normalising (democratising) the host state and thus using this as an excuse or justification for intervention.

For the peacekeeping frameworks, then, this first example of democracy promotion in the Congo arguably expanded peacekeeping's normative frameworks exponentially, particularly for peacekeeping at that time. This, in turn, stretched peacekeeping's red boundary line, taking it much closer to the realm of intervention, potentially breaching this line in instances when the host state had little ability to reject the peacekeeper's actions.

Intervention to Counter Intervention

Further examples of democracy promotion and norm expansion can also be found in the United Nations' later peacekeeping operations in the Congo which also align with the broader development of the norm within UN peacekeeping. In 1999, following the signing of the Lusaka Ceasefire Agreement to end the Second Congo War, UN peacekeeping returned to the Congo in the form of MONUC to oversee the agreement, which, among other things, agreed terms for inter-Congolese political negotiations or an 'Inter-Congolese National Dialogue'.[20] The Dialogue was 'supposed to prepare for a new political dispensation that liberates the Congolese from external occupation and interference',[21] yet in practice numerous external actors were involved in

18 GH Fox and BR Roth (eds) *Democracy and International Law* (Edward Elgar 2020); N Tzouvala, *Capitalism as Civilisation: A History of International Law* (CUP 2020) 5.

19 V Sripati, 'The United Nation's Role in Post-Conflict Constitution-Making Processes: TWAIL Insights' (2008) 10(4) ICLR 411–420, 420.

20 UNSC, 'Ceasefire Agreement' ('Lusaka Ceasefire') (23 July 1999) UN Doc S/1999/815.

21 Crisis Group, 'The Inter-Congolese Dialogue: Political Negotiation or Game of Bluff?' (ICG Africa Report No 37, 16 November 2001).

the process, including the United Nations and EU.[22] Indeed, MONUC was said to have 'had a pretty intrusive role'[23] under their mandate to monitor the implementation of the agreement and issue communiques.[24] Both MONUC and others in the international community also significantly supported the recognition of Kabila as president as he was viewed as a 'much more stable' option for the country.[25] As with ONUC, then, this broad application of the norm of democracy promotion within the Congo meant that MONUC was engaged in sovereign matters, by supporting the establishment of a system of governance and leadership. As such, this could, again, be viewed as coercive action designed to influence change in the host state, and therefore intervention, given the Congolese state's reliance on MONUC at that time. Indeed, any actions which MONUC undertook to foster democratic governance in the Congo could be viewed as coercive as the Congolese state had little voluntary choice in accepting the changes to their state, given the insecurity and lack of stability at that time.

This argument is further compounded by the fact that MONUC's involvement in the Congolese National Dialogue was the first stage in the application of the norm of democracy promotion. The second phase of this application then came with MONUC's role in the Congo's 2006 elections. During this period, 'acting under Chapter VII', MONUC were authorised 'to take all necessary measures, within its means and capabilities' to complete its tasks.[26] This included to 'stabilise a situation', protect civilians and ensure the security and free movement of EUFOR personnel and installations – an EU-led quasi-enforcement mission which was temporarily deployed to support MONUC.[27] The norm was therefore expanded as these new tasks (such as creating a stable environment for elections, supporting EUFOR and providing logistical and strategical support for the organising of elections) were introduced into MONUC's mandate, consequently expanding peacekeeping's normative framework. This expansion also had an impact on peacekeeping's legal framework, particularly the principles of non-use of force and impartiality. The invocation of Chapter VII in MONUC's mandate permitted both MONUC and EUFOR to use an increased level of force in order to complete the democratisation tasks, such as EUFOR thwarting a heavy attack

22 See: E Rogier, 'The Inter-Congolese Dialogue: A Critical Overview' in M Malan and JP Gomes (eds) *Challenges of Peace Implementation: The UN Mission in the Democratic Republic of the Congo* (ISS 2004) 29.

23 Interviewee 16 (n6) 3.

24 UNSC Res 1417 (14 June 2002) UN Doc S/RES/1417, 13-14; UNSC Res 1468 (20 March 2003) UN Doc S/RES/1468, 1.

25 Interview with Congolese Independent Expert ('Interviewee 5') (Oxford, UK, 29 October 2019) DOI: <http://doi.org/10.17639/nott.7119>.

26 ibid, 8.

27 UNSC Res 1671 (25 April 2006) UN Doc S/RES/1671.

against the then-Vice-President Bemba.[28] This therefore pushed the operation closer to intervention, stretching peacekeeping's red boundary line and again highlighting the overlap between the legal and normative frameworks, demonstrating how an expansion or reimagining of one norm or principle may have an impact on the others.

Moreover, the significant efforts of regional actors to resolve the conflict and establish governance could also be viewed as an example of 'African solutions to African problems', as was discussed in Chapter 2.[29] In this instance, however, it is somewhat of a double-edged sword. On the one hand, the Global South states' attempts to take ownership and to provide solutions to a problem within the Global South is, through a TWAIL lens, arguably preferable to externally imposed solutions.[30] On the other hand, the significant involvement of Congo's neighbours exposes a noticeable flaw within the concept of 'African solutions to African problems' – that it may be used to justify or legitimate interventions which are just as 'problematic and riddled with hidden agendas as traditional interventions'.[31] The notion then becomes more troublesome when the dominant role that Western actors, in particular, played in supporting the regional actors' bids to establish an agreement is also considered. That is, the involvement of neighbouring and regional actors could essentially be viewed as a straw man – a front or disguise – which masked the influential role of the dominant powers and institutions that were bankrolling and supporting the Dialogue behind the scenes.

Therefore, from a TWAIL perspective, the Dialogue and the promotion of democracy could be viewed, firstly, as another example of Anghie's dynamic of difference (as noted with ONUC) and as the furtherance of hegemonic standards, ideals and agendas, rather than a suitable or appropriate solution for the Congo. Thus, the peacekeeping operation's democracy promotion tasks could again be compared to the colonial civilising missions as both contain a dominant power attempting to enlighten or transform the subordinate 'other' in order for them to meet hegemonic standards, with little regard for the 'other's' interests and needs.

Secondly, the Dialogue can also be viewed an over-simplified Western solution to a complex problem. It is argued that 'in their Western ideas', MONUC/the United Nations thought it was 'about tribal killing each other

28 See: A Ajello, 'The EU Security Role in the Great Lakes Region' in A Adebajo and K Whiteman (eds) *The EU and Africa: From Eurafrique to Afro-Europa* (Hurst and Company 2012) 291.

29 TM Mays, 'African Solutions for African Problems: The Changing Face of African-Mandated Peace Operations' (2003) 23(1) JConfStud 106–125.

30 ibid.

31 C Ero, 'The Problems with "African Solutions"' (*International Crisis Group*, 2 December 2013) <https://www.crisisgroup.org/africa/problems-african-solutions>. See also: *Case Concerning Armed Activities on the Territory of the Congo (Democratic Republic of the Congo v Uganda)* Judgment of 19 December [2005] ICJ Rep 168.

so therefore if you take one from each group then therefore you are solving the issues which really [it did] not'.[32] The solution to the conflict – the Dialogue to establish democratic governance – could thus be considered, on this occasion, to be another example of the hegemonic powers or international community applying an over-simplified solution to a complex, misunderstood problem,[33] an issue which has been noted throughout this book's exploration of the history of intervention. Indeed, it is also a recurring critique of the approach of the United Nations and the international community to peacekeeping and peacebuilding in the DRC. For many, international actors fail to understand the root causes of violence in the Congo, particularly the way in which local agendas ('micro-level rivalries over lands, resources and traditional or administrative power') play a decisive role in sustaining local, national and regional violence.[34] In particular, it has been argued that the emphasis on holding elections, as opposed to local conflict resolution, ultimately dooms any peacebuilding efforts in the Congo.[35] As such, this example supports arguments for a need to shift peacekeeping's agenda away from a 'narrow focus on state-building, institutional capacity and the extension of state authority' to people-centred peace operations.[36] Indeed, it is a recommendation of this book, like many contemporary reviews of peacekeeping,[37] that there should be a move towards a more bottom-up, people-centred approach to peacekeeping which will, amongst other things, help local communities and societies 'strengthen their own capacities to prevent conflict and sustain peace'.[38]

Furthermore, for peacekeeping's normative frameworks, MONUC's contribution to establishing the foundations for a democratic governance system was a broad application of the norm of democracy promotion, thereby expanding peacekeeping's normative framework and simultaneously undermining the principle of non-intervention. More specifically, it could at times be viewed as a violation of the principle of non-intervention as MONUC's engagement in sovereign matters, through its support of establishing a system of governance and leadership, could be viewed as coercive action designed to influence change in the host state, given the vulnerability or weakness of

32 Interviewee 5 (n25) 10.

33 See, for example: W Easterly, *The White Man's Burden* (OUP 2006) 9.

34 S Autesserre, 'Hobbes and the Congo: Frames, Local Violence and International Intervention' (2009) Intrg 63(2) 349–280, 256.

35 ibid.

36 C de Coning and L Gelot, 'Placing People at the Center of UN Peace Operations' (IPI, 29 May 2020) <https://theglobalobservatory.org/2020/05/placing-people-center-un-peace-operations/>.

37 See, for example: F Carver, 'Linked up Peacekeeping' (Protection Approaches, July 2022) <https://protectionapproaches.org/linked-up-peacekeeping>; Together First, 'People-Centred Peacekeeping' <https://together1st.org/proposals/351#>.

38 de Coning and Gelot (n36).

the Congolese state at that time and its subsequent reliance on MONUC. As such, any actions which MONUC took in an attempt to foster democratic governance in the Congo could be viewed as coercive as the Congolese state had little voluntary choice in accepting the changes to the state, given its vulnerable position. Again, this then links back to the principle of consent and the debate over whether a host state can and should consent to specific peacekeeping tasks during the deployment of an operation. Therefore, like ONUC's role in 1960, MONUC's role throughout the Dialogue could be viewed as amounting to intervention, thereby taking peacekeeping beyond its normative and legal frameworks. As such, a retraction of peacekeeping's boundaries, through a narrower interpretation of this norm (i.e. less peacekeeping involvement in the establishment of democratic institutions) would have been desirable to move peacekeeping away from the intervention line.

Elections: Declining Intervention and Increasing Corruption

A final example of democracy promotion in practice can be found with the United Nations' latest peacekeeping operation in the Congo – MONUSCO. The application of the norm by MONUSCO further demonstrates how norms wax and wane as whilst MONUC provides us with an example of a broad application of the norm, MONUSCO offers a narrower application. That is, whilst the United Nations was heavily involved in the Congo's 2006 election and the development of democracy in the following years – thereby indicating a broad interpretation and application of the norm – this involvement or support decreased for each of the two subsequent elections. Thus, it could be argued that there was a retraction of the expanded interpretation of the norm of democracy promotion and, therefore, a shrinking of peacekeeping's normative framework, with the red, elastic boundary line now being tightened, taking MONUSCO back to a less interventionist operation and thereby supporting the principle of non-intervention.

Indeed, for the Congo's 2011 elections, the Security Council was faced with the dilemma of limiting MONUSCO's role to the protection of civilians in Eastern Congo, as agreed with President Kabila, or expanding its mandate 'in an attempt to enforce democratic principles before the elections at the risk of confronting the incumbent regime'.[39] Indeed, UN personnel have noted that for both the 2011 and 2016 elections (which were delayed until 2018),[40] 'there was a complete rejection of international involvement',

39 A Boutellis and G Lacaille, 'Renewing MONUSCO's Mandate: What Role beyond the Elections?' (IPI Issue Brief, May 2011).

40 H Hoebeke, 'Kabila Shows His Hand in DR Congo's Electoral Poker' (*Crisis Group*, 16 August 2018) <https://www.crisisgroup.org/africa/central-africa/democratic-republic-congo/kabila-shows-his-hand-dr-congos-electoral-poker>.

with the Congolese government refusing to accept MONUSCO's logistical support, even though it was mandated to provide it.[41] For the government, 'even hints at interference in the DRC's sovereignty is, you know, obviously a no no'; it was therefore 'made very clear that they were going to organise their own elections'.[42] MONUSCO therefore could have expanded the norm of democracy promotion, choosing to implement their mandate and go against the will of the state to undertake democratisation tasks, but, instead, chose to play a more limited role, as agreed with the host state.[43] It could be argued that this may reflect a recognition by MONUSCO that, on this occasion, the pursuance of democracy promotion would have amounted to coercive action and, therefore, intervention, taking the operation beyond its peacekeeping boundaries.

Whilst this decreased involvement in elections and subsequent retraction of the boundaries of peacekeeping away from the interventionist line is desirable, it presents a dilemma for the concept of democracy. For some senior UN personnel, it was recognised that the decline in international involvement almost had a 'directly proportional relationship' with 'increasing levels of rigging'.[44] That is, where MONUC played a significant role in the 2006 elections, there were fewer allegations of rigging than in the 2011 and 2018 elections when MONUSCO played less of a role in the organising of elections and violent protests erupted in response to the controversial results[45] and attempts to amend the constitution.[46] The struggle for democracy to take a hold in the DRC therefore supports TWAIL arguments that 'international law does not take global democracy seriously' as it imposes certain obligations on states (such as the need to hold democratic elections) but does not hold it responsible for any further deepening or development of the concept.[47] This, again, reverts back to the issue of what is considered to be a 'successful democracy' and what it means for a peacekeeping operation if these elections are not 'successful'.[48] It could be argued that it is questionable whether the norm of democracy promotion should remain a part of peacekeeping's normative

41 Interviewee 16 (n6).

42 ibid.

43 UNSC Res 1991 (28 June 2011) UN Doc S/RES/1991, 5.

44 Interviewee 16 (n6).

45 Human Rights Watch, 'DR Congo: 24 Killed Since Election Results Announced' (*Human Rights Watch*, 21 December 2011) <https://www.hrw.org/news/2011/12/21/dr-congo-24-killed-election-results-announced>.

46 H Hoebeke (n40); T Wilson, 'Congolese Activists on Hunger Strike after Court Refuses Release' (*The Guardian*, 19 March 2016) <http://www.theguardian.com/world/2016/mar/19/congolese-activists-on-hunger-strike-after-court-refuses-release>.

47 BS Chimni, 'Third World Approaches to International Law: A Manifesto' (2006) 8 ICLR 3–27, 8.

48 B Heldt, 'Peacekeeping Operations and Transitions to Democracy' in H Fjelde and K Höglund (eds) *Building Peace, Creating Conflict* (Nordic Academic Press 2011) 47–71.

framework or whether peacekeeping should focus more on a people-centred, bottom-up rather than state-centric, top-down approach, as argued earlier. Indeed, the political protests prior to, during and after the 2018 elections are said to be 'a clear demonstration of the Congolese population's aspirations for political change',[49] yet these voices are constrained by the patronage power structures and the political elite's desperate bids to cling to power. Therefore, it could be argued that supporting grassroots initiatives may be a more preferable means of developing democracy within the Congo and, ultimately, securing peace, particularly as the Congolese people view electoral concerns, peace and security concerns and economic problems as inextricably linked.[50]

Forcing Democracy?

The interpretation and application of the principle of democracy promotion by the United Nations' peacekeeping operations in the DRC highlight some of the shortcomings of the norm, which were also seen in Chapter 3, namely, the comparisons which can be made with the notion of 'civilisation' and the colonial civilising mission and the suitability of establishing democratic governance in complex, post-conflict settings. In particular, the United Nations' efforts at democracy promotion in the Congo exemplify how simply holding elections does not equate to or result in a deeply penetrating, flourishing democracy. That is, despite holding elections, the reform of Congolese politics and government has been limited,[51] with deeply embedded patronage systems.[52]

Therefore, despite the involvement of the United Nations and the exercise of the norm of democracy promotion, predominantly through the supporting of elections, democracy has failed to take root, with the political culture often cited as the main culprit for Congo's perpetual 'failure to launch'.[53] As such, some UN personnel argue that the United Nations should 'stop doing statebuilding' as peacekeeping 'is a very poor tool' for undertaking such a task, with MONUSCO spending 'a huge amount of money' to support a state 'that has shown no desire or willingness or capacity to play the kind of games that it's being asked to play'.[54] Indeed, the United Nations' emphasis on statebuilding and preoccupation with elections distract from the issues

49 Crisis Group, 'Congo: Is Democratic Change Possible?' (Crisis Group Africa Briefing No 225, 5 May 2015).

50 S Autesserre, *The Frontlines of Peace: An Insider's Guide to Changing the World* (OUP 2021).

51 Crisis Group (n49).

52 G Nzongola-Ntalaja, *The Congo from Leopold to Kabila: A People's History* (Zed Books 2006) 2.

53 T Trefon, *Congo Masquerade: The Political Culture of Aid Inefficiency and Reform Failure* (Zed Books 2011).

54 Interviewee 8 (n9) 16.

whose resolutions are most likely to lead to peace, namely, poverty, unemployment, corruption, poor access to land, the criminal justice system and education.[55] It could be argued, then, that MONUC/MONUSCO's democracy promotion endeavours in the Congo present numerous issues or lessons which could be learned for peacekeeping's normative framework.

The first of these issues is whether a focus on institution or statebuilding is a suitable task for peacekeeping and whether the norm of democracy promotion should therefore be a part of peacekeeping's normative framework. MONUC and MONUSCO's involvement in democracy promotion within the DRC indicates that democracy promotion should perhaps be restricted or even removed from peacekeeping's normative framework. This is not to say that democratisation is not a worthwhile task but, rather, that it is one which should not be undertaken by peacekeeping operations. Indeed, it has been argued that the Council gave MONUC/MONUSCO 'a task they couldn't do', with the statebuilding and central reform mandate 'pie in the sky' after 20 years, with 'almost no meaningful improvement in the SSR side of things'.[56] Therefore, the inclusion of democracy promotion could be viewed as somewhat of an unnecessary expansion of the normative framework of peacekeeping, in part because the operation is ill-equipped to undertake it. This is further compounded by the fact that it has the potential to impact the fundamental principles of peacekeeping and thereby expand or alter peacekeeping's legal framework which, in turn, may undermine the principle of non-intervention. For example, MONUC used significant force to create a 'stabilised' environment in which to hold elections; therefore, the interpretation and application of the norm of democracy promotion had a knock-on effect on the principle of non-use of force. Similarly, the decision to support (or not support) certain actors during electoral processes could be viewed as an infringement on the principle of impartiality. This, in turn, could impact the principle of consent if relationships between the host government and the peacekeeping operation break down – as was seen throughout the Inter-Congolese Dialogue and the 2006 elections. Again, this demonstrates that as the norms and legal principles exist in a competitive arena, there is an inevitability that changes to one norm or principle may impact others. By extension, when these norms are expanded, thus broadening peacekeeping's normative framework, this, consequently, expands the peacekeeping boundaries and constricts the principle of non-intervention.

This then leads to the second notable issue – whether democracy promotion can amount to intervention. As the previous section argued, at

55 S Autesserre, 'What the Uproar over Congo's Elections Misses' (*Foreign Affairs*, 1 March 2017) <https://www.foreignaffairs.com/articles/democratic-republic-congo/2017-03-01/what-uproar-over-congos-elections-misses>.

56 Interviewee 8 (n9) 19.

certain points throughout ONUC, MONUC and MONUSCO's history in the Congo, it is arguable that their promotion of democracy has amounted to coercive action designed to influence change in the host state. ONUC's execution of state functions to establish a governance system and MONUC's robust involvement in the Inter-Congolese Dialogue and 2006 elections, for example, could be viewed as having a coercive impact on the Congolese state's sovereign rights, in an attempt to push the Congo towards changing to democratic governance, thus amounting to intervention. Indeed, this is reinforced by the Congolese government's rejection of MONUSCO's involvement in the more recent elections, with the state explicitly stating that it was a matter of its 'sovereign rights'.[57] This then presents the third key issue which has arisen in the Congo, which is whether there is a more suitable alternative to democracy promotion tasks or statebuilding, such as returning to the more traditional peacekeeping role of supporting agreements such as the 'Peace, Security and Cooperation (PSC) Framework'.[58] It is therefore questionable whether democracy promotion in the form of elections is the best or only way in which UN peacekeeping operations can support the political landscape of its host country, in order to achieve the ultimate goal of maintaining international peace and security. As such, in a similar vein to the first issue, it is arguable that there is a need for a contracting of peacekeeping's normative framework, through a retraction of the norm of democracy promotion.

By extension, this raises a fourth issue which can be drawn from the United Nations' experiences in the Congo – whether peacekeeping should focus more on a people-centred, bottom-up approach, rather than a state-centric, top-down approach. Within this context, it would mean that if peacekeeping operations continued to engage in democracy promotion, they would do so by supporting local and regional actors, which would require peacekeepers to become adaptive, work closely with communities and place emphasis on the resilience of local and national institutions.[59] Had such an approach been adopted in the Congo, it could have perhaps helped to counter some of the problems faced by the UN operations, particularly, from a TWAIL perspective, the failure of the United Nations to recognise the complexities of the Congo and its politics. Indeed, this has, to a certain extent, been recognised by a former head of MONUSCO, Alan Doss, who, in a piece on 'the limits of outside intervention', noted that 'with hindsight' MONUSCO 'did not devote enough of our energy' towards building political trust, social cohesion

57 Interviewee 16 (n6); Crisis Group (n49).

58 UNSC, 'Special Report of the Secretary-General on the Democratic Republic of the Congo and the Great Lakes Region' (27 February 2003) UN Doc S/2013/119, 7.

59 On the adaptive approach, see: C de Coning, 'Adaptive Peacebuilding' (2018) 94(2) International Affairs 301–317.

and community resilience.[60] Similarly, others have argued that democracy itself 'may not be the golden ticket', at least not in the short term, with real lasting peace in the Congo requiring power being given to ordinary citizens.[61]

For peacekeeping's overall frameworks, then, the Congo demonstrates how an expansive interpretation and application of the norm of democracy promotion once again expands peacekeeping's normative framework, with an overlap with the legal principles also impacting the legal framework. This, in turn, expands peacekeeping's red boundary line, taking peacekeeping closer to intervention and thereby undermining or, at times, contravening the principle of non-intervention. This section has therefore suggested that, as was argued in Chapter 5 for the legal principles, a redrawing of peacekeeping's boundaries may be needed, through a significant narrowing of the interpretation and application of the norm of democracy promotion. Ultimately, this would require a review of Security Council mandating,[62] with the need for more realistic, streamlined mandates or, even, 'designer mandates' specifically focused on the particularities of the situation in which the peacekeeping operation is to be deployed.[63]

Protection of Civilians

The interpretation and application of the norm of protection of civilians (PoC) within the United Nations' operations in the DRC is a classic example of the struggle of protection mandates with capabilities and impact or implementation.[64] Indeed, MONUC and MONUSCO have, on occasions, catastrophically failed to protect civilians, resulting in mounting criticisms of the operation and debates over the inclusion of PoC as a priority task for peacekeepers. As was noted in Chapter 4, the Congo has been somewhat of an incubator for the development of the norm of PoC, with numerous policies developed throughout MONUC/MONUSCO's deployment, typically in line with the general developments in the PoC norm but often stepping out on its own, significantly expanding the norm in practice. Therefore, as with the previous norm of democracy promotion and the legal principles discussed

60 A Doss, 'The Congo, Afghanistan and the Limits of Outside Intervention' (*Pass Blue*, 18 January 2021) <https://www.passblue.com/2021/01/18/the-congo-afghanistan-and-the-limits-of-outside-intervention/>.

61 Autesserre (n50).

62 See: P Nadin, 'An Argument for More Focused UN Peacekeeping Mandates' (*Our World, UNU*, 18 February 2014) <https://ourworld.unu.edu/en/an-argument-for-more-focused-un-peacekeeping-mandates>.

63 I Martin, 'All Peace Operations Are Political: A Case for Designer Missions and the Next UN Reform' (CIC Thematic Essay, 2015) <https://cic.nyu.edu/sites/default/files/political_missions_2010_martin_allpeace2.pdf>.

64 See: ND White, 'Empowering Peace Operations to Protect Civilians: Form over Substance?' (2009) 13 JIP 327–355.

in Chapter 5, the broad interpretation and application of the norm of PoC in the Congo have led to an expansion of peacekeeping's normative framework which has undermined and, at times, potentially violated the principle of non-intervention.

Becoming a Priority

Whilst the United Nations' first operation in the Congo, ONUC, undertook protection activities,[65] arguably temporarily expanding peacekeeping's normative framework, it is MONUC's deployment in the early 2000s which best illustrates the expansion of the norm of PoC. In response to three major incidents (Kisangani 2002, Ituri 2003 and Bukavu 2004) which resulted in MONUC gaining a reputation for fleeing conflict, hiding behind its compound walls and failing to protect civilians,[66] MONUC was given a PoC mandate by the Security Council to support MONUC in stabilising the security conditions and, if necessary, 'contribut[ing] to the safety of the civilian population', with a temporary EU-led force – *Operation Artemis* – also deployed.[67] As with the norm of democracy promotion, the Security Council invoked Chapter VII through the inclusion of the ambiguous 'Acting under Chapter VII' clause within the chapeau of the resolution.[68] As such, both MONUC and *Operation Artemis* were permitted to use an expanded level of enforcement-style force to protect civilians, thereby presenting an expanded version of the norm of PoC. However, despite the potential for PoC to be interpreted and applied broadly, including using robust force, MONUC and *Operation Artemis* were 'totally insufficient' for dealing with the crisis in Ituri, only managing to guarantee civilians safety in 'several very limited spaces carved out with great effort'.[69]

Furthermore, MONUSCO's failure or difficulties in implementing the norm of PoC at this point highlight some nuances in the implementation of the norm and shortcomings in communications between peacekeeping and other UN entities, which prevented the norm from being more fully implemented. For example, prior to the Bukavu crisis in 2004, MONUC leadership had

65 Operations Directive No 8 (untitled), February 1961, UN Archives DAG/13/1.6.5.0.0; Operations Directives August 1960–January 1964, Box 3, pp2–3.

66 J Hatcher and A Perry, 'Defining Peacekeeping Downward: The UN Debacle in Eastern Congo' (*Time*, 26 Nov 2012) <http://world.time.com/2012/11/26/defining-peacekeeping-downward-the-u-n-debacle-in-eastern-congo/>; Human Rights Watch, 'War Crimes in Kisangani' (August 2002) 14(6)(A) HRW.

67 UNSC Res 1484 (30 May 2003) UN Doc S/RES/1484.

68 ibid.

69 Médecins Sans Frontières, 'Ituri: Unkept Promises? A Pretense of Protection and Inadequate Assistance' (MSF, 25 July 2003) <https://reliefweb.int/sites/reliefweb.int/files/resources/E4AD40CF77CAAEFBC1256D6E00339499-msf-drc-25jul.pdf>.

been warned on multiple occasions by both UN agencies and from independent sources that the situation was highly explosive.[70] As one UN humanitarian employee, working for the UN Office for the Coordination of Humanitarian Affairs (OCHA) at the time, noted, 'when General Nkunda started the uprising in the east and started with Bukavu, we saw it coming'.[71] OCHA therefore tried to work with their UN colleagues, including warning the UN country team, in anticipation of Nkunda's rebellion.[72] However, the then-head of the Department of Peacekeeping Operations had a 'very very different reading on the situation', arguing it was stable, with matters improving, as talks were happening between groups.[73] Similarly, the then-SRSG, Amos Ngongi, dismissed it as the 'Congolese are fighting among themselves'.[74] Subsequently, MONUC failed to sufficiently act and Bukavu was captured by the rebel group, CNDP, despite the nearby deployment of MONUC troops.[75]

Following this incident, the norm of PoC was more broadly interpreted and applied, with MONUC receiving a new, more expansive PoC mandate from the Security Council. MONUC's PoC responsibilities were extended to include protecting refugees, internally displaced persons, children in armed conflict, humanitarian and human rights workers and victims of sexual violence.[76] Crucially, it also noted that 'the protection of civilians must be given priority in decisions about the use of available capacity and resources'.[77] Thus, the Security Council expanded the norm by recognising its need to be positioned as a priority task, simultaneously expanding the potential for force to be used to fulfil this task. This was later confirmed in MONUC's 2008 mandate, when MONUC became the first UN peacekeeping operation to make PoC its priority task – a priority which has remained in place ever since.[78]

Furthermore, the differing approaches to the Bukavu crisis by the two UN agencies (peacekeeping and humanitarian) weakened the overall UN approach at a time when a joint, coherent approach was clearly needed to protect civilians. As such, following the crisis, the UN Department of Peacekeeping Operations and OCHA began to work more closely, sharing

70 See generally: J Reynaert J, 'MONUC/MONUSCO and Civilian Protection in the Kivus' (IPIS 2010).
71 Interview with Senior UNDP Personnel, formerly OCHA ('Interviewee 1') (Geneva, 20 November 2018) DOI: <http://doi.org/10.17639/nott.7119>.
72 ibid.
73 ibid.
74 Human Rights Watch, 'Ituri: "Covered in Blood"' (July 2003) 15(11)(A) HRW.
75 UN News, 'Rebels Take Bukavu in Eastern DR of Congo, Protesters Target UN' (*UN News*, 2 June 2004) <https://news.un.org/en/story/2004/06/105462-rebels-take-bukavu-eastern-dr-congo-protesters-target-un>.
76 UNSC Res 1794 (21 December 2007) UN Doc S/RES/1794.
77 ibid.
78 UNSC Res 1856 (22 December 2008) UN Doc S/RES/1856; UNSC Res 2556 (18 December 2020) UN Doc S/RES/2556.

security and analysis and trying to find joint solutions, with an unofficial joint framework for collective engagement developing.[79] It could therefore be argued that the norm of PoC was expanded within the Congo by both the inclusion of protection tasks within MONUC's mandate and, to a certain extent, by this collaboration with humanitarian actors. It therefore had a broader, institutional impact which could, again, be viewed as an expansion of peacekeeping's normative framework, on this occasion through the engagement with additional international actors.

PoC Tools

After the protection of civilians was established as a priority task for MONUC, the operation began to significantly develop PoC tools resulting in a much more nuanced or evolved understanding of the norm of PoC. That is, MONUC/MONUSCO's interpretation and implementation of the norm of PoC have created a comprehensive collection of PoC tools which has significantly expanded peacekeeping's normative framework, simultaneously expanding its interventionist potential and thereby undermining the principle of non-intervention.

Often, these tools were developed following a noticeable failure or incident of violence, resulting in the death of civilians. For example, after the massacre of more than 100 people near a MONUC camp in Kiwanja (North Kivu) in 2008, joint protection teams (JPTs) were established.[80] These multidisciplinary teams, composed of military, police and civilian personnel from the peacekeeping mission, are deployed to 'hotspots' or areas needing protection in order to analyse protection needs and outline preventive and responsive measures which may need to be taken.[81] In addition to these teams, the United Nations also developed a 'Must-Should-Could' (PoC) Matrix (MSC), a joint planning exercise between MONUSCO and the humanitarian community.[82] The aim of this matrix is to identify priority areas and to assess the threat level and degree of vulnerability of the local community. It then ranks areas as being 'must protect', 'should protect' and 'could protect'. This information is then passed along to a 'Protection Cluster' and SMG-PP[83] which

79 Interviewee 1 (n71).

80 Human Rights Watch, 'Killings in Kiwanja: The UN's Inability to Protect Civilians' (HRW, 11 December 2018) <https://www.hrw.org/report/2008/12/11/killings-kiwanja/uns-inability-protect-civilians>.

81 See: UN Peacekeeping, 'Protecting Civilians' <https://peacekeeping.un.org/en/protecting-civilians>.

82 See: JA Boutellis, 'From Crisis to Reform: Peacekeeping Strategies for the Protection of Civilians in the Democratic Republic of Congo' (2013) 2(3) 48 Stability 1–11.

83 ibid; see generally: Global Protection Cluster, 'Democratic Republic of Congo' <https://www.globalprotectioncluster.org/field-support/field-protection-clusters/democratic-republic-of-congo/>.

decide on the appropriate action to be taken. Therefore, similarly to the way in which the Bukavu crisis resulted in closer cooperation between peacekeepers and humanitarian actors, the PoC matrix also enhanced cooperation between the UN peacekeeping operation and the wider humanitarian community. Again, this creates a subtle expansion in the norm of PoC by extending peacekeeping's reach into the humanitarian sphere. Whilst this may be well-intentioned, it runs the risk of undermining the work of impartial and unarmed humanitarian actors where their tasks may overlap with those of the UN peacekeepers.[84]

In a similar vein, MONUSCO has developed further tools in order to implement the norm of PoC, focusing on building partnerships at the local level, with Community Liaison Assistants (CLAs) – national staff working alongside troops in military bases to enhance interaction between the Force and local communities.[85] These assistants analyse protection needs and, again, inform protection strategies and plans. Alongside this, Community Alert Networks (CANs) have been established as an early-warning mechanism within communities surrounding MONUSCO bases, communicating via radio or mobile phone to alert one another of an imminent threat.[86] Along with Community Protection Committees[87] and Local Security Committees, these PoC tools demonstrate a broadened interpretation and application of the norm of PoC and mark more of a people-centred, bottom-up approach to peacekeeping which, as has been noted throughout this book, is arguably a more desirable approach to peacekeeping.[88] Indeed, the 2015 HIPPO Report emphasised the significance of local actors to the effectiveness of peace operations, noting that 'they are the main agents of peace'[89] and 'engagement must increasingly be regarded as core to mission success'.[90]

Despite this expansion of the norm of PoC and the development of these tools, designed in order to allow MONUSCO to implement the norm, there

84 J Labbé and A Boutellis, 'Peace Operations by Proxy: Implications for Humanitarian Action of UN Peacekeeping Partnerships with Non-UN Security Forces' (2013) 95(891/892) IRRC 539–559.

85 J Kullenberg, 'Community Liaison Assistants: A Bridge between Peacekeepers and Local Populations' (FMR, October 2016) <https://www.fmreview.org/sites/fmr/files/FMRdownloads/en/community-protection/kullenberg.pdf>.

86 See: CIVIC, 'Community Engagement by MONUSCO with Reduced Field Presence' (CIVIC, May 2018) <https://civiliansinconflict.org/wp-content/uploads/2018/06/MONUSCO_Community-Engagement-Brief.pdf>.

87 See: UNSC, 'Report of the Secretary-General on the United Nations Organisation Stabilisation Mission in the Democratic Republic of the Congo' (25 September 2014) UN Doc S/2014/698.

88 See: Carver (n37).

89 UNGA-SC, 'Report of the High-Level Independent Panel on Peace Operations' ('HIPPO Report') (17 June 2015) UN Doc A/70/95-S/2015/446, 48.

90 ibid, 14.

have still been numerous occasions in which the peacekeeping operation has failed to execute this norm and protect civilians. In particular, there has often been a pattern of failures despite a significant UN presence, with systemic rapes and attacks against civilians occurring in close proximity to MONUSCO bases.[91] On occasions, these have also occurred despite repeated warnings from the local protection committees,[92] suggesting a failure on the part of both MONUSCO and its PoC tools which had been purposefully established to prevent such incidences. This is further compounded by a failure of the operation to adequately respond to the massacres, as occurred in the village of Mutarule, North Kivu, when MONUSCO failed to visit the village until two days after the massacre,[93] simply condemning the attacks and labelling it as a flare of 'inter-ethnic violence'.[94] Once again, this could be viewed as a disregard for the complexities of the Congo and an example of how the norm of PoC may be expanded in theory but not necessarily in practice. Indeed, here, MONUSCO had essentially failed to implement or support the very PoC tools which they had helped to establish. That is, they had failed to respond to alerts from the protection committees that they had helped to create which, for some, consequently results in MONUSCO providing a false sense of security.[95]

This then leads to three main issues which stem from the PoC efforts in the Congo which have been outlined in Chapter 4. Firstly, whether the PoC mandates could be perceived as imposing a duty or obligation on peacekeepers to protect civilians; secondly, if this is a duty which should be placed upon peacekeepers or should, instead, be a priority for the host state; and thirdly, the perception local populations have of UN peacekeeping as protectors of civilians. All these issues, in turn, then pose questions as to how broadly the norm can or should be interpreted and, consequently, to what extent this then impacts peacekeeping's normative frameworks and the principle of non-intervention.

91 Such as the systemic rapes in 13 villages in North Kivu in 2010, 30 kilometres from a MONUSCO base. See: P Worsnip, 'UN's Ban Sends Top Aide to Congo after Mass Rape' (*Reuters*, 24 August 2010) <https://www.reuters.com/article/oukwd-uk-congo-democratic-rape-idAFTRE67N5VQ20100824>; UN Press Release, 'Conference by Special Representative for the Democratic Republic of Congo' (25 August 2010) <https://reliefweb.int/report/democratic-republic-congo/press-conference-special-representative-democratic-republic-congo>.

92 Human Rights Watch, 'DR Congo: Army, UN Failed to Stop Massacre' (*Human Rights Watch*, 2 July 2014) <https://www.hrw.org/news/2014/07/02/dr-congo-army-un-failed-stop-massacre>.

93 ibid.

94 UN News, 'UN Peacekeepers in Eastern DR Congo Help Restore Calm after Inter-Ethnic Violence Flares' (*UN News*, 7 June 2014) <https://news.un.org/en/story/2014/06/470232-un-peacekeepers-eastern-dr-congo-help-restore-calm-after-inter-ethnic-violence>.

95 HRW (n80).

Expectations and Capabilities

The prioritisation of PoC within peacekeeping mandates, in line with the shift to robust peacekeeping, resulted in force being permitted in order to protect civilians. As noted earlier, the often-invoked phrase of 'Acting under Chapter VII' included within PoC mandates introduces enforcement elements into a peacekeeping operation, creating confusion over what this means for both the norm of PoC and the principle of limited use of force. A broader interpretation of PoC may therefore have a knock-on effect on the principle of non-use of force, again demonstrating the co-habitation of peacekeeping's norms and principles and the overlap between the legal and normative frameworks. This shift to a more forceful implementation of PoC is seen in the language of MONUC/MONUSCO's mandates and is posited in such a way that it seemingly places a legal duty or obligation on peacekeepers to protect civilians. In 2003 the Security Council 'authorise[d] MONUC to take the necessary measures' as it deemed 'within its capabilities' to 'protect civilians' under imminent threat of physical violence.[96] Ten years later, the language surrounding PoC changed slightly, with the Security Council authorising MONUSCO to 'take all necessary measures' to 'ensure' the 'effective protection of civilians under imminent threat of physical violence'.[97] This broadening of the language surrounding 'necessary measures' (from 'the' to 'all') arguably invokes more coercive language, implying that a broader range of measures ('all') needed to be taken – including the use of force – rather than simply those measures which the operation could determine, for itself, were within its capabilities. This therefore broadens the already ambiguous notion of 'necessary measures', thereby expanding the norm of PoC and consequently expanding the normative frameworks of peacekeeping, increasing its interventionist potential and consequently undermining the principle of non-intervention. That is, where these measures may include the use of increased levels of force or may impact the state's sovereign rights, then this could amount to coercive action designed to influence change in the host state and, therefore, intervention. This is then compounded by the fact that more recent mandates note that when prioritising tasks, 'the protection of civilians must be given priority in decisions about the use of available capacity and resources'.[98] Again, this reinforces the positioning of PoC as a priority task and emphasises that this places an obligation on MONUSCO to focus its resources on this task.

Indeed, the inclusion of the term 'ensure' also implies that the protection of civilians has become an obligation for MONUSCO peacekeepers. It could therefore be argued that the language within the PoC mandate imposes a legal duty or obligation on MONUSCO peacekeepers to protect

96 UNSC Res 1493 (28 July 2003) UN Doc S/RES/1493, para 25.
97 UNSC Res 2098 (28 March 2013) UN Doc S/RES/2098, para 12.
98 UNSC Res 2502 (19 December 2019) UN Doc S/RES/2502, para 25.

civilians, however they deem necessary, if they are under imminent threat of violence. Further, as these PoC mandates are authorised under Chapter VII, pursuant to Article 25 of the UN Charter, although member states are not obliged to contribute to a peacekeeping operation, if they do, then they become bound by Articles 2 and 25 and must accept and carry out measures within the mandate 'so as to achieve its lawful objectives'.[99] Indeed, both the Department of Peace Operations (DPO, then DPKO) and the Department of Field Support (DFS) have noted that peacekeepers 'are authorized and are duty bound to undertake actions to protect civilians' when the host state is unwilling or unable to do so.[100] Furthermore, in their 2017 Guidelines on the use of force by UN peace operations, the departments argued that if 'the mission is mandated for PoC' then they are under an 'obligation to use force to protect civilians from armed attack', if 'all other unarmed tactics, techniques and procedures fail'.[101] Therefore, as noted in Chapter 4, this creates a two-pronged expansion of peacekeeping's legal and normative frameworks, pushing peacekeeping closer to the intervention boundary line. Firstly, it expands the concept of PoC, confirming it is a priority task and an obligation for peacekeepers to fulfil and, secondly, the stipulation that force can and should be used to fulfil this task simultaneously expands the principle of non-use of force. This ambiguous language in the mandates, combined with the expanded use of force in defence of the mandate (and therefore in defence of tasks such as PoC), expands the norm of PoC exponentially. Thus, by extension, it expands peacekeeping's frameworks and undermines the principle of non-intervention when PoC tasks invoke elements of coercive action that impinge upon states' sovereign rights. As was suggested for the norm of democracy promotion, it could be argued that there needs to be a review and reimagining of the Security Council mandate in order to clarify these legal and practical issues and, in particular, to clarify how much force could or should be used in order to implement a PoC mandate and whether this, in turn, is a legal duty or obligation.

This language of 'duty' and 'obligation' also points to a further issue which is whether or to what extent peacekeepers should be tasked with protecting civilians. Arguably, this language within the mandates places an

99 *Al-Jedda v UK* App No 27021/08 (ECtHR, 7 July 2011) para 34. See also *Namibia*, where the ICJ held that in order to assess the legally binding nature of UNSC Resolutions, one had to consider 'the terms of the resolution to be interpreted, the discussions leading to it, the Charter provisions invoked and, in general, all circumstances that might assist in determining the legal consequences': *Legal Consequences for States of the Continued Presence of South Africa in Namibia (South West Africa) notwithstanding Security Council Resolution 276* (Advisory Opinion) [1971] ICJ Rep 16, para 114.

100 See: DPKO/DFS Policy, 'The Protection of Civilians in United Nations Peacekeeping' (2015) Ref 2015.07. p6.

101 ibid, 23.

undue burden on UN peace operations and could be perceived as both an erosion of host state sovereignty and interventionist behaviour by the peace operation, depending on the 'measure' which is used (e.g. use of force). As previously noted, the very concept of PoC – to protect all civilians – is an impossible task, evidenced in the numerous so-called failures of MONUC and MONUSCO in the Congo. This leads to the question of whether PoC should be the primary responsibility of the peacekeeping operation and thus whether a broad interpretation of the PoC norm is necessary.

This is a poignant issue in states where the peacekeeping operation becomes the primary actor undertaking the protection of civilians, as opposed to the state, thereby creating a reliance on the peacekeeping operation to fulfil protectorate tasks. Indeed, using the Congo example, whilst MONUSCO had created numerous PoC tools and strategies, this strengthened MONUSCO's ability to protect civilians but diminished the primary role of state authorities in assuming their protection of civilians and resulted in 'little success in terms of national ownership and buy-in'.[102] This then raises numerous issues. Firstly, as seen in Chapter 4, it expands the norm of PoC and peacekeeping's normative boundary to its limits, pushing the peacekeeping operation beyond the red boundary line and into the realm of intervention as it is, in essence, undertaking the role of the state as the protection of its citizens is a sovereign right. Therefore, the United Nations is 'basically substituting to regalian powers that the state cannot implement'.[103] As noted in Chapter 4, however, where the state is willing to accept the UN peacekeeping operation undertaking this role, as in the Congo, then an argument could be made that this a 'function of the host state's consent' and, therefore, a form of intervention by invitation.[104]

Secondly, an increased reliance on the peacekeeping operation (both by the state and local populations) to protect civilians is problematic and can create an unrealistic perception of the peacekeepers as protectors of all civilians. As such, when there is an outbreak of violence which leads to loss of civilian life, it 'creates a perfect opportunity … to blame everything on the UN', with both the state and the local population 'pointing the finger at the mission' and 'hardly anyone's asking, well why isn't it the government that is dealing with the problem'.[105] Again, this creates a problematic reliance on a temporary

102 UNSC, 'Transitioning from Stabilization to Peace: An Independent Strategic Review of MONUSCO' ('Strategic Review') (25 October 2019) UN Doc S/2019/842, para 77.

103 Interview with Senior Human Rights Officer in the Office of the UN High Commissioner of Human Rights ('Interviewee 13') (New York, 6 December 2019) DOI: <http://doi.org/10.17639/nott.7119> pg 46.

104 PI Labuda, 'United Nations Peacekeeping as Intervention by Invitation: Host State Consent and the Use of Force in Security Council-Mandated Stabilisation Operations' (2020) JUFIL 1–37.

105 ibid. Interviewee 16 (n6) 24.

peacekeeping operation, which, from a TWAIL perspective, could also be seen as reinforcing patterns of domination and subordination, recreating the colonial archetypal image of the external actor as the enlightened saviour. That is, it is the dominant power that is deemed to be the protectorate of the Congolese peoples, as opposed to the Global South host state. In essence, this reinforces or replicates the colonial dichotomies of the 'civilised' dominant powers and an 'uncivilised' Global South, the latter of which requires the support and protection of the former. As a result of this reliance, interviewees within the Office of the SRSG in Congo have argued that there is a need to ensure that civil society is aware that MONUSCO is not and should not be the main protector of civilians,[106] with others working within MONUSCO also arguing that PoC should be removed as a priority task for MONUSCO and should instead be undertaken by the UN country team.[107] Thus, questions again need to be asked about the tasks contained within peacekeeping mandates and whether there needs to be a shrinking of both these tasks and the interpretation and application of the peacekeeping norms. Furthermore, the reliance on peacekeepers to protect civilians also supports arguments for a people-centred approach to peacekeeping which focus on developing robust domestic mechanisms that would place protection firmly back in the hands of the host state and its people,[108] thereby avoiding some of the issues MONUC/MONUSCO has faced.

MONUSCO's interpretation and application of the norm of PoC therefore demonstrate how a broad understanding expands peacekeeping's normative boundary, thereby undermining the principle of non-intervention and, at times, potentially taking peacekeeping into the realm of intervention. Furthermore, it also highlights a wider issue of how to reconcile people-oriented PoC mandates with the state-centric logic of UN-mandated interventions.[109] This is now demonstrated in the operation's withdrawal as it is engaging with local-level authorities and civil society organisations, thereby seemingly adopting a grassroots, bottom-up approach. As such, it can again be argued that there is a need for the re-drawing of peacekeeping's boundaries and a move to a more bottom-up, insider-led approach.

Prohibition of Sexual Exploitation and Abuse

Similar to the development of the norm of PoC, the interpretation and application of the prohibition of sexual exploitation and abuse (SEA) in practice

106 Interview with Political Adviser in the Office of the SRSG MONUSCO ('Interviewee 18') (Skype, 17 February 2020) DOI: <http://doi.org/10.17639/nott.7119>.

107 Interview with Personnel in MONUSCO's Stabilisation Support Unit ('Interviewee 19') (Skype, 21 February 2020) DOI: <http://doi.org/10.17639/nott.7119>.

108 Carver (n37).

109 PI Labuda, 'With or against the State? Reconciling the Protection of Civilians and Host-State Support in UN Peacekeeping' (IPI 2020).

have resulted in numerous tools and policies, thereby broadening the norm and, consequently, peacekeeping's normative framework. However, as was noted in Chapter 4, the development of this norm, unlike its counterparts, has been somewhat slow, with a disconnect between the Secretary-General and the office of the SG who have promoted the norm, and the Security Council and member states, including the troop-contributing nations (TCNs), which have typically done little to support the norm. Indeed, using the DRC as an example, whilst the Security Council repeatedly 'strongly condemns' sexual violence in conflict, encouraging the government of the DRC to combat such violence and end impunity, particularly when acts are committed by host state forces, this same level of condemnation and drive to implement strategies and roadmaps is not seen for sexual violence committed by UN peacekeepers.[110] These differing standards can, again, be viewed as an example of the hypocrisy or power differentials that are entrenched within peacekeeping, as a TWAIL lens has highlighted throughout the previous chapters. The norm of prohibition of SEA therefore differs from the other principles and norms in that its slow development has resulted in only a limited expansion of peacekeeping's normative framework. For the principle of non-intervention, then, the norm has supported rather than undermined the principle but, as Chapter 4 noted, a broader interpretation of the norm would reinforce the principle further as its aim is to restrict peacekeepers' behaviour and limit their coercive intervention through SEA.

Protectors or Predators?

The application of the norm of prohibition of SEA within the Congo is illustrative of the norm's broader development within peacekeeping. Whilst there were allegations of rape by ONUC peacekeepers in the 1960s,[111] reporting of such incidences in the DRC became most prominent in 2003–2004, around the same time as the General Assembly's report on SEA of refugees by aid workers in West Africa[112] and the subsequent SG's Bulletin on protection from SEA.[113] For example, in 2003 an uncovered memo from the MONUC child protection officer in Kindu to MONUC headquarters in Kinshasa reported fears about allegations of SEA by MONUC forces, yet no action was taken.[114] Similarly, when a gender advisor to MONUC contacted UN

110 S/RES/2556 (n78) paras 9–10.

111 HL Deb 15 March 1962, vol 238, Cols 364-88, 367.

112 UNGA, 'Investigations into Sexual Exploitation of Refugees by Aid Workers in West Africa' (11 October 2002) UN Doc A/57/465; UNGA Res 57/306 (22 May 2003) UN Doc A/RES/57/306.

113 UNSG, 'Secretary-General Bulletin: Special Measures for Protection for Sexual Exploitation and Abuse' (9 October 2003) UN Doc ST/SGB/2003/13.

114 K Holt and S Hughes, 'Will Congo's Women Ever Have Justice?' (*The Independent*, 12 July 2004) <https://www.independent.co.uk/news/world/africa/will-congos-women-ever-have-justice-46938.html>.

headquarters in New York requesting that Moroccan troops in Kisangani not be sent to Bunia, following allegations of extreme sexual abuse, including child pornography, a short-lived investigation was dropped due to a lack of evidence and support for the inquiry.[115] Therefore, whilst allegations were made, during a time when the norm was developing through UNGA and SG documents, this did not translate into any noticeable action with the Congo, indicating that for norm development, there is a lag between theory and practice.

Indeed, it was a year later, in June 2004, when the norm began to be implemented in practice. Following a cable sent from MONUC to UN headquarters, which detailed 50 claims of SEA against minors by MONUC peacekeepers in Bunia,[116] an independent UN investigation team from the Office of Internal and Oversight Services (OIOS) was deployed to Bunia to conduct investigations.[117] This was followed by a special investigative team from the Department of Peacekeeping Operations (DPKO)[118] but details of allegations continued to emerge.[119] In line with the broader development of the norm at that time – the UNSG's newly launched zero tolerance policy – MONUC's resolutions began to recognise the 'grave concern' of allegations of SEA by MONUC personnel.[120] In doing so, it encouraged MONUC to conduct training for personnel and to ensure 'full compliance' with its code of conduct, simultaneously urging TCNs to 'take appropriate disciplinary and other action to ensure full accountability for misconduct'.[121] Similar statements 'expressing grave concern' and calling for training and accountability were also repeated in MONUC's subsequent mandates,[122] with UNSG Kofi Annan introducing 'non-fraternisation' regulations in the DRC which banned

115 ibid; C Lynch, 'UN Sexual Abuse Alleged in Congo' (*The Washington Post*, 16 December 2004) <https://www.washingtonpost.com/archive/politics/2004/12/16/un-sexual-abuse-alleged-in-congo/ae8ed493-29e0-482b-aafc-5be20838cc47/>.

116 K Holt and S Hughes, 'Sex and the UN: When Peacemakers Become Predators' (*The Independent*, 11 January 2005) <https://www.independent.co.uk/news/world/africa/sex-and-the-un-when-peacemakers-become-predators-486170.html>.

117 UNGA, 'Investigation of the OIOS into Allegations of SEA in MONUC' (5 January 2005) UN Doc A/59/661.

118 UN Press Release, 'Press Briefing on Sexual Exploitation Allegations Related to MONUC' (22 November 2004) <https://www.un.org/press/en/2004/lute041122.doc.htm>; UN Press Release, 'Statement by the Secretary-General' (19 November 2004) <https://www.un.org/sg/en/content/sg/statement/2004-11-19/statement-secretary-general-allegations-sexual-exploitation-and>.

119 E Wax, 'Congo's Desperate "One-Dollar UN Girls"' (*The Washington Post*, 21 March 2005) <https://www.washingtonpost.com/archive/politics/2005/03/21/congos-desperate-one-dollar-un-girls/26b5e610-d9ed-42e1-909a-03b2e061377d/>.

120 UNSC Res 1565 (1 October 2004) UN Doc S/RES/1565, 25.

121 ibid.

122 For example: UNSC Res 1635 (28 October 2005) UN Doc S/RES/1635, 8.

peacekeepers from having sexual relations with the local population.[123] This implementation of the norm in the Congo therefore demonstrates the development of the prohibition of SEA, through the UNSG and the Security Council mandates. However, when examining MONUC's subsequent mandates and the positioning of SEA within the peacekeeping operation's list of mandated tasks, it is dubious how much the norm can be said to have developed. That is, it is debatable how much of a priority the norm of prohibition of SEA was in the DRC given that in 2007, in an eight-page mandate, the first and only mention of SEA came on the final page of the mandate in the second to last paragraph.[124] The same phrases were again reiterated and placed low-down on MONUC's list of tasks in the 2008 mandate.[125] This shifted in 2009 in MONUC's final mandate when the issue of SEA became incorporated into MONUC's PoC tasks, with the tackling of SEA by UN peacekeepers therefore essentially moving from the bottom of the task list to the top, surpassing DDR and SSR provisions.[126] Under the umbrella of protection of civilians, including humanitarian and UN personnel, the Council again requested that the UNSG continued to fully investigate the allegations of SEA and take appropriate measures per the 2003 SG Bulletin.[127] Whilst this was still a reiteration of statements that had been made for the previous four years, it could be argued that the absorption of SEA into PoC placed the issue higher on MONUC's task list, placing it within one of its priorities, thereby expanding the norm slightly.

Nuances of Norm Development

The MONUC example therefore highlights the nuances within norm development, including how peacekeeping norms can merge or overlap. For example, whilst ostensibly, the prohibition of SEA was being promoted, to varying degrees within the Congo, what remained problematic was that neither the 2008 nor 2009 mandates made any reference to the role of TCNs in addressing SEA committed by their troops; instead, the mandates called upon the Secretary-General to investigate allegations and to take appropriate measures under the 2003 SG Bulletin.[128] Therefore, the absorption of SEA into PoC, rather than being viewed as placing the norm higher on MONUC's priority list, could instead be seen as detracting from the seriousness of SEA, essentially downgrading it as a problem in and of itself. Indeed, in the next

123 E Leopold, 'UN Bans Peacekeepers from Sex with Congolese' (*Global Policy*, 10 February 2005) <https://archive.globalpolicy.org/security/issues/congo/2005/0210nonfrat.htm>.
124 UNSC Res 1756 (15 May 2007) UN Doc S/RES/1756, 22.
125 S/RES/1856 (n78) 15.
126 UNSC Res 1906 (23 December 2009) UN Doc S/RES/1906, 12–13.
127 ibid.
128 SG Bulletin (n113).

Security Council mandate, as MONUC transitioned into MONUSCO, the norm of SEA was again moved, this time being placed under MONUSCO's second priority task of 'stabilisation and peace consolidation'.[129] With this 2010 mandate, the Council simply stated that the Secretary-General was to take the 'necessary measures to ensure full compliance' of MONUSCO with the United Nations' zero-tolerance policy on SEA and 'to keep the Council informed if cases of such conduct occur'.[130] Within this mandate, then, the reference to SEA by peacekeepers was relatively short, with no reference to the SG Bulletin. This could be viewed as somewhat of a disregard or waning of support for the norm of prohibition of SEA which was reflected in the fact that MONUSCO's 2011 and 2012 mandates did not contain a single reference to SEA committed by UN peacekeepers.[131] This seemingly diminished support for tackling SEA was again evidenced in the 2013, 2014 and 2015 mandates which referred to SEA by peacekeepers but simply repeated the same sentence that had been contained within the 2010 mandate – that the SG was to take the necessary measures to ensure compliance with the United Nations' zero-tolerance policy and to keep the Council informed of any allegations.[132] The implementation of the norm of prohibition of SEA within the Congo during this period therefore demonstrates how peacekeeping's norms and principles, seen in previous chapters, 'wax and wane'[133] and are dependent on external pressures, events and practices. More specifically, it highlights how a lack of support for a norm results in its stagnation.

Indeed, as the peacekeeping environment changed in 2015 following the HIPPO report, the norm of prohibition of SEA, as noted in Chapter 4, was expanded, with renewed support for the United Nations' zero-tolerance policy and the reaffirming of the primary responsibility of troop- and police-contributing countries to investigate allegations.[134] In practice, the impact of the HIPPO report was reflected in MONUSCO's mandates as the Council explicitly referred to the report and their own resolution.[135] Supporting this revival of the norm, the Council again called upon the Secretary-General to ensure compliance of the zero-tolerance policy within MONUSCO but also requested troop- and police-contributing countries to 'take preventative action' including pre-deployment awareness training.[136] This was then reiter-

129 UNSC Res 1925 (28 May 2010) UN Doc S/RES/1925, 15.

130 ibid.

131 S/RES/1991 (n43); UNSC Res 2053 (27 June 2012) UN Doc S/RES/2053.

132 S/RES/2098 (n97) para 26; UNSC Res 2147 (28 March 2014) UN Doc S/RES/2147, para 32; UNSC Res 2211 (26 March 2015) UN Doc S/RES/2211, para 22.

133 J Karlsrud, 'Special Representatives of the Secretary-General as Norm Arbitrators? Understanding Bottom-up Authority in UN Peacekeeping' (2013) 19(4) GG 525–544, 527.

134 HIPPO Report (n89).

135 UNSC Res 2277 (30 March 2016) UN Doc S/RES/2277.

136 ibid.

ated in MONUSCO's mandate the following year, reflecting a broadening of the norm within the Congo, with this noticeable shift from simply reporting allegations to now undertaking pro-active, preventative steps in the form of pre-deployment training. There was therefore an expansion of the norm of prohibition of SEA and peacekeeping's frameworks, which simultaneously supported the principle of non-intervention as it attempted to prevent violence by peacekeepers against civilians.

The norm was then expanded further within the Congo following a strategic review of MONUSCO, which noted the need to enhance the authority of the SRSG to ensure accountability of MONUSCO staff.[137] Alongside the pre-established tasks of the SG and the TCC's provision of pre-deployment training and investigating allegations, a performance management framework was also introduced.[138] The Secretary-General was now mandated to conduct a comprehensive performance review of all MONUSCO units in accordance with the Operational Readiness Assurance and Performance Improvement Policy and the zero-tolerance policy on SEA.[139] This demonstrated how a renewed support for the norm within the broader UN Secretariat had filtered into peacekeeping practice. Thus, it reflects how the peacekeeping agenda is very much influenced and shaped by the dominant states and agendas, again highlighting the entrenched power differentials within the UN system and peacekeeping. It also emphasises the key role of the Office of the Secretary-General in shaping peacekeeping practices through its interpretation and application of the peacekeeping principles and norms and its reporting to the Security Council.

Through this broadened norm, in 2019 and 2020 similar reiterations of the SG and TCC's role in the implementation of the norm were included within MONUSCO's mandate, this time shifting the task from under the heading of 'Gender, Sexual Violence and SEA' to 'Mission Effectiveness'.[140] In particular, the mandates also emphasised the crucial role of the SRSG noting that when the SG was to implement the zero-tolerance policy on SEA it was to do so 'including by making full use of the existing authority of the SRSG to ensure accountability of the Mission's staff and through effective mission support arrangement'.[141] It also repeated the same phrase that had been used within earlier mandates – that the SG was to 'take all necessary measures to ensure full compliance of all personnel' with the zero-tolerance

137 UNSC, 'Special Report of the Secretary-General on the Strategic Review of the United Nations Organisation Stabilisation Mission in the Democratic Republic of the Congo' (29 September 2017) UN Doc S/2017/826, para 98.

138 UNSC Res 2409 (27 March 2018) UN Doc S/RES/2409, paras 4, 40, 57, 60.

139 ibid.

140 S/RES/2502 (n98) para 45; S/RES/2556 (n78) para 47.

141 S/RES/2556 (n78) para 47.

policy.[142] Crucially for the development of the norm, in the 2019 mandate, when referring to the troop- and police-contributing countries (T/PCCs) the Council explicitly stated that, in addition to providing training, reporting allegations and 'hold[ing] perpetrators accountable', the T/PCCs were to 'repatriate units when there is credible evidence of widespread or systematic [SEA] or other serious misconduct by those units'.[143] This therefore expands the norm further as it explicitly instructs T/PCCs to remove its troops from the peacekeeping operation, going one step further than simply requiring states to investigate and hold personnel to account. Within these mandates, then, the approach to responding to SEA was made much more explicit than in previous years, with the Council outlining roles for the SG, SRSG and T/PCCs. This more expansive approach to the prohibition of SEA has not been repeated, however, in the 2021 and 2022 mandates, although elements from the previous mandates have remained.

In MONUSCO's 2021 mandate, SEA was still noted under the subheading of 'mission effectiveness' but this time was contained within a bullet-pointed list of activities which the Secretary-General was to implement in the 'planning and conduct of MONUSCO's operations within the limits of the mandate and area of operation and in line with existing United Nations guidelines and regulations'.[144] Unlike the 2019 and 2020 mandates, on this occasion, the mandate only referred to the SG (not the SRSG) implementing the United Nations' zero-tolerance policy on SEA and reporting any cases of misconduct to the Security Council. Furthermore, in a list of 16 activities contained within paragraph 42 of the mandate, the reference to implementing the zero-tolerance policy featured last in the list, indicating, once again, that it was not a high priority for the mission. Despite this, later in the mandate, under the sub-heading of 'mission effectiveness and safety and security of peacekeepers', the same reference to the role of the T/PCCs was incorporated, including the need for states to repatriate units.[145] This same paragraph was then included in MONUSCO's most recent mandate but is the sole reference to SEA; that is, only the role of the T/PCCs is discussed, with no mention of the SG or SRSG.[146]

Whilst MONUSCO's most recent mandates may indicate a narrowing or slower development of the norm of prohibition of SEA, activities undertaken in recent years indicate how the norm may still be more broadly implemented in practice. For example, projects have been undertaken through the UN Trust Fund (created by the UNSG in 2016[147]) to support victims of SEA.

142 ibid.
143 S/RES/2502 (n98), para 45.
144 UNSC Res 2612 (20 December 2021) UN Doc S/RES/2612, para 42.
145 ibid, para 47.
146 UNSC Res 2666 (20 December 2022) UN Doc S/RES/2666, para 37.
147 See: UNGA, 'Special Measures for Protection from Sexual Exploitation and Sexual Abuse' (13 February 2015) UN Doc A/69/779.

This has included six projects in the DRC in 2021 which involved supporting victims with activities such as developing skills, funding school fees and strengthening communities' capacity in addressing SEA.[148]

A Stuttering Norm

From the examples of the interpretation and application of the prohibition of SEA in the UN peacekeeping operations in the Congo, it is evident that the norm has been much slower to develop than the other two norms explored within the book. From a TWAIL perspective, it highlights how norms are slow to develop when they do not receive significant support or do not feature highly on the agendas of the dominant powers within the United Nations which set the peacekeeping agendas – i.e. the members of the Security Council. That is, as the prohibition of SEA is evidently not a priority for member states, given that it requires them to potentially address issues within their own state troops or within another TCC, then it is, consequently, not a focus within the peacekeeping agenda. Indeed, it is a task which is primarily offloaded to the Secretary-General, despite the fact that it is an issue directly stemming from member states. In essence, then, the norm is highly politicised, with member states seemingly more concerned with losing the support of a TCC or souring relations between states than they are of addressing SEA amongst its peacekeepers. Indeed, senior personnel within the UN Secretariat have noted that the United Nations 'can definitely do more', particularly the Secretary-General, but a fear of the severe backlash from member states limits the SG from speaking out more.[149]

The politics of peacekeeping and its impact on norm development is, again, exemplified in peacekeeping in the Congo where the TCC with the highest number of SEA allegations – South Africa[150] – has remained a key contributor of troops, playing a pivotal role within the FIB[151] and, more recently,

148 UN News, 'Trust Fund Seeks Sustained Support as It Empowers Victims of Sexual Abuse and Exploitation by UN Personnel' (12 September 2022) <https://monusco.unmissions.org/en/trust-fund-seeks-sustained-support-it-empowers-victims-sexual-abuse-and-exploitation-un-personnel>. UN, 'Trust Fund in Support of Victims of Sexual Exploitation and Abuse: Annual Report' <https://www.un.org/en/content/psea-trust-fund-report-2022/>.

149 Interview with Senior UN DPO Personnel, Policy, Evaluation and Training Division ('Interviewee 10') (New York, 3 December 2019) DOI: <http://doi.org/10.17639/nott.7119>.

150 See: UN Conduct in Field Missions, 'Sexual Exploitation and Abuse: Table of Allegations' <https://conduct.unmissions.org/table-of-allegations>; SM Cold-Ravnkilde and T Mandrup, 'When Peacekeepers Do Damage: Sexual Exploitation and Abuse in the Democratic Republic of Congo' (Danish Institute for International Studies 2017).

151 SADC (n17); P Fabricius, 'Asking the Right Questions about the Force Intervention Brigade' (*ISS*, 21 August 2020) <https://issafrica.org/iss-today/asking-the-right-questions-about-the-force-intervention-brigade>.

the SADC contingent.[152] This highlights two key issues – firstly, the inherent power differentials or hypocrisy embedded within the UN system, as whilst sexual violence committed by host state forces or armed groups is routinely condemned within Security Council mandates, there is little to no accountability for SEA committed by UN peacekeepers. Secondly, it highlights the problem of the United Nations' reliance on TCCs to prosecute their personnel and provide adequate training pre-deployment. The United Nations is therefore beholden to member states and, as has been demonstrated within the Congo, this has limited the development of the norm of prohibition of SEA, consequently restricting peacekeeping's normative framework which, in turn, has the effect of undermining the principle of non-intervention because it does little to prevent these acts against civilians being committed.

Conclusions: Regaining Peacekeeping's Boundaries

Whilst Chapter 5 demonstrated how the fundamental principles of peacekeeping have been interpreted and applied within the United Nations' peacekeeping operations in the DRC, this chapter has explored peacekeeping's norms of democracy promotion, protection of civilians and the prohibition of sexual exploitation and abuse. Adopting the same approach as the previous chapter, this chapter has examined how an interpretation and application of these norms has either expanded or contracted peacekeeping's normative framework. This once again demonstrates the fluidity of these frameworks and the red boundary line that surrounds peacekeeping, which consequently may reinforce or undermine the principle of non-intervention, depending on how broadly the norms are interpreted. Throughout this exploration, a TWAIL lens has also continued to be applied, with the chapter noting instances when the norms of peacekeeping may contribute to the maintenance of power differentials (which have been explored in the previous chapters) and how these norms are frequently driven or based upon the dominant states interests and agendas.

More specifically, the chapter has found that, firstly, like peacekeeping's legal principles, the norms cohabit in a competitive arena in which they are rebalanced for each operation and, even, each mandate.[153] In particular, it has highlighted how these norms have waxed and waned, typically in keeping with international trends but, often, in response to changes within the Congo, thereby reinforcing the notion that the DRC has frequently been used as a test bed for UN peacekeeping. Indeed, MONUSCO is considered to be an innovative operation which has been 'quite proactive in initiating changes from within the mission, rather than waiting for the Council or waiting for

152 Fabricius (n17).
153 J Karlsrud (n1).

headquarters to tell them'.[154] At times, then, it is the Congo which has shaped UN peacekeeping, rather than peacekeeping shaping the Congo.

Secondly, the chapter has highlighted that whilst the norms form a part of peacekeeping's broader normative framework, which surrounds peacekeeping's core legal framework, there is, at times, a degree of overlap. For example, whilst the concept of democracy promotion could perhaps only be considered as a norm, failing to amount to a legal principle, PoC and the prohibition of SEA have clearer legal underpinnings in areas such as international humanitarian and human rights law, thus providing a subsidiary contribution to peacekeeping's legal framework. Similarly, where a broader interpretation and application of these norms have been taken in the Congo, this has had a knock-on effect on the legal principles with, for example, democracy promotion and PoC invoking questions over impartiality and an increased level of force, thereby expanding the principles of impartiality and non-use of force. The chapter has therefore demonstrated how the principles and norms exist in a competitive arena, waxing, waning and rebalancing each time they are re-interpreted and applied within each peacekeeping operation both in the field (in practice) and in the drafting of the mandate.

This then leads to the third matter which this chapter has noted – the impact of these frameworks on the principle of non-intervention. It has been argued that the broader understanding of democracy promotion and PoC, which has been implemented in the DRC, has led to an expansion of peacekeeping's normative frameworks that has consequently undermined and at times contravened the principle of non-intervention. Indeed, it is argued that, at times, this broadened application of these norms has resulted in the peacekeeping operation undertaking coercive action designed to influence change in the host state and, therefore, intervention – such as MONUC's involvement in the Congo's National Dialogue or MONUSCO's substitution for the state in the protection of civilians. Conversely, it has been found that of the three norms, the prohibition of SEA is the only norm to have not been rapidly developed and broadly interpreted, thereby only providing a limited contribution to the normative framework. However, as seen in Chapter 4, it has been argued that, unlike its democracy and PoC counterparts, a narrow application of the norm, seemingly based predominantly on member states reluctance to support the norm, effectively permits SEA and thereby undermines, rather than supports, the principle of non-intervention. Therefore, in essence, the only norm to support the principle of non-intervention is the one that is least developed.

Finally, the chapter has argued that the significant expansion of peacekeeping's normative framework in the Congo, through the norms of democracy promotion and PoC, in particular, has pushed peacekeeping to its very limits.

154 Interviewee 10 (n149) 37.

As such, the chapter has advocated for the need to re-draw the normative boundaries of peacekeeping (by narrowing the interpretation and application of these norms) in the hope of retracting peacekeeping's interventionist potential and reinforcing the principle of non-intervention. In other words, the chapter has highlighted instances when it would be preferable to shrink peacekeeping's normative boundaries thereby retreating from the large, multi-dimensional operations, with their ambiguous Christmas tree mandates, to a more traditional model of peacekeeping. This, in turn, would go some way in helping to clarify the legal issues which this book has explored (including peacekeeping's Charter basis) and more appropriately match the mandates to peacekeeping capabilities. As this chapter has suggested, this may therefore require a review of Security Council mandating and a move to a people-centred approach to peacekeeping. Indeed, such recommendations – to streamline peacekeeping mandates and adopt a people-centred approach to peacekeeping – are not new suggestions and have recently gained further support in the United Nations' 'New Agenda for Peace', which recognises, amongst other things, a need for 'the Security Council not to burden peace operations with unrealistic mandates'.[155]

References

Al-Jedda v UK App No 27021/08 (ECtHR, 7 July 2011)

Ajello A, 'The EU Security Role in the Great Lakes Region' in A Adebajo and K Whiteman (eds) *The EU and Africa: From Eurafrique to Afro-Europa* (Hurst and Company 2012)

Autesserre S, 'Hobbes and the Congo: Frames, Local Violence and International Intervention' (2009) Intrg 63(2) 349–280

Autesserre S, 'What the Uproar Over Congo's Elections Misses' (*Foreign Affairs*, 1 March 2017) <https://www.foreignaffairs.com/articles/democratic-republic-congo/2017-03-01/what-uproar-over-congos-elections-misses>

Autesserre S, *The Frontlines of Peace: An Insider's Guide to Changing the World* (OUP 2021)

Blair RA, Di Salvatore J, Smidt HM, 'When Do UN Peacekeeping Operations Implement Their Mandates?' (2021) 66(3) American Journal of Political Science 664–680

Bothe M, 'UN Peace Operations' in D Fleck (ed) *The Handbook of the Law of Visiting Forces* (2nd edn, OUP 2018)

Boutellis JA, 'From Crisis to Reform: Peacekeeping Strategies for the Protection of Civilians in the Democratic Republic of Congo' (2013) 2(3):48 Stability 1–11

Boutellis A and Lacaille G, 'Renewing MONUSCO's Mandate: What Role Beyond the Elections?' (IPI Issue Brief, May 2011)

Carver F, 'Linked Up Peacekeeping' (Protection Approaches July 2022) <https://protectionapproaches.org/linked-up-peacekeeping>

155 New Agenda for Peace (n11) 24.

Charter of the United Nations "UN Charter" (24 October 1945)

Chimni BS, 'Third World Approaches to International Law: A Manifesto' (2006) 8 ICLR 3–27

CIVIC, 'Community Engagement by MONUSCO with Reduced Field Presence' (CIVIC, May 2018) <https://civiliansinconflict.org/wp-content/uploads/2018/06/MONUSCO_Community-Engagement-Brief.pdf>

Cold-Ravnkilde SM and Mandrup T, 'When Peacekeepers Do Damage: Sexual Exploitation and Abuse in the Democratic Republic of Congo' (Danish Institute for International Studies 2017)

Crisis Group, 'The Inter-Congolese Dialogue: Political Negotiation or Game of Bluff?' (ICG Africa Report No 37, 16 November 2001)

Crisis Group, 'Congo: Is Democratic Change Possible?' (Crisis Group Africa Briefing No 225, 5 May 2015)

Day A, 'The Future of Multidimensional Peacekeeping' (*IPI*, 15 September 2020) <https://theglobalobservatory.org/2020/09/future-multidimensional-peacekeeping/>

de Coning C, 'Adaptive peacebuilding' (2018) 94(2) International Affairs 301–317

de Coning C and Gelot L, 'Placing People at the Center of UN Peace Operations' (*IPI*, 29 May 2020) <https://theglobalobservatory.org/2020/05/placing-people-center-un-peace-operations/>

Dobbins J, Jones SG, Crane K, Rathmell A, Steele B, Teltschik R and Timilsina A, *The UN's Role in Nation-Building: From the Congo to Iraq* (RAND Corporation 2005)

Doss A, 'The Congo, Afghanistan and the Limits of Outside Intervention' (*Pass Blue*, 18 January 2021) <https://www.passblue.com/2021/01/18/the-congo-afghanistan-and-the-limits-of-outside-intervention/>

DPKO/DFS Policy, 'The Protection of Civilians in United Nations Peacekeeping' (2015) Ref 2015.07

Easterly W, *The White Man's Burden* (OUP 2006)

Ero C, 'The Problems with "African Solutions"' (International Crisis Group, 2 December 2013) <https://www.crisisgroup.org/africa/problems-african-solutions>

Fabricius P, 'Asking the Right Questions About the Force Intervention Brigade' (ISS, 21 August 2020) <https://issafrica.org/iss-today/asking-the-right-questions-about-the-force-intervention-brigade>

Fabricius P, 'SADC Prepares to go Back to the Future in Eastern DRC' (*ISS*, 19 May 2023) <https://issafrica.org/iss-today/sadc-prepares-to-go-back-to-the-future-in-eastern-drc>

Fox GH and Roth BR (eds) *Democracy and International Law* (Edward Elgar 2020)

Global Protection Cluster, 'Democratic Republic of Congo' <https://www.globalprotectioncluster.org/field-support/field-protection-clusters/democratic-republic-of-congo/>

Goulding M, 'The Evolution of United Nations Peacekeeping' (1993) 69(3) IntAff 451–464

Hatcher J and Perry A, 'Defining Peacekeeping Downward: The UN Debacle in Eastern Congo' (*Time*, 26 November 2012) <http://world.time.com/2012/11/26/defining-peacekeeping-downward-the-u-n-debacle-in-eastern-congo/>

Heldt B, 'Peacekeeping Operations and Transitions to Democracy' in H Fjelde and K Höglund (eds) *Building Peace, Creating Conflict* (Nordic Academic Press 2011)

HL Deb 15 March 1962, vol 238, Cols 364–88

Hoebeke H, 'Kabila Shows His Hand in DR Congo's Electoral Poker' (*Crisis Group*, 16 August 2018) <https://www.crisisgroup.org/africa/central-africa/democratic-republic-congo/kabila-shows-his-hand-dr-congos-electoral-poker>

Holt K and Hughes S, 'Will Congo's Women Ever Have Justice?' (*The Independent*, 12 July 2004) <https://www.independent.co.uk/news/world/africa/will-congos-women-ever-have-justice-46938.html>

Holt K and Hughes S, 'Sex and the UN: When Peacemakers Become Predators' (*The Independent*, 11 January 2005) <https://www.independent.co.uk/news/world/africa/sex-and-the-un-when-peacemakers-become-predators-486170.html>

Human Rights Watch, 'War Crimes in Kisangani' (August 2002) 14(6)(A) HRW

Human Rights Watch, 'Ituri: "Covered in Blood"' (July 2003) 15(11)(A) HRW

Human Rights Watch, 'DR Congo: 24 Killed Since Election Results Announced' (*Human Rights Watch*, 21 December 2011) <https://www.hrw.org/news/2011/12/21/dr-congo-24-killed-election-results-announced>

Human Rights Watch, 'DR Congo: Army, UN Failed to Stop Massacre' (*Human Rights Watch*, 2 July 2014) <https://www.hrw.org/news/2014/07/02/dr-congo-army-un-failed-stop-massacre>

Human Rights Watch, 'Killings in Kiwanja: The UN's Inability to Protect Civilians' (HRW, 11 December 2018) <https://www.hrw.org/report/2008/12/11/killings-kiwanja/uns-inability-protect-civilians>

Interview with Senior UNDP Personnel, formerly OCHA ('Interviewee 1') (Geneva, 20 November 2018) DOI: <http://doi.org/10.17639/nott.7119>

Interview with Congolese Independent Expert ('Interviewee 5') (Oxford, 29 October 2019) DOI: <http://doi.org/10.17639/nott.7119>

Interview with Independent Expert and Former UN Political Adviser ('Interviewee 8') (New York, 26 November 2019) DOI: <http://doi.org/10.17639/nott.7119>

Interview with Senior UN DPO Personnel, Policy, Evaluation and Training Division ('Interviewee 10') (New York, 3 December 2019) DOI: <http://doi.org/10.17639/nott.7119>

Interview with Senior Human Rights Officer in the Office of the UN High Commissioner of Human Rights ('Interviewee 13') (New York, 6 December 2019) DOI: <http://doi.org/10.17639/nott.7119>

Interview with Senior Political Affairs Officer, UN DPO ('Interviewee 16') (New York, 10 December 2019) DOI: <http://doi.org/10.17639/nott.7119>

Interview with Political Adviser in the Office of the SRSG MONUSCO ('Interviewee 18') (Skype, 17 February 2020) DOI: <http://doi.org/10.17639/nott.7119>

Interview with Personnel in MONUSCO's Stabilisation Support Unit ('Interviewee 19') (Skype, 21 February 2020) DOI: <http://doi.org/10.17639/nott.7119>

IPI, 'COVID-19 Crisis an Opportunity to "Rethink and Develop UN Peacekeeping Further"' (IPI, 7 October 2020) <https://www.ipinst.org/2020/10/un-peace-ops-during-covid-19-high-level-dialogue#3>

Karlsrud J, 'Special Representatives of the Secretary-General as Norm Arbitrators? Understanding Bottom-up Authority in UN Peacekeeping' (2013) 19(4) GG 525–544

Kullenberg J, 'Community Liaison Assistants: A Bridge Between Peacekeepers and Local Populations' (FMR, October 2016) <https://www.fmreview.org/sites/fmr/files/FMRdownloads/en/community-protection/kullenberg.pdf>

Labbé J and Boutellis A, 'Peace Operations by Proxy: Implications for Humanitarian action of UN Peacekeeping Partnerships with Non-UN Security Forces' (2013) 95(891/892) IRRC 539–559

Labuda PI, 'United Nations Peacekeeping as Intervention by Invitation: Host State Consent and the Use of Force in Security Council-Mandated Stabilisation Operations' (2020) JUFIL 1–37

Labuda PI, 'With or Against the State? Reconciling the Protection of Civilians and Host-State Support in UN Peacekeeping' (IPI 2020).

Legal Consequences for States of the Continued Presence of South Africa in Namibia (South West Africa) notwithstanding Security Council Resolution 276 (Advisory Opinion) [1971] ICJ Rep 16

Leopold E, 'UN Bans Peacekeepers From Sex With Congolese' (*Global Policy*, 10 February 2005) <https://archive.globalpolicy.org/security/issues/congo/2005/0210nonfrat.htm>

Lynch C, 'UN Sexual Abuse Alleged in Congo' (*The Washington Post*, 16 December 2004) <https://www.washingtonpost.com/archive/politics/2004/12/16/un-sexual-abuse-alleged-in-congo/ae8ed493-29e0-482b-aafc-5be20838cc47/>

Martin I, 'All Peace Operations Are Political: A Case for Designer Missions and the Next UN Reform' (CIC Thematic Essay, 2015) <https://cic.nyu.edu/sites/default/files/political_missions_2010_martin_allpeace2.pdf>

Mays TM, 'African Solutions for African Problems: The Changing Face of African-Mandated Peace Operations' (2003) 23(1) JConfStud 106–12

Médecins Sans Frontières, 'Ituri: Unkept Promises? A Pretense of Protection and Inadequate Assistance' (MSF, 25 July 2003) <https://reliefweb.int/sites/reliefweb.int/files/resources/E4AD40CF77CAAEFBC1256D6E00339499-msf-drc-25jul.pdf>

Nadin P, 'An Argument For More Focused UN Peacekeeping Mandates' (*Our World, UNU*, 18 February 2014) <https://ourworld.unu.edu/en/an-argument-for-more-focused-un-peacekeeping-mandates>

Nzongola-Ntalaja G, *The Congo from Leopold to Kabila: A People's History* (Zed Books 2006)

Operations Directive No 8 (untitled), February 1961, UN Archives DAG/13/1.6.5.0.0; Operations Directives August 1960–January 1964, Box 3

Reynaert J, 'MONUC/MONUSCO and Civilian Protection in the Kivus' (IPIS 2010)

Rogier E, 'The Inter-Congolese Dialogue: A Critical Overview' in M Malan and JP Gomes (eds) *Challenges of Peace Implementation: The UN Mission in the Democratic Republic of the Congo* (ISS 2004)

SADC, 'SADC Prepares to go Back to the Future in Easter DRC' (*ISS*, 19 May 2023) <https://issafrica.org/iss-today/sadc-prepares-to-go-back-to-the-future-in-eastern-drc>

SADC Press Release, 'SADC Reiterates Its Position for a Stable and Peaceful DRC' (*SADC*, 29 May 2020) <https://reliefweb.int/report/democratic-republic-congo/sadc-reiterates-its-position-stable-and-peaceful-drc>

Schneider M, 'Examining the Role of Rwanda in the DRC Insurgency' (*Crisis Group*, 19 September 2012) <https://www.crisisgroup.org/africa/central-africa/democratic-republic-congo/examining-role-rwanda-drc-insurgency>

Sripati V, 'The United Nation's Role in Post-Conflict Constitution-Making Processes: TWAIL Insights' (2008) 10(4) ICLR 411–420

Tamm H, 'Status Competition in Africa: Explaining the Rwandan-Ugandan Clashes in the Democratic Republic of Congo' (2019) 118(472) AfrAff 509–530

Together First, 'People-Centred Peacekeeping' <https://together1st.org/proposals/351#>

Trefon T, *Congo Masquerade: The Political Culture of Aid Inefficiency and Reform Failure* (Zed Books 2011)

Tzouvala N, *Capitalism as Civilisation: A History of International Law* (CUP 2020)

UN, 'Our Common Agenda Policy Brief 9: A New Agenda for Peace' (July 2023) <https://dppa.un.org/en/a-new-agenda-for-peace>

UN Conduct in Field Missions, 'Sexual Exploitation and Abuse: Table of Allegations' <https://conduct.unmissions.org/table-of-allegations>

UN, 'Trust Fund in Support of Victims of Sexual Exploitation and Abuse: Annual Report' <https://www.un.org/en/content/psea-trust-fund-report-2022/>

UN News, 'Rebels Take Bukavu in Eastern DR of Congo, Protesters Target UN' (*UN News*, 2 June 2004) <https://news.un.org/en/story/2004/06/105462-rebels-take-bukavu-eastern-dr-congo-protesters-target-un>

UN News, 'UN Peacekeepers in Eastern DR Congo Help Restore Calm after Inter-Ethnic Violence Flares' (*UN News*, 7 June 2014) <https://news.un.org/en/story/2014/06/470232-un-peacekeepers-eastern-dr-congo-help-restore-calm-after-inter-ethnic-violence>

UN News, 'Trust Fund Seeks Sustained Support as it Empowers Victims of Sexual Abuse and Exploitation by UN Personnel' (12 September 2022) <https://monusco.unmissions.org/en/trust-fund-seeks-sustained-support-it-empowers-victims-sexual-abuse-and-exploitation-un-personnel>

UN Peacekeeping, 'Protecting Civilians' <https://peacekeeping.un.org/en/protecting-civilians>

UN Press Release, 'Statement by the Secretary-General' (19 November 2004) <https://www.un.org/sg/en/content/sg/statement/2004-11-19/statement-secretary-general-allegations-sexual-exploitation-and>

UN Press Release, 'Press Briefing on Sexual Exploitation Allegations Related to MONUC' (22 November 2004) <https://www.un.org/press/en/2004/lute041122.doc.htm>

UN Press Release, 'Conference by Special Representative for the Democratic Republic of Congo' (25 August 2010) <https://reliefweb.int/report/democratic-republic-congo/press-conference-special-representative-democratic-republic-congo>

UNGA, 'Investigations into Sexual Exploitation of Refugees by Aid Workers in West Africa' (11 October 2002) UN Doc A/57/465; UNGA Res 57/306 (22 May 2003) UN Doc A/RES/57/306

UNGA, 'Investigation of the OIOS into Allegations of SEA in MONUC' (5 January 2005) UN Doc A/59/661

UNGA, 'Special Measures for Protection from Sexual Exploitation and Sexual Abuse' (13 February 2015) UN Doc A/69/779

UNGA-SC, 'Report of the High-level Independent Panel on Peace Operations' ("HIPPO Report") (17 June 2015) UN Doc A/70/95-S/2015/446

UNSC, 'Ceasefire Agreement' ("Lusaka Ceasefire") (23 July 1999) UN Doc S/1999/815

UNSC, 'Report of the Secretary-General on the United Nations Organisation Stabilisation Mission in the Democratic Republic of the Congo' (25 September 2014) UN Doc S/2014/698

UNSC, 'Joint Strategy on the Progressive Drawdown of MONUSCO' (27 October 2020) UN Doc S/2020/1041
UNSC, 'Report of the Secretary General' (30 November 2020) UN Doc S/2020/1150
UNSC, 'Transitioning from Stabilization to Peace: An Independent Strategic Review of MONUSCO' ("Strategic Review") (25 October 2019) UN Doc S/2019/842
UNSC Report, 'Is Christmas Really Over? The Mandating of Peace Operations' (UNSC, 22 February 2019) <https://www.securitycouncilreport.org/atf/cf/%7B65BFCF9B-6D27-4E9C-8CD3-CF6E4FF96FF9%7D/research_report_council_mandating_february_2019.pdf>
UNSC Res 143 (14 July 1960) UN Doc S/RES/143
UNSC Res 1325 (31 October 2000) UN Doc S/RES/1325
UNSC Res 1417 (14 June 2002) UN Doc S/RES/1417
UNSC Res 1468 (20 March 2003) UN Doc S/RES/1468
UNSC Res 1484 (30 May 2003) UN Doc S/RES/1484
UNSC Res 1493 (28 July 2003) UN Doc S/RES/1493
UNSC Res 1565 (1 October 2004) UN Doc S/RES/1565
UNSC Res 1635 (28 October 2005) UN Doc S/RES/1635
UNSC Res 1671 (25 April 2006) UN Doc S/RES/1671
UNSC Res 1756 (15 May 2007) UN Doc S/RES/1756
UNSC Res 1794 (21 December 2007) UN Doc S/RES/1794
UNSC Res 1856 (22 December 2008) UN Doc S/RES/1856
UNSC Res 1906 (23 December 2009) UN Doc S/RES/1906
UNSC Res 1925 (28 May 2010) UN Doc S/RES/1925
UNSC Res 1991 (28 June 2011) UN Doc S/RES/1991
UNSC Res 2053 (27 June 2012) UN Doc S/RES/2053
UNSC Res 2098 (28 March 2013) UN Doc S/RES/2098
UNSC Res 2147 (28 March 2014) UN Doc S/RES/2147
UNSC Res 2211 (26 March 2015) UN Doc S/RES/2211
UNSC Res 2277 (30 March 2016) UN Doc S/RES/2277
UNSC Res 2409 (27 March 2018) UN Doc S/RES/2409
UNSC Res 2502 (19 December 2019) UN Doc S/RES/2502
UNSC Res 2556 (18 December 2020) UN Doc S/RES/2556
UNSC Res 2612 (20 December 2021) UN Doc S/RES/2612
UNSC Res 2666 (20 December 2022) UN Doc S/RES/2666
UNSC, 'Special Report of the Secretary-General on the Democratic Republic of the Congo and the Great Lakes Region' (27 February 2003) UN Doc S/2013/119
UNSC, 'Special Report of the Secretary-General on the Strategic Review of the United Nations Organisation Stabilisation Mission in the Democratic Republic of the Congo' (29 September 2017) UN Doc S/2017/826
UNSC, 'Report of the Secretary-General' (18 March 2020) UN Doc S/2020/214
UNSC, 'Report of the Secretary-General' (21 September 2020) UN Doc S/2020/919
UNSG, 'Secretary-General Bulletin: Special Measures for Protection for Sexual Exploitation and Abuse' (9 October 2003) UN Doc ST/SGB/2003/13
Van Reybrouck D, *Congo: The Epic History of a People* (Fourth Estate 2015)
Wax E, 'Congo's Desperate "One-Dollar UN Girls"' (*The Washington Post*, 21 March 2005) <https://www.washingtonpost.com/archive/politics/2005/03/21/congos-desperate-one-dollar-un-girls/26b5e610-d9ed-42e1-909a-03b2e061377d/>

Weiss TG and Kuele G, 'The Global South and UN Peace Operations' (*E-International Relations*, 3 February 2019) <https://www.e-ir.info/2019/02/03/the-global-south-and-un-peace-operations/#_ftn2>

White ND, 'Peacekeeping and International Law' in J Koops, N MacQueen, T Tardy and PD Williams (eds) *The Oxford Handbook of United Nations Peacekeeping Operations* (OUP, 2016)

White ND, 'Empowering Peace Operations to Protect Civilians: Form over Substance?' (2009) 13 JIP 327–355

Wilson T, 'Congolese Activists on Hunger Strike After Court Refuses Release' (*The Guardian*, 19 March 2016) <http://www.theguardian.com/world/2016/mar/19/congolese-activists-on-hunger-strike-after-court-refuses-release>

Worsnip P, 'UN's Ban Sends Top Aide to Congo After Mass Rape' (*Reuters*, 24 August 2010) <https://www.reuters.com/article/oukwd-uk-congo-democratic-rape-idAFTRE67N5VQ20100824>

Chapter 7

Conclusion

Introduction

This book has highlighted, through an exploration of peacekeeping's frameworks in the Democratic Republic of the Congo, the interventionist nature of peacekeeping and the potential for peacekeeping to cross the thin red boundary line between peacekeeping and intervention, thereby becoming a form of intervention. That is, both peacekeeping and intervention are ill-defined with no pre-determined or explicit frameworks creating set boundaries around the concepts. As such, both concepts are fluid, open to being re-interpreted and contorted, particularly by dominant powers, in order to justify interventions or meet the needs and agendas of these dominant actors. Throughout an exploration of these issues, the book has also uniquely adopted a TWAIL perspective, seeking to offer, not a totalising destructive critique of intervention and UN peacekeeping, but, rather, a constructive critique, highlighting instances when colonial patterns and dichotomies of domination and subordination are replicated within intervention and peacekeeping practices. It has therefore provided an alternative view to the prevailing Western narratives of the development of UN peacekeeping and its current status within international law.

The book has explored all of these issues in somewhat of a pyramid structure. Beginning with the top of this pyramid, Chapter 2 explored the development of the principle of non-intervention before Chapters 3 and 4 moved on to explore the second layer – the most prevalent form of intervention today, UN peacekeeping. These chapters also exposed the legal and normative frameworks surrounding peacekeeping and how those laws and norms interact with the principle of non-intervention. The final layer of the pyramid then examined peacekeeping in practice, with Chapters 5 and 6 exploring how the legal and normative frameworks are interpreted and applied within the United Nations' peacekeeping operations in the DRC. The book therefore provides a deep analysis of intervention and peacekeeping in order to determine the relationship between the two and to question whether peacekeeping is, at times, intervention. At various points throughout the book, it has been argued that peacekeeping has, at times, constricted or even contravened the principle of non-intervention. The book therefore argues that when peacekeeping's

DOI: 10.4324/9781003371649-7

principles and norms have been broadly interpreted and applied, it has resulted in peacekeeping evolving too far and thus it is suggested that: (1) peacekeeping boundaries need to be constricted with more realistic, streamlined mandates and (2) in doing so, a people-centred approach should also be adopted.

Intervention as Peacekeeping

To begin with, Chapter 2 traced the development of the principle of non-intervention, with intervention defined as any action taken by a state, state actor or international organisation such as the United Nations, which may be deemed coercive, in order to force change within the host state. The chapter then highlighted how the concept and practice of intervention have been somewhat cyclical. That is, there has been a constant fluctuation in intervention and non-intervention rhetoric with, often, a disparity between rhetoric and practice. In other words, whilst the principle of non-intervention may have been emphatically supported, in practice, interventions have continually occurred, as was seen, for example, with the Cold War proxy wars. These cycles of interventionist practice have therefore had the impact of either supporting or undermining the principle of non-intervention. Unpicking all of this, the chapter began by examining the historical development or roots of non-intervention, including the Peace of Westphalia and colonialism; it then went on to examine key tipping points such as the formulation of the United Nations and then, most crucially, the decolonisation period. It is this latter period that this book has argued was a crucial moment for the formulation of the principle of non-intervention as it evolved from a principle which exclusively benefited the European hegemonic powers, to one that applied to the newly independent Global South states. The principle therefore transformed from a European or Western principle to a universal one and was 'professed equally emphatically in the East, West and Third World'.[1] Having clarified the composition of the principle of non-intervention, which had been significantly developed within the UN system, particularly with General Assembly Resolutions and Declarations, the chapter then went on to explore the nuances within the principle. It examined how, through the International Court of Justice (ICJ) and regional organisations, a greater understanding of the principle in practice began to develop, with the ICJ, in particular, condemning intervention in the Global South and, for the first time, addressing intervention by the Global South within the Global South.[2]

1 W Grewe, *The Epochs of International Law* (Walter de Gruyter & Co; Rev Ed edition 2000) 654.
2 See: *Case Concerning Military and Paramilitary Activities in and against Nicaragua (Nicaragua v United States of America)* [1986] ICJ Rep 14; *Case Concerning Armed Activities on the Territory of the Congo (Democratic Republic of the Congo v Uganda)* Judgment of 19 December [2005] ICJ Rep 168.

From this, the chapter continued to explore how the firmly established principle of non-intervention developed throughout the post-Cold War era and into the twenty-first century. It noted how intervention began to diversify, with the end of the Cold War sparking a shift in attitude towards intervention, which undermined the principle of non-intervention, as there was greater support for intervention. The increased optimism about the potential for the United Nations during this period, combined with the perceived failures of the international community, such as the Rwandan genocide and Srebrenica massacre, resulted in a move from unilateral to multilateral intervention. There was then a revival of UN peacekeeping, through the justification of collective security intervention, and a return to humanitarian-based interventions, with the introduction of the concept of the responsibility to protect (R2P). During this period, Chapter 2 argued that the principle of non-intervention was both challenged by these increasing justifications for intervention and simultaneously further developed as the principle began to grapple with regional interventions, with ICJ decisions, again, providing some clarity on how these related to the principle.[3] This diversification in the forms of intervention therefore contributed to a more nuanced understanding of the principle of non-intervention and its application in the ever-changing modern era. This was then further developed in the post-9/11 era which, Chapter 2 argued, was another tipping point for the principle, as intervention shifted from a military to security approach. Threats to international peace and security now included, not just armed conflict but civil violence, organised crime, terrorism, weapons of mass destruction, poverty, infectious disease and 'environmental degradation', permitting states to 'take advantage of any relevant security system' in order to counter these issues.[4] This shift was, in turn, reflected in UN peacekeeping with a move to robust, multi-dimensional, 'stabilisation' operations which pushed peacekeeping into the realm of intervention. The chapter then began to question whether UN peacekeeping, as the most prevalent form of intervention today, could be considered to be, at times, a form of coercive action designed to influence change in the host state and, therefore, intervention.

Whilst exploring this development of the principle of non-intervention, Chapter 2 also applied a TWAIL lens which highlighted numerous issues, such as the unequal global order, the lack of a Third World or Global South voice within both international law and the international system, and the use of international law to maintain hierarchies, including colonial legacies and patterns of domination and subordination. Indeed, the chapter argued that the formulation of the principle of non-intervention during the decolonisation

3 See: ibid, *DRC v Uganda*.

4 B Simma, DE Khan, G Nolte, A Paulus and N Wessendorf (eds) *The Charter of the United Nations: A Commentary, Vol 1* (3rd ed, OUP 2012) 111.

period was largely driven by the newly independent Global South states and could therefore be viewed, from a TWAIL perspective, as a prime example of the Global South challenging both the dominance of the hegemonic powers and the international law and institutions which maintained this hierarchical system. Furthermore, Chapter 2 also argued that the structure of the United Nations, particularly the veto-wielding Security Council, legitimised hegemony through the 'cloak of universality'[5] and exploited the unclear Charter basis of peacekeeping, meaning the Council can move from non-interventionist Chapter VI peacekeeping operations to interventionist Chapter VII operations. That is, regardless of the influx of Global South states into the UN General Assembly, the inherently biased Security Council enshrines the power of the hegemonic permanent five (P5) states, perpetually maintaining the dichotomies of domination and subordination, whilst espousing principles of universality and equality. Chapter 2 then highlighted how this filters down into the UN system and into its activities, such as peacekeeping, with this argument explored further in Chapters 3 and 4.

Alongside this, following Anghie's argument on the influence of colonialism in shaping international law,[6] Chapter 2 argued that the principle of non-intervention had also been animated by colonialism, providing examples of this colonial influence, such as when the principle had ostensibly applied to the Global South but had been used by the dominant powers to legitimise extensive intervention – as occurred in the Congo in 1960 with the deployment of ONUC and throughout the 1990s with the humanitarian-based interventions. The chapter further argued that remnants of colonialism or colonial practices could be found within intervention today, particularly within UN peacekeeping. It was argued that comparisons may be drawn between the two forms of intervention, not least given that both were (or are) the most illustrious forms of intervention in their era – colonialism in the nineteenth and twentieth centuries and peacekeeping in the twenty-first century. Chapter 2 also argued that both peacekeeping and colonialism invoked, for example, elements of domination and subordination and were largely motivated or shaped by the interests and will of the hegemonic powers.

Peacekeeping as Intervention

Flowing on from this comparison, Chapters 3 and 4 explored the second layer of the pyramid – UN peacekeeping – finding that, despite the lack of an explicit framework, there do exist principles and norms which, together, form a complex peacekeeping framework. The chapters argued that peacekeeping possesses both legal and normative frameworks which establish an invisible

5 M Mutua, 'What Is TWAIL?' (2000) 94 ASILPROC 31–38, 37.
6 A Anghie, *Imperialism, Sovereignty and the Making of International Law* (CUP 2007).

red boundary line around peacekeeping that divides peacekeeping from intervention. The chapters found that, along with the broad framework of the UN Charter, the fundamental principles of consent, impartiality and non-use of force constituted peacekeeping's legal framework, whilst the newer, more controversial norms of democracy promotion, protection of civilians (PoC) and the prohibition of sexual exploitation and abuse (SEA) constituted peacekeeping's normative framework. It was argued that the legal framework sits at peacekeeping's core and is surrounded by the much broader normative framework. However, the chapters highlighted how these frameworks do not exist in total isolation but, rather, overlap at certain points. In particular, Chapter 4 showed how the norms of PoC and prohibition of SEA contain legal underpinnings, thereby potentially invoking elements of international humanitarian, criminal and human rights law and consequently making a secondary contribution to peacekeeping's legal framework. It was further argued that these principles and norms do not exist harmoniously and instead 'exist in a competitive arena' with the normative composition of a peacekeeping operation being 're-balanced each time'.[7] Therefore, if, for example, one principle is interpreted broadly, this may have an impact on another principle or norm, thereby altering peacekeeping's overall framework. These frameworks could therefore be viewed as a fluid, red elastic band, constantly expanding and contracting, as the principles and norms within them are routinely re-interpreted and contorted within each peacekeeping operation and each peacekeeping mandate.

The chapters therefore highlighted how the six principles and norms are continually contorted, re-interpreted and re-shaped which results in peacekeeping's frameworks being continually contracted and expanded. That is, the chapters explored each principle or norm in turn and found that, whether in isolation or taken together, if the principles are interpreted narrowly, then this constricts peacekeeping's frameworks, thereby firming the boundary between peacekeeping and intervention and consequently reinforcing the principle of non-intervention. However, with the exception of the prohibition of SEA, when the principles and norms are interpreted broadly (as is frequently the case with contemporary, multi-dimensional stabilisation operations) then this expands peacekeeping's frameworks, blurring the line between peacekeeping and intervention and therefore undermining the principle of non-intervention or, at times, potentially contravening it. It also found that these evolutions within peacekeeping were often in line with the interventionist trends which Chapter 2 explored. That is, where the principle of non-intervention was emphatically supported, such as during decolonisation, peacekeeping operations followed the traditional model

7 J Karlsrud, 'Special Representatives of the Secretary-General as Norm Arbitrators? Understanding Bottom-up Authority in UN Peacekeeping' (2013) 19(4) GG 525–544, 527.

of peacekeeping, with the principles narrowly interpreted and peacekeeping deemed to be non-interventionist in nature. Conversely, when there has been support for intervention, such as in the post-Cold War era with the calls for humanitarian-based interventions and democratisation, peacekeeping's boundaries have been expanded, leading to the introduction of, for example, robust peacekeeping and multi-dimensional operations. As a result of this interconnectedness, any changes to peacekeeping's boundary line, by extension, result in changes to the boundaries of the principle of non-intervention – a narrow interpretation of the peacekeeping boundaries reinforces the principle of non-intervention, whilst a broadened or expanded interpretation results in a constriction of contravening of the principle.

The only exception to this pattern is the norm of prohibition of SEA, as the chapter found that a broader interpretation and greater application of this norm would reinforce the principle of non-intervention as it places a restriction on peacekeepers' behaviour with the aim of preventing them from committing a violent form of intervention. Thus, unlike the other two norms of peacekeeping – democracy promotion and PoC – Chapter 4 found that the prohibition of SEA was not, in itself, interventionist but was instead designed to prevent intervention. However, it found that this norm, unlike its counterparts, had not evolved as rapidly nor had it received the same level of support from member states, arguably due to the fact that it places restrictions upon the dominant, intervening actors and condemns their misconduct. Thus, from a TWAIL perspective, this highlights how the moulding or reimagining of peacekeeping's frameworks is shaped by the dominant powers to meet their interests and agendas.

Indeed, a TWAIL lens was, again, applied throughout these chapters and highlighted how the same dynamics and patterns of domination and subordination which were found within the principle of non-intervention could also be found within UN peacekeeping. In particular, an application of the TWAIL lens demonstrated how the principles and norms are predominantly based upon Western values and standards and their interpretation and application are often based upon the hegemonic powers' interests and agendas – as was seen with the norm of democracy promotion and PoC. It also highlighted examples of where Anghie's dynamic of difference is recreated within peacekeeping and noted how peacekeeping's frameworks and their application, can, at times, maintain the colonial dichotomies of domination and subordination, particularly when peacekeeping is taken closer to the intervention line and could be viewed as coercive action designed to influence change in the host state – such as through the use of force or PoC.

Peacekeeping in Practice: The DRC – Peacekeeping's Laboratory

Chapters 3 and 4 therefore illuminated peacekeeping's legal and normative frameworks, demonstrating their fluidity and ability to constantly expand or contract, depending on how the principles and norms are interpreted and applied. Chapters 5 and 6 then took the analysis further by examining peacekeeping and its frameworks in practice. The chapters used the DRC as a case study as it has hosted three UN peacekeeping operations since 1960 and has often been used a test bed for peacekeeping. A case study of peacekeeping in the DRC therefore provides a wealth of examples of the how the frameworks are implemented in practice, highlighting the nuances of the frameworks and reinforcing arguments made in Chapters 3 and 4.

To begin with, Chapter 5 focused on the legal framework – the principles of consent, impartiality and non-use of force – and examined how each principle has been interpreted and applied within the United Nations' peacekeeping operations in the Congo. The chapter found that, firstly, as was argued in Chapter 3, the principles and norms do not exist harmoniously but, instead, overlap and are continually re-interpreted, re-applied and re-balanced through each mandate renewal and, even, in reaction to changes in the field, such as an increase in armed group violence. The chapter found that when one of the principles is expanded, such as when MONUSCO has embarked upon joint operations with the Congolese armed forces, then this broader interpretation of impartiality has simultaneously expanded the principle of limited use of force, which has also impacted the principle of consent when relations during these operations break down. This, in turn, leads to the second notable finding – that is, when these principles have been broadly interpreted, they have expanded peacekeeping's legal frameworks, stretching the invisible red boundary line around peacekeeping, taking it much closer to the realm of intervention, and thereby undermining the principle of non-intervention. Indeed, the chapter argued that, at times, ONUC, MONUC and MONUSCO have all crossed this boundary line, potentially violating the principle of non-intervention, as they have undertaken coercive action designed to influence change in the host state and, thus, intervention. The chapter argued that ONUC's involvement in the Katangan secession, MONUC's shift to a stabilisation operation, joint operations conducted by both MONUC and MONUSCO and the implementation of the Human Rights Due Diligence Policy (HRDDP) could all be cited as examples of this coercive action, rendering the peacekeeping operations a form of intervention. In particular, the chapter explored the conducting of joint operations between MONUSCO and the Congolese armed forces (FARDC), arguing that these operations are difficult to reconcile with peacekeeping's 'holy trinity' of legal principles and could, perhaps, be best viewed as a form of intervention by invitation.

Throughout this exploration of the three legal principles in the Congo, Chapter 5 also continued to apply a TWAIL lens highlighting the continual patterns of domination and subordination. It argued that this was particularly the case when the peacekeeping operation could be deemed to be undertaking coercive action – such as the pressure exerted on states to provide consent to a mandate renewal or the imposition of conditions or standards (through the HRDDP) which must be met before joint operations are conducted.

Continuing this analysis of peacekeeping's frameworks in the DRC, Chapter 6 explored peacekeeping's normative framework, analysing the three norms of democracy promotion, protection of civilians (PoC) and the prohibition of sexual exploitation and abuse (SEA). Again, as with the legal frameworks, it found that these norms do not exist harmoniously, with a degree of overlap between these norms and the legal principles, particularly when, for example, an application of democracy promotion or PoC invokes the use of force. The chapter also found that, as highlighted in Chapter 4, these norms, although not amounting to legal principles, may at times contribute to peacekeeping's legal frameworks where they may trigger broader elements of international law. As with the legal principles, it also found that where the norms of democracy promotion and PoC are expanded and interpreted more broadly, this results in an expansion of peacekeeping's frameworks, thereby stretching the red elastic boundary line surrounding peacekeeping. Chapter 6 therefore once again demonstrated the fluidity of peacekeeping's frameworks and its boundaries which has, consequently, resulted in a constantly fluctuating support or undermining of the principle of non-intervention.

In particular, the chapter found that a broader application of the norms of democracy promotion and PoC within the Congo had, again, resulted in ONUC, MONUC and MONUSCO, at times, undertaking coercive action to influence change in the host state and, therefore, intervention. For example, the chapter argued that MONUC's involvement in the Congo's National Dialogue, established by the Lusaka Ceasefire Agreement, and MONUSCO's substitution for the state in protection of civilian tasks amounted to coercive action and thereby intervention. Chapter 6 also found that the outlier to this pattern of continually broadening norms was the norm of prohibition of SEA. It found that although there has been a troubling level of SEA committed by peacekeepers within MONUSCO, there has not been the same level of commitment to the expansion of the norm of prohibition of SEA as there has been with the norms of democracy promotion and PoC. It has been argued that this has, in part, been due to a reluctance of member states to engage in the matter, highlighting how the United Nations is, again, beholden to its member states, particularly the hegemonic powers. Indeed, as with the previous chapters, a TWAIL lens was again applied throughout Chapter 6 demonstrating how the patterns of domination and subordination and the furtherance of hegemonic interests had been recreated in, for example, the pursuance of democratisation in the Congo, despite it clearly failing to take hold due to the persistent authoritarian regimes and patronage systems of governance. Similarly, the chapter noted how the expansion of MONUSCO's PoC tools and policies created a reliance on the peacekeeping operation, often resulting in MONUSCO undertaking the role of the state. As such, Chapter 6 argued that the broadening of the norms of democracy promotion and PoC within the Congo had been taken too far. It suggested that these norms had expanded peacekeeping's normative framework to its very limits, requiring a re-drawing of the normative boundaries of peacekeeping, through a constriction or even retraction of these two norms. In order to achieve this, it was noted that this may require a change in the approach taken by the Security Council to mandating peacekeeping operations, including a move back towards the more traditional concept of peacekeeping and a shift to a people-centred approach to peacekeeping.

Recommendations

This book's analysis of peacekeeping, its frameworks and its relationship with the principle of non-intervention has identified two key recommendations.

Realistic, Streamlined Mandates

The first main recommendation is that peacekeeping's boundaries need to be re-drawn through a move away from large, multi-dimensional operations towards operations with more realistic, streamlined mandates. The analysis of peacekeeping's frameworks in Chapters 3–6 has highlighted how the expansive interpretation and application of peacekeeping's principles and norms have pushed peacekeeping to its very limits. As such, it is argued that there needs to be a re-drawing or constricting of these boundaries – i.e. the principles and norms need to be interpreted more narrowly. Within Chapter 6, it was also debated whether some norms, such as democracy promotion and PoC, should be removed from peacekeeping mandates altogether, not because they are tasks which should not be pursued but because they are tasks which peacekeepers are ill-suited to undertake. A considerable review of peacekeeping tasks is therefore much needed, as noted in the recent 'New Agenda for Peace', which recognised a need for 'the Security Council not to burden peace operations with unrealistic mandates'.[8] It is therefore proposed that there needs to be a reflection on the Security Council mandating process and the tasks assigned to peacekeepers to ensure that these align with peacekeeping's resources and capabilities.

People-Centred Approach

The second main recommendation is that there is also a need for a shift from a 'narrow focus on state-building, institutional capacity and the extension of state authority' to people-centred peace operations.[9] This book therefore proposes,

8 UN, 'Our Common Agenda Policy Brief 9: A New Agenda for Peace' (July 2023) <https://dppa.un.org/en/a-new-agenda-for-peace> 24.
9 C de Coning and L Gelot, 'Placing People at the Center of UN Peace Operations' (IPI 29 May 2020) <https://theglobalobservatory.org/2020/05/placing-people-center-un-peace-operations/>.

like other contemporary reviews of peacekeeping,[10] that there should be a move towards a more bottom-up, people-centred approach to peacekeeping which will, amongst other things, help local communities and societies 'strengthen their own capacities to prevent conflict and sustain peace'.[11] Indeed, within Chapters 5 and 6, the discussions of the application of consent, democracy promotion and protection of civilians highlighted how a move to a people-centred approach could be beneficial in amplifying the effectiveness of peacekeeping and creating sustainable peace. This would, again, require a review of the mandating process alongside a focus on the role of the heads of peacekeeping operations in the field – the Special Representatives of the Secretary-General (SRSG) – who play a pivotal part in implementing the mandates and acting as liaison between the local or national actors and the United Nations.

Conclusion

The book has therefore examined the relationship between peacekeeping and intervention, demonstrating how, at times, an expansion of peacekeeping's legal and normative frameworks results in the undermining or potential violation of the principle of non-intervention. The book has therefore imagined these frameworks as forming an invisible red, elastic boundary line around peacekeeping which constantly expands and contracts with each re-interpretation or reimagining of peacekeeping's principles and norms. Through an exploration of peacekeeping in practice it has been argued that in recent times the continual expansion of these principles and norms has resulted in the red boundary line being stretched to its very limits and, even, beyond. Therefore, in answer to the question posed at the very beginning of this book – peacekeeping is, at times, intervention.

Whilst it could be argued that those operations which are mandated by the Security Council under Chapter VII cannot amount to intervention, due to the exception embedded within Article 2(7), this book has argued that these operations should be considered to be, at times, a form of intervention, not peacekeeping. That is, these operations stretch the traditional understanding of peacekeeping, blurring the lines with peace enforcement and expanding peacekeeping far beyond its intended purpose. Indeed, the move to robust peacekeeping, Cruz Report[12] and Action for Peacekeeping initiative[13] all appear

10 See, for example: F Carver, 'Linked up Peacekeeping' (Protection Approaches July 2022) <https://protectionapproaches.org/linked-up-peacekeeping>; Together First, 'People-Centred Peacekeeping' <https://together1st.org/proposals/351#>.

11 de Coning and Gelot (n9).

12 CA Dos Santos Cruz, WR Phillips and S Cusimano, 'Improving Security of United Nations Peacekeepers: We Need to Change the Way We Are Doing Business' ('Santos Cruz Report') (19 December 2017) <https://peacekeeping.un.org/sites/default/files/improving_security_of_united_nations_peacekeepers_report.pdf>.

13 UN Peacekeeping, 'A4P+ Priorities for 2021–2023' <https://peacekeeping.un.org/sites/default/files/a4p_background_paper.pdf>.

to promote a more aggressive form of peacekeeping which this book has demonstrated results in an increase in intervention. The contemporary multi-dimensional operations and their extensive Christmas tree mandates permit broader interpretations of peacekeeping's principles and norms in an attempt to fulfil the mandated tasks. This results in an expansion of peacekeeping's frameworks and an increase in peacekeeping's interventionist potential, along with unrealistic expectations of an operation that has neither the resources nor capabilities to fulfil such mandates. Moreover, this book's unique application of a TWAIL lens has demonstrated how this move towards increased intervention is not just legally and practically problematic but also reinforces patterns of domination and subordination, creating a concept of peacekeeping which is made in the image of the hegemonic Security Council, thus contradicting the intent and purpose of the United Nations as a universal, global organisation.[14]

It could therefore be argued that peacekeeping has evolved too far. The grandiose forms of intervention, through multi-dimensional stabilisation operations, appear to be reaching a natural end. Whilst these operations were an innovative response to the conflict of their day, it is questionable whether they remain an appropriate model of peacekeeping in the current climate. As such, this book has demonstrated how there is a need for a narrowing of these peacekeeping frameworks and a move away from multi-dimensional operations back to a more traditional model of peacekeeping – a move which would be consistent with peacekeeping's cyclical nature. Now, in 2023, as there has been a gradual decline of multi-dimensional operations over the last five years as a result of budget pressures, a divided Security Council, contested track records and the impact of the COVID-19 pandemic,[15] the time is arguably ripe for this shift in peacekeeping.

In order to achieve this, there needs to be a review of peacekeeping operations, with a reflection on what and who contributes to peace. More specifically, two key factors could help to effect this change – one stemming from the Security Council and another coming from the overall approach to peacekeeping. Firstly, there needs to be a revision of Security Council mandates, including a re-structuring of the mandate which would assist in debates over peacekeeping's Charter basis and the blurring of peacekeeping and peace enforcement. That is, the Council should reconsider the catch-all phrase of 'Acting under Chapter VII' which is placed into the introductory section or chapeau of some resolutions, including that of MONUSCO.[16] Instead, the

14 See Chapter 1, Charter of the United Nations (24 October 1945).

15 A Day, 'The Future of Multidimensional Peacekeeping' (*IPI*, 15 September 2020) <https://theglobalobservatory.org/2020/09/future-multidimensional-peacekeeping/>; IPI, 'COVID-19 Crisis an Opportunity to "Rethink and Develop UN Peacekeeping Further"' (7 October 2020) <https://www.ipinst.org/2020/10/un-peace-ops-during-covid-19-high-level-dialogue#3>.

16 UNSC Res 2556 (18 December 2020) UN Doc S/RES/2556.

invocation of Chapter VII should only occur within specific paragraphs, clarifying which tasks, such as PoC, are mandated under this provision. This could then provide some clarity over peacekeeping's legal basis and assist peacekeepers in the implementation of the mandate, whilst simultaneously firming the boundaries between peacekeeping and peace enforcement. As such, it would go some way towards remedying the interventionist shift within peacekeeping, which this book has highlighted.

In a similar vein, the Council should also consider a revision of its Christmas tree mandates, reducing the list of mandated tasks which it sets for a peacekeeping operation and creating more realistic, streamlined mandates. This would assist in clarifying some of the legal and practical issues which this book has explored. Indeed, if interviewees of this research have noted that 'constraints of the Security Council mandate' were 'the major framework for us to make decisions', as opposed to general international law, then it follows that the key to retracting peacekeeping's frameworks is through a shrinking or reimagining of the mandate.[17]

Secondly, as this book has suggested at various points, the United Nations should also re-consider its state-centric, outsider-led, top-down approach to peacekeeping, moving, instead, to one which is people-centred, bottom-up and insider-led, focused on including the input of actors on the ground. Put simply, peacekeeping should be a concept for 'we the people' rather than a concept for member states, thus better reflecting the broader, fundamental purposes of the United Nations.[18] This shift in approach may then create more sustainable solutions to conflict and violence, particularly in complex settings such as the DRC. It would also challenge the lingering colonial dichotomies and patterns of domination and subordination, within intervention and peacekeeping, which a TWAIL lens has demonstrated still exist within the two concepts. Therefore, a reimagining of peacekeeping, through a move to a more people-centred approach, could challenge these power dynamics and give a greater voice to peoples of the Global South in the hope of establishing sustainable peace and security within conflict and post-conflict situations.

These are not easy problems to solve, but just because they are difficult does not mean that they cannot be, at the very least, attempted. Indeed, as Secretary-General Dag Hammarskjöld famously stated, the United Nations 'was not created in order to bring us to heaven, but to save us from hell'.[19] Peacekeeping should therefore not be expected to fulfil unrealistic lists of tasks set by a body dominated by hegemonic powers but, rather, to support host states and their

17 Interview with Independent Expert and Former UN Political Adviser ('Interviewee 8') (New York, 26 November 2019) DOI: <http://doi.org/10.17639/nott.7119>.

18 UN, '"We the People" for the Global Goals' <https://www.un.org/sustainabledevelopment/blog/2015/09/we-the-people-for-the-global-goals/>.

19 UN Press Release, 'Address by Secretary-General Dag Hammarskjöld' (13 May 1954) UN Doc SG/382, 7.

peoples in developing sustainable peace and security. Thus, as peacekeeping is in a transitional period, there needs to be a reflection on what model or approach peacekeeping should adopt in order to amplify its effectiveness as a tool for maintaining international peace and security in the modern era.

References

Anghie A, *Imperialism, Sovereignty and the Making of International Law* (CUP 2007)

Carver F, 'Linked Up Peacekeeping' (Protection Approaches, July 2022) <https://protectionapproaches.org/linked-up-peacekeeping>;

Case Concerning Military and Paramilitary Activities in and Against Nicaragua (Nicaragua v United States of America) [1986] ICJ Rep 14

Case Concerning Armed Activities on the Territory of the Congo (Democratic Republic of the Congo v Uganda) Judgment of 19 December [2005] ICJ Rep 168

Charter of the United Nations (24 October 1945).

Day A, 'The Future of Multidimensional Peacekeeping' (*IPI*, 15 September 2020) <https://theglobalobservatory.org/2020/09/future-multidimensional-peacekeeping/>

de Coning C and Gelot L, 'Placing People at the Center of UN Peace Operations' (*IPI*, 29 May 2020) <https://theglobalobservatory.org/2020/05/placing-people-center-un-peace-operations/>

Dos Santos Cruz CA, Phillips WR and Cusimano S, 'Improving Security of United Nations Peacekeepers: We need to change the way we are doing business' ("Santos Cruz Report") (19 December 2017) <https://peacekeeping.un.org/sites/default/files/improving_security_of_united_nations_peacekeepers_report.pdf>.

Grewe W, *The Epochs of International Law* (Rev edn, Walter de Gruyter & Co 2000)

Interview with Independent Expert and Former UN Political Adviser ('Interviewee 8') (New York, 26 November 2019) DOI: <http://doi.org/10.17639/nott.7119>

IPI, 'COVID-19 Crisis an Opportunity to "Rethink and Develop UN Peacekeeping Further"' (7 October 2020) <https://www.ipinst.org/2020/10/un-peace-ops-during-covid-19-high-level-dialogue#3>

Karlsrud J, 'Special Representatives of the Secretary-General as Norm Arbitrators? Understanding Bottom-up Authority in UN Peacekeeping' (2013) 19(4) GG 525–544

Mutua M, 'What Is TWAIL?' (2000) 94 ASILPROC 31–38

Simma B, Khan DE, Nolte G, Paulus A, Wessendorf A (eds) *The Charter of the United Nations: A Commentary, Vol 1* (3rd edn, OUP 2012)

Together First, 'People-Centred Peacekeeping' <https://together1st.org/proposals/351#>

UN, 'Our Common Agenda Policy Brief 9: A New Agenda for Peace' (July 2023) <https://dppa.un.org/en/a-new-agenda-for-peace>

UN, '"We the People" for the Global Goals' <https://www.un.org/sustainabledevelopment/blog/2015/09/we-the-people-for-the-global-goals/>

UN Peacekeeping, 'A4P+ Priorities for 2021–2023' <https://peacekeeping.un.org/sites/default/files/a4p_background_paper.pdf>

UN Press Release, 'Address by Secretary-General Dag Hammarskjöld' (13 May 1954) UN Doc SG/382

UNSC Res 2556 (18 December 2020) UN Doc S/RES/2556

Index